SwimTime Corp. v. Water-Fun, Inc.

SwimTime Corp. v. Water-Fun, Inc.

Ryan H. Flax

A2L Consulting
and
American University
Washington College of Law

National Institute for Trial Advocacy

Address inquiries to:

Reprint Permission
National Institute for Trial Advocacy
1685 38th Street, Suite 200
Boulder, CO 80301-2735
Phone: (800) 225-6482
Fax: (720) 890-7069
E-mail: permissions@nita.org

ISBN 978-1-60156-501-3
eISBN 978-1-60156-514-3
FBA 1501

Printed in the United States of America

Official co-publisher of NITA.
WKLegaledu.com/NITA

Contents

Acknowledgements

The author thanks first Nikole, Chloe, and Mason—the reason the effort is worth it—and Mom and Dad. Also, with great appreciation, the author thanks Patrick Hanes of Williams Mullen LLP, A2L Consulting, Mark Austrian of Kelley Drye & Warren LLP, and the faculty of American University's Washington College of Law.

INTRODUCTION

This case concerns a patent infringement claim by one midsized player in the consumer aquatic leisure market, brought in U.S. federal court in the Eastern District of Nita against another midsized competitor in this market. This case file contains materials for a civil trial based upon allegations of patent infringement and defenses to these allegations, including allegations of patent invalidity and non-infringement.

These materials are designed to provide opportunities for users of the case file to address the key issues relating to U.S. patent infringement litigation both before the court and a jury, including patent analysis, claim construction, summary judgment, expert testimony, and evidence. A heavy emphasis is put on the presentation of both fact evidence and demonstrative evidence. The case file will take students through the case from the complaint stage, to patent claim construction (called the *Markman* hearing stage after the U.S. Supreme Court case settling the issue of claim construction as a matter of law for the court), to summary judgment, and finally to trial.

It is the author's hope that this case file with not only familiarize attorneys and students with the challenges inherent to patent litigation and basic trial preparation in modern, high-tech courtrooms, but also to the importance of case presentation and the use of demonstrative evidence to persuasion in this environment.

All events and individuals represented in this case file are fictional. Any resemblance to actual people or events is unintentional.

CASE SUMMARY

This case concerns a patent infringement claim by one midsized player in the consumer aquatic leisure market, plaintiff SwimTime Corp. ("SwimTime"), brought in U.S. federal court in the Eastern District of Nita against another midsized competitor in this market, defendant Water-Fun, Inc. ("Water-Fun"). SwimTime is the owner of and employs the inventors of U.S. Patent No. 8,197,517 (the '517 patent) directed to pool float products shaped roughly like oblong seats. The '517 patent is being asserted against Water-Fun.

SwimTime entered the pool and water leisure market during the pool industry's heyday of the late 1970s and early 1980s. SwimTime develops and sells products such as pool floats, pool games, poolside lounges, and pool toys. Over the years, SwimTime has sold its products across the country in big-box retail stores, such as Walmart, Kmart, and Target. SwimTime also sells its products in pool and water recreation-focused stores, such as Wings and Ron Jon Surf Shop, as well as via catalogs, such as Herrington and Frontgate. SwimTime has a strong online presence, selling its products on its own website and on Amazon.com, among others.

Morgan Miller is the chief executive officer of SwimTime (only the second person to hold this position) and has been for the past thirteen years. Miller has led SwimTime from a small player in the industry to become one of the top five largest brands and the number-one "luxury" pool accessory brand. Miller's philosophy has been to market and advertise heavily and invest heavily in research and development (R&D) and intellectual property protection to bring new "high-design" products to consumers.

About eleven years ago, Miller hired a new head of R&D, Eric Flax. Miller made it Flax's mission to design and develop high-luxury pool accessory products that would have wide-market appeal. Miller emphasized that Flax should use the latest in materials and technology to achieve this goal. Miller gave Flax the budget necessary to hire a staff of engineers and designers.

About a year after his hiring, Flax's team developed what would become the bestselling and most profitable pool float product in SwimTime's history: the Spring Float. The product hit the market in YR-9 and remains one of the bestselling SwimTime products today with very little change in design. The Spring Float uses luxury, aquatic fabrics and high design to provide a very desirable water lounge chair that includes an internal wire rim allowing the lounge to be twist-folded in half for storage and opens for use merely by releasing the lounge and allowing the spring to expand.

Water-Fun is in the business of designing, manufacturing, and selling various recreational aquatic products, primarily swimming and pool-related products. Examples of products sold by Water-Fun are swim masks, fins, pools, beach toys and games, and various floating products such as lounges and chairs. Water-Fun has been in this industry since YR-45. Water-Fun sells its products to a variety of retailers, including Walmart, Target, Sam's Club, Costco, Toys "R" Us, Dick's Sporting Goods, Sports Authority, Walgreens, CVS, Rite Aid, Publix Albertsons, Kroger, various "mom and pop" stores, and pool retail stores.

Water-Fun is a fierce competitor of SwimTime and has been selling pool floats for decades, but over the last fifteen years has lost considerable market share to SwimTime. Water-Fun has recently introduced a new product that is strikingly similar to the top-selling SwimTime Spring Float product and, at least superficially, bears many similarities to the invention described in the '517 patent. The Water-Fun product is called the Recliner Fabric Comfort Lounge.

About four years ago, Water-Fun's CEO, Glenn Berenson, hired a new head of R&D named Barry Kim. Kim was tasked with closing the gap between Water-Fun's and SwimTime's market share by developing new products. Kim was responsible for the development of the new Water-Fun Recliner Fabric Comfort Lounge.

SwimTime became aware of Water-Fun's sales of the Recliner Fabric Comfort Lounge and brought suit for patent infringement in the U.S. District Court for the Eastern District of Nita. SwimTime is the owner, by assignment, of U.S. Patent Number 8,197,517 (herein called "the '517 patent"), which is the asserted patent or patent-in-suit. The '517 patent is titled "Collapsible Flotation Device" and issued October 26, YR-6. It was filed as application number 12/123,456 in the United States Patent Office (USPTO) in YR-8 and claims priority as a continuation application of U.S. patent application number 11/234,567, which was filed in the USPTO on May 31, YR-9, which itself claims priority as a continuation application of U.S. patent application number 10/345,678, which was filed in the USPTO on February 21, YR-10. Each of these three patent applications shares identical drawings and specifications. The '517 patent has three claims, each being an independent claim.

Instructions

Evidence is provided for both plaintiff and defendant. Use only the evidentiary exhibits provided in this case file. Basic litigation graphics—i.e., demonstrative evidence—are also provided. These graphics illustrate or support basic concepts on infringement and invalidity and important points to be made relating to each. It is hoped, however, that over the course of the class students will develop more advanced demonstrative evidence customized to their case presentation.

Court orders are provided on summary judgment and claim construction—these are determinative on the issues and are to be used in subsequent class activities, e.g., the mock trial. However, the motions and briefing relating to these orders are not provided. It is intended that a part of the curriculum for this course (time permitting) include students' preparing the briefing for and/or arguing these motions. Therefore, the orders for such briefing should be withheld until the proper time during the course—after the motions have been "filed" and argued. The provided lists of relevant issues preceding these orders in this case file should be used in preparing the motions and briefs and oral arguments.

Unless otherwise instructed, parties need not call all of the witnesses on their list. All witnesses are gender-neutral and can be played by a man or a woman. Witness statements are sworn testimony.

Plaintiff's Witness List

Morgan Miller—Chief Executive Officer, SwimTime

Eric (Erica) Flax—first named inventor on '517 patent; Head of Research & Development, SwimTime

Pat Thurman—expert witness for SwimTime (infringement and validity)

Defendant's Witness List

Glenn Berenson—Chief Executive Officer, Water-Fun

Barry Kim—Head of Research & Development, Water-Fun

Drew Clark—expert witness for Water-Fun (invalidity and non-infringement)

Please note that all years in the fictional, narrative portions of these materials are stated in the following form:

YR-0 indicates the actual year in which the case is being tried (i.e., the present year);

YR-1 indicates the preceding year (please use the actual year);

YR-2 indicates the next preceding year (please use the actual year); et cetera.

True, Gregorian-calendar years are used in citations to actual court cases and where actual historical times and events are described.

Stipulations

1. The parties agree that all fact evidence is authenticated, unless a specific objection is raised to the contrary.

2. The parties agree that the correct inventors are named on the face of the '517 patent.

3. The parties agree that SwimTime Corp. is the lawful assignee and owner of the '517 patent.

4. The parties agree that all procedural requirements relating to the prosecution of the '517 patent and to the filings in this litigation have been met.

5. The parties agree that the Terminal Disclaimer filed by the applicants during the prosecution of the '517 patent was correct and accurate.

6. The parties agree that the defendant sells the accused devices in the United States and in Nita.

7. The parties agree that, should the defendant's liability on infringement be proven on any claim of the '517 patent, damages shall be awarded based on a five percent reasonable royalty on $18 million net sales of the accused products, amounting to $900,000.

8. The parties agree that willful infringement cannot be proven.

9. The parties agree that no pretrial actions give rise to any claim for enhancement of damages or an award of attorney fees.

10. The parties agree that the defense of inequitable conduct cannot be proven.

11. The parties agree that U.S. Patent Nos. 3,401,020 and 4,249,454 are not infringed by the Water-Fun products.

Note: As of the trial, the parties have cross-moved (*Daubert* challenges) the court to exclude the other's proffered experts from testifying as expert witnesses on the grounds that said proffered experts are not qualified as such. The court denies all such motions.

Case Materials and Exhibits

UNITED STATES DISTRICT COURT
FOR THE DISTRICT OF NITA

Nita City Division

SWIMTIME CORPORATION, Plaintiff,	)	Civil Action No. 1:Y00-cv-00100
v.	)	JURY TRIAL DEMANDED
WATER-FUN, INC., Defendant.	)	

COMPLAINT

Plaintiff, SwimTime Corporation ("SwimTime"), by counsel, for its Complaint against Defendant Water-Fun Industries, Inc. ("Water-Fun" or "Defendant") alleges as follows:

Parties

1. Plaintiff SwimTime is a Nita corporation with its principal place of business at 5816 Main Avenue, Nita City, Nita 20815.
2. Defendant Water-Fun, upon information and belief, is a Nita corporation with its principal place of business at 525 Broadway Street, Nita City, Nita 22314.

Jurisdiction and Venue

3. This is an action for patent infringement arising under the Patent Act, 35 U.S.C. §§ 1 *et seq*.
4. This Court has jurisdiction over the subject matter of this action pursuant to 28 U.S.C. §§ 1331 and 1338(a).
5. Venue is proper in this district pursuant to 28 U.S.C. § 1391(c) because it is a district in which Defendant is subject to personal jurisdiction.
6. This Court has personal jurisdiction over Water-Fun because Water-Fun has committed, directed, authorized, endorsed, and/or approved of acts of infringement in the District of Nita; Water-Fun has caused tortious injury to SwimTime in the District of Nita, Nita City Division; and Water-Fun has transacted substantial business in this judicial district.

Facts

7. SwimTime is a worldwide manufacturer of innovative and commercially successful leisure and recreational water products. The SwimTime brand has been around for over thirty-five years, and SwimTime continues to invest substantial resources into its product design and development to create unique, quality products that are leaders in the industry. SwimTime's products can be found in thousands of major retailers and individual pool dealers, both in the United States and abroad.

8. SwimTime's products also include a line of Spring Float® inflatable pool floats (the "SwimTime Products"), an example of which is attached hereto as Exhibit A. SwimTime owns all right, title, and interest to U.S. Patent No. 8,197,517 ("the '517 patent"), which was duly and legally issued on October 26, YR-6. The '517 patent covers flotation devices, as shown and described therein and as embodied in the SwimTime Products, which, at all pertinent times, have been marked with the '517 patent number. A true and accurate copy of the '517 patent is attached hereto as Exhibit B.

9. The SwimTime Products have been advertised through various media, including on the Internet and substantial advertising dollars have been spent in connection with the products. The SwimTime Products have appeared in print media, newspapers, trade journals, magazines, promotional materials, and on the Internet, in addition to retail locations.

10. On information and belief, Water-Fun markets its infringing products through various advertising media, and certain of those products are available for sale at retail locations throughout the United States. On information and belief, sales are imminent for certain other infringing products as described in more detail below.

11. Water-Fun sells a Recliner Fabric Comfort Lounge ("Water-Fun Recliner") that infringes at least one claim of the '517 patent. A comparison of Figure 1 from the '517 patent, which discloses a claimed embodiment, next to the Water-Fun Recliner appears below.

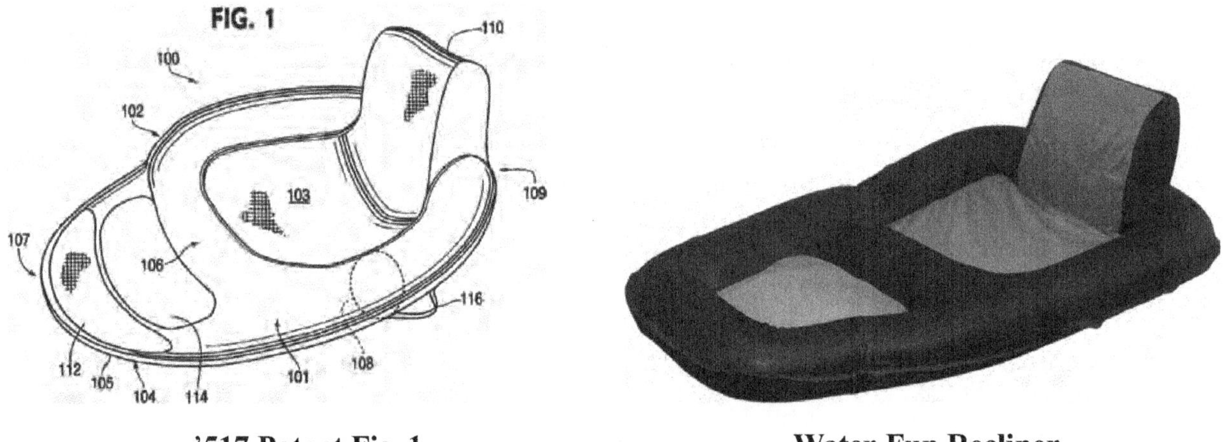

'517 Patent Fig. 1 **Water-Fun Recliner**

[*Note*: To view images in color, please refer to the CD-ROM accompanying this book.]

Count One
(Infringement of the '517 patent)

12. Plaintiff repeats and re-alleges, as if fully set forth herein, each and every allegation contained in the foregoing paragraphs.

13. Water-Fun manufactures, distributes, sells, offers to sell, and/or imports the infringing Water-Fun Recliner throughout the United States in the stream of interstate commerce. SwimTime purchased a Water-Fun Recliner at a Costco in Nita City, Nita.

14. The Water-Fun Recliner embodies and infringes the '517 patent in violation of SwimTime's statutory rights under 35 U.S.C. §§ 1 *et seq.*

15. Water-Fun does not have license or authorization from SwimTime to utilize the '517 patent.

16. Water-Fun's conduct also constitutes contributory and/or induced infringement of the '517 patent.
17. Upon information and belief, Water-Fun's infringement of the '517 patent has been and continues to be willful.

The foregoing acts of patent infringement by Water-Fun have caused, and unless enjoined by this Court, will continue to cause immediate and irreparable injury and damage to SwimTime, leaving it with no adequate remedy at law.

Prayer for Relief

WHEREFORE, Plaintiff prays:

a. that this Court issue preliminary and permanent injunctive relief against Water-Fun, its respective officers, agents, servants, employees, attorneys, parent and subsidiary corporations, assigns and successors in interest, and those persons in active concert or participation with them, enjoining them from continued acts of infringement of the '517 patent, including, without limitation, an injunction against future sales of the Water-Fun Recliner;

b. a judgment that the '517 patent is duly and legally issued, valid, and enforceable;

c. a judgment that Water-Fun has infringed one or more claims of the '517 patent;

d. an accounting and award of compensatory and enhanced damages under 35 U.S.C. § 284 including, but not limited to, Plaintiff's lost profits, but in any event not less than a reasonable royalty, resulting from Water-Fun's infringement of the '517 patent, together with prejudgment and post-judgment interest;

e. that this be adjudged an exceptional case and that Plaintiff be awarded attorney fees pursuant to 35 U.S.C. § 285 in addition to other authority;

f. that this Court award Plaintiff its costs incurred herein; and

g. for such other and further relief as this Court deems just.

Jury Demand

Pursuant to Federal Rule of Civil Procedure 38, Plaintiffs hereby demands a trial by jury on all issues so triable.

Dated: October 5, YR-1

SWIMTIME CORPORATION

By:
Jim W. Brady
Counsel for Plaintiff
GEORGE BRENT & DAPKUS LLP
1869 Deacon Blvd.
Nita City, Nita 20854
Telephone: (311) 555-8800

Exhibit A

SwimTime Spring Float Products Photos

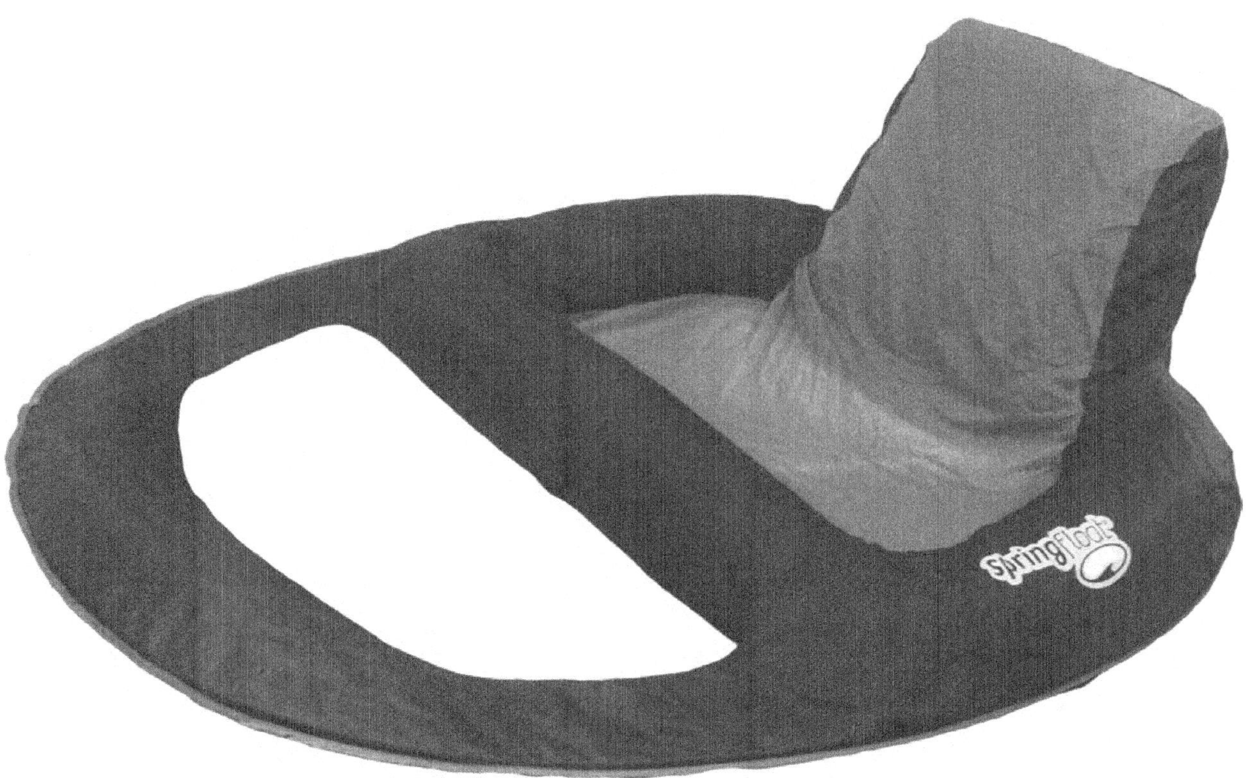

[*Note*: To view the following images in color, please refer to the CD-ROM accompanying this book.]

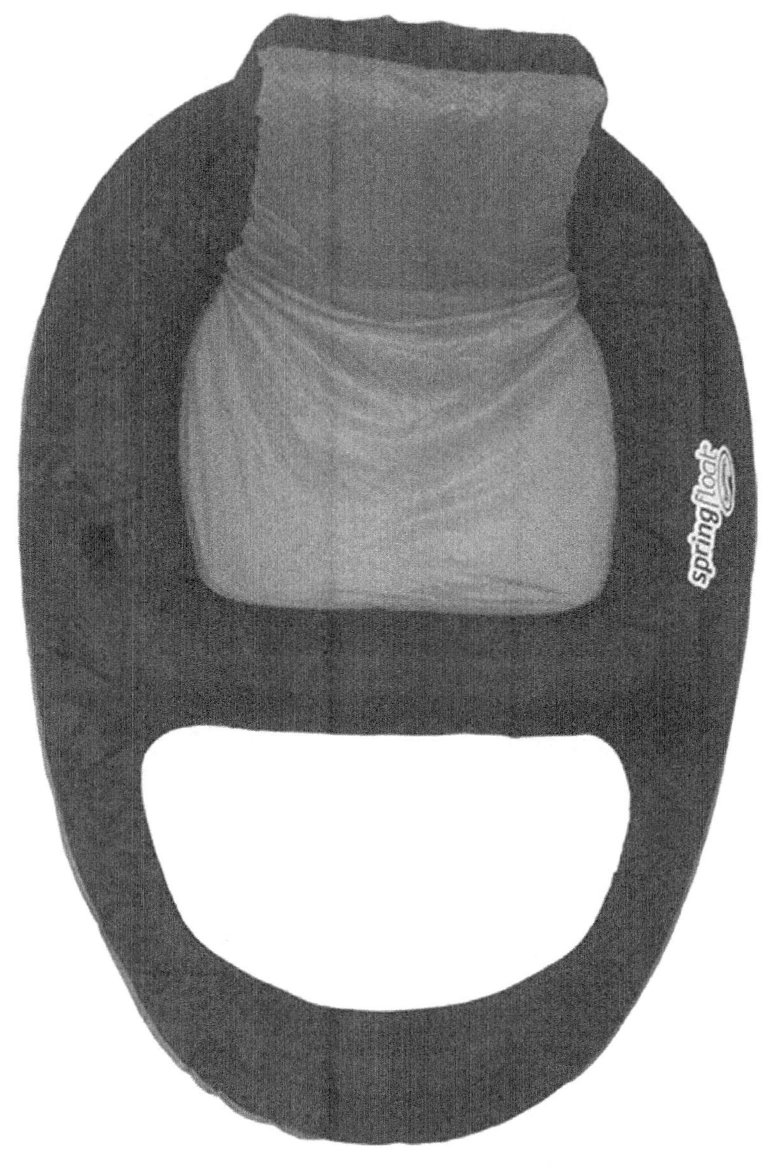
springfloat

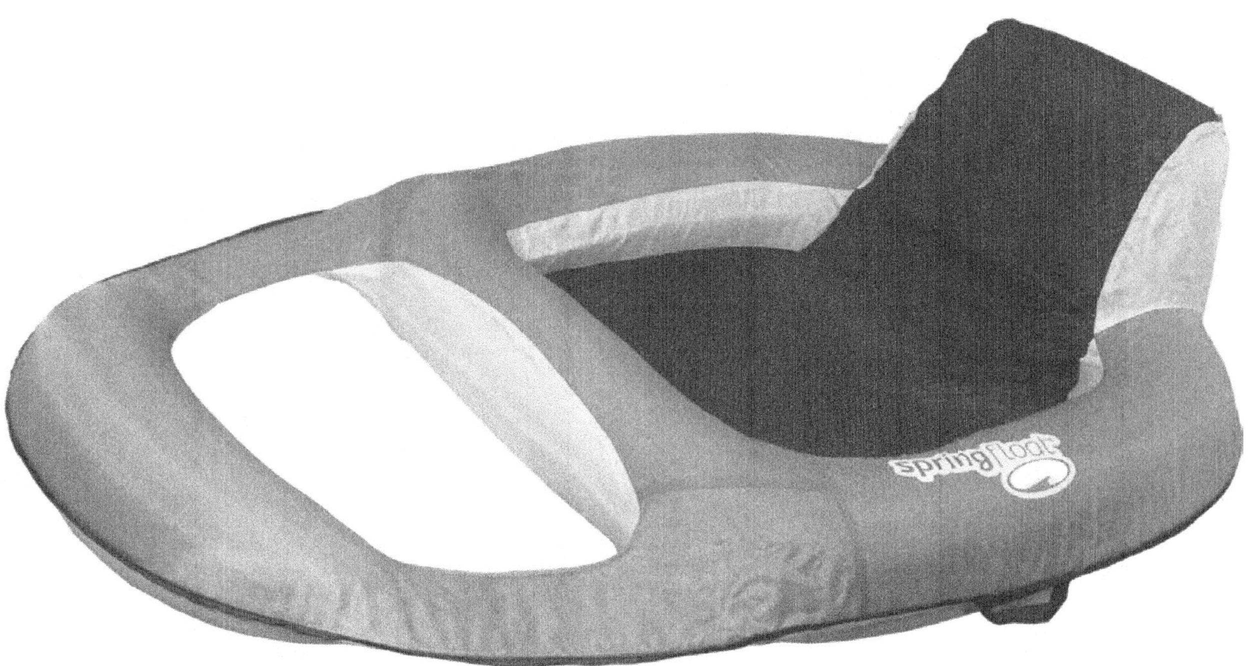
springfloat

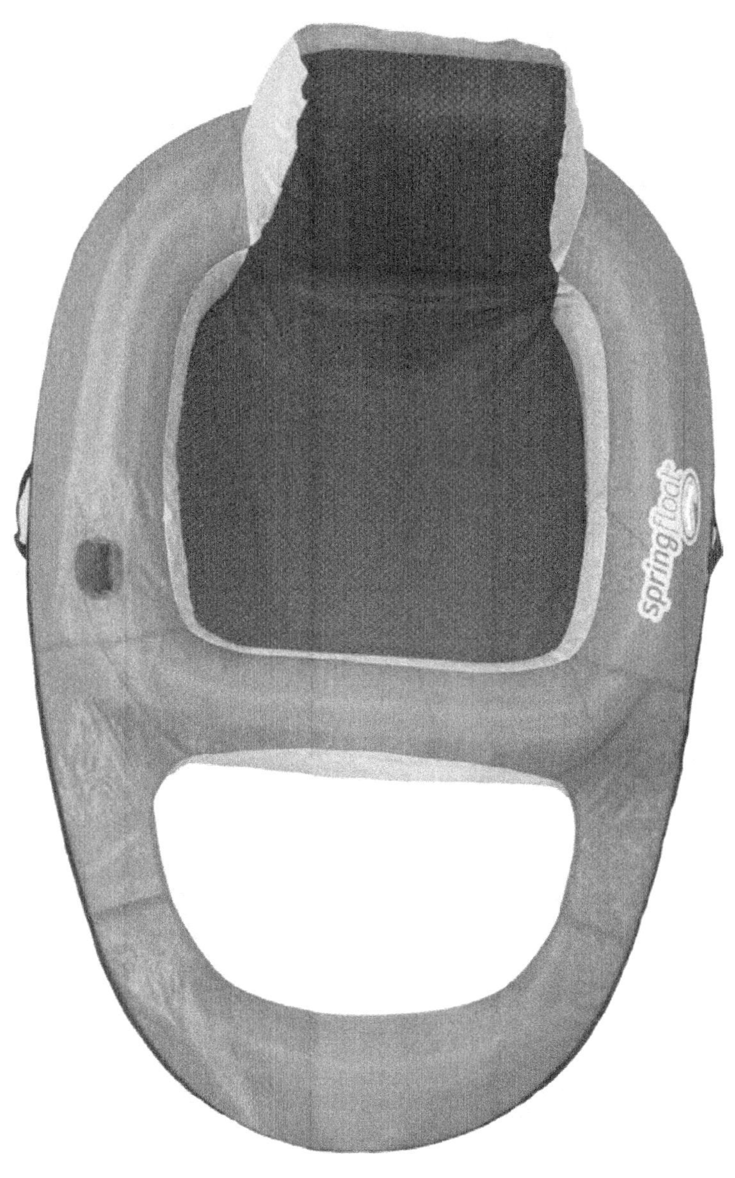
springfloat

Exhibit B

’517 Patent

(12) **United States Patent**
Flax et al.

(10) **Patent No.: US 8,197,517 B2**
(45) **Date of Patent: *Oct. 26, YR-6**

(54) **COLLAPSIBLE FLOTATION DEVICE**

(75) Inventors: **Eric Flax**, Nita City, NT (US); **Richard Pruitt**, Nita City, NT (US); **August LaCata**, Nita City, NT (US); **Reba Sparks**, Nita City, NT (US); **Leon Holbrook**, Nita City, NT (US); **Susan Kolb**, Nita City, NT (US)

(73) Assignee: **SwimTime Corp.**, Nita City, NT (US)

(*) Notice: Subject to any disclaimer, the term of this patent is extended or adjusted under 35 U.S.C. 154(b) by 0 days.

This patent is subject to a terminal disclaimer.

(21) Appl. No.: **12/123,456**

(22) Filed: **Oct. 15, YR-8**

(65) **Prior Publication Data**

US 2010/0233924 A1 Sep. 16, YR-7

Related U.S. Application Data

(63) Continuation of application No. 11/234,567 filed on May 31, YR-9 now Pat. No. 4,249,454, which is a continuation of application No. 10/345,678, filed on Feb. 21 YR-10 now Pat. No. 3,401,020

(51) **Int. Cl.**
B63C 9/08 (2006.01)
B63C 9/28 (2006.01)

(52) **U.S. Cl.** **441/130**

(58) **Field of Classification Search** .... 441/129-132; 297/188.14, 452.41, DIG. 3; 472/129
See application file for complete search history.

(56) **References Cited**

U.S. PATENT DOCUMENTS

1,190,743	A	7/1916	Fageol
1,479,903	A	1/1924	Erland
1,960,474	A	5/1934	Browne

(Continued)

FOREIGN PATENT DOCUMENTS

EP 0 974 293 A2 1/2000

OTHER PUBLICATIONS

International Search Report and Written Opinion for PCT/US04/04517, mailed on Jul. 29, 2004; 10 pages.

(Continued)

Primary Examiner — Daniel V Venne
(74) *Attorney, Agent, or Firm* — Clark Nikole LLP

(57) **ABSTRACT**

A collapsible flotation device is provided that uses a coilable spring coupled to a panel to collapse the device when the spring is coiled, and to expand the device when the spring is uncoiled configuration. The spring can be contained within a sleeve along the outer portion of the panel. A support member that traverses the panel is provided. An inflatable bladder disposed about a part of the outer portion of the panel and coupled to the support member buoyantly supports a body weight of a user. The combination of the inflatable bladder and the support member provide support for a user in a seated position on the panel. Many configurations are disclosed, including a multi-user collapsible flotation device, multiple connected single-user flotation devices, and so forth. A back support member and a headrest, both of which can be inflatable, provide additional support for a user to maintain a seated position on the panel. A foot support member is provided for the comfort of the user.

3 Claims, 10 Drawing Sheets

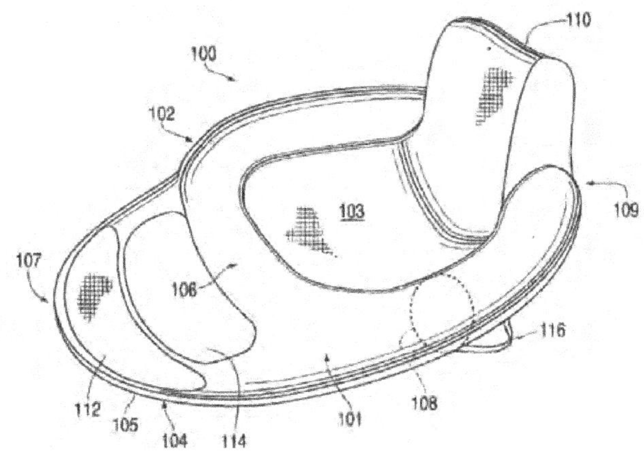

US 8,197,517 B2

Page 2

U.S. PATENT DOCUMENTS

Number	Kind		Date	Name	Class
2,119,023	A		5/1938	Pickard	
2,173,963	A		9/1939	Eubank	
2,190,566	A		2/1940	Julian	
2,344,010	A		3/1944	Walsh	
2,357,789	A		9/1944	Levy	
2,420,344	A		5/1947	Alexander	
2,442,105	A		5/1948	Vacheron	
2,637,861	A		5/1953	Kethledge	
2,731,997	A		1/1956	Muth et al.	
2,803,291	A		8/1957	Meyer	
2,803,839	A		8/1957	Mosley	
2,870,464	A		1/1959	Lalick	
3,052,895	A		9/1962	Lo Vico	
3,336,610	A		8/1967	Geddings	
3,602,930	A		9/1971	Channon	
3,775,782	A		12/1973	Rice et al	
3,860,976	A		1/1975	Suyama	
3,862,876	A		1/1975	Graves	
3,960,161	A		6/1976	Norman	
3,990,463	A		11/1976	Norman	
4,097,944	A		7/1978	Yulish	
4,200,942	A		5/1980	Case	
4,231,125	A		11/1980	Tittl	
D261,464	S		10/1981	Smith	
4,296,788	A		10/1981	Slater	
4,478,587	A		10/1984	Mackal	
4,512,049	A		4/1985	Henry	
4,561,480	A		12/1985	Underwood et al.	
4,576,375	A		3/1986	Roberts	
D289,075	S		3/1987	Wolfe	
D293,012	S		12/1987	Storey et al.	
4,709,430	A		12/1987	Nicoll	
4,766,918	A		8/1988	Odekirk	
4,815,784	A		3/1989	Zheng	
4,825,892	A		5/1989	Norman	
4,858,634	A		8/1989	McLeese	
4,905,332	A		3/1990	Wang	
4,942,838	A		7/1990	Boyer et al	
4,944,707	A		7/1990	Silverglate	
4,946,067	A		8/1990	Kelsall	
4,951,333	A		8/1990	Kaiser et al.	
4,976,642	A		12/1990	Wilkie	
5,004,296	A	*	4/1991	Ziegenfuss, Jr.	297/188.14
5,024,262	A		6/1991	Huang	
5,038,812	A		8/1991	Norman	
5,045,011	A		9/1991	Lovik	
5,056,172	A		10/1991	Kaiser et al.	
5,059,463	A		10/1991	Peters	
5,070,807	A		12/1991	Lewis	
D325,489	S		4/1992	Pratt	
5,116,273	A		5/1992	Chan	
5,123,869	A		6/1992	Schipmann	
5,163,192	A		11/1992	Watson	
5,163,461	A		11/1992	Ivanovich et al.	
5,206,964	A		5/1993	Wilson, Sr.	
5,213,147	A		5/1993	Zheng	
5,261,131	A		11/1993	Kilby	
5,299,331	A		4/1994	Badillo	
D349,593	S		8/1994	Hensley	
5,334,067	A		8/1994	Henry et al.	
5,345,627	A		9/1994	Cammarata	
5,358,440	A		10/1994	Zheng	
5,385,518	A		1/1995	Turner	
5,396,917	A		3/1995	Hazinski et al.	
5,430,980	A		7/1995	Ferrier	
5,433,433	A		7/1995	Armell	
5,435,025	A		7/1995	Gerard et al.	
5,454,643	A		10/1995	Sullivan	
5,467,794	A		11/1995	Zheng	
5,476,404	A	*	12/1995	Price	441/131
D366,161	S		1/1996	Arcouette	
D366,177	S		1/1996	Dean	
5,507,674	A		4/1996	Yeung	
5,520,561	A		5/1996	Langenohl	
D371,252	S		7/1996	Chaput	
5,533,653	A		7/1996	Kaufman	
5,560,385	A		10/1996	Zheng	
5,571,036	A		11/1996	Hannigan	
5,579,799	A		12/1996	Zheng	
5,592,961	A		1/1997	Chin	
5,618,110	A		4/1997	Sullivan	
5,618,246	A		4/1997	Zheng	
RE35,571	E		7/1997	McLeese	
5,644,807	A		7/1997	Battistella	
D384,721	S		10/1997	Peterson	
5,688,052	A		11/1997	Compton	
5,693,398	A		12/1997	Granger	
D389,362	S		1/1998	Boulatian	
5,718,612	A		2/1998	Elsholz	
5,729,846	A		3/1998	Sullivan	
5,730,529	A		3/1998	Fritz et al.	
5,810,695	A		9/1998	Sass	
D400,749	S		11/1998	Bechtold, Jr	
D406,299	S		3/1999	Huston	
5,885,123	A		3/1999	Clifford	
D416,063	S		11/1999	Scheurer et al.	
5,976,023	A		11/1999	Cho	
6,030,300	A		2/2000	Zheng	
D425,357	S		5/2000	Waring	
D426,415	S		6/2000	Le Gette et al.	
6,073,283	A		6/2000	Zheng	
6,113,453	A		9/2000	Stuffelbeam	
6,170,100	B1		1/2001	Le Gette et al	
6,173,671	B1		1/2001	Casull	
D437,283	S		2/2001	Peterson	
6,192,635	B1		2/2001	Zheng	
6,223,673	B1		5/2001	Mears et al.	
6,257,943	B1		7/2001	Peterson	
6,276,979	B1		8/2001	Saltel et al.	
D447,661	S		9/2001	Le Gette et al	
D449,193	S		10/2001	Le Gette et al.	
D465,540	S		11/2002	Peterson	
6,485,344	B2		11/2002	Arias	
D485,593	S		1/2004	Muci	
6,971,936	B2		12/2005	Le Gette et al	
7,097,524	B2		8/2006	Arias	
7,147,528	B2		12/2006	Arias	
D610,216	S		2/2010	Le Gette et al	
7,727,038	B2		6/2010	Le Gette et al.	
2003/0232551	A1		12/2003	Zheng	
2004/0224583	A1		11/2004	Zheng	

OTHER PUBLICATIONS

Office Action for Chinese Patent Application No. 200410005842.2, mailed on May 11, 2007; 9 pages.

Office Action for Chinese Patent Application No. 200410005842.2, mailed on Nov. 2, 2007; 4 pages.

Supplementary European Search Report for European Application No. 04711822.9, dated Apr. 28, 2010; 5 pages.

Office Action for European Application No. 04711822.9, dated Oct. 8, 2010; 6 pages.

* cited by examiner

U.S. Patent **Oct. 26, YR-6** **Sheet 1 of 10** **US 8,197,517 B2**

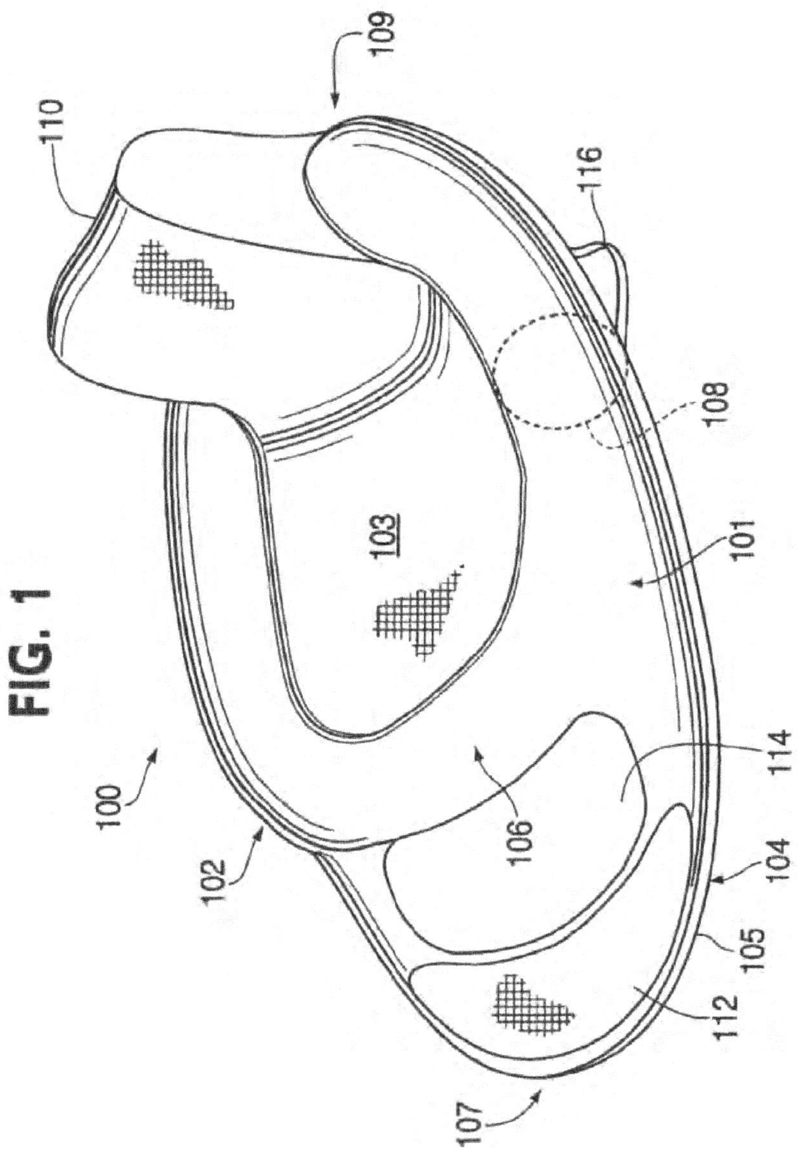

U.S. Patent Oct. 26, YR-6 Sheet 2 of 10 US 8,197,517 B2

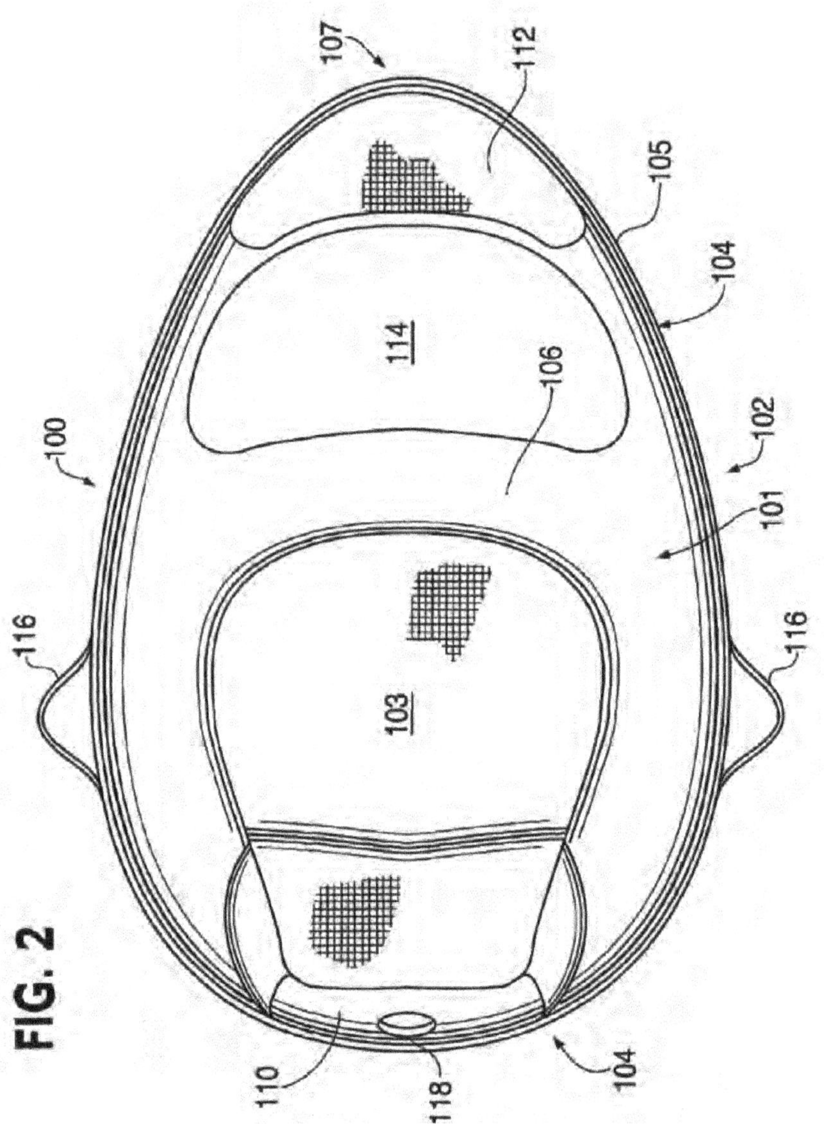

U.S. Patent **Oct. 26, YR-6** **Sheet 3 of 10** **US 8,197,517 B2**

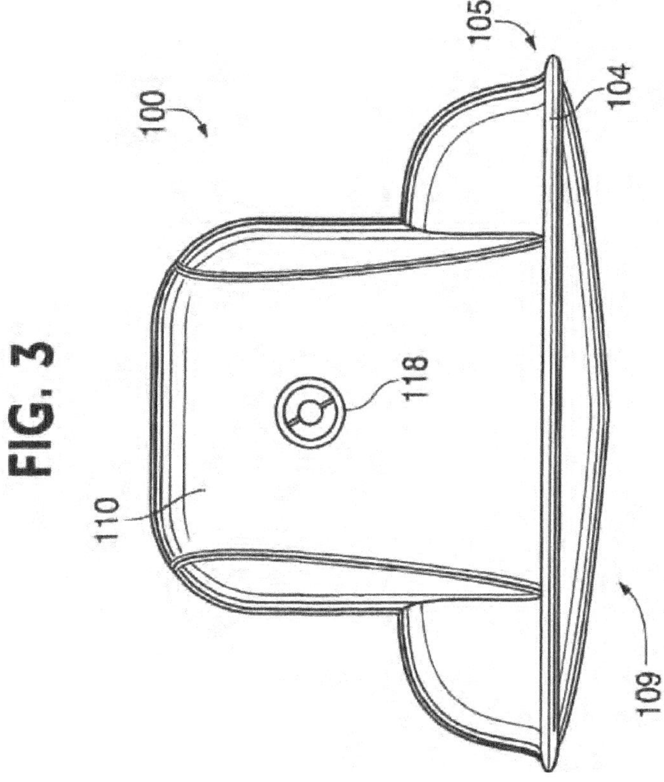

FIG. 3

U.S. Patent Oct. 26, YR-6 Sheet 4 of 10 US 8,197,517 B2

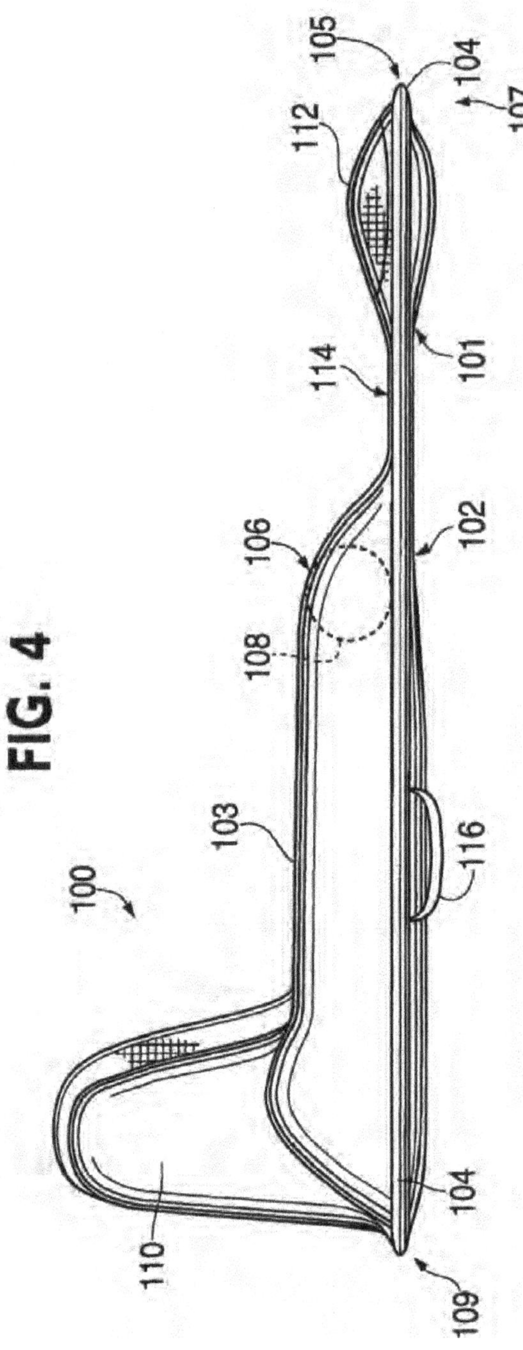

U.S. Patent Oct. 26, YR-6 Sheet 5 of 10 **US 8,197,517 B2**

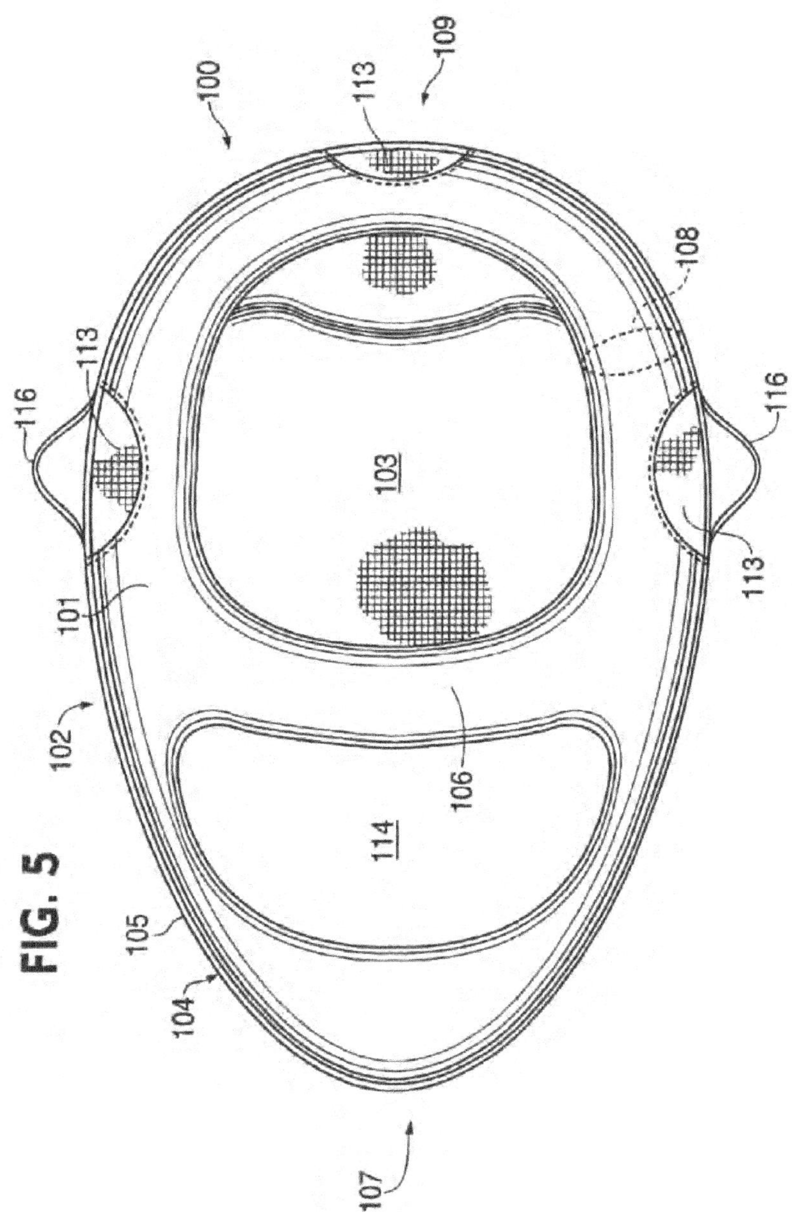

FIG. 5

U.S. Patent Oct. 26, YR-6 Sheet 6 of 10 US 8,197,517 B2

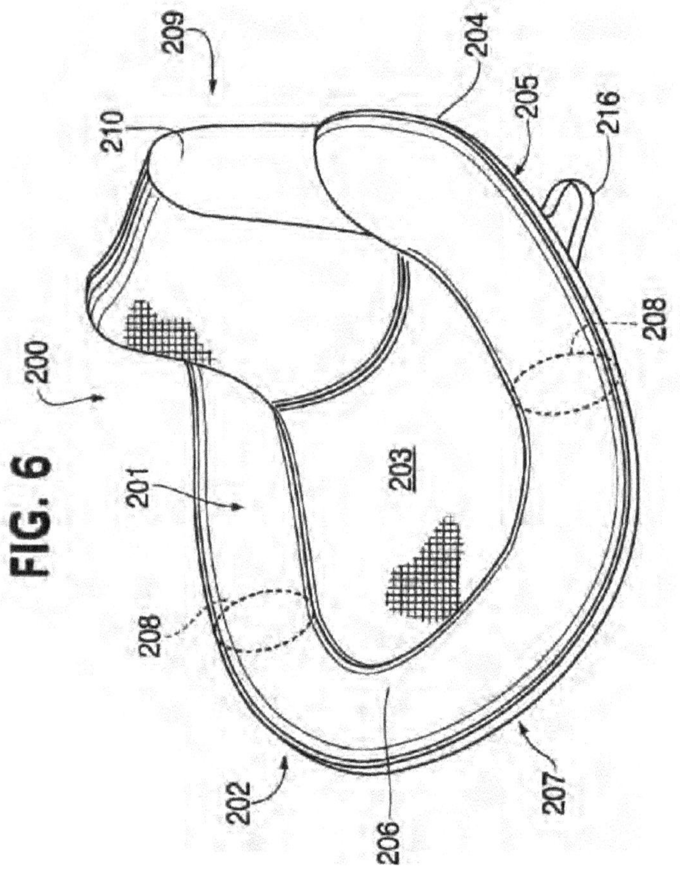

U.S. Patent **Oct. 26, YR-6** **Sheet 7 of 10** **US 8,197,517 B2**

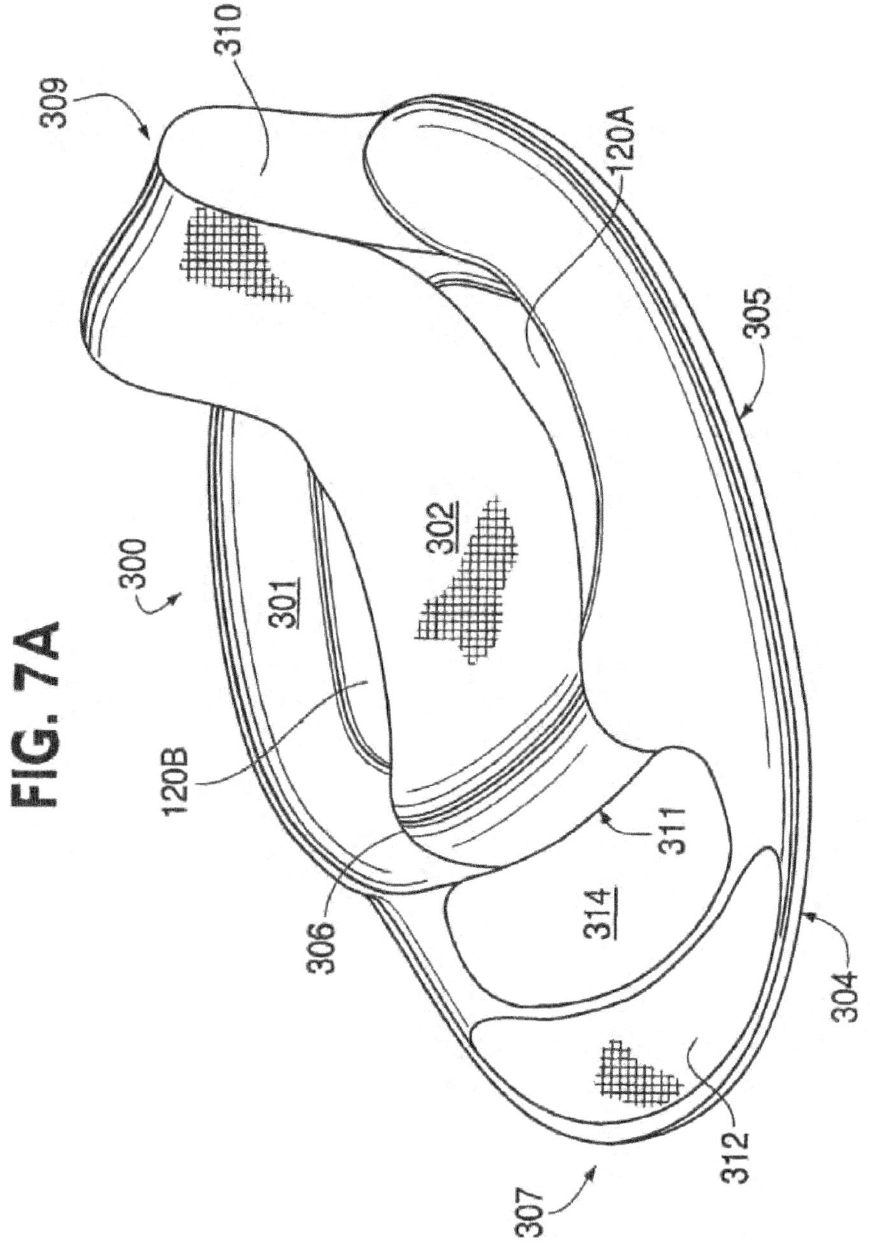

U.S. Patent Oct. 26, YR-6 Sheet 8 of 10 US 8,197,517 B2

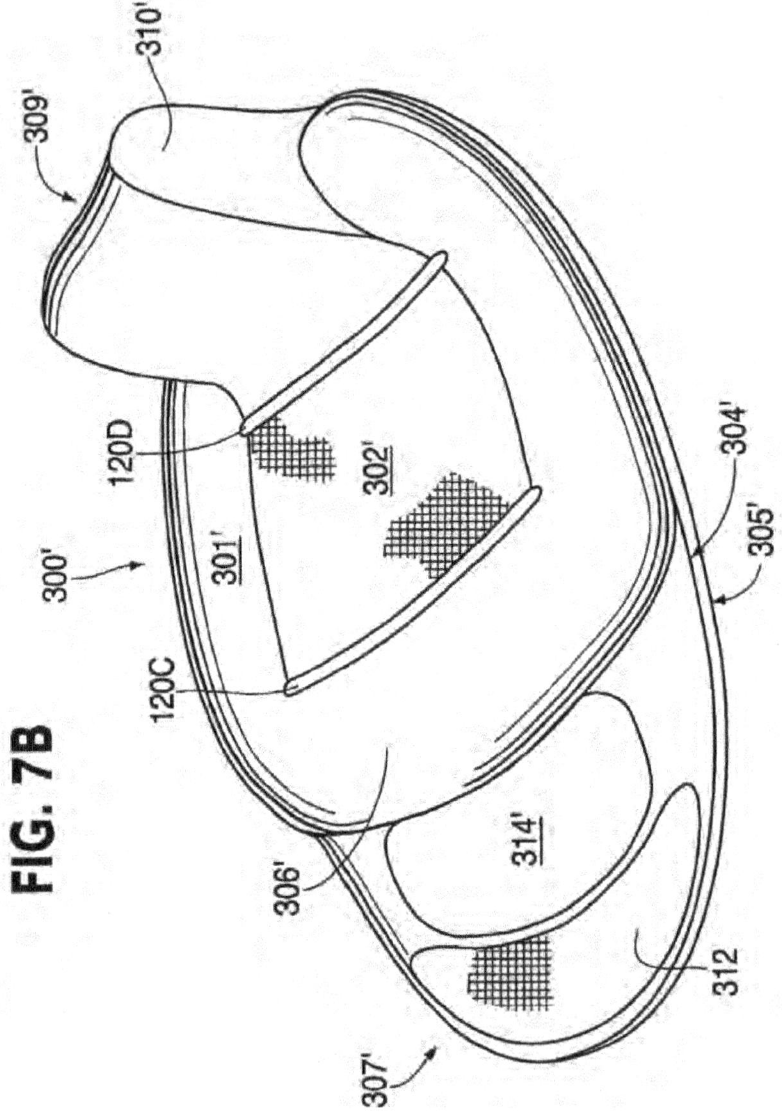

FIG. 7B

U.S. Patent Oct. 26, YR-6 Sheet 9 of 10 **US 8,197,517 B2**

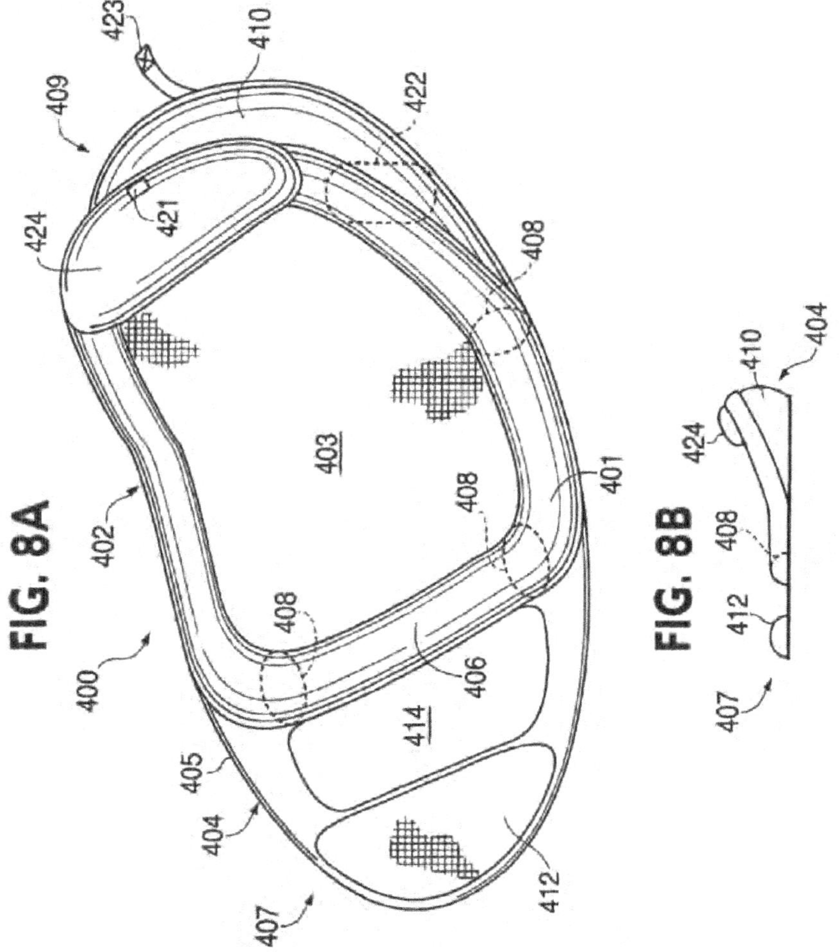

FIG. 8A

FIG. 8B

U.S. Patent Oct. 26, YR-6 Sheet 10 of 10 US 8,197,517 B2

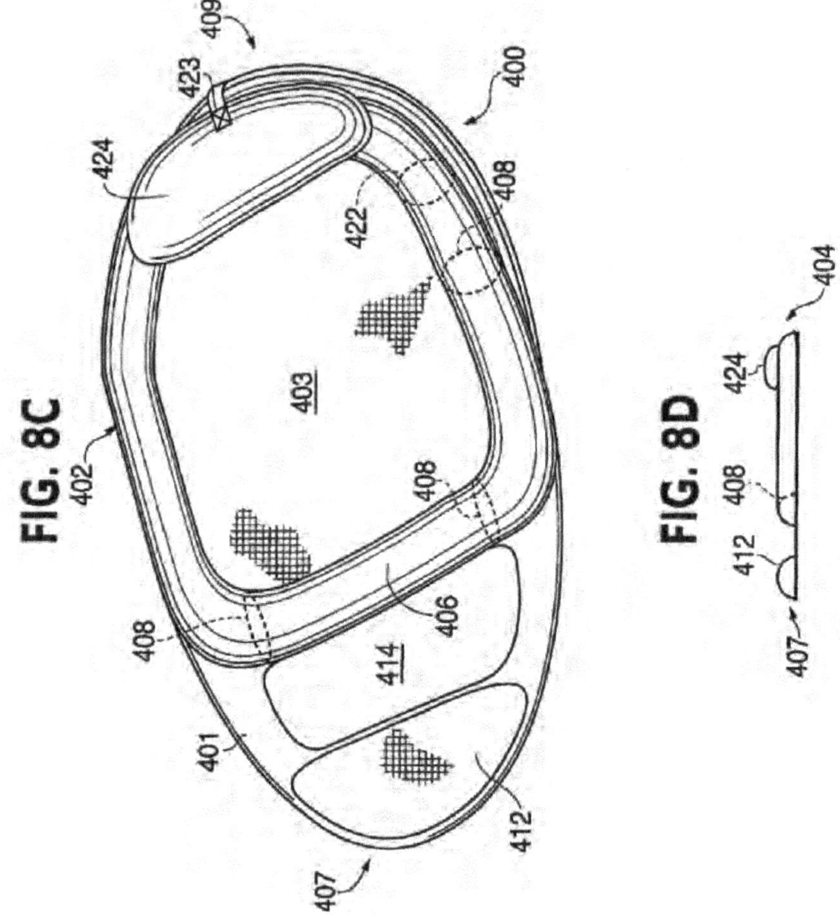

US 8,197,517 B2

1

COLLAPSIBLE FLOTATION DEVICE

CROSS-REFERENCE TO RELATED APPLICATIONS

This application is a continuation of U.S. application Ser. No. 11/234,567 filed May 31 YR-9 now U.S. Pat. No. 4,249, 454, which is a continuation of U.S. application Ser. No. 10/345,678, filed Feb. 21 YR-10, now U.S. Pat. No. 3,401,020 each of the disclosures of which is incorporated herein by reference in its entirety.

FIELD OF THE INVENTION

The invention relates to collapsible flotation devices. More specifically, the invention is directed to a collapsible flotation device having a support member that allows a user to float thereon in a seated position.

BACKGROUND

Inflatable flotation devices are well-known, such as floats, rafts, lifeboats, life preservers, and other similar devices. Standard flotation devices generally maintain their shape by the air pressure of the device alone, and collapse when deflated. One example of a typical inflatable flotation device is the inflatable rescue raft described in U.S. Pat. No. 3,775, 782 to Rice, et al. Like many other inflatable flotation devices that are commonly known, this inflatable rescue raft maintains its shape by way of its air pressure, and loses its shape when deflated, which allows the raft to be rolled, folded, or stored in a compact, deflated size.

More recently, collapsible flotation devices that use collapsible springs to assist in retaining the device's shape have become known. Because of the use of collapsible springs, less air may be used since air pressure is not entirely relied upon to maintain the device's shape. An example of a collapsible flotation device that makes use of collapsible springs to help maintain the device's shape and inflatable portions to provide buoyancy when used in water is described in U.S. Pat. No. 6,485,344 to Arias, the disclosure of which is incorporated herein by reference in its entirety. As is the case with many flotation devices, the flotation device of the Arias patent is generally used by a person in a laying or prone position.

It would be desirable to provide a collapsible flotation device with all of the attendant advantages of known collapsible flotation devices, which would have the added advantage of being easily used by a user in a seated position. Having a collapsible flotation device that is configured to be used in a seated position would be desirable for many activities in which a laying or prone position is less advantageous.

2

SUMMARY

A collapsible device provides a panel with an inner portion and an outer portion. A spring is disposed about the outer portion of the panel and is movable between a coiled configuration and an uncoiled configuration. A support member that traverses the panel is also provided. An inflatable bladder is disposed about at least a part of an outer portion of the panel, and is disposed proximate to the support member. The inflatable bladder is configured to buoyantly support the body weight of a user disposed on the panel.

Further features of the invention, and the advantages offered thereby, are explained in greater detail hereinafter with references to specific embodiments illustrated in the accompanying drawings, wherein like elements are indicated by like reference designators.

BRIEF DESCRIPTION OF THE DRAWINGS

FIG. **1** is a perspective view of a collapsible flotation device, in accordance with an embodiment of the invention.

FIG. **2** is a top view of a collapsible flotation device, in accordance with an embodiment of the invention.

FIG. **3** is a back view of a collapsible flotation device, in accordance with an embodiment of the invention.

FIG. **4** is a side view of a collapsible flotation device, in accordance with an embodiment of the invention.

FIG. **5** is a bottom view of a collapsible flotation device, in accordance with an embodiment of the invention.

FIG. **6** is a perspective view of a collapsible flotation device, in accordance with an embodiment of the invention.

FIG. **7**A is a perspective view of a collapsible flotation device, in accordance with an embodiment of the invention.

FIG. **7**B is a perspective view of a collapsible flotation device, in accordance with an embodiment of the invention.

FIG. **8**A is a perspective view of a collapsible flotation device, showing an inflatable bladder, in accordance with an embodiment of the invention.

FIG. **8**B is a side view of a collapsible flotation device, in accordance with an embodiment of the invention.

FIG. **8**C is a perspective view of a collapsible flotation device, showing an inflatable bladder, in accordance with an embodiment of the invention.

FIG. **8**D is a side view of a collapsible flotation device, in accordance with an embodiment of the invention.

DETAILED DESCRIPTION

To facilitate an understanding of the principles and features of the invention, it is explained hereinafter with reference to its implementation in illustrative embodiments. In particular, the invention is described in the context of a collapsible flotation device configured to support a user, or multiple users, in a seated position. Various configurations are disclosed herein, each of which is considered to be encompassed within embodiments of the invention. Each of these configurations and embodiments are designed to support a user in a seated position while floating on water.

Multiple embodiments of collapsible flotation devices are disclosed that are configured to allow a user, or users, to remain in a seated position while floating on water. Generally speaking, the various embodiments of the invention allow a user, or users, to buoyantly float near the surface of the water, while only a portion of the user's body is submerged within the water.

The various collapsible flotation devices of the invention are formed from a panel including an inner portion and an outer portion, and a spring disposed about the outer portion of the panel, the spring being movable between a coiled configuration and an uncoiled configuration. The spring operates to change the shape of the flotation device. The spring can be a coiled, or folded upon itself, causing the collapsible flotation device to assume a collapsed configuration, which generally occupies less space and can be advantageous for storage. When the spring is uncoiled, the collapsible flotation device unfolds into its expanded configuration for use, in which it occupies more space. According to embodiments of the invention, the spring may be disposed within a sleeve that is disposed about the outer portion of the panel.

The panel according to embodiments of the invention is a device that may take on various shapes and forms, and is not necessarily flat. In accordance with embodiments of the invention, the panel may define an extended region, and may be formed from flexible or semi-flexible materials, such as textiles, membranes, or the like. The outer portion of the panel includes the panel's perimeter as well as some portion within the perimeter. The panel has an interior portion that does not include the perimeter or the outer portion of the panel. According to various embodiments of the invention, the interior portion may be disposed proximate to the outer portion. The interior portion can include multiple portions, including but not limited to an inner portion, a seating area, or the like. In accordance with some embodiments of the invention, the outer portion of the panel can include one or more buoyant members (e.g., an inflatable bladder), one or more support members (e.g., a spring, rigid support member, or semi-rigid member), one or more foot support members, one or more back support members, and so forth, and the interior portion of the panel may include an inner portion, a seating area, a support member, a hole or opening, and so forth. Alternatively, according to other embodiments of the invention, elements associated above with the outer portion of the panel may be associated with the interior portion of the panel, and elements associate with the interior portion may be associate with the outer portion of the panel.

The various embodiments of the invention make use of a support member that traverses the panel of the flotation device. This support member can provide the support required to allow a user to remain in a seated position while floating on water. An inflatable bladder is disposed about at least a part of the outer portion of the flotation device's panel, and is coupled to the support member. The inflatable bladder is configured to buoyantly support the body weight of a user on the panel, and the combination of this inflatable bladder and the support member is configured to support a user in a seated position on the panel, while floating in or on water. A back support, which may be inflatable, is also provided in connection with embodiments of the invention. The back support can be configured to support a user in a seated position in combination with the inflatable bladder and the support member.

Because of the positioning of the support member, and the inflatable bladder coupled thereto, a user can easily sit on the panel, and need not remain in a lying or prone position. The collapsible flotation device of the invention can be configured in a variety of shapes and designs to provide maximum utility. In accordance with an embodiment of the invention, the flotation device is an oval or elliptical shape. In accordance with other embodiments of the invention, however, the flotation device of the invention can comprise a variety of shapes including, but not limited to, elliptical, circular, rectangular, triangular, diamond-shaped, hourglass shaped, and so forth.

The collapsible flotation device of the invention may also make use of a variety of configurations to provide maximum utility to a user. For example, the flotation device may make use of multiple inflatable bladders instead of a single bladder. Additional bladders can be added to provide additional buoyancy, seating position support, adjustable back support, headrest support, and so forth. For example, an inflatable foot support member, upon which a user's feet may be rested, is provided according to embodiments of the invention. According to other embodiments of the invention, an inflatable headrest may be provided. Additionally, the back support may be configured to recline at various angles associated with various levels of inflation of the back support. Various pockets, straps, coverings, containers, valves, mechanical devices, and so forth are also used in connection with the collapsible flotation device according to various embodiments of the invention to provide a user with a variety of desired functionalities.

The flotation device of the invention can be constructed from a variety of different materials. For example, the panel may be made from a water permeable material, such as a mesh or similar material, which allows for a user disposed thereon to be seated partially within the water upon which the flotation device is floating. Water impermeable material may be used to protect portions or components of the flotation device that are sensitive to water exposure.

In accordance with embodiments of the invention, the collapsible flotation device may be configured to allow more than one user to be supported thereon. Specifically, the shape of the flotation device can be altered such that it provides sitting areas for multiple users. Alternatively, one or more flotation devices configured to support a single user can be connected by way of a connecting portion.

An example of a collapsible flotation device **100** according to an embodiment of the invention is shown in FIG. **1** in a perspective view. The flotation device **100** includes a panel **102** that has an outer portion **101** and an interior portion. The outer portion **101** may include, for example, a sleeve **105**, one or more inflatable bladders **108**, a back support member **110**, and a foot support member **112**, or portions of the panel proximate thereto. The interior portion may include, for example, an inner portion **103** (e.g., a seating area), a support member **106**, a back support member **110**, a headrest (not shown in FIG. **1**), a foot support member **112**, a hole **114**, or portions of the panel proximate thereto.

A rigid support member, or shape-retaining member, **104** (e.g., a coilable spring) is disposed about the outer portion **101** of the panel **102**. According to an embodiment of the invention, the rigid support member **104** may be, for example, a permanently rigid or semi-rigid member. Alternatively, the rigid support member **104** may be a coilable spring configured to change between a coiled and an uncoiled position.

As illustrated in FIG. **1**, the inner portion **103** of the panel **102** may be constructed from a material that is different than the material of the outer portion **101** of the panel **102**. For example, in accordance with an embodiment of the invention, the inner portion **103** of the panel **102** could be a membrane made from a mesh, or similar material, while the material of the outer portion **101** of the panel **102** could be a nylon, or other suitable material. When the flotation device **100** has a user seated thereon, the inner portion **103** of the panel **102** is partially submerged in water. Therefore, using a mesh, or other similar material, water can freely pass, thereby partially submerging a user seated in the inner portion **103** of the panel **102**.

The coilable spring **104** provides rigidity to the flotation device **100** while the flotation device **100** is in an expanded configuration. Advantageously, however, the coilable may be folded upon itself, or coiled, into a coiled configuration, thereby collapsing the flotation device **100** into a space-saving collapsed configuration. According to embodiments of the invention, the coilable spring **104** may be disposed within a sleeve **105**, which is disposed about the outer portion **101** of the panel **102**.

An example of a coilable spring used for rigidity in a collapsible device, and the technique of transforming a collapsible device between a collapsed configuration and an expanded configuration can be seen in U.S. Pat. No. 6,170,100 to Le Gette et al., the disclosure of which is incorporated by reference herein in its entirety. The coilable spring used in connection with the flotation device **100** generally has an elongated cross section, such as a rounded rectangular cross section, that provides rigidity in the plane of the coilable spring when uncoiled, but which allows the spring to be folded onto itself. The Le Gette et al. patent illustrates the manner in which the collapsible flotation device **100** of the invention can be folded to a collapsed configuration for storage, or to minimize the space that it occupies.

The coilable spring **104** of the flotation device **100** has a generally rounded, or circular shape when uncoiled. The spring **104** can be coupled to the panel **102** (e.g., by way of a sleeve **105**, etc.) in such a manner that the shape of the panel **102** changes the shape of the spring **104**. Thus, when the panel **102** is an oval shape, the spring **104** takes on an oval-like shape to support a generally oval-shaped device **100**. The sleeve **105** is shown circumscribing the outer portion **101** of the panel **102**, although the sleeve **105** may be located in a variety of locations.

The flotation device **100** also has a support member **106** that traverses the panel **102**. In the embodiment illustrated in FIG. **1**, the support member **106** is located at approximately one-third of the distance from the foot end **107** of the flotation device **100**. However, it will be appreciated that the precise location of the support member **106** may be varied, according to various design parameters and objectives. For example, to allow a user to be seated within the inner portion **103** of the panel **102**, the location of the support member **106** may vary according to the anticipated girth of the user. Moreover, the support member **106** can be adjustable, removable, and attachable, in accordance with embodiments of the invention.

An inflatable bladder is disposed about at least a part of the outer portion of the panel **102**, and is coupled to the support member **106**. A cross-section of the inflatable bladder **108** is shown by a broken line as being contained within the outer portion **101** of the panel **102**. According to embodiments of the invention, the inflatable bladder **108** can also be contained within the support member **106**. Thus, the inflatable bladder **108** forms a substantially oval-shape or U-shape. The exact shape of the bladder may vary according to various embodiments of the invention. The inflatable bladder may be made up of multiple inflatable portions, or multiple inflatable bladders. The inflatable bladder **108** is configured to buoyantly support the body weight of a user. When used in combination with the support member **106** and the back support member, the inflatable bladder is configured to support a user in a seated position on the panel **102**. To further provide support to a user in a seated position, the inflatable bladder **108** may be shaped in such a way to provide some support to a user's back.

In contrast to known collapsible flotation devices, the device **100** shown in FIG. **1**, as well as the devices according to the alternative embodiments of the invention, allow a user to easily remain in a seated position while floating on water because of the location of the support member **106**. Specifically, when a user is seated on an inner portion **103** of the panel **102**, the relative proximity of the support member **106** to the user's rear end supports the user's legs, and in combination with the inflatable bladder **108**, allows a user to remain in a seated position.

The collapsible flotation device **100** illustrated in FIG. **1** also makes use of a back support member **110**. This back support member **110** provides additional support for a user to remain in a seated position on the inner portion **103** of the panel **102**. In the particular embodiment illustrated in FIG. **1**, the back support member **110** is inflatable. Alternatively, the back support member **110** can have a variety of configurations relative to the panel **102**, thereby providing adequate support for a user to remain in a seated position. In embodiments where the back support member **110** is inflatable, it can be inflated by a separate inflatable bladder. In another embodiment, the inflatable bladder **108** can also be shaped so that it also inflates within the back support member **110**. In yet another embodiment, the back support member can be inflated by an inflatable bladder portion integrally formed with bladder **108**. The back support member **110** can be shaped so that it supports a user's back, while the user is in an upright-seated position and the user's head, while the user is in a reclined position between an upright-seated position and a prone position. Additionally, the back support member **110** can be inflatable to different levels to provide a plurality of reclining support levels.

The collapsible flotation device **100** illustrated in FIG. **1** also has other convenient features. One such feature is a foot support member **112** located at the foot end **107** of the flotation device **100** opposite the head end **109**. In accordance with an embodiment of the invention, the foot support member **112** may be inflatable or otherwise buoyant. The foot support member can alternatively be made from a cushioning material to provide a comfortable footrest for a user seated on the panel **102**. In embodiments where the foot support member **112** is a cushion, it may be made, for example, from foam, or other suitable material that is able to be used or that floats in water. It may be desirable to make the foot support member from a material that is resistant to water damage. In embodiments where the foot support member **112** is inflatable, it may be inflated by using a separate inflatable bladder, or by connecting the inflatable bladder **108**, or another inflatable bladder in the device **100**, to the foot support member **112** to provide air pressure within the foot support member **112**.

According to an embodiment of the invention, the foot support member may be attached to the flotation device **100** by some means other than the panel **102** or the spring **104**. For example, the foot support member **112** can be attached to the flotation device **100** by way of a rigid support member (e.g., plastic rods, etc.), or by way of a non-rigid connection device (e.g., tethers). When attached by a rigid support member, the foot support member **112** would not need to be buoyant; however, in the case of a non-rigid connection device, the foot support member **112** would likely need to be buoyant.

The collapsible flotation device **100** illustrated in FIG. **1** shows a configuration in accordance with an embodiment of the invention that has a hole **114**, through which water may pass or a user may place the user's legs. The inclusion or placement of such a hole **114** is subject to a variety of design parameters and objectives. Accordingly, the invention is intended to encompass collapsible flotation devices with or

US 8,197,517 B2

7

without such holes, or with holes shaped differently, or placed in different locations, than the hole 114 shown in FIG. 1. The presence of an foot support member 112 is entirely optional, as the foot support member 112 could be removed, allowing the hole 114 to be larger and more easily accommodate a user's legs.

Additionally, numerous optional elements can be added to the collapsible flotation device 100 illustrated in FIG. 1, in accordance with various embodiments of the invention that are intended to be embraced within the scope of the inventions. Many of these elements will be illustrated in the various figures. One such element is a strap 116, which is provided, for example, for convenience in removing the device 100 from the water and carrying or transporting the collapsible flotation device 100. While many such features will be illustrated in the drawings and described below, some will not be illustrated, but will merely be described. The invention is intended to embrace those elements shown in the drawings and described below, as well as some items not shown, but readily added.

FIG. 2 is a top view of the collapsible flotation device 100 illustrated in FIG. 1. This top view illustrates many of the same elements described in connection with FIG. 1. Additionally, the top view provides a better angle for viewing various shapes associated with the embodiment of the invention illustrated therein. In addition to features described in connection with FIG. 1, an inflation valve 118 can be seen in FIG. 2, and more clearly in the back view of the flotation device 100 illustrated in FIG. 3.

The inflation valve 118 may be a variety of suitable valves. For example, a standard oral inflation valve could be used, whereby a user could inflate the bladder within the back support member 110 orally. Additionally, other types of valves could be used, such as one-way valves, valves configured to be used with pumps, or other suitable valves. It should be noted that, in addition to inflating the back support member 110, the valve 118 could be used to inflate the inflatable bladder 108 in embodiments where the inflatable bladder 108 is shaped to also provide air pressure within the back support member 110. Alternatively, in an embodiment wherein the back support member 110 has a separate inflatable bladder from the inflatable bladder 108, the valve location could house multiple valves to inflate these multiple inflatable bladders. Although the valve 118 is shown in a specific location, the valve, or a plurality of valves, can be located anywhere on the device 100 according to various preferences.

FIG. 4 is a side view of the collapsible flotation device 100. This view illustrates many of the same features shown in FIGS. 1-3. Additionally, the broken line 108 illustrates a cross-section of the inflatable bladder where it passes through the support member 106.

FIG. 5 is a bottom view of the collapsible floatation device 100 in accordance with an embodiment of the invention. Features illustrated in FIG. 5 can be used in connection with the various embodiments of the invention, and are not limited to the device 100. The bottom view shown in FIG. 5 shows drain areas 113 that allow water to drain from within the panel 102 (e.g., from within the sleeve 105). Thus, water that accumulates within the device 100 as it is used in the water drains from the device 100 via the drain areas 113 as the device 100 is pulled from the water (e.g., by way of the handles 116). The drain areas may be made of any material suitable to allow the passage of water, such as a mesh or other porous material and can be located anywhere on the flotation device 100.

FIG. 6 is a perspective view of a collapsible flotation device 200, in accordance with another embodiment of the invention. This flotation device 200 differs from the flotation

8

device illustrated in FIGS. 1-4, in that it does not have a foot support member at the foot end 207 of the panel 202. Like the flotation device 100 illustrated in FIGS. 1-4, however, the flotation device 200 also uses a panel 202 having an inner portion 203 and an outer portion 201, a spring 204, a support member 206, an inflatable bladder 208 (the cross section of which is represented by broken lines), and a back support member 210. According to an embodiment of the invention, the support member 206 and the inflatable bladder 208 form an integral piece. In other embodiments, the support member 206, the inflatable bladder 208, and the back support member 210 can form an integral piece. The spring 204 is disposed within a sleeve 205, which is disposed about the outer portion 201 of the panel 202. Other features can be provided associated with the flotation device 200 that are not shown, such as a pillow-shaped headrest, pockets, and so forth.

The flotation device 200 of FIG. 6 provides similar support for a user in a seated position to the flotation device 100 illustrated in FIGS. 1-4 by way of the support member 206, the inflatable bladder 208, and the back support member 210. By way of the combination of the support member 210 positioned at the head end 209 of the panel, the inflatable bladder 208, and the back support member 210, a user can remain comfortably seated within the inner portion 203 of the panel 202 while the flotation device 200 floats in water. The height of the back support member can be adjusted either by way of differing inflation amounts or otherwise, according to a user's comfort preferences. Additionally, a handle 216 is provided for convenience in removing the device 200 from the water or carrying the device.

FIGS. 7A and 7B are perspective views of collapsible flotation devices in accordance with embodiments of the invention. The flotation device 300, 300' is similar to the flotation devices 100 and 200 described above. The flotation device 300, 300' is a chair including a seat portion 301, 301' and a membrane 302, 302'. The membrane 302, 302' has a first and a second end, each of the ends being coupled to one of the seat portion 301, 301' and the back portion 310, 310'. The spring 304, 304', which may be disposed within a sleeve 305, 305', is coupled to at least a part of the seat portion 301, 301' of the chair 300, 300'.

The embodiments of the flotation device 300, 300' illustrated in FIGS. 7A and 7B provide a somewhat suspended, hammock-like membrane 302, 302' within a seating area, about which the seat portion 301, 301' is disposed. When a user is seated on the membrane 302, 302', and the flotation device 300, 300' is on water, water is allowed to pass through the holes 120A, 120B, 120C, 120D, and the user remains partially supported by the membrane 302, 302' while being partially submerged in the water. Also provided is a footrest 312, 312' at the foot end 307, 307' of the device 300, 300'.

The flotation device shown in FIG. 7A has a membrane 302, which is coupled to a section 311 of the seat portion 301 and the back portion 310 located at a head end 309 of the device 300. The membrane 302 is shown as being coupled to the back portion 310 at the top of the back portion; however, the membrane can be attached to the back portion 310 along any part of the back portion 310. Additionally, the end of the membrane 302 coupled to the back portion 310 can be coupled to both the back portion 310 and the seat portion 301 proximate to the back portion 310. The flotation device shown in FIG. 7B has a membrane 302' that is oriented in a different direction, and is coupled to two locations of the seat portion 301'. Although the membrane 302' is not shown as coupled to the back support member 310' in FIG. 7B, according to another embodiment of the invention it can be coupled to two locations of the seat portion 301' and to the back support

US 8,197,517 B2

9

member 310'. Alternatively, the membrane 302' could be attached to multiple locations of the seat portion 301'. For example, according to an embodiment of the invention, the membrane 302' could be attached to 3 locations of the seat portion 301' (e.g., the two locations shown, and a third location opposite the back portion 310').

FIGS. 8A-D illustrate a flotation device 400 that provides a user support in a variety of reclined seating positions, being able to move between a range of seated positions, ranging from an upright seated position to a prone position. Thus, the flotation device can move between a first configuration corresponding to an upright-seated position to a second configuration corresponding to a prone position. FIG. 8A is the perspective view and FIG. 8B is a side view of the flotation device 400 with the back support member 410 being in a partially reclined position. FIG. 8C is a perspective view and FIG. 8D is a side view of the flotation device with the back support member 410 in a fully reclined, or prone position.

FIG. 8A shows a perspective view of the flotation device 400 with the back support member in a partially reclined position. The inflatable bladder 408 is shown by way of a series of broken lines. This illustration shows that the inflatable bladder is disposed about at least a part of the outer portion 401 of the panel 402, and is coupled to the support member 406 (i.e., in this embodiment it is disposed within the support member 406). Additionally, the location of an additional inflatable bladder 422, used to inflate the back support member 410, is illustrated by way of a broken line. As this additional inflatable bladder 422 is inflated, the position of the back support member 410 is changed such that a user may be supported in a variety of reclined seating positions, as well as the upright seated and prone positions. As the bladder 422 within the back support member 410 becomes increasingly inflated, the back support member 410 becomes less and less reclined, and a user approaches an upright seated position.

As discussed above, the back support member 410 may or may not be inflated by way of a separate bladder 422. In accordance with embodiments of the invention, the inflatable bladder 408 may be shaped such that it inflates portions of the panel 402 as well as the back support member 410. Furthermore, the support member 406 may be inflated by way of the inflatable bladder 408, or by way of a separate support member inflatable bladder, which is represented by the broken lines shown within the support member 406.

A headrest 424 is shown as being coupled to the back support member 410. The headrest 424 may be attached to the back support member 410 in a variety of ways. For example, as will be discussed below, the headrest may be fixedly attached to the support member 410, or may be detachable. As discussed above, the back support member 410 can itself provide the basic function of a headrest when the user is seated in certain positions. The headrest 424 may, therefore, be considered to be an additional headrest, providing cushioning in addition to any headrest-like cushioning provided by the back support member 410.

FIG. 8C shows a perspective view of the flotation device 400 with the back support member in a fully reclined or prone position. This prone position is achieved by deflating the inflatable bladder 422 within the back support member 410. A range of reclined positions can be achieved by way of inflating the additional inflatable bladder 422, which can include a range between an upright-seated position and a prone position.

Although the configuration shown in FIGS. 8C and 8D most comfortably supports a user in a prone position, the combination of the support member 406 and inflatable bladder 408 can accommodate a user in a seated position. The

10

flotation device 400 of FIGS. 8A-D also includes a foot support member 412 at the foot end 407, and may include a sleeve 405 within which the spring 404 can be disposed. A connector 423 can be removably attached to a receptor 421 on the headrest 424 or the back support member 410 to secure the back support member 410 or the headrest 424, when the back support member 410 is deflated in the position shown in FIGS. 8C and 8D.

From the foregoing, it can be seen that the present invention provides a variety of collapsible flotation devices, which can be used to support a user in a seated position while floating on water. Additionally, according to various embodiments of the invention, the collapsible flotation devices may be provided with numerous convenient features, to provide additional functionality desired by users. Furthermore, various embodiments of the present invention provide for multiuser or multiple connected collapsible flotation devices, which may be used by multiple users.

The invention can be embodied in other specific forms without departing from the spirit or essential characteristics thereof. For example, while the invention has been described in the context of a device that makes use of an inflatable bladder, the floatation devices according to embodiments of the invention can make use of other buoyant members in the place of inflatable bladders that provide a buoyancy similar to the buoyancy provided by the inflatable bladder or bladders described above. One such buoyant member, for example, can be a foam insert that can be coupled to the device to provide adequate buoyant support to a user seated in the device.

Additionally, the embodiments of the collapsible flotation devices shown in the figures, multiple features could be added to these flotation devices according to a user's need, market demand, design specifications, or the like. Moreover, additional convenient features can be readily added to the flotation devices described above. For example, a fastening means could be provided to attach the flotation device of the present invention to a boat, or other vehicle. Likewise, an anchor could be added to maintain a position of the flotation device on a body of water. Other mechanical apparati could be added to the flotation devices of the present invention, such as holders for ores, holders for fishing poles, propellers, paddles, foot pedals to power the paddles, solar panels to power electronic devices, and the like.

Furthermore, it will be appreciated that the choice of materials and size and shape of the various elements of the invention could be varied according to particular design specifications or constraints requiring a flotation device according to the invention.

The presently disclosed embodiments are, therefore, considered in all respects to be illustrative and not restrictive. The scope of the invention is indicated by the appended claims, rather than the foregoing description, and all changes that come within the meaning and range of equivalents thereof are intended to be embraced therein.

What is claimed is:

1. An apparatus, comprising:

a panel including an inner portion, an outer portion and a back support portion, the inner portion of the panel having a first edge and a second edge on an opposite side of the inner portion of the panel from the first edge, a distance between the first edge of the inner portion of the panel and the second edge of the inner portion of the panel defining a width of the inner portion of the panel, the inner portion of the panel being substantially planar across the width of the inner portion of the panel, the back support portion being inflatable; and

a buoyant member disposed about at least the inner portion

US 8,197,517 B2

11 12

of the panel, at least a portion of the buoyant member being disposed within at least a portion of the outer portion of the panel, the buoyant member having a first portion and a second portion different from the first portion, the first portion of the buoyant member and the second portion of the buoyant member being disposed at opposite locations of the inner portion of the panel and separated by the width of the inner portion of the panel, the inner portion of the panel extending continuously between the first portion of the buoyant member and the second portion of the buoyant member without an intervening buoyant member,

at least one of the outer portion of the panel within which the first portion of the buoyant member is at least partially disposed or the first portion of the buoyant member being in contact with the first edge of the inner portion of the panel,

at least one of the outer portion of the panel within which the second portion of the buoyant member is at least partially disposed or the second portion of the buoyant member being in contact with the second edge of the inner portion of the panel,

the buoyant member having an outermost width that substantially defines an outermost width of the apparatus, the apparatus being configured to support a user in a seated position.

2. An apparatus, comprising:

a panel including an inner portion, an outer portion and a back support portion, the inner portion of the panel including a mesh material, the panel defining an opening configured to collectively receive a user's legs therethrough, the opening being outside the inner portion of the panel, the back support portion being inflatable; and

a buoyant member disposed about at least a portion of the outer portion of the panel, the buoyant member having a front portion, the front portion of the buoyant member and the back support member being disposed at opposite locations of the inner portion of the panel and separated by a length of the inner portion of the panel, the front portion of the buoyant member being disposed between the inner portion of the panel and the opening,

the combination of the buoyant member, the panel and the back support portion being collectively configured to support the user in a seated position.

3. An apparatus, comprising:

a panel including an inner portion, an outer portion and a back support portion, the inner portion of the panel including a mesh material, the panel defining an opening, the back support portion being inflatable, the mesh material being disposed at least between the back support portion and a support portion defined by the panel;

a buoyant member disposed about at least a portion of the outer portion of the panel, the combination of the buoyant member, the panel and the back support portion being collectively configured to support a user in a seated position; and

a foot support disposed at an end portion of the panel, the opening disposed between the foot support and the support portion, the foot support configured to buoyantly support a weight of the user's feet.

* * * * *

UNITED STATES DISTRICT COURT
FOR THE DISTRICT OF NITA

Nita City Division

SWIMTIME CORPORATION, Plaintiff, v. WATER-FUN, INC., Defendant.	)))))))	Civil Action No. 1:Y00-cv-00100

ANSWER

Defendant Water-Fun Industries, Inc. ("Water-Fun") hereby answers the separately numbered allegations of the plaintiff's Complaint as follows:

1. Admitted.
2. Admitted.
3. No response is required.
4. Admitted.
5. Admitted.
6. Water-Fun denies that it has committed any acts of infringement, otherwise admitted.
7. Water-Fun is without information sufficient to admit or deny the averments of this paragraph and requests plaintiff provide such information, if material.
8. Water-Fun is without information sufficient to admit or deny the averments of this paragraph and requests plaintiff provide such information, if material.
9. Water-Fun is without information sufficient to admit or deny the averments of this paragraph and requests plaintiff provide such information, if material.
10. Water-Fun admits that it markets its products through various advertising media, and certain of those products are available for sale at retail locations throughout the United States and that Water-Fun is an innovative company that has new products in various stages of development and on the way to market, otherwise denied and particularly denied to the extent that patent infringement is alleged.
11. Water-Fun admits that it sells a recliner fabric comfort lounge, otherwise denied and particularly denied to the extent that patent infringement is alleged.
12. Water-Fun repeats and re-alleges its responses to paragraphs 1 through 11, as if fully set forth herein.

13. Denied to the extent the paragraph alleges patent infringement, otherwise Water-Fun is without sufficient information to admit or deny.
14. Denied.
15. Admitted.
16. Denied.
17. Denied.
18. Denied to the extent that the paragraph alleges patent infringement.

First Affirmative Defense

19. On information and belief, one or more claims of the patent in suit are invalid, null, void, and/or unenforceable for failure to comply with the requirements of Title 35, United States Code, including, without limitation, §§ 101, 102, 103, and/or 112 thereof.

Second Affirmative Defense

20. The defendant does not infringe and has not infringed either directly, jointly, contributorily, or by inducement any valid and enforceable claim of any of the patents in suit, either literally or under the doctrine of equivalents.

Additional Affirmative Defenses

21. The defendant reserves the right to assert, and hereby gives notice that it intends to rely upon any other defense that may become available or appear during discovery proceedings or otherwise in this case, and hereby reserves the right to amend its Answer to assert any such defense.

Jury Demand

DEFENDANT HEREBY REQUESTS A TRIAL BY JURY ON ALL CLAIMS SO TRIABLE.

Dated: November 5, YR-1

WATER-FUN, INC.

By: Sal Tambo ____________________

Sal Tambo
Counsel for Defendant
PRUITT MILLER LLP
100 Main Street
Suite 3200
Nita City, Nita 20854
Telephone: (311) 867-5309

CERTIFICATE OF SERVICE

I hereby certify that on November 5, YR-1, I electronically filed the foregoing with the Clerk of the Court using the CM/ECF system, which will send a Notice of Electronic Filing (NEF) to the following counsel of record:

Jim W. Brady
Counsel for Plaintiff
GEORGE BRENT & DAPKUS LLP
1869 Deacon Blvd.
Nita City, Nita 20854
Telephone: (311) 555-8800
Counsel for SWIMTIME CORPORATION

Sal Tambo
Counsel for Defendant
PRUITT MILLER LLP
100 Main Street
Suite 3200
Nita City, Nita 20854
Telephone: (311) 867-5309

Statement of Eric(a) Flax

My name is Eric(a) Flax, and I am forty years old. I reside at 10 Hempstead Drive in Nita City. I am not married, and I have no children. I make this written statement freely and voluntarily and without reservation.

I am the head of Research & Development at SwimTime, Inc. I have worked at SwimTime for the last eleven years and have been in this same position all this time. I was hired in YR-11 by the CEO of SwimTime, Morgan Miller. At the time of my hiring, Miller had been in his position as CEO for several years and hired me with the goal of boosting SwimTime's product line and market share.

I am a mechanical engineer and earned my Bachelor of Science degree from Nita College in YR-19. Upon graduating from Nita College, my first job was with Wilson Sporting Goods as an engineer, where I designed sporting equipment. I was employed with Wilson for about ten years and gradually rose in the ranks there until I was head of a product development team in goal-focused team sports products. In YR-11, I left Wilson and began my employment with SwimTime.

Soon after beginning my employment as head of the SwimTime Research & Development division, I hired a staff of other mechanical engineers and product designers to help develop new water-related products. My staff consisted of Richard Pruitt, August LaCata, Reba Sparks, Leon Holbrook, and Susan Kolb. CEO Miller had tasked me with developing a new line of high-luxury products that would be attractive to pool-owning homeowners, country clubs, resorts, and the like. My team and I got started right away on this project.

Coming from the sporting goods industry, I'd known of and designed many products that included internal mechanisms for rigidly opening and collapsing the products for use and storage, respectively. Such products included things like soccer goals, lacrosse nets, hockey nets, and throwing disks, and I also knew of other products like camping tents and others. I had designed such products to include a metal wire ring in a border hem around the devices' perimeters that can be squeezed between two hands and twisted to collapse the device in half or even a third or less of its opened size for easy storage in an accompanying case. Likewise, when the device was desired to be used, one need only remove it from the case and release it so that the internal wire expands and opens the net or tent or goal to its full size. I knew of the popularity of these products and believed that a similar apparatus would be equally popular in the water accessories market.

My team and I designed a new floating pool lounge chair that incorporated such a design. This lounge chair product was eventually called the Spring Float. We designed the Spring Float to have an internal metal wire coil to allow it to be collapsed and opened in the ways I've described so that it is easy for a homeowner or country club or resort management to store the devices when not in use and also easy to open the devices to use. We also incorporated high-luxury materials, such as high-quality neoprene fabrics and meshes, into the Spring Float designs. Also, we designed the Spring Float to have an ideal sitting position for the user when floating in water. The Spring Float has an optimized seat panel and foot support. It also has a superior back support and high-quality buoyancy components. All of these factors make the Spring Float a winning design and highly desirable to our customers.

Based on our initial concepts for the Spring Float product, my team and I submitted an invention disclosure memorandum to Morgan Miller to notify Miller that we believed we had some patentable innovations. Our initial disclosure focused on the spring opening/closing and support structure of the product, the layout of buoyancy devices within the device, and the overall configuration of features making up the floating recliner. The spring coil design was initially disclosed to include an embodiment where the recliner could be collapsed via a single twist in the coil to roughly about half the overall size of the expanded device. A second embodiment was also disclosed where a double twist in the coil would collapse the float to roughly one third the original expanded size. Another embodiment positioned the spring coil inside a hemmed border of the recliner. A final embodiment left large portions of the coil exposed and retained the spring to the recliner via loops around the perimeter.

Our invention disclosure also identified several buoyancy mechanisms to float the device. A first embodiment disclosed internal and inflatable bladders positioned around the seat component of the recliner. We disclosed an embodiment where only a single inflatable bladder was used and one where two were positioned within the seat perimeter and an embodiment with many inflatable bladders in various locations within the recliner panel. The seat back could also be an inflatable bladder, or not.

Our invention disclosure also identified the general layout and configuration of the floating recliner. We imagined a water-passing, mesh seat to support a user's posterior, surrounded by a large fabric panel and a back support. A foot support was also contemplated where either another mesh panel could support the user's feet or a through-hole could be provided as an opening to the water for the feet.

We worked with outside counsel, the law firm Clark Nikole LLP based in Nita City, to develop a patent application on these concepts. This process took about six months. Our first patent application was filed in the U.S. Patent and Trademark on February 21, YR-10. The application was given the number 10/345,678 by the patent office. We worked with the patent attorney during that applications prosecution to seek allowance of the claims and issuance of the patent, which did eventually issue as U.S. Patent 3,401,020. This patent had claims directed to the spring opening/closing feature I described above in this statement. Before this patent issued, we instructed our patent attorney to file a related patent application—number 11/234,567, filed May 31, YR-9—to cover other inventions disclosed in the original filing. This second application had claims directed to the layout and different materials of the buoyancy components of the product, as I've discussed above in this statement. This second application issued as U.S. Patent 4,249,454. We filed the application that became U.S. Patent 8,197,517 or the '517 patent based on this second application.

I've seen the Water-Fun Recliner products at issue in this case in person. I'm not terribly impressed with their design, although it sure is an improvement over their prior product designs, which had zero innovation whatsoever. The Water-Fun Recliners do seem to copy many aspects of my Spring Float product design, such as the fabric panel covering, the separate seat and foot areas, the back support, etc. They do not include the spring, which really diminishes the overall structural integrity of their products. I am no patent lawyer, but I believe they infringe the '517 patent's claims.

STATEMENT OF MORGAN MILLER

I am Morgan Miller, and I'm the chief executive officer—CEO—of SwimTime Corporation. I swear under oath that this written statement is the truth under penalty of perjury.

I am sixty-nine years old. I reside at 100 Western Avenue, Nita City. I am married and have three children: Brittany, age 21; William, age 19; and Katherine, age 16.

Prior to joining SwimTime in YR-13, I was the senior executive vice president of Product Management for Mattel, Inc. I am well known for my work in making SwimTime the market leader in water leisure products. I have received recognition by my peers in industry publications and have received awards from industry groups. When I was brought on as CEO of SwimTime by its board of directors, the company was ranked in the mid-range of its competitors in the aquatic leisure products market and had net sales of about $25 million per year. Since joining the company, I have raised net sales to over $60 million per year, introduced many fantastic new products to the marketplace, and positioned SwimTime in the top five of industry leaders.

An important first step in my elevation of SwimTime within the industry was focusing the company on the important niches of the market—an important one being luxury pool products. Another important step was my focusing the company on innovation. To each of these ends, I hired Eric(a) Flax, an industry stand-out in product design, as the company's head of Research & Development. I immediately tasked Flax with developing a winning new design for luxury pool float products and provided the resources to do it.

The Spring Float product has been our most successful product ever and is one of the most successful pool accessory products in history. We have three patents covering the technology of the Spring Float product—that is, U.S. Patent No. 3,401,020; U.S. Patent No. 4,249,454; and U.S. Patent No. 8,197,517. The '020 patent covers the spring opening and collapsing mechanism of the Spring Float product. The '454 patent covers some of the innovative materials of which the Spring Float is composed. The '517 patent, the patent asserted against Water-Fun, covers the way the component parts of the Spring Float are combined into a superior water lounge product.

In YR-3, I learned that Water-Fun was selling a product called the Recliner Fabric Comfort Lounge. One of my sales representatives had seen the Water-Fun product for sale at a Target store. He told me that it looked just like our Spring Float products and was being sold right alongside them on the shelf. I had my sales team look into it further and was informed that the Water-Fun Recliner product was being sold in this way in the same stores as our Spring Float all over the U.S. and online.

Upon learning that Water-Fun had commenced selling its Recliner products across the country, including here in Nita, I immediately contacted our patent attorneys and brought this lawsuit. SwimTime simply will not abide having its intellectual property stolen by a second-rate competitor.

Statement of Glenn Berenson

I am Glenn Berenson and I am the CEO of Water-Fun, Inc. I am 58 years old. I reside at 111 Bradley Avenue, Nita City. I am married and have one child—Ashley, 23. I have been the CEO of Water-Fun since YR-25.

Historically, Water-Fun has been one of the leaders in the industry. From the company's beginnings in the 1970s and through the 1980s, we had well over twenty-five percent market share in pool accessory sales. Water-Fun has introduced many very popular water accessories into the marketplace, such as the integrated water float and squirt gun and the water lounge with an integrated beverage holder.

Over the last few years, our market share has slowly declined—due to a significant change in the economy causing fewer and fewer homeowners to install home pools. When I joined Water-Fun, we had a ten percent market share and over the last fifteen years it has dropped to about eight percent, as new Internet-based companies joined the marketplace and many foreign companies have entered the U.S. Regardless of the cause, as the leader of our company it was my duty to point us in the right direction toward profitability and market leadership.

About four years ago, I hired Barry Kim, a new head of Research & Development for Water-Fun, in an effort to jumpstart a rise for the company in the marketplace. I tasked Kim to develop new products across our spectrum of water accessories.

Around YR-3, Kim's team developed a new water lounge product called the Water-Fun Recliner Fabric Comfort Lounge. This has been a terrific new product that our customers have been very excited about. We have sold a record number of recliner products. We sell two variants of the recliner, one with a through-foot hole and one with a mesh-covered foot support.

I know that SwimTime accuses us of ripping off its design for our recliner, but it's simply not true. I was aware of the SwimTime Spring Float when it was released and was aware of its generally decent sales. But, I recognized it to be basically a rehash of many old water recliner lounge designs that had been on the market for decades. A floating seat is nothing new, but SwimTime did have an excellent product. It was made of terrific materials and was very attractive. I saw no need, however, for the Spring Float's internal wire mechanism to collapse it down to a smaller package. This was an "innovation" no one was looking for and no one needs. Our products certainly don't have this feature and, instead, are completely collapsible with no rigid parts to keep you from crushing the recliners down to as small a package as possible once deflated.

Also, I think our product looks very different from the SwimTime Spring Float. Our Comfort Lounges are much more polygonally shaped, like rounded rectangles, where the Spring Floats are egg-shaped. We use a single, seat-perimeter inflatable tube as a buoyancy mechanism. It is also the same tube that supports a user's feet—unlike the Spring Float, which has many tubes and costs a lot more. Also, we use less expensive materials to lower the customers' costs to purchase our products-they're a much better value that SwimTime's products.

I also know SwimTime's CEO, Morgan Miller. Miller's got a tremendous ego. Miller thinks that he has reinvented the water accessory industry. He may be riding high now, but he'll see that these things come in high and low tides and he'll be floating down on the tide soon enough. We'll see how the Miller ego looks then.

Statement of Barry Kim

My name is Barry Kim, and I am thirty-four years old. I live at 328 Taylor Drive, Nita City. I am not married and have no children. I make this written statement under penalty of perjury.

I am the head of Research and Development for Water-Fun, Inc. I was hired in YR-4 by the company's CEO Glenn Berenson. Prior to working with Water-Fun, I was in the Research and Development division of O'Brien Watersports. I have a mechanical engineering degree from Southwest Nita University.

Since joining Water-Fun, I have directed the development of several important new products, including the Water-Fun Aqua Leisure Above-Ground Pool, the Dolphin Above-Head Snorkel and Mask combo, the WF Inflatable Stand Up Paddleboard (WFISUP), and the Water-Fun Recliner Fabric Comfort Lounge. It is the last of these products upon which Water-Fun has been sued by SwimTime.

Water-Fun is certainly a company on the rebound. For several years before I joined the company, little innovation had occurred and few interesting new products were sold. It has been my goal and Glenn Berenson's mission to change this. Of all the new products we've developed and brought to market during my time at Water-Fun, the most important has been the Recliner.

In YR-4, I received an email from Glenn Berenson asking me to "get cracking" on a product to compete with the SwimTime Spring Float. His email came well after I'd already had a team of engineers actively developing a new pool lounge—the lounge that ultimately became the Water-Fun Recliner Fabric Comfort Lounge.

In designing the Water-Fun Recliner, I used my knowledge of the many examples of similar recliners in the industry—there are many, many such floating seats for pool use—and, although I was aware of the Spring Float when I designed the Water-Fun Recliner, I neither found it particularly innovative nor worth copying. The primary basis for the new recliner design was actually Water-Fun's old recliner float. We simply improved it and gave it a nice, new fabric cover.

What I noted as somewhat new in the design of the Spring Float was the internal metal coil provided about its perimeter, similar to those found in some sports equipment goals or tent structure for collapsing those devices. The Spring Float incorporates such a "spring" so that it can be twisted and collapsed and stored more easily in a bag. The spring gives the float some rigidity—which I found undesirable in such a device. I did not incorporate an internal spring in the Water-Fun Recliner. I attribute the recliner's warm reception by our customers to its soft fabric covering and superior seat design, as well as to its price, which is considerably lower than that of the Spring Float.

UNITED STATES DISTRICT COURT
FOR THE DISTRICT OF NITA

Nita City Division

SWIMTIME CORPORATION, Plaintiff, v. WATER-FUN, INC., Defendant.	)))))))	Civil Action No. 1:Y00-cv-00100

CLAIM TERMS FOR THE COURT'S CONSTRUCTION

(over which parties disagree)

Term 1: "panel" (claims 1, 2, 3)

Term 2: "substantially planar" (claim 1)

Term 3: "different" (claim 1)

Term 4: "disposed about" (claims 1, 2, 3)

Term 5: "seated position" (claims 1, 2, 3)

Term 6: "foot support" (claim 3)

(*Note:* If you are engaging in claim construction arguments and a mock *Markman* hearing in this exercise, refrain from reviewing the remainder of this book, beginning with the Court's Claim Construction Order, until after such practical exercise.)

UNITED STATES DISTRICT COURT
FOR THE DISTRICT OF NITA

Nita City Division

SWIMTIME CORPORATION,	)	
Plaintiff,	)	Civil Action No. 1:Y00-cv-00100
	)	
v.	)	
	)	
WATER-FUN, INC.,	)	
Defendant.	)	

COURT'S ORDER CONSTRUING CLAIMS

This matter comes before the Court pursuant to *Markman v. Westview Instruments, Inc.*, 52 F.3d 967 (Fed. Cir. 1995) (en banc), *aff'd*, 517 U.S. 370 (1996), to construe certain terms contained in U.S. Patent Number 8,197,517 ("the '517 patent"). The Court conducted a *Markman* hearing and the parties have fully briefed the issue.

Phillips v. AWH Corp., 415 F.3d 1303 (Fed. Cir. 2005), and its progeny enunciate the principles of claim construction. In deciding the following claim constructions, the Court finds that the patent claims, the patent specification, and the prosecution history provide the necessary guidance to define the terms in dispute and, thus, has looked only at the "intrinsic evidence" of the patent. *See Id.* at 1317-19.

The Court gives the words of a claim the ordinary and customary meaning that they would have to a person or ordinary skill in the art. *Id.* at 1312-13. "[T]he person of ordinary skill in the art is deemed to read the claim term not only in the context of the particular claim in which the disputed term appears, but in the context of the entire patent, including the specification." *Id.* at 1313. "In some cases, the ordinary meaning of claim language as understood by a person of skill in the art may be readily apparent even to lay judges, and claim construction in such cases involves little more than the application of the widely accepted meaning of commonly understood words." *Id.* at 1314 (citing *Brown v. 3M*, 265 F.3d 1349, 1352 (Fed. Cir. 2001)). Further, "the specification 'is always highly relevant to the claim construction analysis. Usually, it is dispositive; it is the single best guide to the meaning of a disputed term.'" *Id.* at 1315 (quoting *Vitronics Corp v. Conceptronic, Inc.*, 90 F.3d 1576, 1582 (Fed. Cir. 1996)). Moreover, "the prosecution history can often inform the meaning of the claim language by demonstrating how the inventor understood the invention and whether the inventor limited the invention in the course of prosecution, making the claim scope narrower than it would otherwise be. *Id.* at 1317 (citing *Vitronics Corp.*, 90 F.3d at 1582-83). The parties dispute the meaning of six terms.

Term 1: "panel" (claims 1, 2, 3)

SwimTime Corp. (hereinafter "SwimTime") proposes that the term "panel" needs no construction and should be given its plain and ordinary meaning.

Water-Fun, Inc. (hereinafter "Water-Fun") proposes that the term "panel" means "a layer of flexible material having a circumferentially attached spring for collapsing or expanding the layer as desired."

The Court defines the term "panel" as "*a layer of material that is mostly flat, but does not necessarily contain a spring.*"

Water-Fun proposes that the Court limit "panel" to always including a collapsible spring. The Court finds no support in the claims themselves for this limitation. The Federal Circuit has clearly stated that a court's claim construction "must not import limitations from the specification into the claims." *Deere & Co. v. Bush Hog, LLC*, 703 F.3d 1349, 1354 (Fed. Cir. 2012) (citing *Phillips*, 415 F.3d at 1323)). Thus, following the Federal Circuit's guidance, this Court will not limit the term "panel" based on limitations found only in the specification. The Court defines "panel" as a layer of material that is mostly flat and does not necessarily contain a spring.

Term 2: "substantially planar" (claim 1)

SwimTime proposes that the term "substantially planar" needs no construction and should be given its plain and ordinary meaning.

Water-Fun proposes that the term "substantially planar" means "flat or level."

The Court defines the term "substantially planar" as "*mostly flat.*"

Water-Fun argues that the term "substantially planar" is indefinite and not amenable to construction. The Court disagrees, the term is not indefinite. A claim term is indefinite only if, "read in light of the specification delineating the patent, and the prosecution history, [it] fail[s] to inform, with reasonable certainty, those skilled in the art about the scope of the invention." *Nautilus, Inc. v. Biosig Instruments, Inc.*, 134 S.Ct. 2120, 2124 (June 2, 2014). Moreover, a claim term is not indefinite if "the boundaries of the claim, as construed by the court, [are] discernible to a skilled artisan based on the language of the claim, the specification, and the prosecution history, as well as [the skilled artisan's] knowledge of the relevant field of art." *Power-One, Inc. v. Artesyn Tech.*, 599 F.3d 1343, 1350 (Fed. Cir. 2010). Thus, if a claim (term) can be construed, it is not indefinite. *Aero Prods. Int'l, Inc. v. Intex Recreation Corp.*, 466 F.3d 1000 (Fed. Cir. 2006). The Court finds that this term can be construed. The Court defines the term "substantially planar" as mostly flat.

Term 3: "different" (claim 1)

SwimTime proposes that the term "different" needs no construction and should be given its plain and ordinary meaning.

Water-Fun proposes that the term "different" means "the first portion of the buoyant member be not alike in character or quality; dissimilar."

The Court determines that no construction of the term "different" is necessary and that this term shall have its plain and ordinary meaning. The plain and ordinary meaning of the term does not require the limitation that different members be dissimilar in character or quality.

This claim term represents an instance in which "the ordinary meaning of claim language as understood by a person of skill in the art [is] readily apparent even to lay judges, and claim construction... involves little more than the application of the widely accepted meaning of commonly understood words." *Phillips*, 415 F.3d at 1314 (citing *Brown*, 265 F.3d at 1352). Thus, the Court finds the plain and ordinary meaning of "different" applies, which does not have the limitation proposed by Water-Fun. For items to be "different," as that term is used in the claims, they do not have to be dissimilar in character or quality.

Term 4: "disposed about" (claims 1, 2, 3)

SwimTime proposes that the term "disposed about" needs no construction and should be given its plain and ordinary meaning.

Water-Fun proposes that the term "disposed about" means "disposed on all sides of."

The Court defines the term "disposed about" to mean "*around but not necessarily on all sides.*"

Once again, Water-Fun asks this Court to limit the definition of a term. The limited definition Water-Fun proposes is inconsistent with the claim's own language. A person skilled in the art, after having read the claims, would not limit "disposed about" to mean that an item must be disposed on all sides of another item. Thus, the term "disposed about" means around—its plain and ordinary meaning.

Term 5: "seated position" (claims 1, 2, 3)

SwimTime proposes that the term "seated position" needs no construction and should be given its plain and ordinary meaning.

Water-Fun proposes that the term "seated position" means "having the torso erect and legs bent with the body supported on the buttocks."

The Court defines the term "seated position" to mean "includes an upright-seated position and reclined seated position, but not a prone position."

The Court finds that the definition of "seated position" includes both upright-seated and reclined-seated, but not prone position. This definition stays true to the claim language and most naturally aligns with the use of the term in the patent's specification and claims. Nothing in the prosecution history or the claims requires this Court to limit the definition of "seated" to a fully erect, ninety-degree angle. The Court finds no support for Water-Fun's position that the patentee disavowed "reclined" from the construction of the term "seated."

Term 6: "foot support" (claim 3)

SwimTime proposes that the term "foot support" needs no construction and should be given its plain and ordinary meaning.

Water-Fun proposes that the term "foot support" means "a member, different than the buoyant member, which is configured to buoyantly support the weight of the user's feet."

The Court defines the term "foot support" to mean "*a member that supports a user's feet, but not necessarily different or separate from the buoyant member.*"

This term also represents an instance in which, "the ordinary meaning of claim language as understood by a person of skill in the art [is] readily apparent even to lay judges, and claim construction... involves little more than the application of the widely accepted meaning of commonly understood words." *Phillips*, 415 F.3d at 1314 (citing *Brown*, 265 F.3d at 1352). A "foot support" consists of a member that supports a user's feet. Nothing in the claims or the specification requires this Court to limit the definition of "foot support" to a different member from the buoyant member.

It is SO ORDERED.

The Court directs the clerk to send a copy of this Order to all counsel of record.

UNITED STATES DISTRICT COURT
FOR THE DISTRICT OF NITA

Nita City Division

SWIMTIME CORPORATION, Plaintiff,	))	Civil Action No. 1:Y00-cv-00100
	)	
v.	)	
	)	
WATER-FUN, INC., Defendant.	))	

PLAINTIFF'S EXPERT REPORT ON INFRINGEMENT

I. INTRODUCTION

1. I, Pat Thurman, am a United States citizen residing in Deaconville, Nita. I have been retained by the Plaintiff in this case as a technical expert in this action for patent infringement filed against Water-Fun, Inc. ("Water-Fun").

II. BACKGROUND AND QUALIFICATIONS

2. I have been involved in product development and new product innovation for over twenty years, serving in various positions in both the corporate and consulting settings. I have been involved with both large and small consulting firms and worked with a wide range of clients in areas ranging from housewares, kitchen appliances, inflatable toys, electronics, automotive components, medical devices, and industrial equipment. I have designed, developed, and managed all aspects of the product development process including research, design, engineering, packaging, graphics, merchandising, manufacturing, and quality control. I have been part of numerous cases involving utility and design patent infringement. I am named as inventor on over fifty design and utility patents. My formal education includes a Bachelor's of Fine Arts in industrial design from University of Nita, a Master's of Science in Product Development from Northwestern Nita University, and many years of industry-related seminars and management training. A copy of my curriculum vitae is appended hereto as Exhibit A. I have not authored any publications within the past ten years.

3. I am being compensated for my work on this case on an hourly basis at my usual and customary rate of $500 per hour. My compensation is not related in any way to the outcome of this case.

III. SUMMARY OF OPINIONS TO BE EXPRESSED

4. I have been asked by counsel to provide my opinion regarding Water-Fun's infringement of the asserted claims of U.S. Patent No. 8,197,517 ("the '517 Patent"), entitled "COLLAPSIBLE FLOTATION DEVICE." In preparation of this report, I have reviewed the '517 Patent and the prosecution history of the '517 Patent. I have also reviewed the materials listed in Exhibit B.

5. Briefly, it is my opinion that the accused products infringe the '517 Patent. As explained in detail in the following sections of this report, the Water-Fun (Holey) Recliner meets each and every limitation of, and therefore infringes, claims 1, 2, and 3 of the '517 Patent. The Water-Fun (Mesh) Recliner meets each and every limitation of, and therefore infringes, claims 1 and 3 of the '517 Patent. I have analyzed infringement using the claim constructions adopted by the Court in its *Markman* Order. It is my opinion that the accused products literally infringe the asserted claims.

IV. LEGAL FRAMEWORK FOR ANALYSIS

6. In developing my opinions on the infringement of the '517 patent set forth herein, I have relied upon the following legal framework.

Claim Construction

7. The property right protected by a patent is defined by the claims of the patent, which appear as numbered paragraphs at the end of the text. Each claim stands on its own when determining infringement or validity. These are the "metes and bounds" that define the scope of the property right. Thus, the first step in analyzing either the infringement or validity of a patent claim begins with an analysis of the claim itself, also referred to as "claim construction."

8. The first step in construing a claim is an analysis of how the claim language would be understood by a person having ordinary skill in the art. To understand the perspective of a person of ordinary skill in the art, one must determine the field of art to which the patent pertains, and then the background of one of ordinary skill in that art. Dictionaries, encyclopedias, and treatises may be used to demonstrate how one skilled in the art would understand a specific term or phrase recited in a claim. Such terms or phrases are also referred to as "claim limitations," because, as discussed below, they limit what is covered by a claim.

9. After reviewing the precise language used in the claim, the patent specification and prosecution history are reviewed to ensure that they do not alter the way one skilled in the art would understand a claim limitation. At times, the specification might provide further clarification as to the meaning of a claim limitation.

10. Statements and amendments made by a patent applicant during prosecution of the patent application might provide further clarification as to the meaning of a claim limitation. For example, the applicant may argue that certain prior art raised by the examiner is outside the scope of a claim because it fails to disclose a certain claim limitation. The claims cannot be construed to cover that which was surrendered during prosecution. In addition to the claim language, patent specification, and prosecution history, which are the preferred sources for claim construction, outside sources may be referenced to construe a claim limitation.

Patent Infringement

11. Some claims are referred to as "independent" claims, meaning claims that do not incorporate limitations of other claims by reference. Other claims are "dependent" claims in that they incorporate the limitations of other claims by reference. For example, a dependent claim may read, "the apparatus of claim 1 further comprising...," meaning that, to find infringement, all limitations of claim 1 must be present in addition to those following the word "comprising." It follows from this that a dependent claim cannot be infringed unless the independent claim from which it depends also is infringed. Here, we deal only with independent claims.

12. A patent claim is literally infringed when the accused product includes every limitation exactly as recited in the claim (as properly construed). For example, if a claim recites the limitations of A, B, and C, the accused product literally infringes the claim if it includes A, B, and C.

13. When a claim is not literally infringed, it may still be infringed under the doctrine of equivalents if the "equivalent" of the limitation not literally present is still found in the accused product, assuming there is no bar to the doctrine of equivalents (an issue I do not address in this report). A common test for mechanical equivalents is whether the accused product contains an element that performs substantially the same function as the claim limitation in substantially the same way as the claim limitation to obtain substantially the same result as the claim limitation. Thus, if a claim recites A, B, and C, and the accused product includes A, B, and D, the accused product will infringe the claim under the doctrine of equivalents if one skilled in the art would understand D to be an equivalent of C.

14. I understand that in addition to direct infringement, as described above, patent infringement can occur indirectly, either by induced infringement or contributory infringement. For induced infringement, one party must know of the patent at issue and encourage, instruct, cause, or aid others (e.g., a customer) to infringe the patent, when it knew or should have known that its actions would cause others to infringe. For contributory infringement, a party must know of the patent at issue and sell accused products that form a material part of the claimed invention, when it knew or should have known that the products were specially made or adapted for a use that would infringe the patent at issue; others must infringe the patent at issue by using the accused products; and those products must have no substantial non-infringing uses.

V. BACKGROUND ON THE '517 PATENT AND THE ASSERTED CLAIMS

Summary of the '517 Patent

15. The '517 patent discloses a collapsible flotation device. Figure 1 (reproduced below) provides a perspective view of a collapsible flotation device 100 according to one embodiment of the invention. The flotation device 100 includes a panel 102 that has an outer portion 101 and an inner portion. The outer portion includes a back support member 110 and a foot support member 112. An inner portion 103 provides a seating area. The inner portion 103 of the panel 102 can be a membrane made from a mesh, or similar material, while the material of the outer portion 101 of the panel 102 can be a nylon, or other suitable material. When the flotation device 100 has a user seated thereon, the inner portion 103 of the panel 102 is partially submerged in water. By using a mesh, or other similar material, for the inner portion 103, water can freely pass, thereby partially submerging a user seated in the inner portion 103 of the panel 102. The flotation device 100 can also include a coilable spring 104 to provide rigidity to the flotation device 100 while the flotation device 100 is in an expanded configuration. The flotation device 100 can include a hole or opening 114 through which water may pass or through which a user may place his legs.

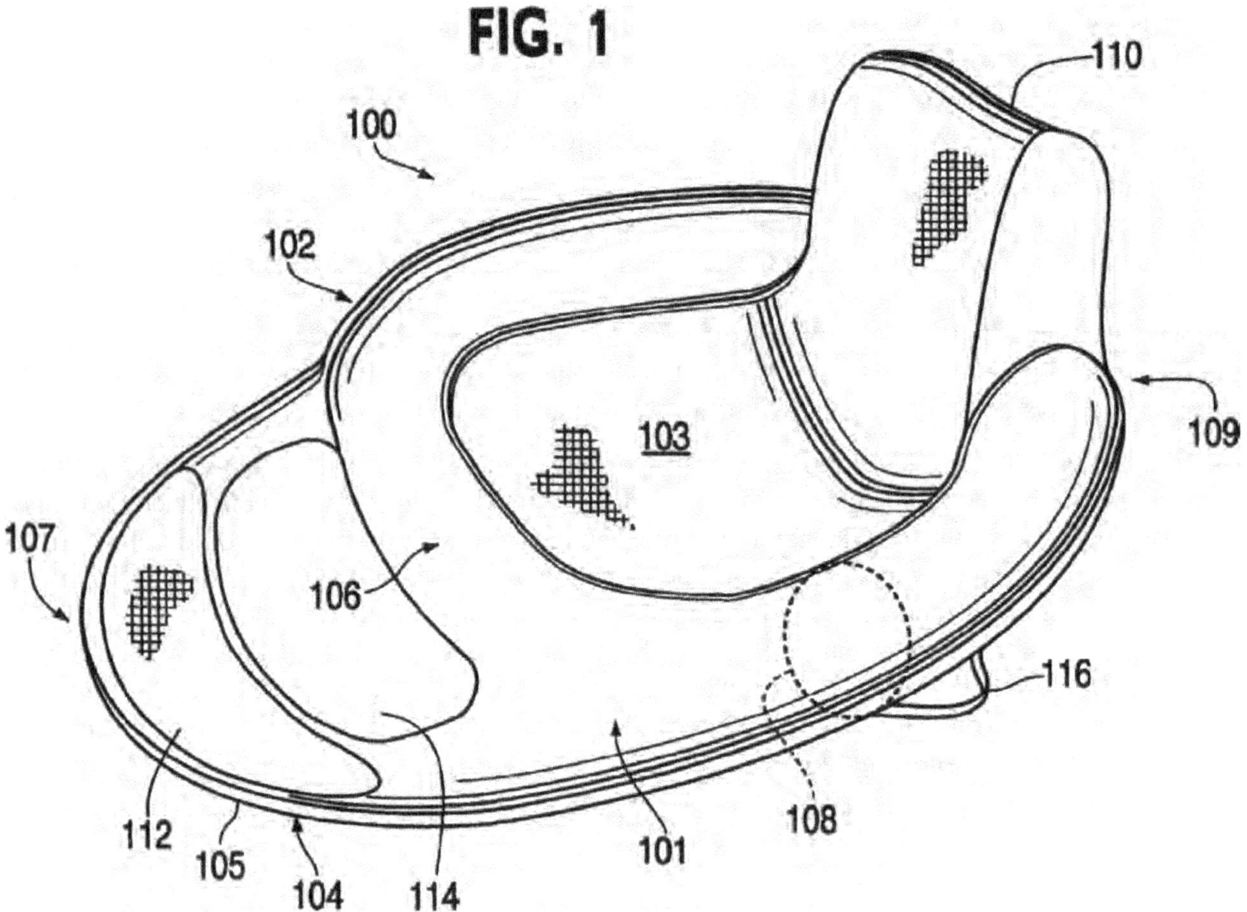

Asserted Claims of the '517 Patent

16. It is my understanding that Plaintiff is currently asserting infringement of claims 1, 2, and 3.

The Court's Claim Construction of Disputed Terms

17. I have performed my infringement analysis using the claim constructions adopted by the Court. Those constructions are summarized below:

> *The Court defines the term "panel" as "a layer of material that is mostly flat, but does not necessarily contain a spring."*
>
> *The Court defines the term "substantially planar" as "mostly flat."*
>
> *The Court determines that no construction of the term "different" is necessary and that this term shall have its plain and ordinary meaning. The plain and ordinary meaning of the term does not require the limitation that different members be dissimilar in character or quality.*
>
> *The Court defines the term "disposed about" to mean "around but not necessarily on all sides."*
>
> *The Court defines the term "seated position" to mean "includes an upright-seated position and reclined seated position, but not a prone position."*

The Court defines the term "foot support" to mean "a member that supports a user's feet, but not necessarily different or separate from the buoyant member."

Person Having Ordinary Skill in the Art

18. For purposes of this analysis, I have considered the characteristics of a person having ordinary skill in the art with respect to the inventions claimed in the '517 Patent and have concluded that, at a minimum, such a person would have 1) at least two years' experience in designing inflatable products, or 2) a bachelor's degree in industrial design or mechanical engineering.

19. I am a person having at least this level of skill in the art, and, in fact, I possess skill significantly beyond this level as a result of my education and experience. Furthermore, I am familiar with this level of skill in the art and levels of skill beyond that. For example, I have worked with designers and technicians who have little or no formal engineering training, but who have worked with such systems in a design and manufacturing capacity.

20. I understand that Water-Fun has not identified what it considers to be the skill level of one having ordinary skill in the art despite having been asked to provide this information through discovery. If a different level of ordinary skill in the art were found to be applicable, my opinion that the asserted claims are literally infringed would not change.

VI. INFRINGEMENT ANALYSIS

The Accused Products

21. The accused Water-Fun products are the Water-Fun (Mesh) Recliner and the Water-Fun (Holey) Recliner.

22. Photographs of the accused products are provided below.

23. Water-Fun (Holey) Recliner (photos attached as Exhibit C):

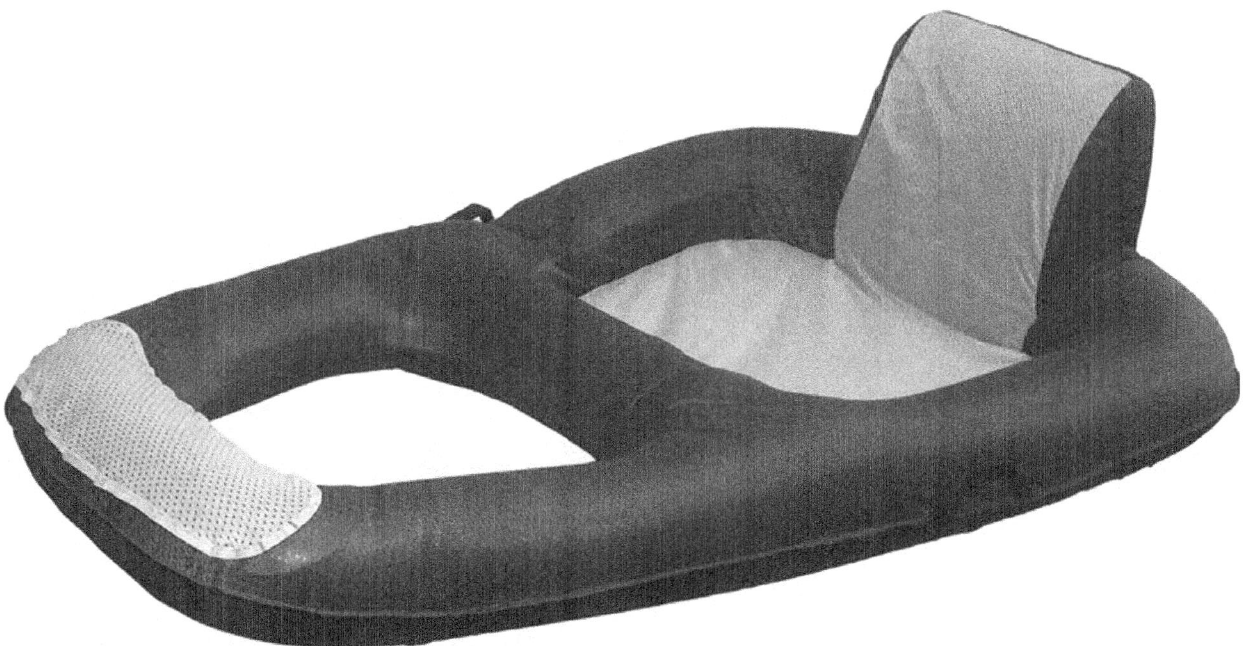

[*Note*: To view the following images in color, please refer to the CD-ROM accompanying this book.]

24. Water-Fun (Mesh) Recliner (photos attached as Exhibit D):

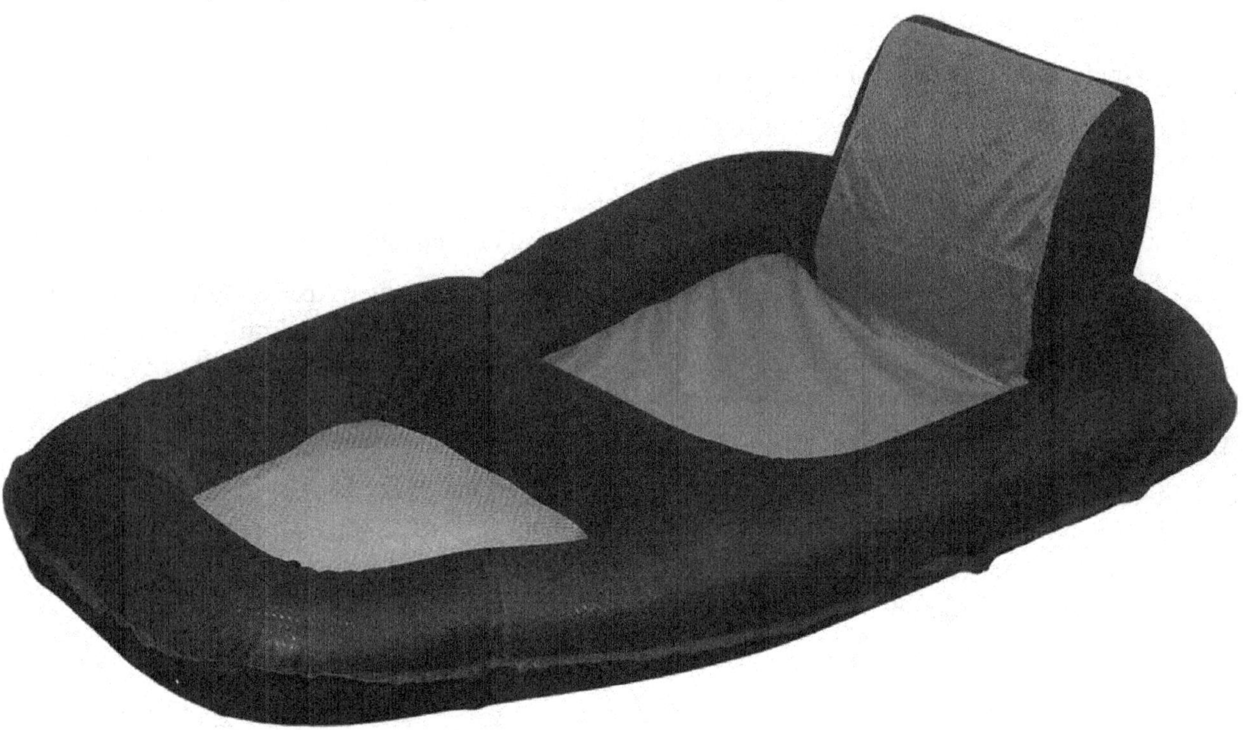

25. These two products are substantially similar, but for one (Holey) having a through-opening at the foot portion and one (Mesh) having a mesh panel covered opening at the foot portion, as shown in the photos of the products, above.

26. A claim chart illustrating how each and every limitation of Claim 1 is met by the Water-Fun (Holey) Recliner is provided below:

Claim 1 Limitation	Water-Fun (Holey) Recliner
1. An apparatus, comprising:	The Water-Fun (Holey) Recliner is an apparatus.
a panel including an inner portion, an outer portion and a back support portion,	The Water-Fun (Holey) Recliner includes a panel—a layer that is mostly flat. The panel of the Water-Fun (Holey) Recliner defines the overall footprint of the product. The panel includes an inner portion, an outer portion, and a back support as shown below. 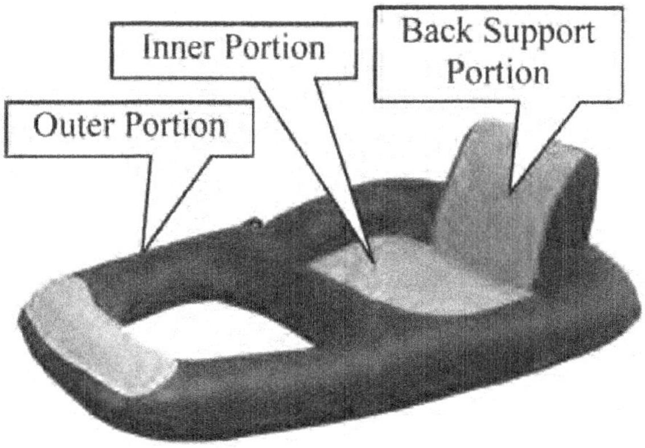 Inner Portion Back Support Portion Outer Portion
the inner portion of the panel having a first edge and a second edge on an opposite side of the inner portion of the panel from the first edge, a distance between the first edge of the inner portion of the panel and the second edge of the inner portion of the panel defining a width of the inner portion of the panel,	The inner portion of the product's panel includes a first and a second edge on opposite sides. The distance between the first and second edges defines a width of the inner portion.

[*Note*: To view the following images in color, please refer to the CD-ROM accompanying this book.]

Claim 1 Limitation	Water-Fun (Holey) Recliner
	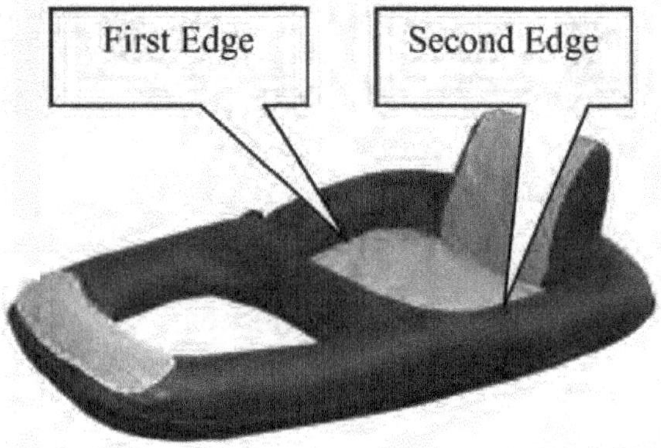
the inner portion of the panel being substantially planar across the width of the inner portion of the panel,	As shown in the photos, the panel inner portion of the accused product is substantially planar—mostly flat—across its width. 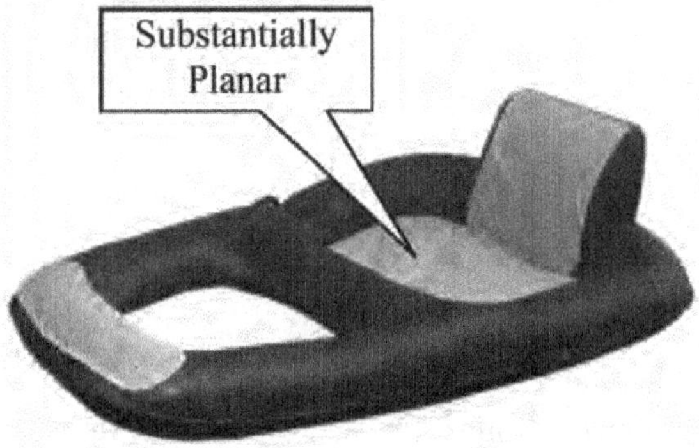
the back support portion being inflatable; and	The back support potion of the product is inflatable.

Claim 1 Limitation	Water-Fun (Holey) Recliner
	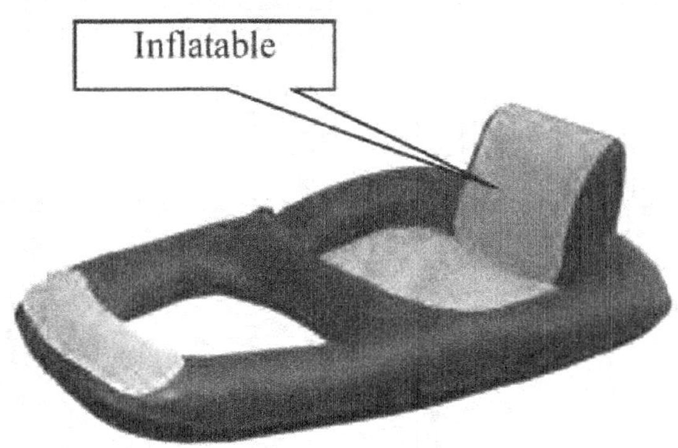
a buoyant member disposed about at least the inner portion of the panel, at least a portion of the buoyant member being disposed within at least a portion of the outer portion of the panel,	The Water-Fun (Holey) Recliner includes an inflatable raft that is a buoyant member. As shown in the photo, this buoyant member is disposed about the panel's inner portion and the buoyant member is disposed within at least a portion of the panel's outer portion. 
the buoyant member having a first portion and a second portion different from the first portion, the first portion of the buoyant member and the second portion of the buoyant member being disposed at opposite locations of the inner portion of the panel and separated by the width of the inner portion of the panel,	The buoyant member includes first and second portions that are disposed at opposite locations of the panel's inner portion and separated by the width of the panel's inner portion.

Claim 1 Limitation	Water-Fun (Holey) Recliner
	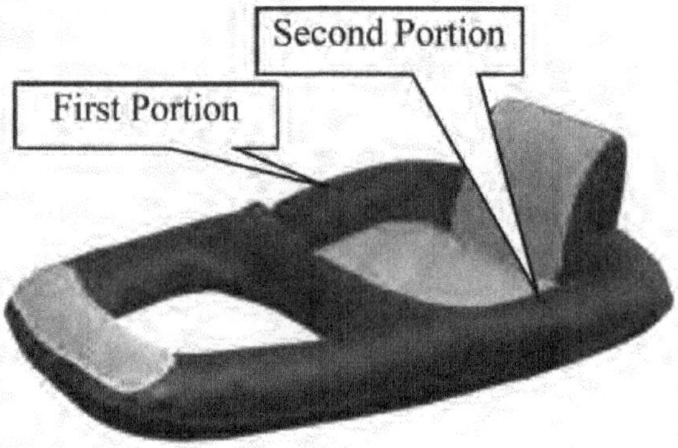 Second Portion First Portion
the inner portion of the panel extending continuously between the first portion of the buoyant member and the second portion of the buoyant member without an intervening buoyant member,	As shown in the photo, the panel's inner portion extends continuously between the first and second portions of the buoyant member without an intervening buoyant member. 
at least one of the outer portion of the panel within which the first portion of the buoyant member is at least partially disposed or the first portion of the buoyant member being in contact with the first edge of the inner portion of the panel,	The outer portion of the panel within which the first portion of the buoyant member is at least partially disposed is in contact with the first edge of the panel's inner portion.

Claim 1 Limitation	Water-Fun (Holey) Recliner
	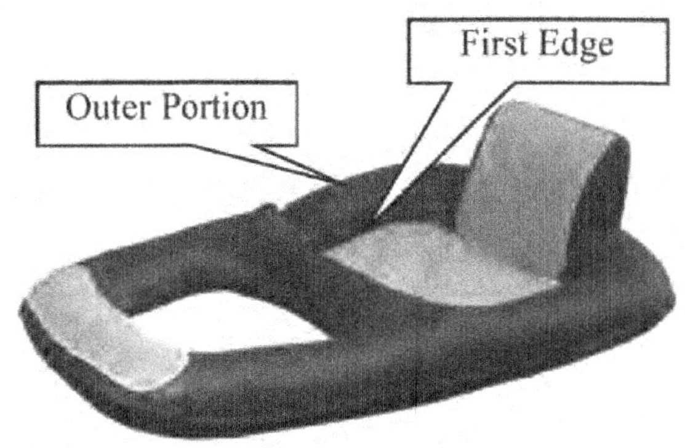
at least one of the outer portion of the panel within which the second portion of the buoyant member is at least partially disposed or the second portion of the buoyant member being in contact with the second edge of the inner portion of the panel,	The outer portion of the panel within which the second portion of the buoyant member is at least partially disposed is in contact with the second edge of the panel's inner portion. 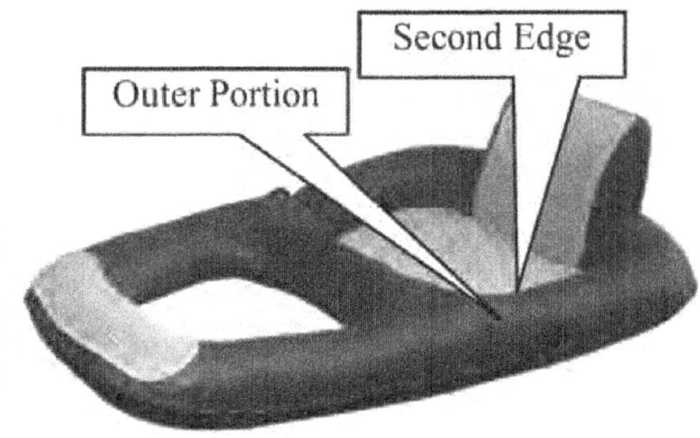
the buoyant member having an outermost width that substantially defines an outermost width of the apparatus, the apparatus being configured to support a user in a seated position.	As shown in the photo, the buoyant member has an outermost width that defines an outermost width of the apparatus. The apparatus is configured to support a user in a seated position as that term has been construed by the Court—encompassing both and upright seated position and a reclined seated position.

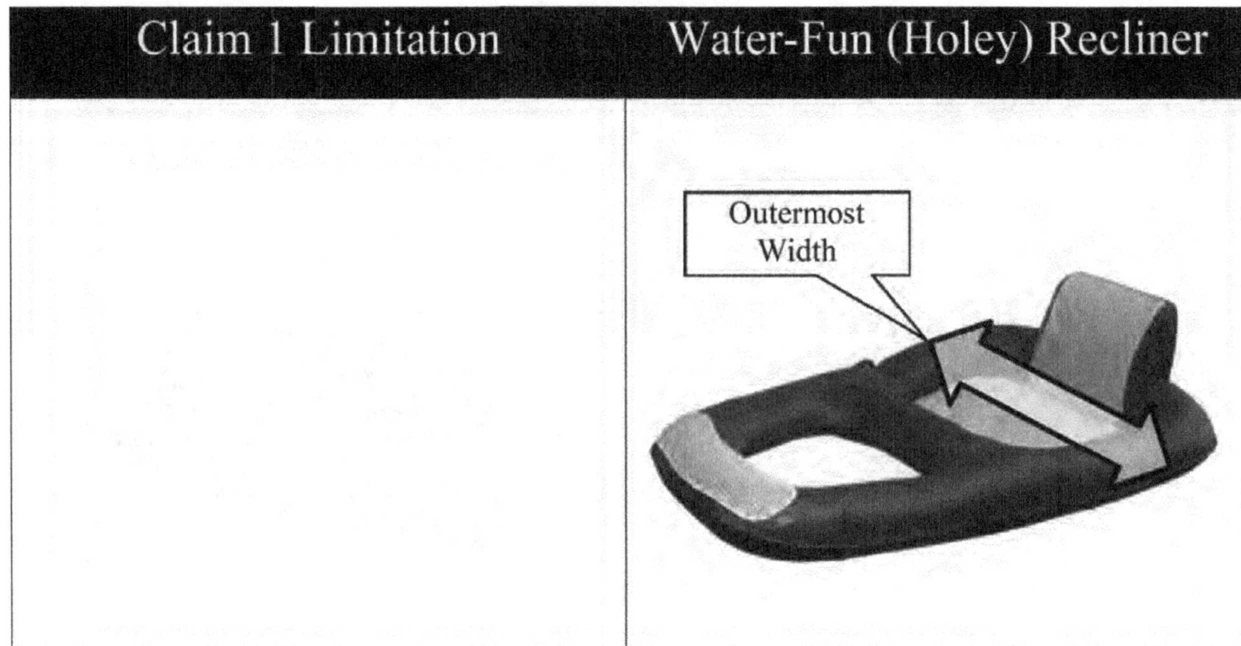
Claim 1 Limitation
Water-Fun (Holey) Recliner
Outermost Width

27. A claim chart illustrating how each and every limitation of Claim 1 is met by the Water-Fun (Mesh) Recliner is provided below:

Claim 1 Limitation	Water-Fun (Mesh) Recliner
1. An apparatus, comprising:	The Water-Fun (Mesh) Recliner is an apparatus.
a panel including an inner portion, an outer portion and a back support portion,	The Water-Fun (Mesh) Recliner includes a panel—a layer that is mostly flat. The panel of the Water-Fun (Mesh) Recliner defines the overall footprint of the product. The panel includes an inner portion, an outer portion, and a back support as shown below. 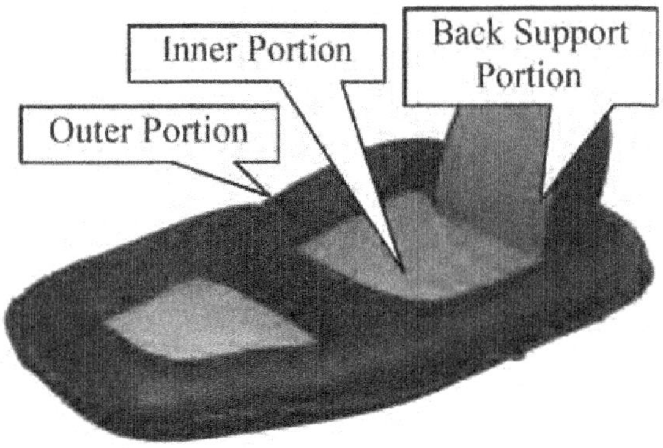
the inner portion of the panel having a first edge and a second edge on an opposite side of the inner portion of the panel from the first edge, a distance between the first edge of the inner portion of the panel and the second edge of the inner portion of the panel defining a width of the inner portion of the panel,	The inner portion of the product's panel includes a first and a second edge on opposite sides. The distance between the first and second edges defines a width of the inner portion.

Claim 1 Limitation	Water-Fun (Mesh) Recliner
	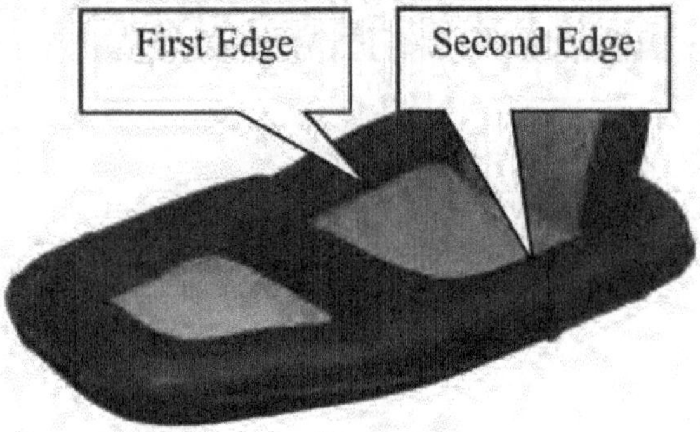 First Edge Second Edge
the inner portion of the panel being substantially planar across the width of the inner portion of the panel,	As shown in the photos, the panel inner portion of the accused product is substantially planar—mostly flat—across its width.  Substantially Planar
the back support portion being inflatable; and	The back support potion of the product is inflatable.

Claim 1 Limitation	Water-Fun (Mesh) Recliner
	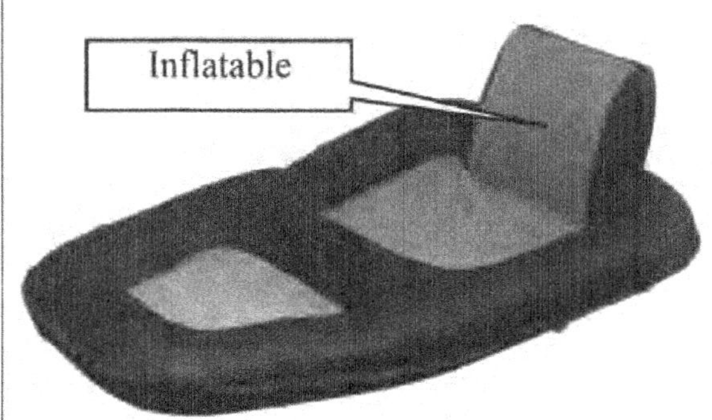
a buoyant member disposed about at least the inner portion of the panel, at least a portion of the buoyant member being disposed within at least a portion of the outer portion of the panel,	The Water-Fun (Mesh) Recliner includes an inflatable raft that is a buoyant member. As shown in the photo, this buoyant member is disposed about the panel's inner portion and the buoyant member is disposed within at least a portion of the panel's outer portion. 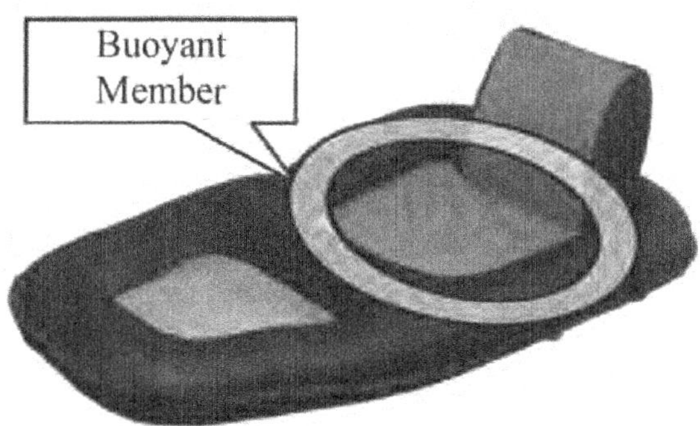
the buoyant member having a first portion and a second portion different from the first portion, the first portion of the buoyant member and the second portion of the buoyant member being disposed at opposite locations of the inner portion of the panel and separated by the width of the inner portion of the panel,	The buoyant member includes first and second portions that are disposed at opposite locations of the panel's inner portion and separated by the width of the panel's inner portion.

Claim 1 Limitation	Water-Fun (Mesh) Recliner
	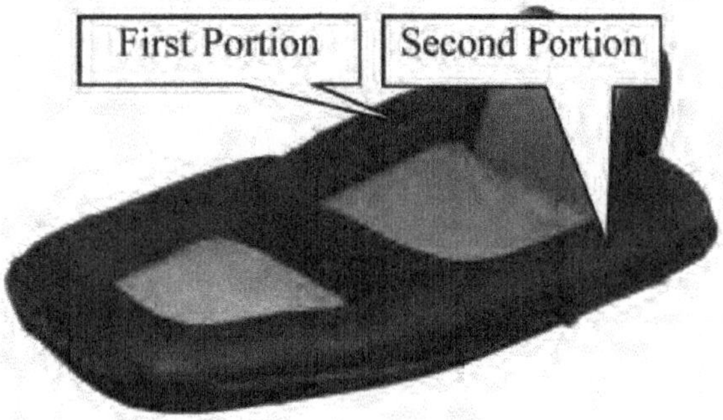 First Portion Second Portion
the inner portion of the panel extending continuously between the first portion of the buoyant member and the second portion of the buoyant member without an intervening buoyant member,	As shown in the photo, the panel's inner portion extends continuously between the first and second portions of the buoyant member without an intervening buoyant member. 
at least one of the outer portion of the panel within which the first portion of the buoyant member is at least partially disposed or the first portion of the buoyant member being in contact with the first edge of the inner portion of the panel,	The outer portion of the panel within which the first portion of the buoyant member is at least partially disposed is in contact with the first edge of the panel's inner portion.

Claim 1 Limitation	Water-Fun (Mesh) Recliner
	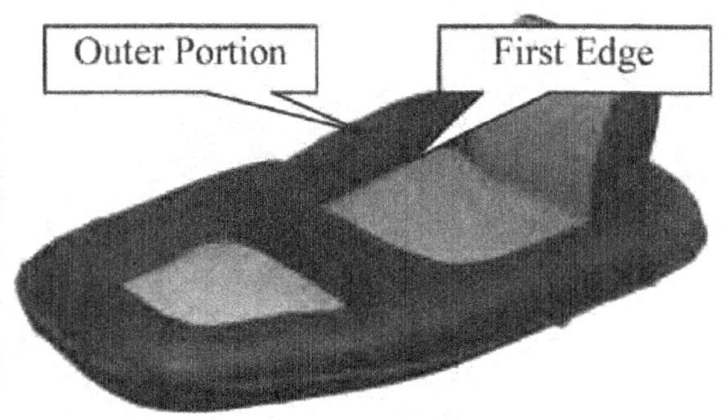
at least one of the outer portion of the panel within which the second portion of the buoyant member is at least partially disposed or the second portion of the buoyant member being in contact with the second edge of the inner portion of the panel,	The outer portion of the panel within which the second portion of the buoyant member is at least partially disposed is in contact with the second edge of the panel's inner portion. 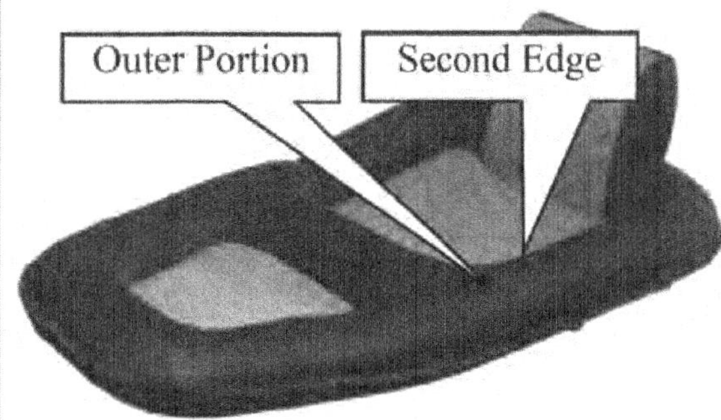
the buoyant member having an outermost width that substantially defines an outermost width of the apparatus, the apparatus being configured to support a user in a seated position.	As shown in the photo, the buoyant member has an outermost width that defines an outermost width of the apparatus. The apparatus is configured to support a user in a seated position as that term has been construed by the Court—encompassing both and upright seated position and a reclined seated position.

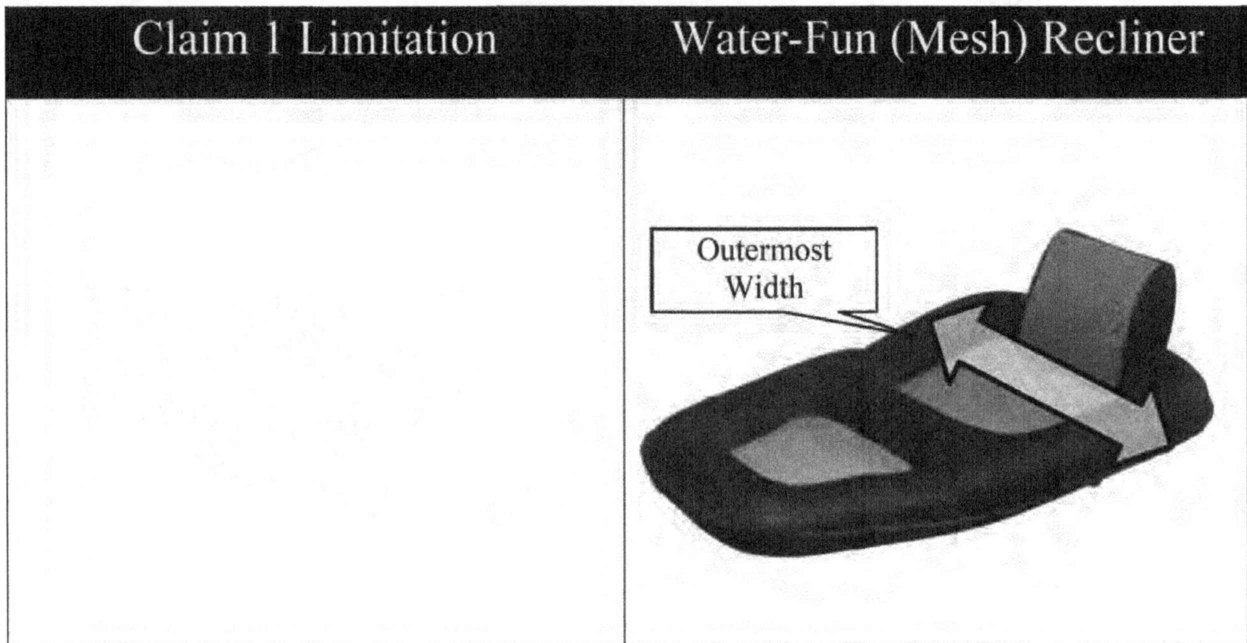

Claim 1 Limitation	Water-Fun (Mesh) Recliner

Independent Claim 2

28. A claim chart illustrating how each and every limitation of Claim 2 is met by the Water-Fun (Holey) Recliner is provided below:

Claim 2 Limitation	Water-Fun (Holey) Recliner
2. An apparatus, comprising:	The Water-Fun (Holey) Recliner is an apparatus.
a panel including an inner portion, an outer portion and a back support portion, the inner portion of the panel including a mesh material,	The Water-Fun (Holey) Recliner includes a panel—a layer of material that is mostly flat. The panel of the Water-Fun (Holey) Recliner defines the overall footprint of the product. The panel includes a mesh inner portion, an outer portion, and a back support portion as shown below. 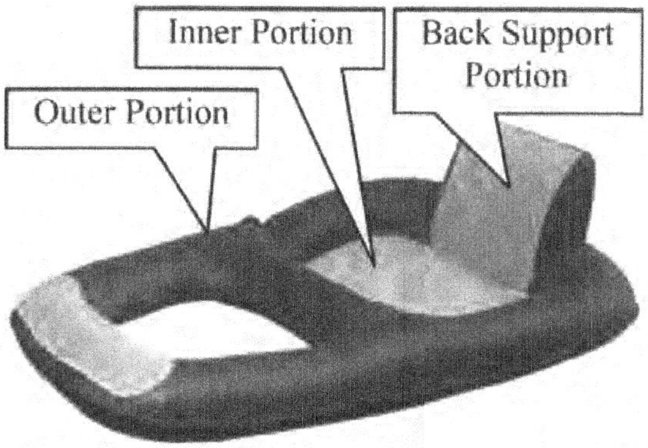
the panel defining an opening configured to collectively receive a user's legs therethrough, the opening being outside the inner portion of the panel,	The panel includes an opening configured to collectively receive a user's legs therethrough. The opening is located outside of the panel's inner portion.

	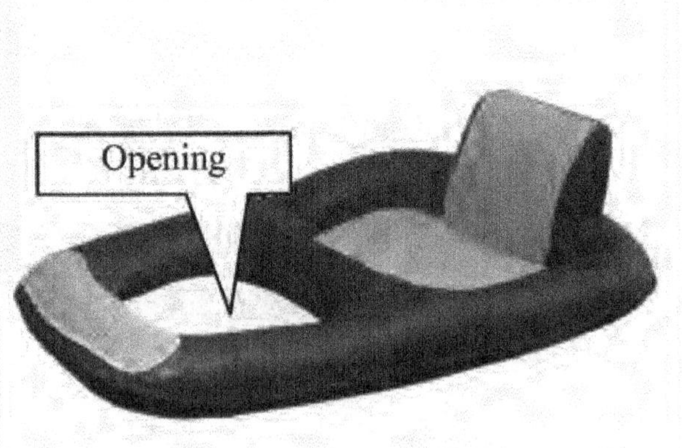
the back support portion being inflatable; and	The back support portion of the accused product is inflatable. 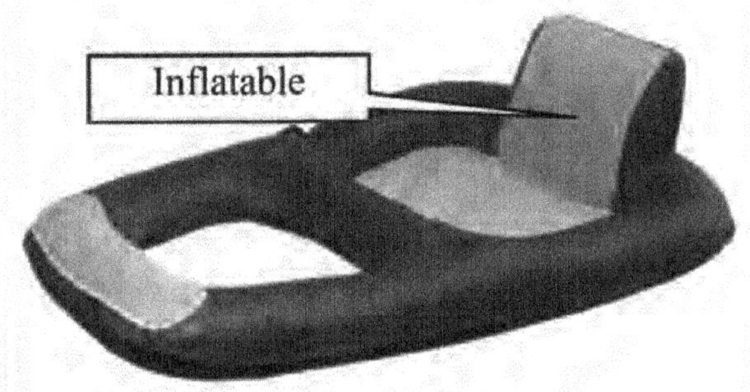
a buoyant member disposed about at least a portion of the outer portion of the panel, the buoyant member having a front portion, the front portion of the buoyant member and the back support member being disposed at opposite locations of the inner portion of the panel and separated by a length of the inner portion of the panel,	The product includes an inflatable raft that is a buoyant member. The buoyant member is disposed about at least a portion of the panel's outer portion. The buoyant member includes a front portion. The front portion of the buoyant member and the back support member are disposed at opposite locations of the panel's inner portion and are separated by a length of the panel's inner portion.

	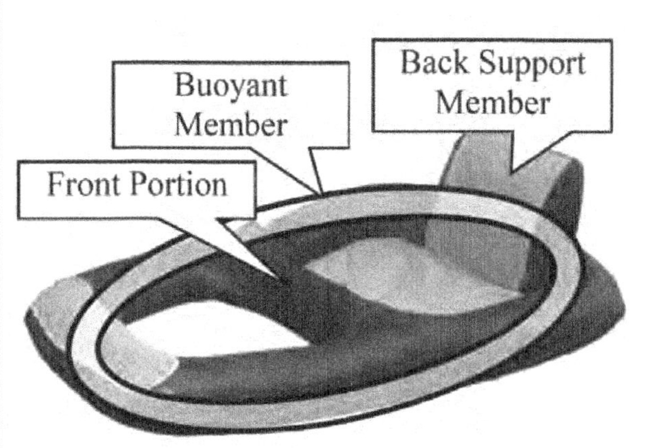
the front portion of the buoyant member being disposed between the inner portion of the panel and the opening,	The buoyant member's front portion is disposed between the panel's inner portion and the opening. 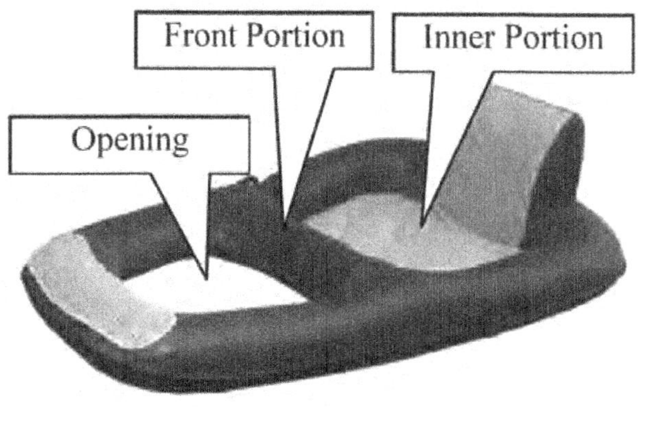

the combination of the buoyant member, the panel and the back support portion being collectively configured to support the user in a seated position.	The combination of the buoyant member, the panel, and the back support are collectively configured to support a user in a seated position as that term has been construed by the Court—encompassing both an upright seated position and a reclined seated position. 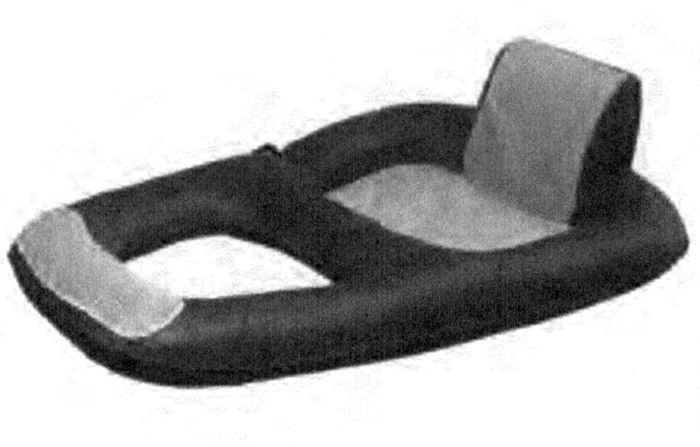

Independent Claim 3

29. A claim chart illustrating how each and every limitation of Claim 3 is met by the Water-Fun (Holey) Recliner is provided below:

Claim 3 Limitation	Water-Fun (Holey) Recliner
3. An apparatus, comprising:	The Water-Fun (Holey) Recliner is an apparatus.
a panel including an inner portion, an outer portion and a back support portion,	The Water-Fun (Holey) Recliner includes a panel—a layer of material that is mostly flat. The panel of the product defines the overall footprint of the product. The panel includes an inner portion, an outer portion, and a back support portion, as shown below. 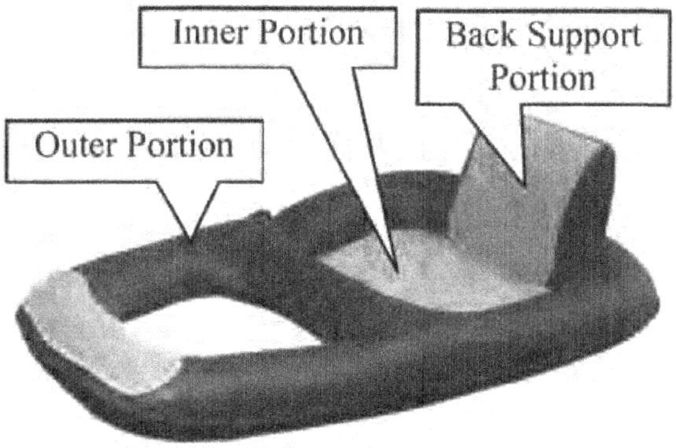
the inner portion of the panel including a mesh material,	The panel's inner portion includes a mesh material.

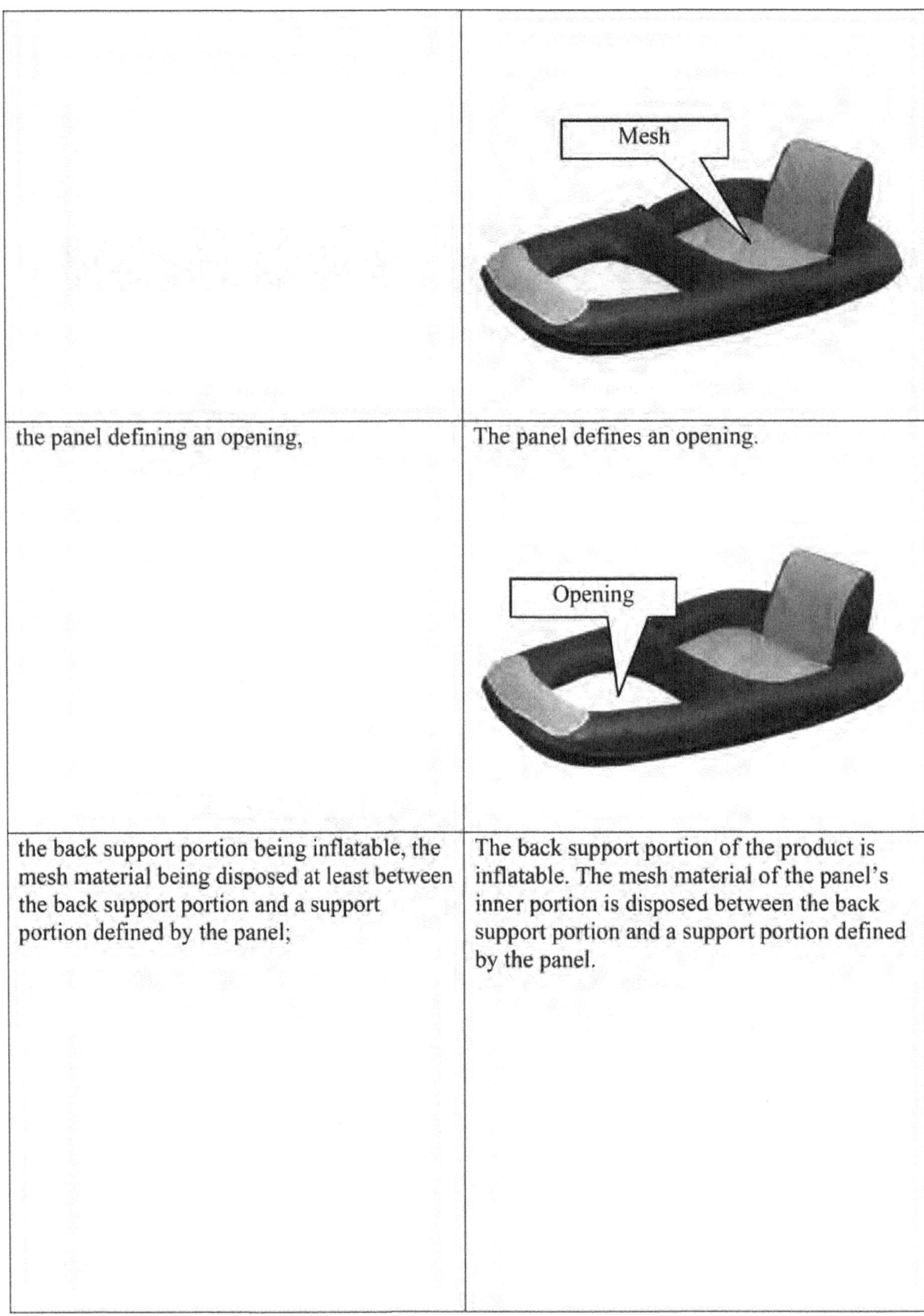

the panel defining an opening,	The panel defines an opening.
the back support portion being inflatable, the mesh material being disposed at least between the back support portion and a support portion defined by the panel;	The back support portion of the product is inflatable. The mesh material of the panel's inner portion is disposed between the back support portion and a support portion defined by the panel.

	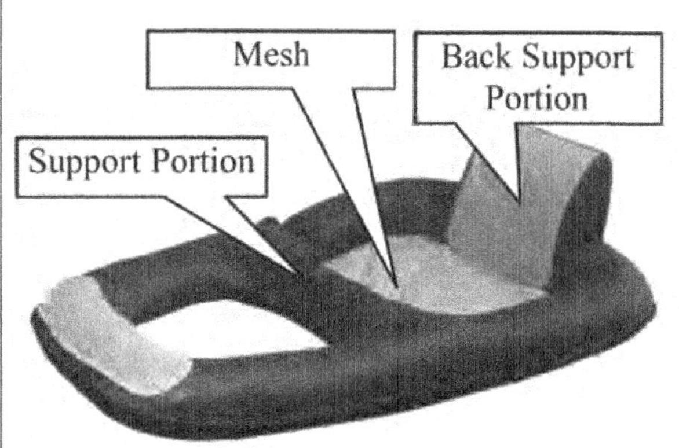
a buoyant member disposed about at least a portion of the outer portion of the panel, the combination of the buoyant member, the panel and the back support portion being collectively configured to support a user in a seated position; and	The product includes an inflatable raft that is a buoyant member. The buoyant member is disposed about at least a portion of the panel's outer portion. The combination of the buoyant member, the panel and the back support portion are collectively configured to support a user in a seated position as that term has been construed by the Court—encompassing both an upright seated position and a reclined seated position. 
a foot support disposed at an end portion of the panel, the opening disposed between the foot support and the support portion, the foot support configured to buoyantly support a weight of the user's feet.	The product includes a foot support disposed at an end portion of the panel. The opening is disposed between the foot support and the support portion. The foot support is configured to buoyantly support the weight of a user's feet.

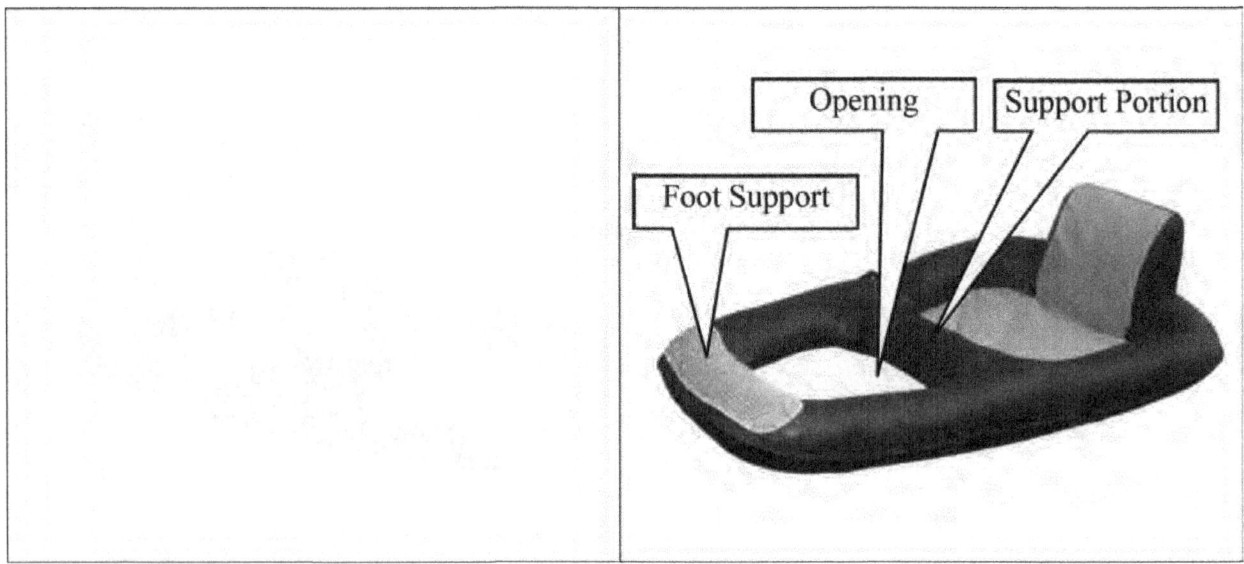
Opening
Support Portion
Foot Support

30. A claim chart illustrating how each and every limitation of Claim 3 is met by the Water-Fun (Mesh) Recliner is provided below:

Claim 3 Limitation	Water-Fun (Mesh) Recliner
3. An apparatus, comprising:	The Water-Fun (Holey) Recliner is an apparatus.
a panel including an inner portion, an outer portion and a back support portion,	The Water-Fun (Holey) Recliner includes a panel—a layer of material that is mostly flat. The panel of the product defines the overall footprint of the product. The panel includes an inner portion, an outer portion, and a back support portion, as shown below. 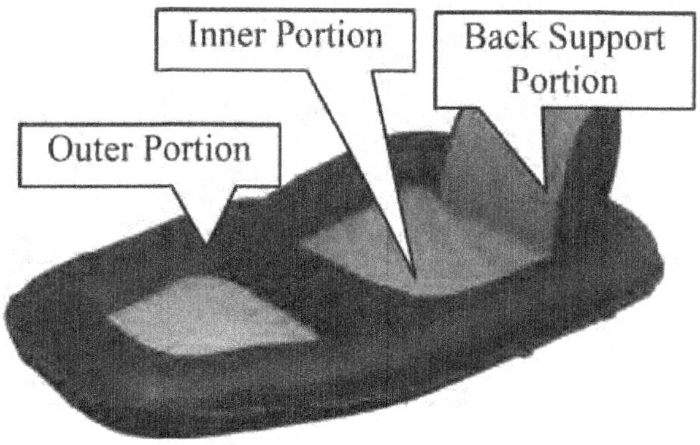
the inner portion of the panel including a mesh material,	The panel's inner portion includes a mesh material. 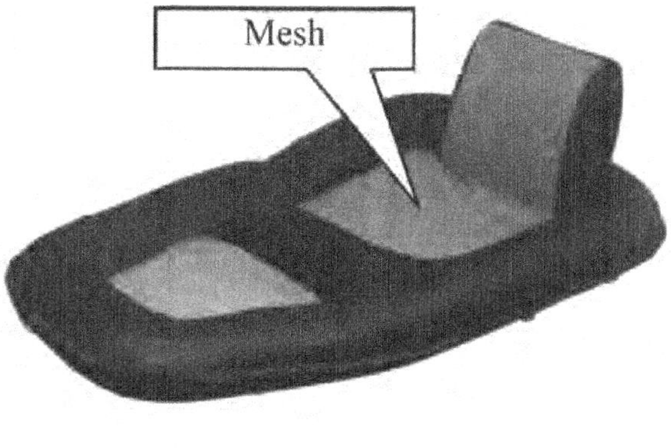

the panel defining an opening,	The panel defines an opening. 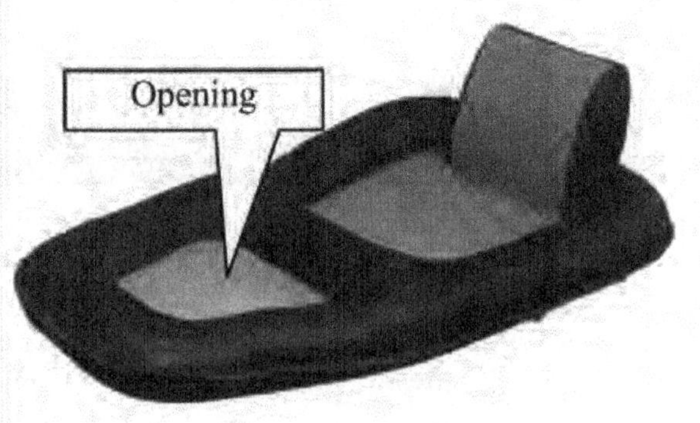
the back support portion being inflatable, the mesh material being disposed at least between the back support portion and a support portion defined by the panel;	The back support portion of the product is inflatable. The mesh material of the panel's inner portion is disposed between the back support portion and a support portion defined by the panel. 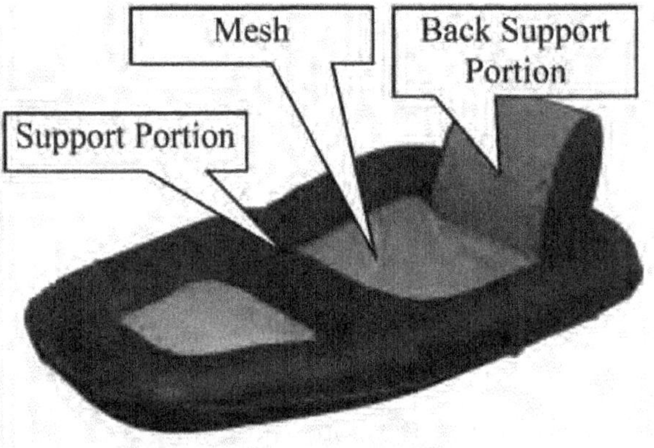
a buoyant member disposed about at least a portion of the outer portion of the panel, the combination of the buoyant member, the panel and the back support portion being collectively configured to support a user in a seated position; and	The product includes an inflatable raft that is a buoyant member. The buoyant member is disposed about at least a portion of the panel's outer portion. The combination of the buoyant member, the panel and the back support portion are collectively configured to support a user in a seated position as that term has been construed by the Court—encompassing both an upright seated position and a reclined seated position.

a foot support disposed at an end portion of the panel, the opening disposed between the foot support and the support portion, the foot support configured to buoyantly support a weight of the user's feet.	The product includes a foot support disposed at an end portion of the panel. The opening is disposed between the foot support and the support portion. The foot support is configured to buoyantly support the weight of a user's feet. 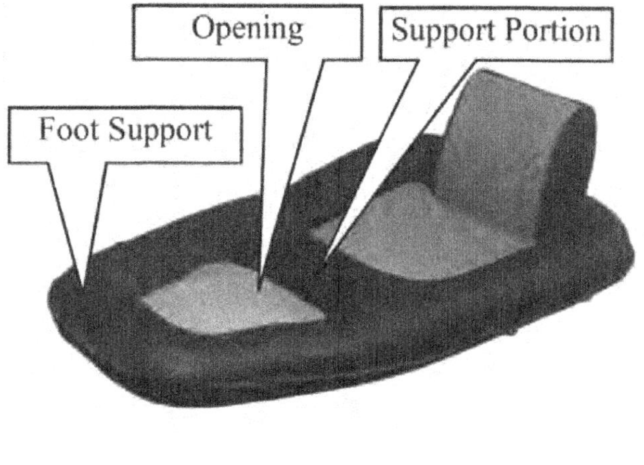

VII. CONCLUSION

For the reasons discussed and illustrated above, it is my opinion that each of the elements of claims 1, 2, and 3 of the '517 Patent are found in the Water-Fun (Holey) Recliner and therefore the '517 Patent is infringed by the Water-Fun (Holey) Recliner. It is also my opinion that each of the elements of claims 1 and 3 of the '517 Patent is found in the Water-Fun (Mesh) Recliner and, therefore, the '517 Patent is infringed by this product.

Respectfully Submitted,

Pat Thurman

Exhibit A

Resume/CV

PAT THURMAN

816 S. Spring Avenue
Deaconville, Nita 20000
(H) 700-555-2457
(C) 700-555-2458
pthurman@global.nita

CAREER BRIEF

Product development and design specialist with more than twenty-two years of product development experience within the consumer, industrial, and commercial markets. An innovative product developer who has successfully researched, designed, engineered, and developed products in numerous categories including consumer housewares, medical equipment, industrial equipment, toys, automotive, lighting, and fitness equipment.

PROFESSIONAL HISTORY

Sunshine Corporation

Director of Product Development and Innovation, YR-7 to present

Sunshine Corporation is one of the largest manufacturers of outdoor products in the U.S. I was recruited to fill a new position coordinating the Marketing, Design, and Engineering departments in an effort to improve the product development process and double the company's profit in two years.

Responsibilities include new product and channel strategy development, market research, marketing, branding, design, and engineering.

Fit Solid, Inc.

Director of Product Development, YR-9 to YR-7

Fit Solid, Inc. is one of the largest manufacturers of fitness equipment in the U.S. Recruited to be part of a new management team taking the company over from the original three partners, I was asked to rebuild the company's development process, which had lapsed in the previous years. Initially responsible for developing and bringing to market a limited number of new products, the new department and process ultimately designed, developed, and managed production on over fifty new products in under two years.

Responsibilities included new product and channel strategy development, market research, design, engineering, and cost reduction. Product categories included specialty fitness equipment for home and commercial fitness equipment, including strength, cardio, and accessories.

Lava Lamp International, Inc.

Manager of Product Development, YR-11 to YR-9

A family-owned business for over forty years, the team was tasked with turning the company into a more commercially viable and salable company. I was asked to redevelop and extend the product line, including moving all production to Asia.

Responsibilities included product and channel strategy development, design, engineering and cost reduction, and manufacturing supervision. Product categories ranged from indoor and outdoor tabletop and specialty lighting, battery-powered and AC and fluid-based novelty products.

Home International, Inc.

Director of New Product Development, YR-13 to YR-11

HII is a large housewares manufacturer comprised of a number of national and international manufacturing facilities.

As department head, I was responsible for designing and launching major plastic product lines along with developing products for Michael Graves and Martha Stewart. Product lines included plastic injection molded products for the kitchen, bath, and storage markets, as well as metal and fabric products for the laundry market.

Responsibilities included all aspects of product development, including managing the manufacturing of current product lines, establishing new product directions, and directing the company's design, engineering, and prototyping process.

The Center Group

Design Director, YR-16 to YR-13

The Center Group was a small firm specializing in strategic planning, market research, product development, category management, and merchandising. Responsible for all aspects of the development process, including new business development, program management, design engineering, prototyping, and production.

Clients included Black & Decker, Bemis, Price Pfister, Sunshine Corp., HII, Fellowes, True Temper, Murray, TDK

Insight Development

Project Manager, YR-25 to YR-16

Insight Development is a consulting product development firm offering research, industrial design, engineering, and manufacturing vendor liaison. Originally starting with the company as one of the first employees and progressed from staff designer to senior project manager. Over the 9.5-year relationship, responsibilities included initial client contact and sales, project organization and proposal generation, research and conceptual design, preliminary and production engineering, prototype development, and vendor sourcing and liaison.

Clients included Baxter Healthcare, First Alert, Fellowes, Panduit Corp., Woods Wire, ACCO, Motorola, Skil/Bosch, Sunshine Corp.

EDUCATION

Northwestern Nita University

Master's degree in new product development, June YR-9

University of Nita

BFA in industrial design, June YR-25

PROFESSIONAL SKILLS AND DEVELOPMENT

Specialist in new product conceptualization, sketch and presentation rendering development, plastic and metal part engineering development, 3D prototype development, including engineering mechanisms and breadboards. Extensive knowledge of high- and low-volume manufacturing processes, including injection molding, blow molding, sheet metal fabrication, and composite processing. Computer skills include Microsoft Office, Project, and Excel; Adobe InDesign, AutoCAD, and SolidWorks. Extensive experience with the patent development process and registered design expert witness with testimony in twelve patent infringement cases.

Exhibit B

Materials Considered

MATERIALS CONSIDERED

U.S. Patent 8,197,517

The USPTO file history of the '517 patent

SwimTime's Complaint

Water-Fun's Answer to the Complaint

Court's Order Construing the Claims of the '517 patent

Physical sample of the Water-Fun (Holey) Recliner

Physical sample of the Water-Fun (Mesh) Recliner

Exhibit C

Photos of Water-Fun (Holey) Recliner

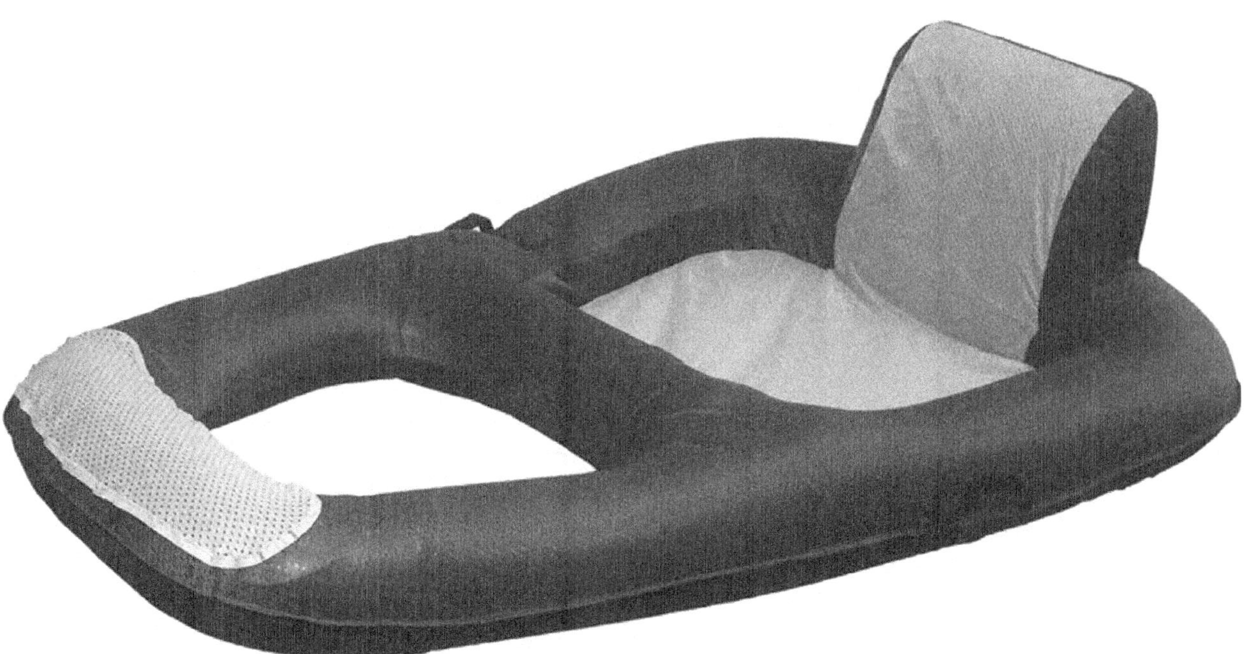

[*Note*: To view the following images in color, please refer to the CD-ROM accompanying this book.]

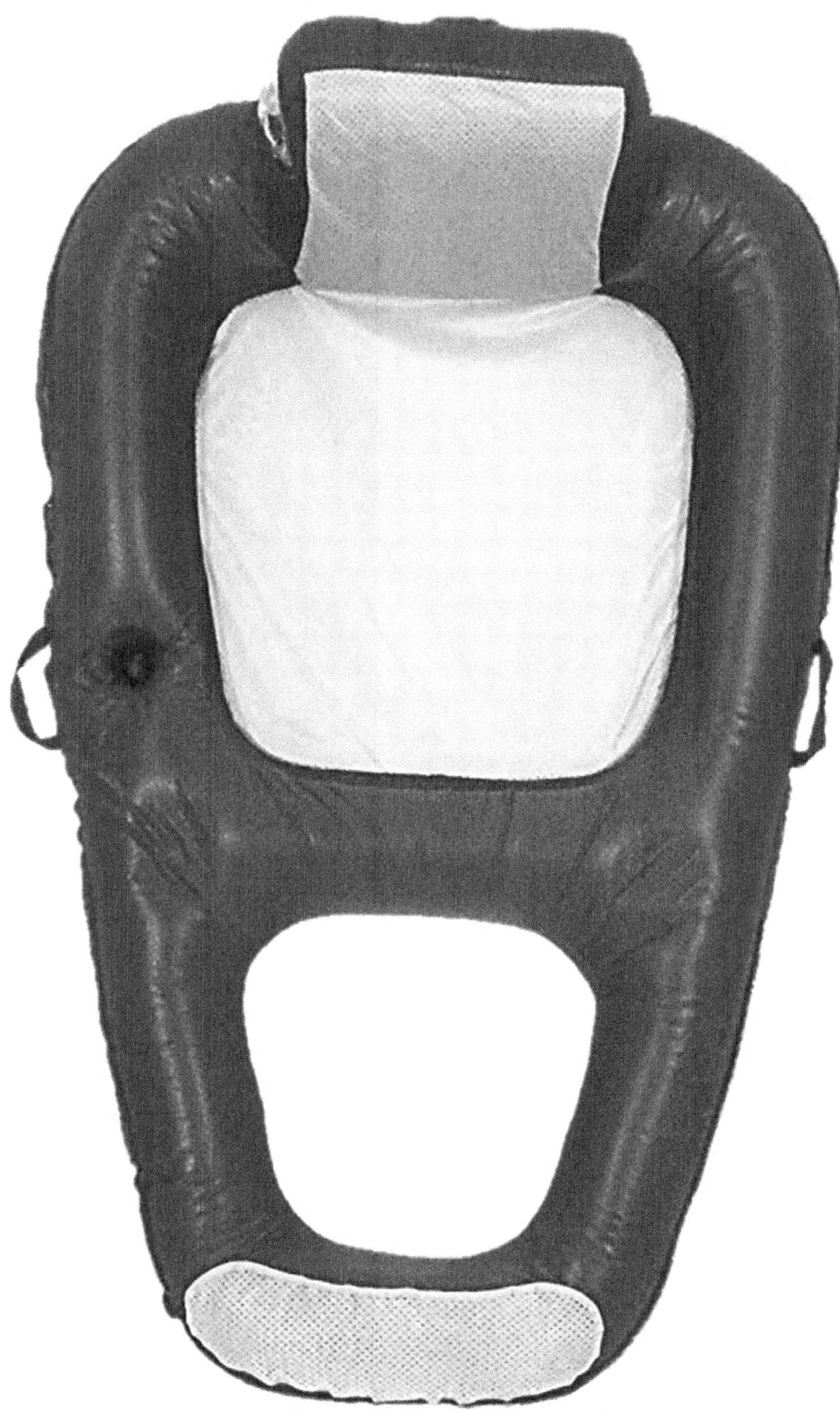

Exhibit D

Photos of Water-Fun (Mesh) Recliner

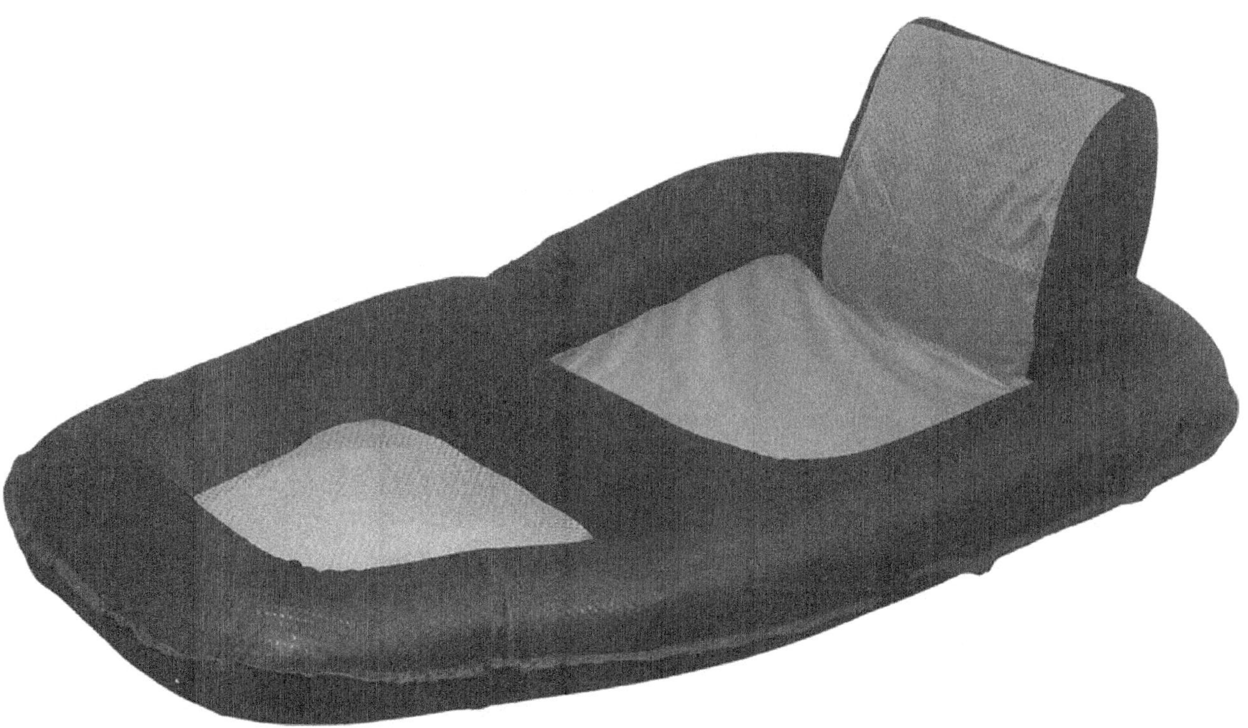

[*Note*: To view the following images in color, please refer to the CD-ROM accompanying this book.]

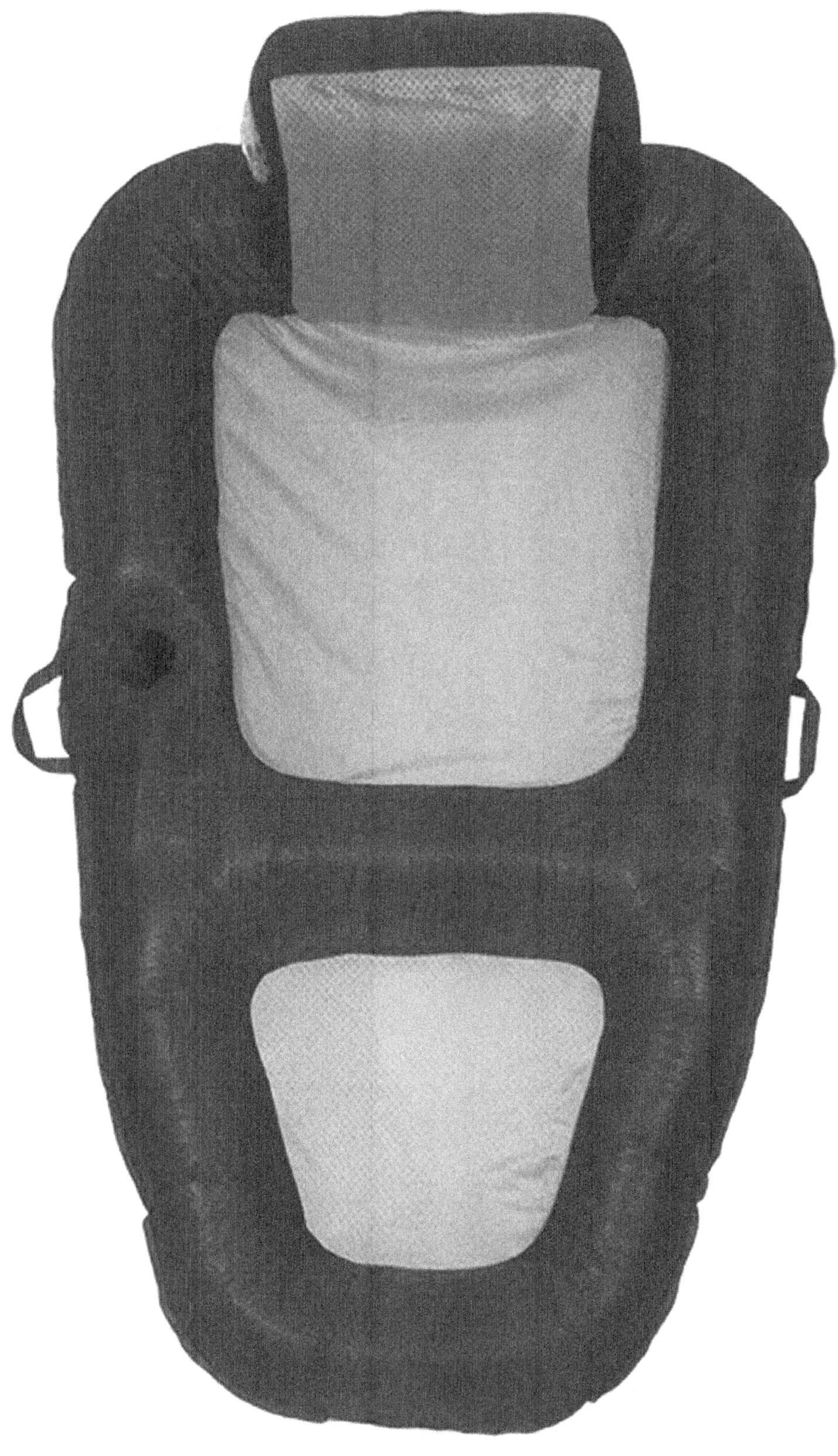

UNITED STATES DISTRICT COURT
FOR THE DISTRICT OF NITA

Nita City Division

SWIMTIME CORPORATION, Plaintiff, v. WATER-FUN, INC., Defendant.	)))))))	Civil Action No. 1:Y00-cv-00100

DEFENDANT'S EXPERT REPORT ON INVALIDITY

This report is submitted by the undersigned pursuant to Rule 26(a)(2)(B) of the Federal Rules of Civil Procedure.

I. QUALIFICATIONS

My name is Drew Clark. I have been retained by counsel for Water-Fun, Inc. (hereinafter "Water-Fun") to review materials relating to the above-referenced patent infringement matter and to provide my opinion on the validity the claims of U.S. Patent Number 8,197,517 to Flax et al. and owned by SwimTime Corp. (hereinafter "SwimTime").

I am being compensated at the rate of $600 per hour for my efforts in this matter.

I am retired from my position as the senior vice president of Research & Development at Water-Fun (my resume/CV is attached hereto as Exhibit A). I held that position from YR-34 until my retirement in YR-19. Water-Fun is in the business of designing, manufacturing, and selling various recreational products, primarily, swim- and pool-related products. Examples of products sold by Water-Fun are masks, snorkels, fins, pools, beach toys and games, and various types of floating lounges and chairs. Water-Fun has been in this industry since YR-45.

I started with Water-Fun in YR-44. Over the years, I played many roles with Water-Fun. When I first started with the company, my role was production management. In YR-37, I was named as the vice president of Research & Development. In YR-34, I was promoted to senior vice president of Research & Development. My primary responsibilities included the overseeing of all new product development functions. Under my management and supervision, Water-Fun has developed hundreds of new and innovative and commercially successful water and pool accessory products. Dozens of these have included pool floats.

I have not authored any publications in the past ten years.

In addition, I am the holder of seven U.S. patents for various products in our field, including the following: an inflatable water slide and pool, dive masks, a buoyant swim suit, a buoyant swim vest, a swim mask, and a swim fin. Further, I am one of the designers and developers of Water-Fun's Deluxe

Inflatable Recliner, a predecessor product to the accused products in this case. The Deluxe Inflatable Recliner first went on sale in the U.S. in YR-25 and was a good seller over that entire time.

At all times during my time in the water and pool accessory industry, I studied and I continue to study the products that are being sold by Water-Time's competitors and I have been familiar with the state of the art in the recreation and swim products areas and with regard to various floating lounge and chair products, in particular.

II. PREPARATION

I am not a lawyer and do not hold myself out as an expert in the field of patent law. I am not offering any legal conclusions in this report. Rather, the opinions in this report are based upon my review and analysis of applicable materials and the following information and factual data:

1. The Complaint in this action;
2. A copy of United States Patent Number 8,197,517 ("the '517 Patent"), as well as the prosecution history for the '517 Patent;
3. A review of the prior art disclosed by defendant in this action (attached at Exhibit C).
4. The Court's *Markman* Order.

My report is also based upon my extensive knowledge and experience in the swim and pool industry and my knowledge of the state of the art. I reserve the right to amend or supplement this report in the future.

III. TOPICS ON WHICH I HAVE BEEN ASKED TO EXPRESS OPINIONS

Based upon my review of the materials listed above, and my knowledge and experience, I have formed the following opinions in this case:

1. A person having ordinary skill in the art would understand that each of the elements of claim 1 of the '517 Patent are present in U.S. Patent Nos. 5,476,404 ("the '404 Patent), 3,871,042 ("the '042 Patent"), 6,465,344 ("the '344 Patent"), and 1,960,474 ("the '474 Patent"), so as to anticipate claim 1.
2. A person having ordinary skill in the art would understand that each of the elements of claim 2 of the '517 Patent are present in the '344 Patent and the '474 Patent, so as to anticipate claim 2.
3. A person having ordinary skill in the art would understand that each of the elements of claim 3 of the '517 Patent are present in the '404 patent, the '344 Patent, and the '474 patent, so as to anticipate claim 3.
4. It would have been obvious to a person having ordinary skill in the art as of the date of invention to combine the teachings of the disclosed prior art products with the flotation devices of the '042, '474, '344 and '404 Patents, as well as with the Intrex King Kool Lounge product and other disclosed prior art, with a resulting flotation device that contains all of the elements of claims 1, 2, and 3 of the '517 Patent. There would have been ample motivation to make such combinations to achieve new water lounge devices, and it would have been obvious to try to do so and there would have been a reasonable expectation and likelihood of successfully doing so with little or no experimentation necessary.

5. The original written description in the application that issued as the '517 patent does not convey to a person having ordinary skill in the art that, at the time of the filing of the patent application, the inventor had invented a flotation device that did not contain a spring for collapsing the device.
6. A person having ordinary skill in the art, with respect to the patent-in-suit and its claimed inventions and the issues in this lawsuit, is someone with a competency and skill level comparable to a college degree and at least three to five years' experience in the recreational flotation device industry. However, I would not be surprised to learn there are persons "having ordinary" skill who have never gone to college and perhaps have additional experience in the relevant industry. My opinions will not change even if I am incorrect on the level of ordinary skill in the art.

IV. OPINIONS

A. A person having ordinary skill in the art would understand that each of the elements of claims 1, 2, and 3 of the '517 Patent are present in one or more of the '042, '474, '344, and/or '404 Patents.

I understand that the plaintiff asserts that the accused products infringe claims 1 through 3 of the '517 Patent. I have reviewed those claims. The chart attached hereto as Exhibit B, accurately reflect the bases for my opinions concerning the '517 Patent. Specifically, the chart attached as Exhibit B accurately discloses the bases for my opinion that a person having ordinary skill in the art would understand that each of the elements of claim 1, 2, and 3 of the '517 Patent is present in at least one of the '042 Patent, the '474 Patent, the '344 Patent, and the '404 Patent.

B. It would have been obvious to a person having ordinary skill in the art to combine the teachings of the '042, '474, '344, and '404 Patents, as well as the Intex King Kool Lounge and other prior art, with a resulting flotation device that contains all of the elements of claims 1, 2, and 3 of the '517 Patent.

I am familiar with the state of the art for floating lounges and chairs as of the earliest priority date for the '517 Patent. As of that time, the use of a foot opening in a floating lounge or chair was well known in the industry. The chart attached as Exhibit B discloses a number of the lounges and chairs that were on the market prior to the '517 Patent's priority date and contain such a foot opening, as well as a buoyant foot rest on the edge of the foot opening. In my opinion, it would have been obvious to a person having ordinary skill in the art to incorporate the opening and foot rest of the prior art products with the flotation devices of the '042 and '474 Patents to afford the user the option of keeping his or her feet on the buoyant foot rest, making the reclined position more comfortable, or dangling them in the water. A combination of the '042 Patent or the '474 Patent and any of the prior art products with openings would result in a flotation device that contains all of the elements of claims 2 and 3 of the '517 Patent.

For the same reasons set forth in the immediately preceding paragraph, and as shown in the chart attached as Exhibit B, it is my opinion that it would have been obvious to a person having ordinary skill in the art to incorporate the opening and foot rest of the Intex King Kool Lounge with the flotation device of the '042 Patent, with a resulting flotation device that contains all of the elements of claims 1 through 3 of the '517 Patent. In my opinion, in the event that any of the accused products are determined to contain all of the elements of claims 1 through 3 of the '517 patent, the Intex King Kool Lounge similarly contains all of the elements of those claims.

Additionally, it is my opinion that it would have been obvious to a person having ordinary skill in the art to incorporate the opening and foot rest of the disclosed prior art products with the flotation devices of the '344 Patent to afford the user the option of keeping his or her feet on the buoyant foot rest, making the reclined position more comfortable, or dangling them in the water. As shown in Exhibit B, a combination of the '344 Patent and any of the prior art products with openings would result in a flotation device that contains all of the elements of claims 2 and 3 of the '517 Patent.

Also, in my opinion, it would have been obvious to a person having ordinary skill in the art to incorporate the opening and foot rest of the prior art products with the flotation devices of the '404 Patent to afford the user the option of keeping his or her feet on the buoyant foot rest, making the reclined position more comfortable, or dangling them in the water. Thus, as shown in Exhibit B, a combination of the '404 Patent and any of the prior art products with openings would result in a flotation device that contains all of the elements of claims 2 and 3 of the '517 Patent.

C. The original written description in the application that issued as the '517 Patent does not convey to a person having ordinary skill in the art that, at the time of the filing of the patent application, the inventor had invented a flotation device that did not contain a spring for collapsing the device.

The original description of the invention of the '517 Patent filed with the USPTO, describes the invention as "a collapsible flotation device having a support member that allows the user to float thereon in a seated position." That description also provides that "[t]he various collapsible flotation devices of the invention are formed from a panel including an inner portion and an outer portion, and a spring disposed about the outer portion of the panel, the spring being movable between a coiled configuration and an uncoiled configuration. The spring operates to change the shape of the flotation device." In fact, every single embodiment and the totality of the description of "the invention" claimed relates to an apparatus having a spring, i.e., rigid support member/shape-retaining member/coilable spring 104 (Fig. 1), spring 204 (Fig. 5), spring 304/ 304' (Figs. 7A and 7B), spring 404 (Fig. 8A et seq.). Thus, in my opinion, the original written description conveys to a person having ordinary skill in the art that at the time of the application the inventor had invented a flotation device that contained (required) a spring to allow the device to collapse, and contained a support member that allowed the user to float in a seated position.

Claims 1 through 3 of the '517 Patent do not recite a spring to collapse the flotation device. However, in my opinion the original written description does not convey to a person having ordinary skill in the art that, at the time of the filing of the patent application, the inventory had invented a flotation device that did not contain a spring for collapsing the device.

D. Person Having Ordinary Skill in the Art.

It is my understanding that the term "person having ordinary skill in the art" is a legal term used by courts in patent cases. It is not an actual person, but rather a hypothetical one. While I am certainly not a legal expert, I understand this term to be based upon many factors.

Based upon the information known at this time, I believe that person is someone with a competency and skill level comparable to a college degree and at least three to five years' experience in the recreational flotation device industry. This person must understand and appreciate the realities of recreational products, particularly flotation devices; customer demands and requests; and the advantages and disadvantages of the various products on the market. I use this measure as an example only. I would not be surprised to learn there are persons "having ordinary" skill who have never gone to college and perhaps have additional experience in the industry. To some degree, I base this on my own abilities, as someone with nearly thirty years of experience designing recreational products, including flotation devices.

V. PREVIOUS EXPERT TESTIMONY

In the past four years, I have not testified as an expert in any matters.

Signed under the penalties of perjury.

Drew Clark

Exhibit A

Resume/CV

DREW CLARK

7500 Wake Lane
Nita City, Nita

Professional History

Currently retired Since YR-19

Senior Vice President of Research & Development YR-34 to YR-19

Water-Fun, Inc.

Supervised the development and production of Water-Fun's recreational, swim- and pool-related products.

Vice President of Research and Development YR-37 to YR-34

Water-Fun, Inc.

Oversaw the development of all new products.

Product Designer YR-44 to YR-37

Water-Fun, Inc.

Designed and worked to develop new recreational, water-use products.

Educational Background

Bachelor of Science, mechanical engineering

Nita University, YR-44

Achievements

I am a named inventor on seven U.S. patents.

Exhibit B

Invalidity Claim Charts

Claim 1 Limitation	PRIOR ART DISCLOSURE
1. An apparatus, comprising:	The '404 patent discloses an apparatus, which is a inflatable recreational inner tube toy. The '344 patent discloses an apparatus, which is a collapsible flotation device. The '474 patent discloses an apparatus, which is a buoyant bathing device. The '042 patent discloses an apparatus, which is an inflatable vehicle construction. The Intex King Kool Lounge is an apparatus—it is an inflatable pool lounge.
a panel including an inner portion, an outer portion and a back support portion,	The '404 patent discloses a panel with an inner portion, an outer portion and a back support portion. 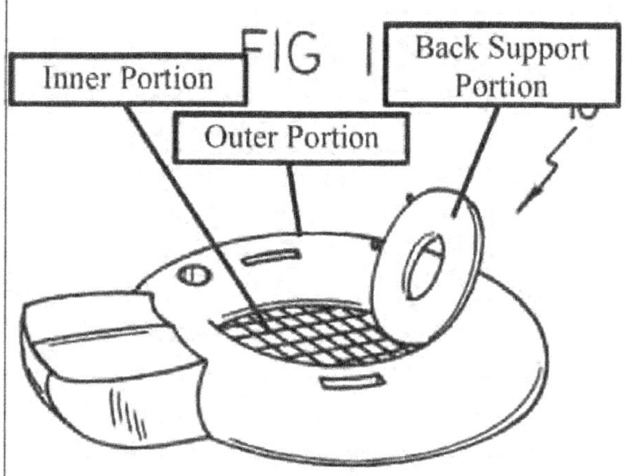 FIG 1 Inner Portion Outer Portion Back Support Portion The '344 patent discloses a panel with an inner portion, an outer portion and a back support portion.

[*Note*: To view the following images in this claims chart in color, please refer to the CD-ROM accompanying this book.]

Claim 1 Limitation	PRIOR ART DISCLOSURE
	FIG. 9 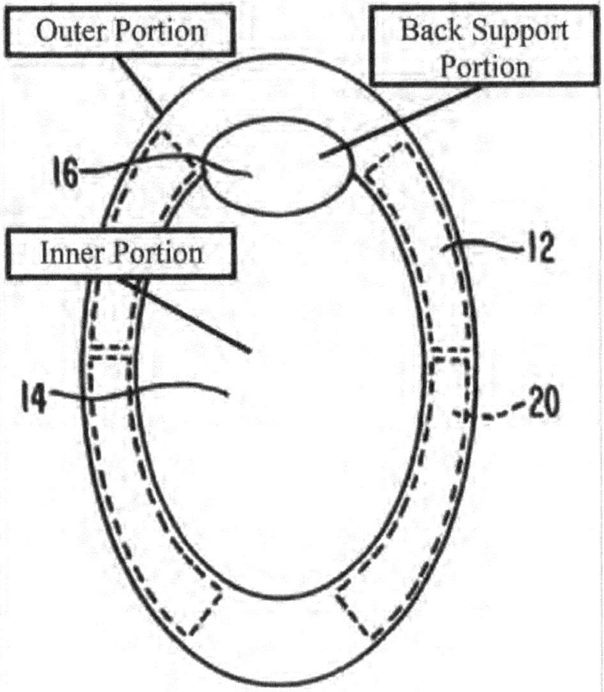 The '474 patent discloses a panel with an inner portion, an outer portion and a back support portion. 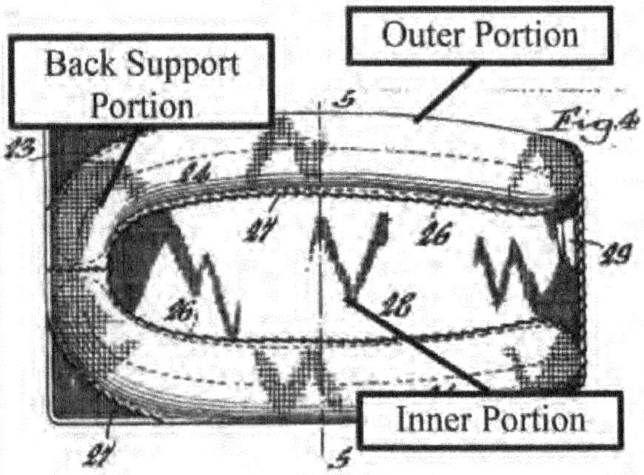

Claim 1 Limitation	PRIOR ART DISCLOSURE
	The '042 patent discloses a panel with an inner portion, an outer portion and a back support portion. 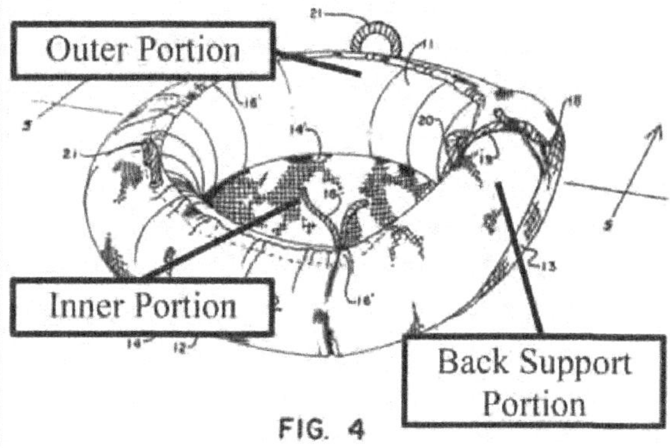 FIG. 4 The Intex King Kool Lounge discloses a panel with an inner portion, an outer portion and a back support portion. 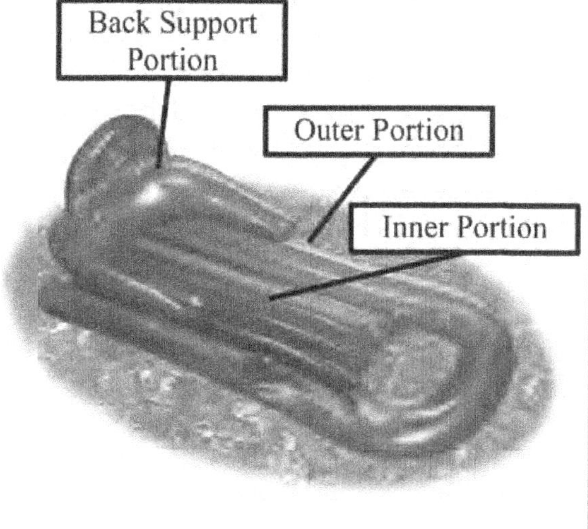
the inner portion of the panel having a first edge and a second edge on an opposite side of the inner portion of the panel from the first edge, a distance between the first edge of the inner portion of the panel and the second edge	The '404 patent discloses the inner portion of the panel has a first edge and a second edge on the opposite side thereof, where the

Claim 1 Limitation	PRIOR ART DISCLOSURE
of the inner portion of the panel defining a width of the inner portion of the panel,	distance between these two edges defines a width of the inner portion. 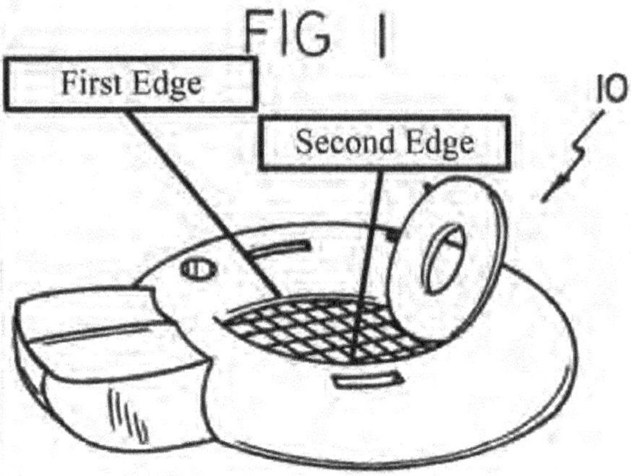 The '344 patent discloses the inner portion of the panel has a first edge and a second edge on the opposite side thereof, where the distance between these two edges defines a width of the inner portion.

<table>
<tr><th>Claim 1 Limitation</th><th>PRIOR ART DISCLOSURE</th></tr>
<tr><td></td><td>

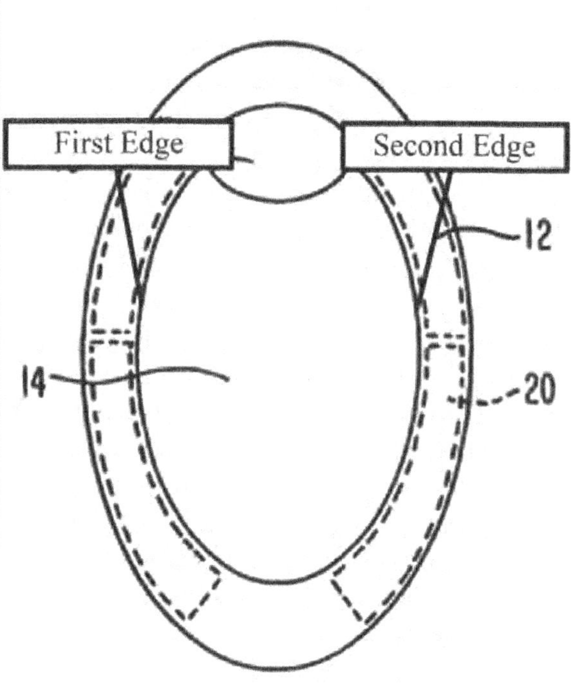

The '474 patent discloses the inner portion of the panel has a first edge and a second edge on the opposite side thereof, where the distance between these two edges defines a width of the inner portion.

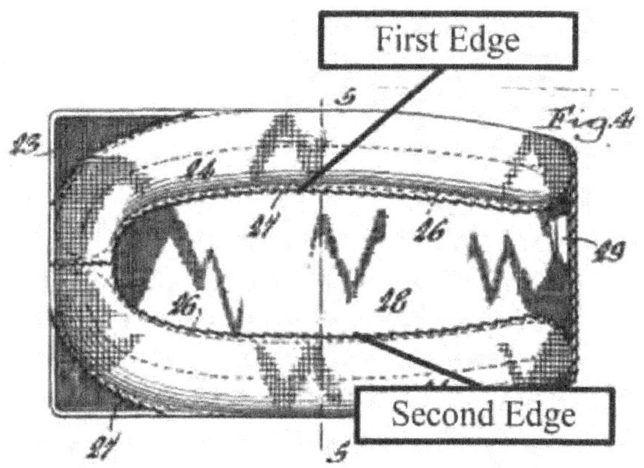

</td></tr>
</table>

Claim 1 Limitation	PRIOR ART DISCLOSURE
	The '042 patent discloses the inner portion of the panel has a first edge and a second edge on the opposite side thereof, where the distance between these two edges defines a width of the inner portion. 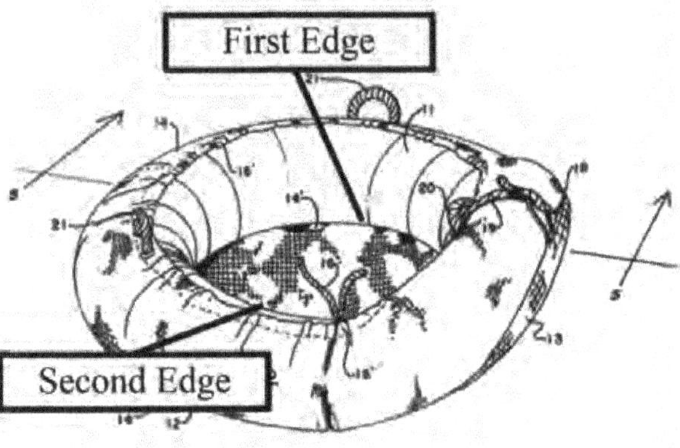 FIG. 4 The Intex King Kool Lounge discloses the inner portion of the panel has a first edge and a second edge on the opposite side thereof, where the distance between these two edges defines a width of the inner portion.

Claim 1 Limitation	PRIOR ART DISCLOSURE
	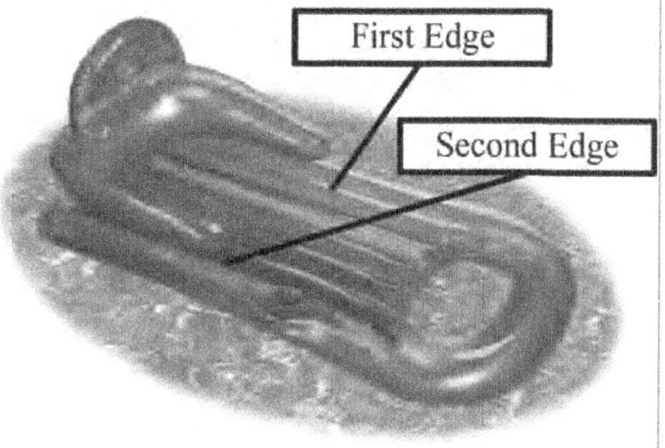 First Edge Second Edge
the inner portion of the panel being substantially planar across the width of the inner portion of the panel,	The '404 patent discloses the inner portion being substantially planar across the width. FIG 1  10 The '344 patent discloses the inner portion being substantially planar across the width.

Claim 1 Limitation	PRIOR ART DISCLOSURE
	FIG. 9 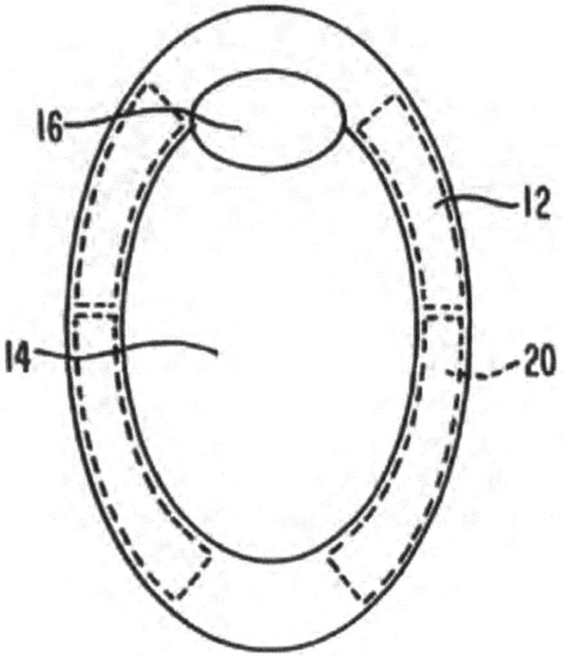 16 12 14 20 The '474 patent discloses the inner portion being substantially planar across the width. 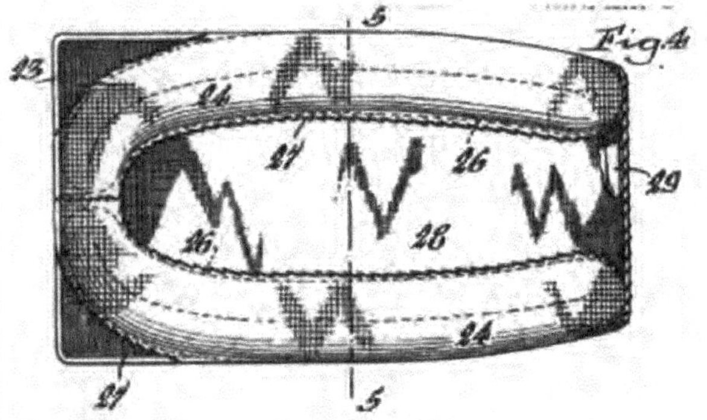 Fig. 4

Claim 1 Limitation	PRIOR ART DISCLOSURE
	The '042 patent discloses the inner portion being substantially planar across the width. 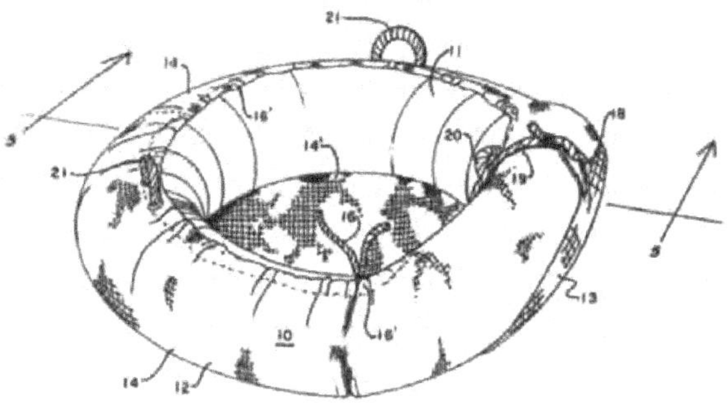 FIG. 4 The Intex King Kool Lounge discloses the inner portion being substantially planar across the width. 
the back support portion being inflatable; and	The '404 patent discloses the back support is inflatable.

Claim 1 Limitation	PRIOR ART DISCLOSURE
	FIG 1  The '344 patent discloses the back support is inflatable. FIG. 9 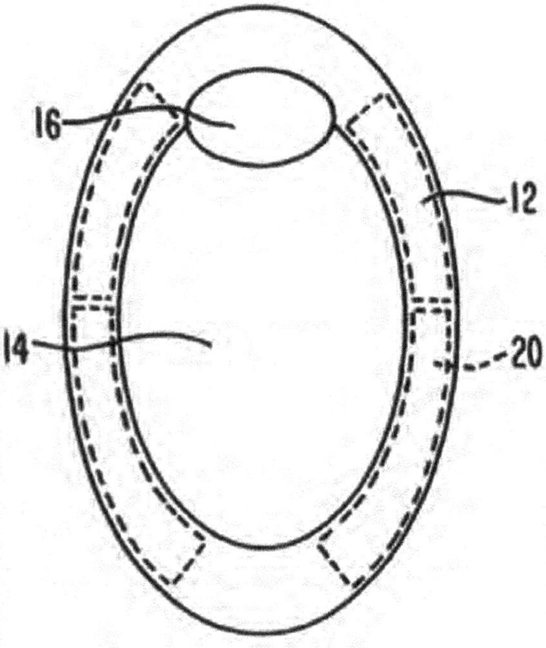

Claim 1 Limitation	PRIOR ART DISCLOSURE
	The '474 patent discloses the back support is inflatable. 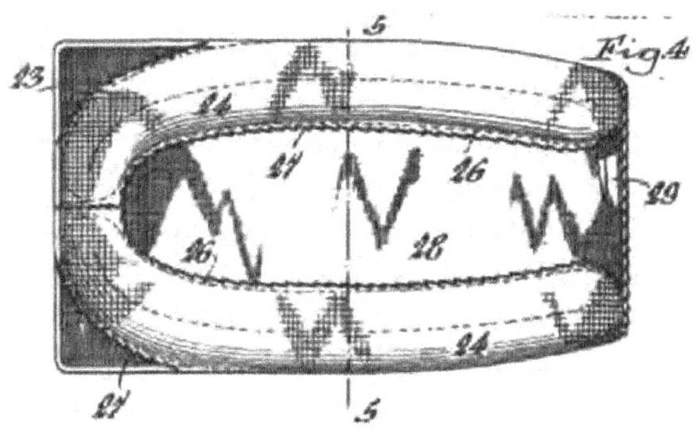 The '042 patent discloses the back support is inflatable. 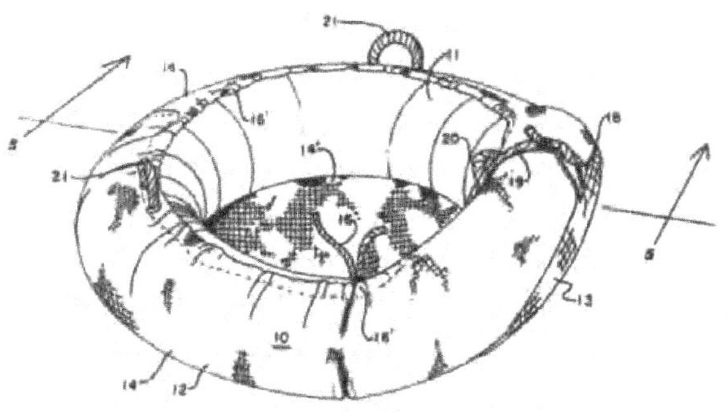 FIG. 4 The Intex King Kool Lounge discloses the back support is inflatable.

Claim 1 Limitation	PRIOR ART DISCLOSURE

a buoyant member disposed about at least the inner portion of the panel, at least a portion of the buoyant member being disposed within at least a portion of the outer portion of the panel,	The '404 patent discloses a buoyant member around the inner portion and at least partially disposed in a portion of the outer portion. 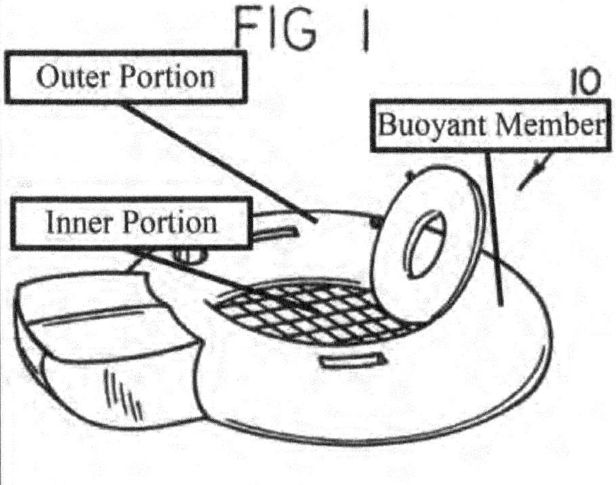 FIG 1 The '344 patent discloses a buoyant member around the inner portion and at least partially disposed in a portion of the outer portion.

Claim 1 Limitation	PRIOR ART DISCLOSURE
	FIG. 9 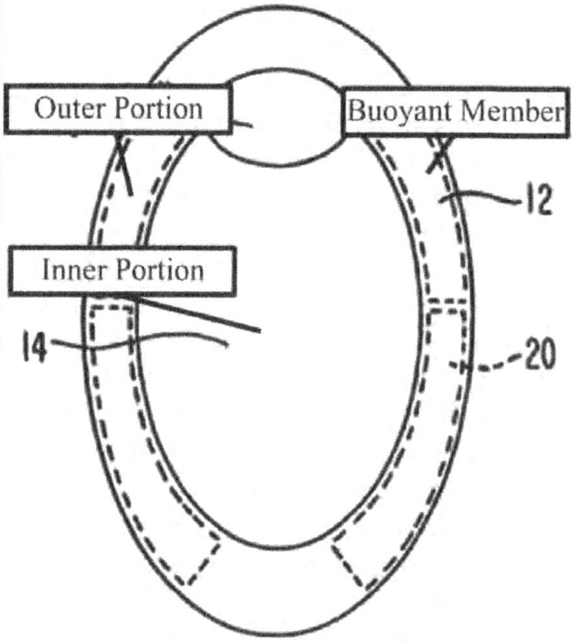 The '474 patent discloses a buoyant member around the inner portion and at least partially disposed in a portion of the outer portion. 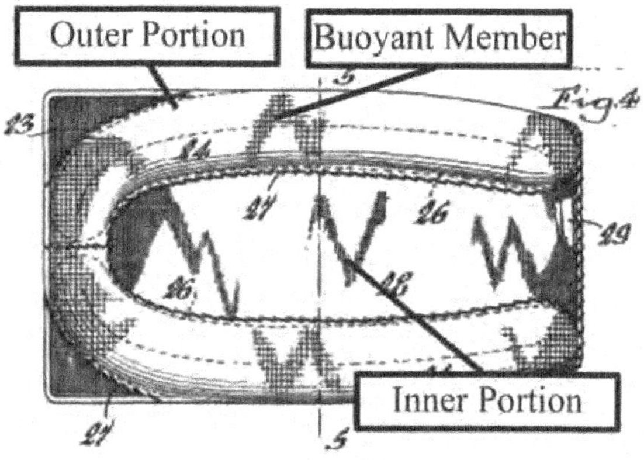

Claim 1 Limitation	PRIOR ART DISCLOSURE
	The '042 patent discloses a buoyant member around the inner portion and at least partially disposed in a portion of the outer portion. 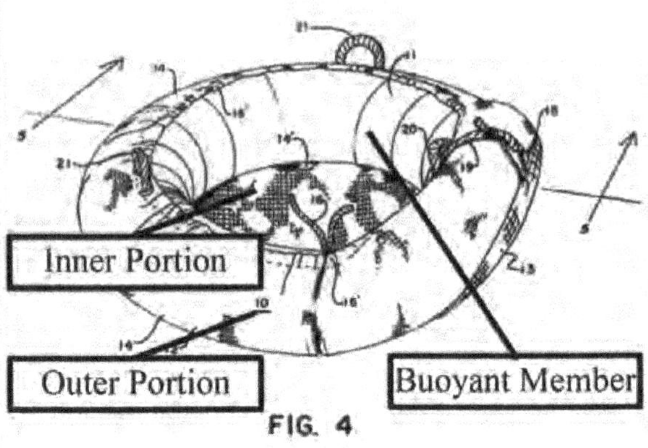
the buoyant member having a first portion and a second portion different from the first portion, the first portion of the buoyant member and the second portion of the buoyant member being disposed at opposite locations of the inner portion of the panel and separated by the width of the inner portion of the panel,	The '404 patent discloses that the buoyant member has a first and a second portion, each different, where they are disposed at opposite locations of the inner portion of the panel and separated by its width. 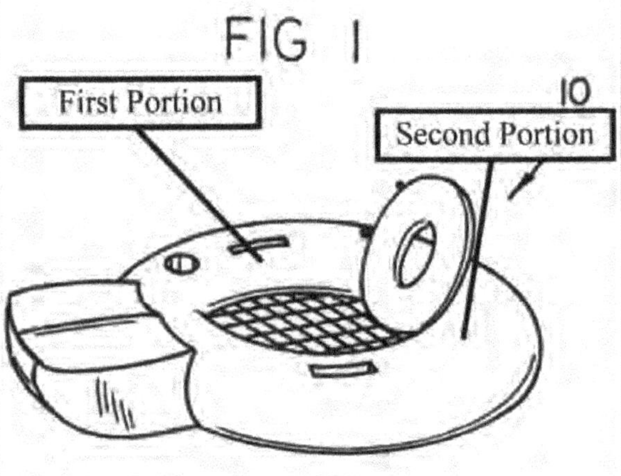 The '344 patent discloses that the buoyant member has a first and a second portion, each different, where they are disposed at opposite

Claim 1 Limitation	PRIOR ART DISCLOSURE
	locations of the inner portion of the panel and separated by its width. 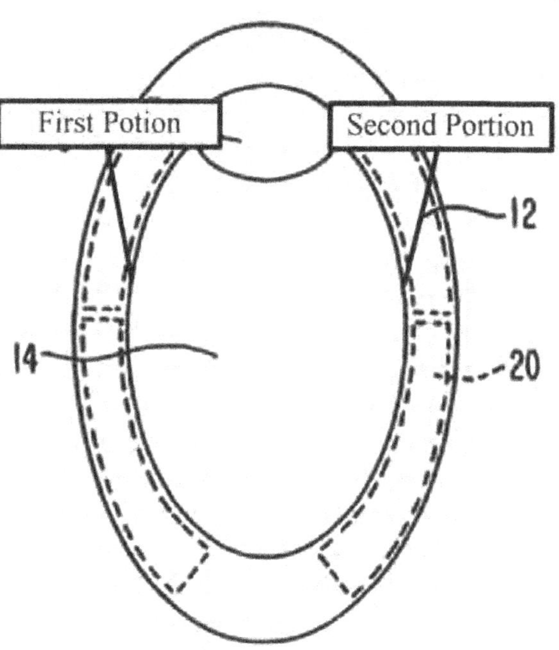 The '474 patent discloses that the buoyant member has a first and a second portion, each different, where they are disposed at opposite locations of the inner portion of the panel and separated by its width.

Claim 1 Limitation	PRIOR ART DISCLOSURE
	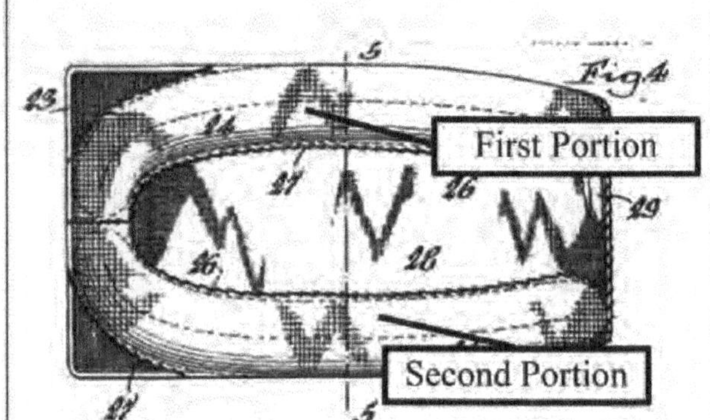 The '042 patent discloses that the buoyant member has a first and a second portion, each different, where they are disposed at opposite locations of the inner portion of the panel and separated by its width. 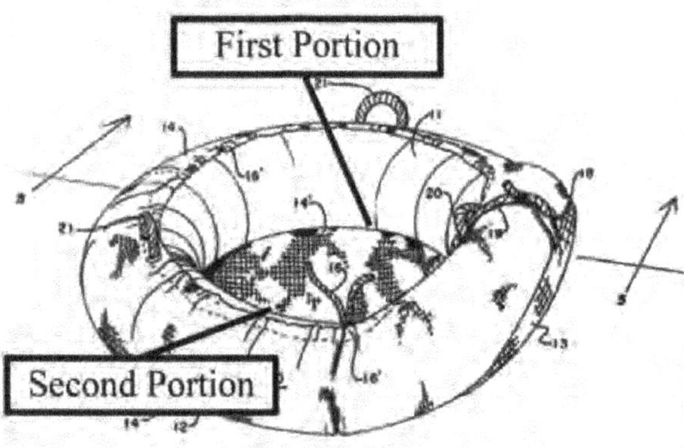 FIG. 4 The Intex King Kool Lounge discloses that the buoyant member has a first and a second portion, each different, where they are disposed at opposite locations of the inner portion of the panel and separated by its width.

Claim 1 Limitation	PRIOR ART DISCLOSURE
	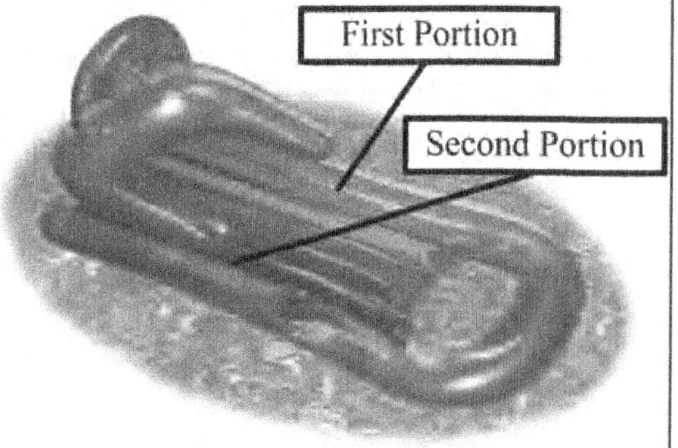 First Portion Second Portion
the inner portion of the panel extending continuously between the first portion of the buoyant member and the second portion of the buoyant member without an intervening buoyant member,	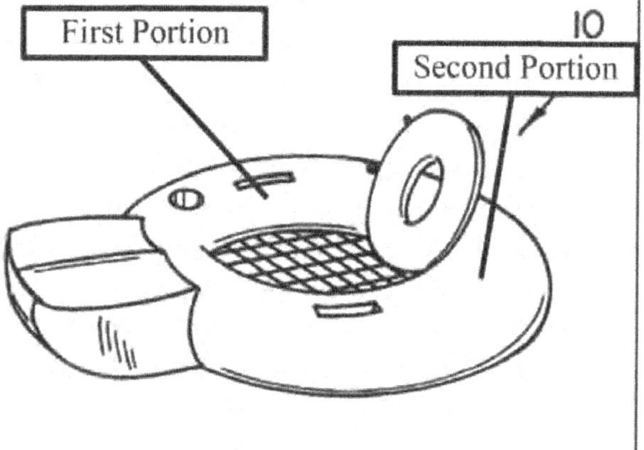 The '404 patent discloses that the inner portion of the panel extends continuously between the first and second portions of the buoyant member without an intervening buoyant member. FIG 1 First Portion 10 Second Portion The '344 patent discloses that the inner portion of the panel extends continuously between the first and second portions of the

Claim 1 Limitation	PRIOR ART DISCLOSURE
	buoyant member without an intervening buoyant member. 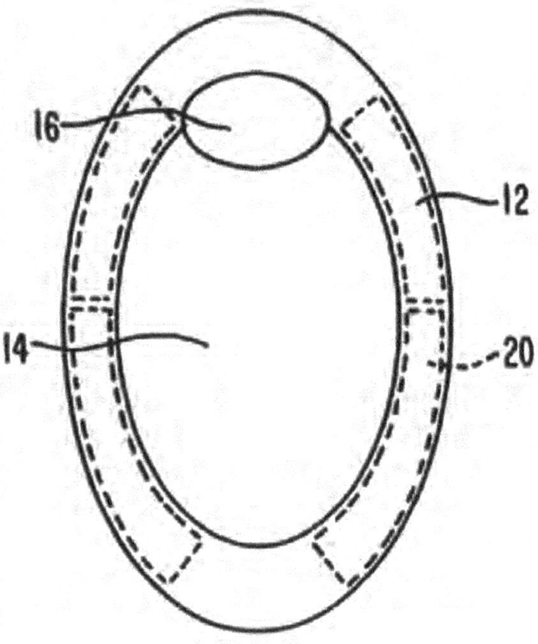 The '474 patent discloses that the inner portion of the panel extends continuously between the first and second portions of the buoyant member without an intervening buoyant member.

Claim 1 Limitation	PRIOR ART DISCLOSURE
	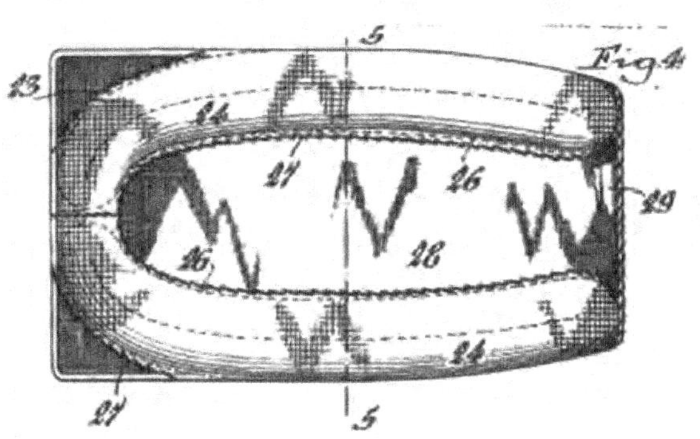 The '042 patent discloses that the inner portion of the panel extends continuously between the first and second portions of the buoyant member without an intervening buoyant member. 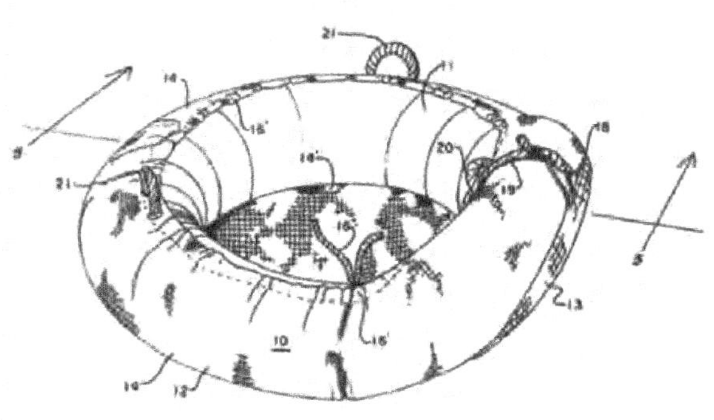 FIG. 4
at least one of the outer portion of the panel within which the first portion of the buoyant member is at least partially disposed or the first portion of the buoyant member being in contact with the first edge of the inner portion of the panel.	The '404 patent discloses that the outer portion and/or the first portion of the buoyant member within that part of the outer portion contacts the first edge of the inner portion.

Claim 1 Limitation	PRIOR ART DISCLOSURE
	FIG 1 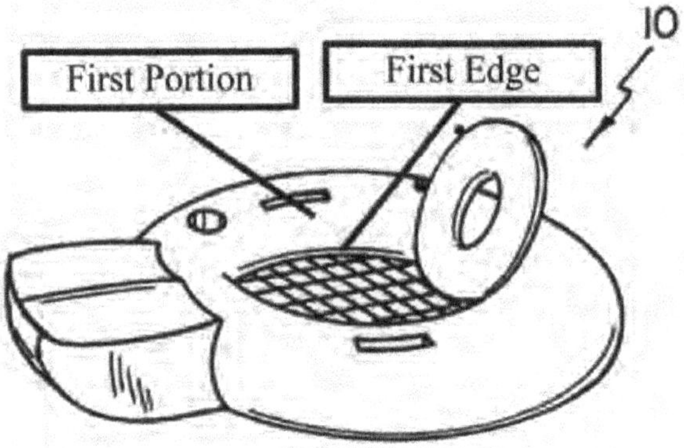 First Portion First Edge 10 The '344 patent discloses that the outer portion and/or the first portion of the buoyant member within that part of the outer portion contacts the first edge of the inner portion.

Claim 1 Limitation	PRIOR ART DISCLOSURE
	FIG. 9 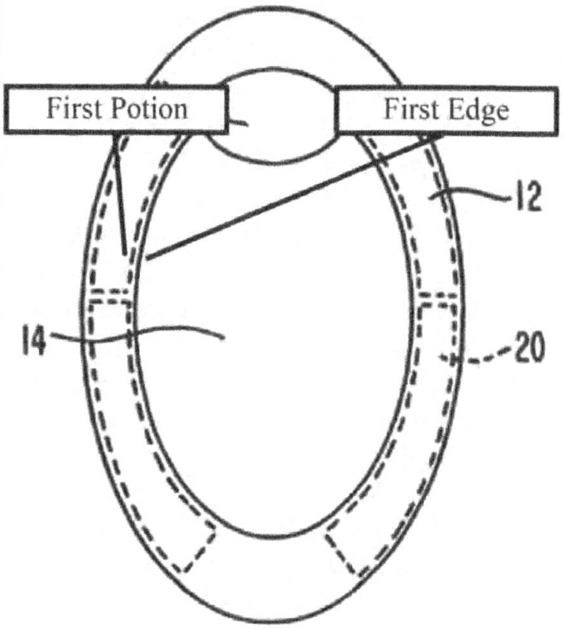 First Potion First Edge 12 14 20 The '474 patent discloses that the outer portion and/or the first portion of the buoyant member within that part of the outer portion contacts the first edge of the inner portion. 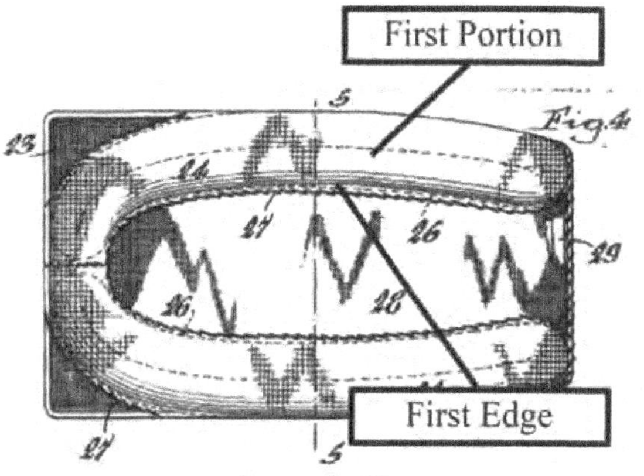 First Portion First Edge

Claim 1 Limitation	PRIOR ART DISCLOSURE
	The '042 patent discloses that the outer portion and/or the first portion of the buoyant member within that part of the outer portion contacts the first edge of the inner portion. 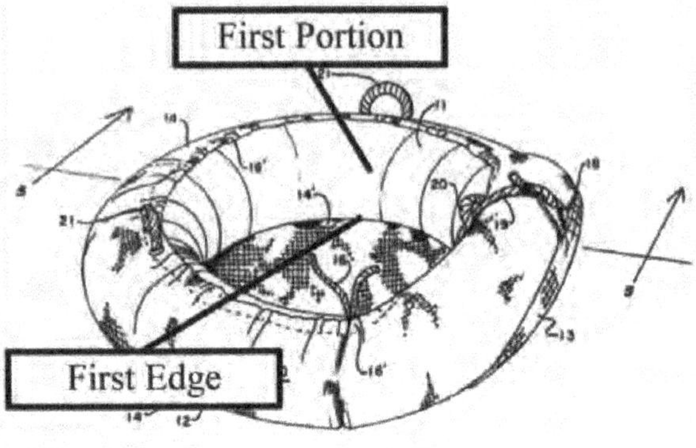 First Portion First Edge FIG. 4 The Intex King Kool Lounge discloses that the outer portion and/or the first portion of the buoyant member within that part of the outer portion contacts the first edge of the inner portion. 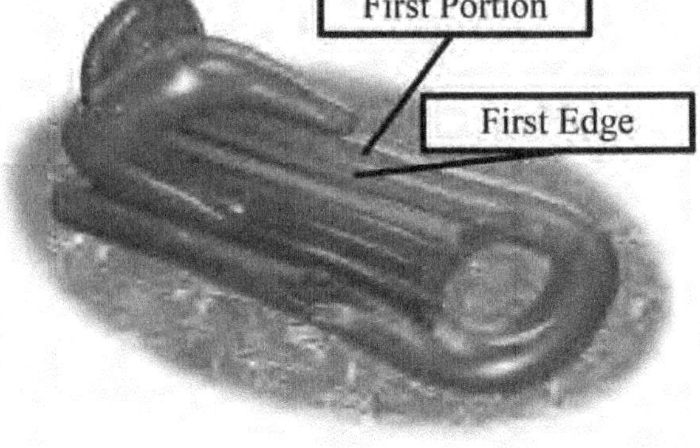 First Portion First Edge

Claim 1 Limitation	PRIOR ART DISCLOSURE
at least one of the outer portion of the panel within which the second portion of the buoyant member is at least partially disposed or the second portion of the buoyant member being in contact with the second edge of the inner portion of the panel,	The '404 patent discloses that the outer portion and/or the second portion of the buoyant member within that part of the outer portion contacts the second edge of the inner portion. 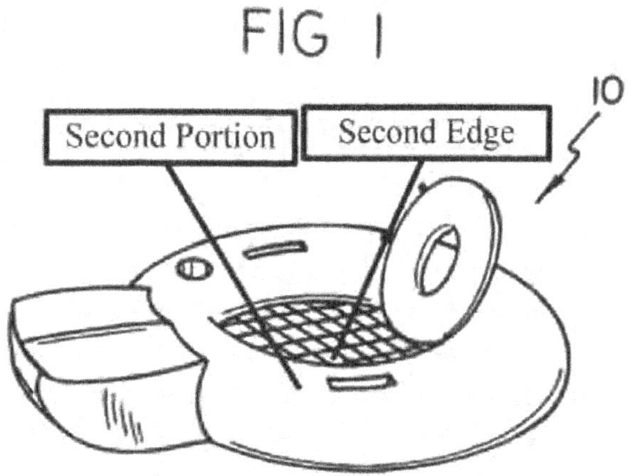 The '344 patent discloses that the outer portion and/or the second portion of the buoyant member within that part of the outer portion contacts the second edge of the inner portion.

Claim 1 Limitation	PRIOR ART DISCLOSURE
	FIG. 9 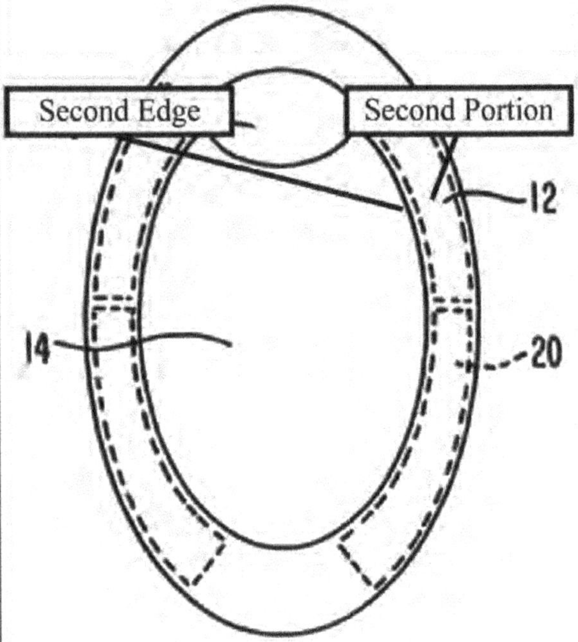 The '474 patent discloses that the outer portion and/or the second portion of the buoyant member within that part of the outer portion contacts the second edge of the inner portion. 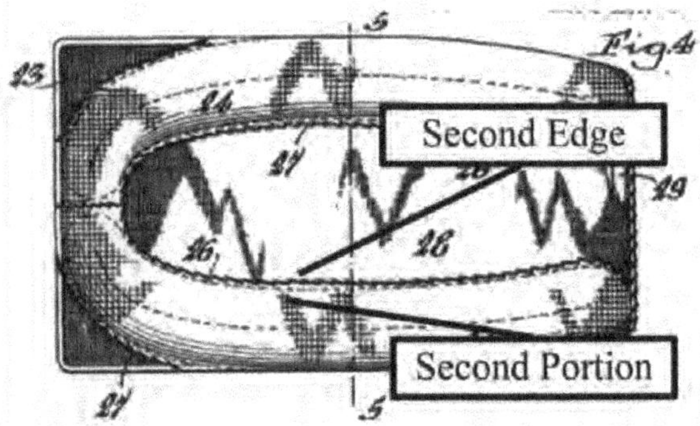

Claim 1 Limitation	PRIOR ART DISCLOSURE
	The '042 patent discloses that the outer portion and/or the second portion of the buoyant member within that part of the outer portion contacts the second edge of the inner portion. 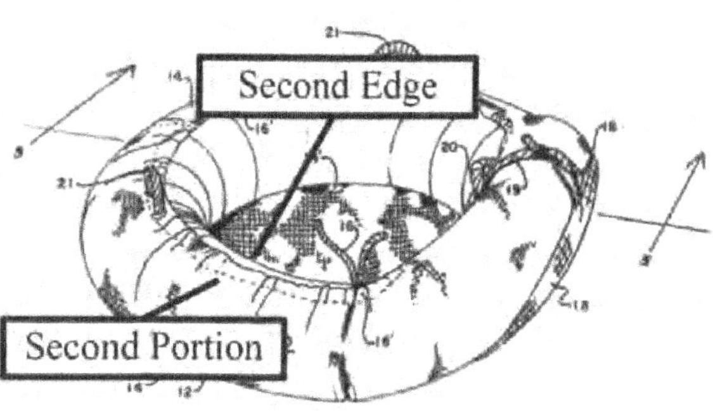 FIG. 4 The Intex King Kool Lounge discloses that the outer portion and/or the second portion of the buoyant member within that part of the outer portion contacts the second edge of the inner portion.

Claim 1 Limitation	PRIOR ART DISCLOSURE
	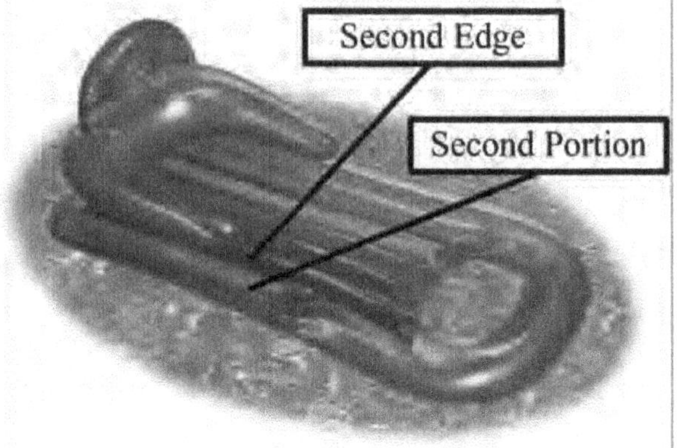 Second Edge Second Portion
the buoyant member having an outermost width that substantially defines an outermost width of the apparatus, the apparatus being configured to support a user in a seated position.	The '404 patent discloses that the buoyant member has an outermost width defining the outermost width of the apparatus and that the apparatus is configured to support a user in a seated position. FIG 1 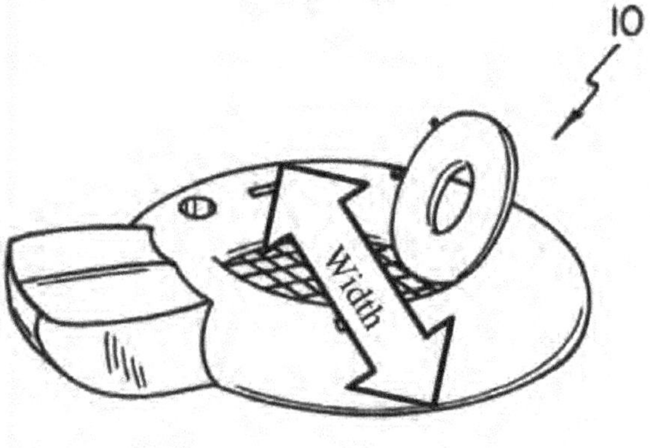 10 Width The '344 patent discloses that the buoyant member has an outermost width defining the outermost width of the apparatus and that the

Claim 1 Limitation	PRIOR ART DISCLOSURE
	apparatus is configured to support a user in a seated position. 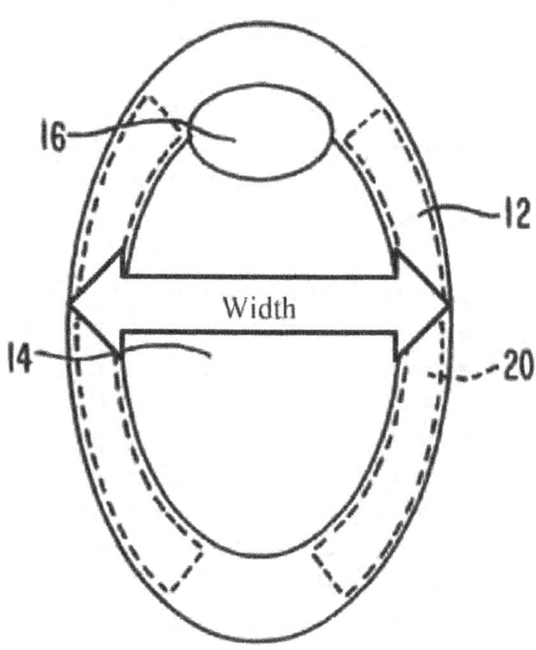 The '474 patent discloses that the buoyant member has an outermost width defining the outermost width of the apparatus and that the apparatus is configured to support a user in a seated position.

Claim 1 Limitation	PRIOR ART DISCLOSURE
	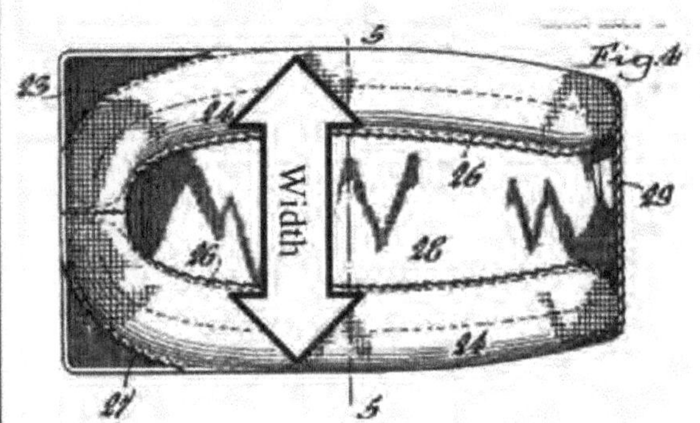 The '042 patent discloses that the buoyant member has an outermost width defining the outermost width of the apparatus and that the apparatus is configured to support a user in a seated position. 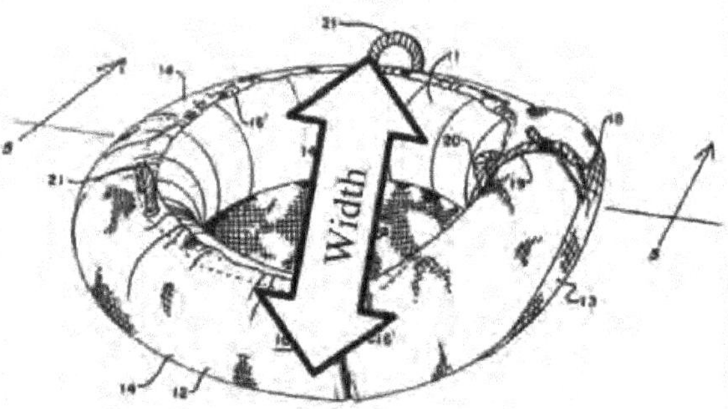 FIG. 4 The Intex King Kool Lounge discloses that the buoyant member has an outermost width defining the outermost width of the apparatus and that the apparatus is configured to support a user in a seated position.

Claim 1 Limitation	PRIOR ART DISCLOSURE

Claim 2 Limitation	PRIOR ART DISCLOSURE
2. An apparatus, comprising:	The '404 patent discloses an apparatus, which is an inflatable recreational inner tube toy. The '344 patent discloses an apparatus, which is a collapsible flotation device. The '474 patent discloses an apparatus, which is a buoyant bathing device. The '042 patent discloses an apparatus, which is an inflatable vehicle construction. The Intex King Kool Lounge is an apparatus—it is an inflatable pool lounge
a panel including an inner portion, an outer portion and a back support portion, the inner portion of the panel including a mesh material,	The '404 patent discloses a panel with an inner portion, an outer portion, and a back support portion, where the inner portion includes mesh material.

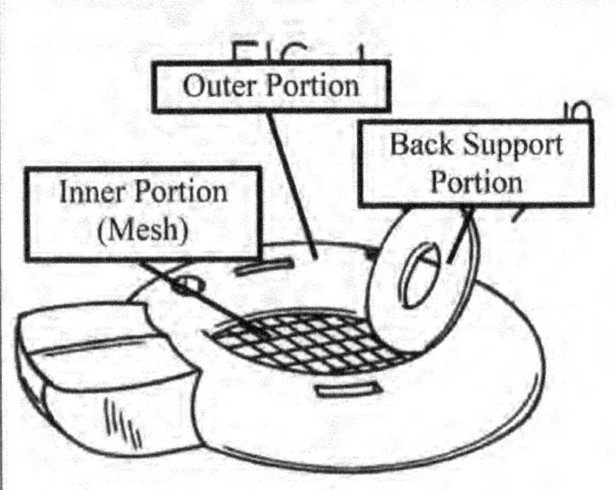

The '344 patent discloses a panel with an inner portion, an outer portion, and a back support portion, where the inner portion includes mesh material.

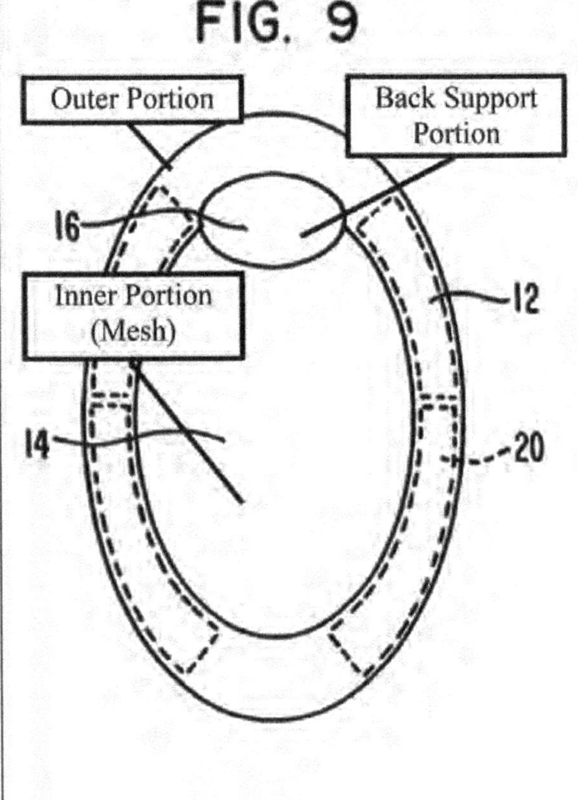

	The '474 patent discloses a panel with an inner portion, an outer portion, and a back support portion, where the inner portion includes mesh material. 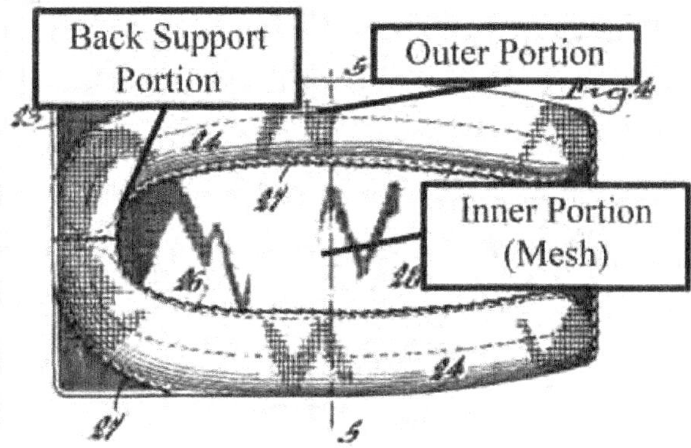 The '042 patent discloses a panel with an inner portion, an outer portion, and a back support portion, where the inner portion includes mesh material. 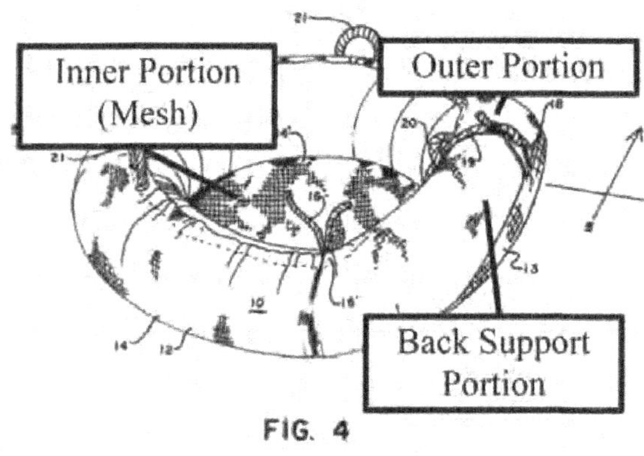
the panel defining an opening configured to collectively receive a user's legs therethrough, the opening being outside the inner portion of the panel,	The '344 patent discloses an opening to receive a user's legs therethrough, which is outside the inner portion of the panel.

	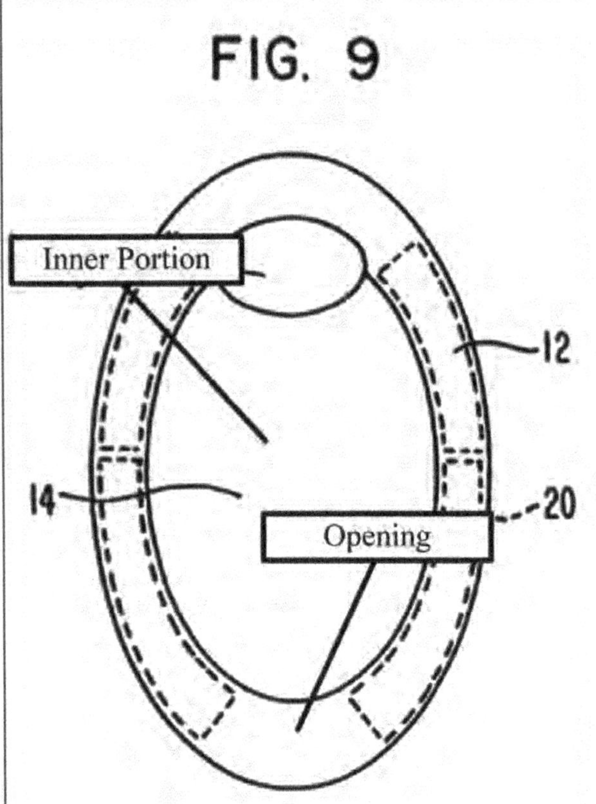 The '474 patent discloses an opening to receive a user's legs therethrough, which is outside the inner portion of the panel. 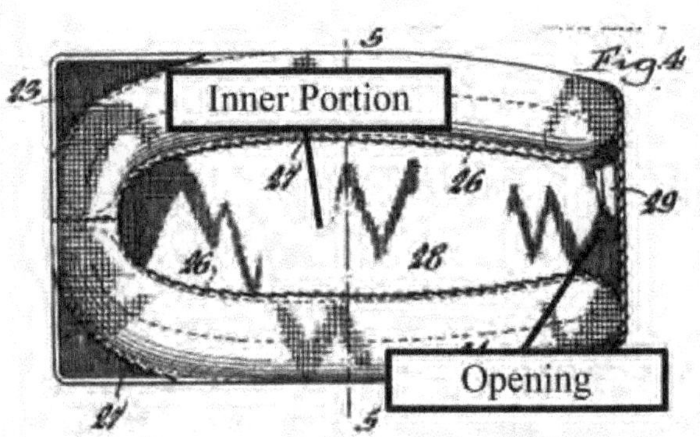 The Intex King Kool Lounge discloses an opening to receive a user's legs therethrough,

	which is outside the inner portion of the panel. 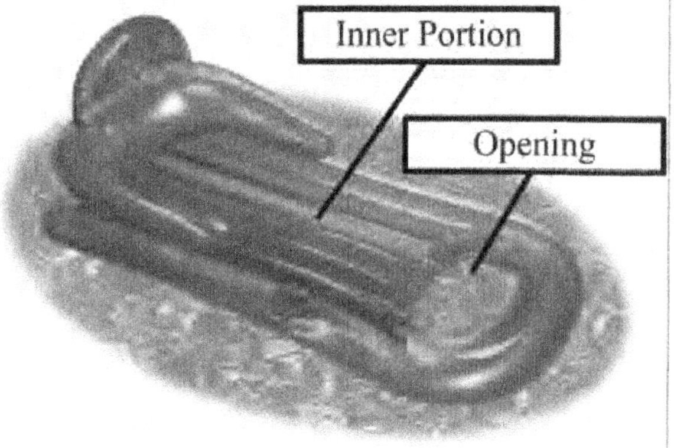 Inner Portion Opening
the back support portion being inflatable; and	The '404 patent discloses that its back support is inflatable. The '344 patent discloses that its back support is inflatable. The '474 patent discloses that its back support is inflatable. The '042 patent discloses that its back support is inflatable. The Intex King Kool Lounge discloses that its back support is inflatable.
a buoyant member disposed about at least a portion of the outer portion of the panel, the buoyant member having a front portion, the front portion of the buoyant member and the back support member being disposed at opposite locations of the inner portion of the panel and separated by a length of the inner portion of the panel,	The '404 patent discloses a buoyant member around the inner portion and at least partially disposed in a portion of the outer portion; the buoyant member has a front portion at an opposite side of the inner portion from the back support member, separated by its length.

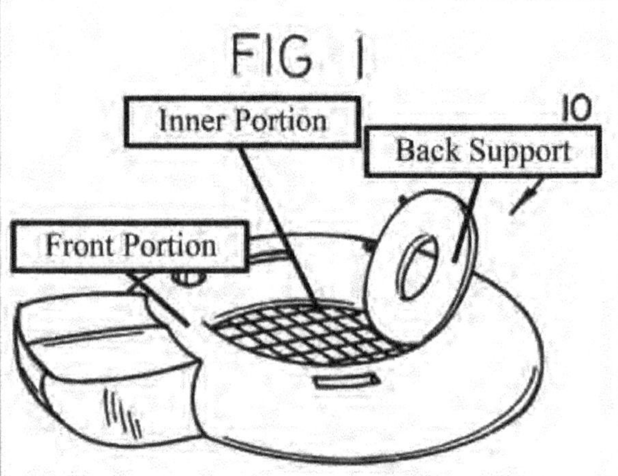

The '344 patent discloses a buoyant member around the inner portion and at least partially disposed in a portion of the outer portion; the buoyant member has a front portion at an opposite side of the inner portion from the back support member, separated by its length.

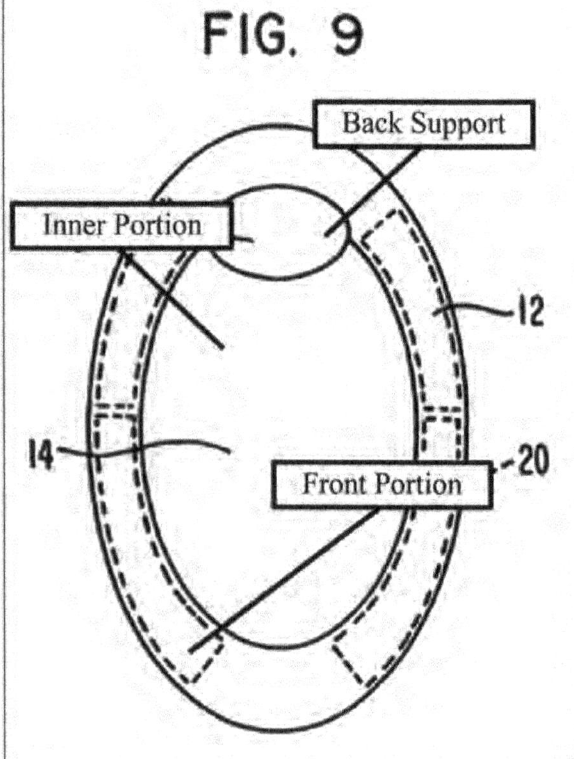

The '474 patent discloses a buoyant member around the inner portion and at least partially disposed in a portion of the outer portion; the buoyant member has a front portion at an opposite side of the inner portion from the back support member, separated by its length.

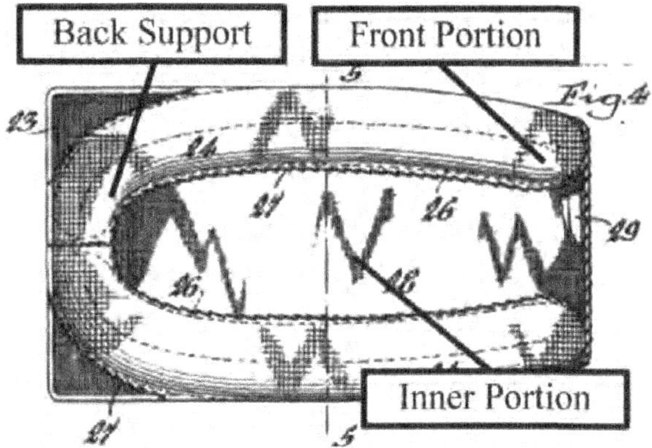

The '042 patent discloses a buoyant member around the inner portion and at least partially disposed in a portion of the outer portion; the buoyant member has a front portion at an opposite side of the inner portion from the back support member, separated by its length.

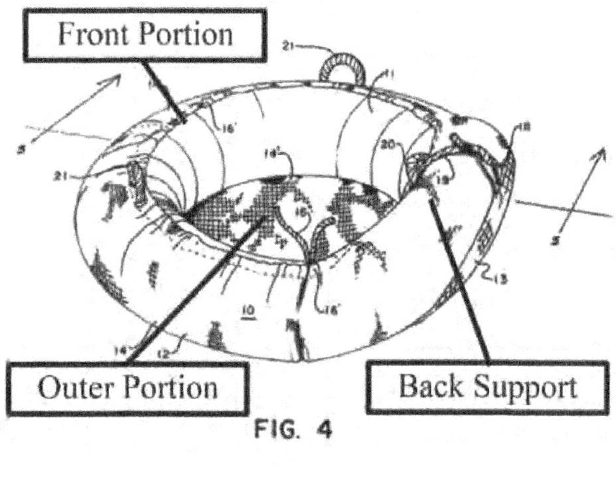

FIG. 4

the front portion of the buoyant member being disposed between the inner portion of the panel and the opening,	The '344 patent discloses that the front portion of the buoyant member is between the inner portion and the opening. 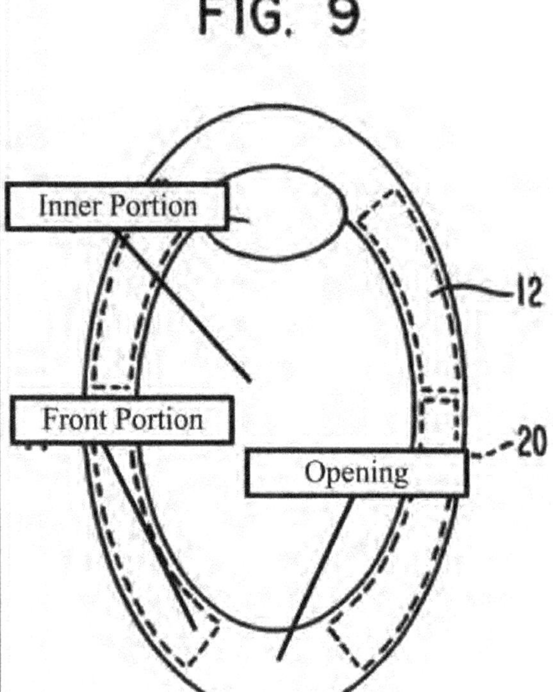 The '474 patent discloses that the front portion of the buoyant member is between the inner portion and the opening. 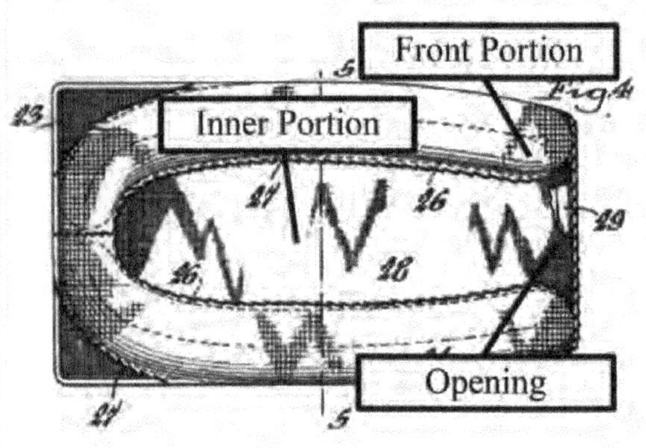

	The Intex King Kool Lounge discloses that the front portion of the buoyant member is between the inner portion and the opening. 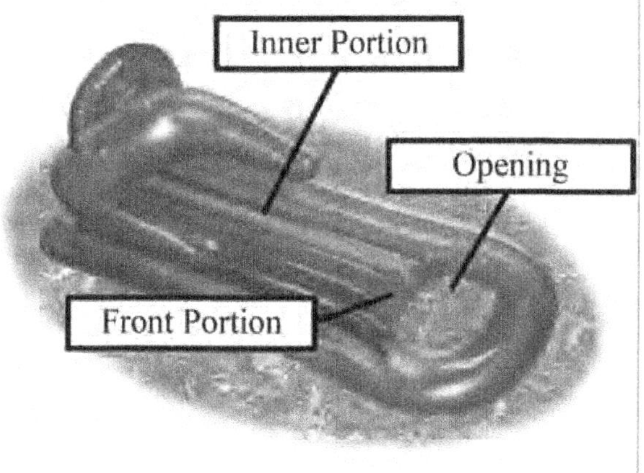
the combination of the buoyant member, the panel and the back support portion being collectively configured to support the user in a seated position.	The '404 patent discloses that its combination of the buoyant member, panel, and back support are configured to support a user in a seated position. The '344 patent discloses that its combination of the buoyant member, panel, and back support are configured to support a user in a seated position. The '474 patent discloses that its combination of the buoyant member, panel, and back support are configured to support a user in a seated position. The '042 patent discloses that its combination of the buoyant member, panel, and back support are configured to support a user in a seated position. The Intex King Kool Lounge discloses that its combination of the buoyant member, panel, and back support are configured to support a user in a seated position.

Claim 3 Limitation	PRIOR ART DISCLOSURE
3. An apparatus, comprising:	The '404 patent discloses an apparatus, which is an inflatable recreational inner tube toy. The '344 patent discloses an apparatus, which is a collapsible flotation device. The '474 patent discloses an apparatus, which is a buoyant bathing device. The '042 patent discloses an apparatus, which is an inflatable vehicle construction. The Intex King Kool Lounge is an apparatus—it is an inflatable pool lounge
a panel including an inner portion, an outer portion and a back support portion,	The '404 patent discloses a panel with an inner portion, an outer portion, and a back support portion. 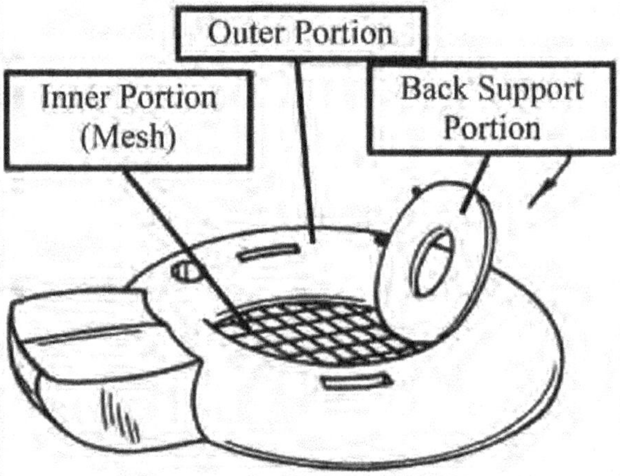 Outer Portion Inner Portion (Mesh) Back Support Portion The '344 patent discloses a panel with an inner portion, an outer portion, and a back support portion.

	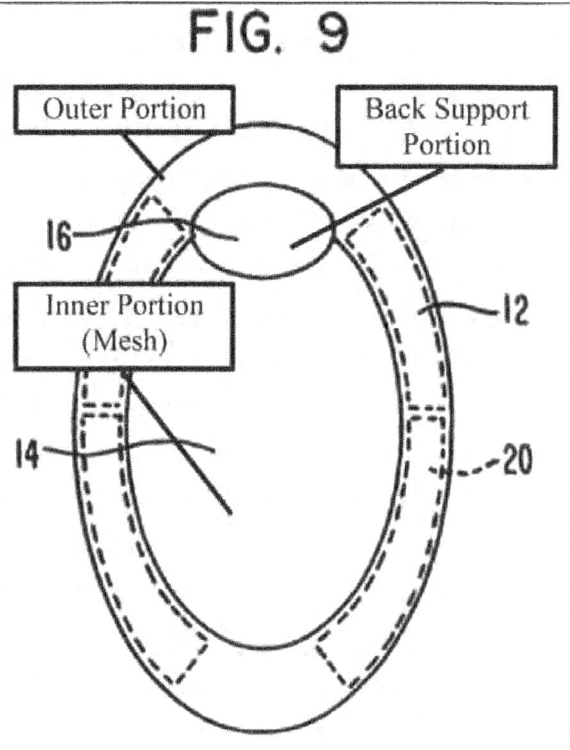 The '474 patent discloses a panel with an inner portion, an outer portion, and a back support portion. 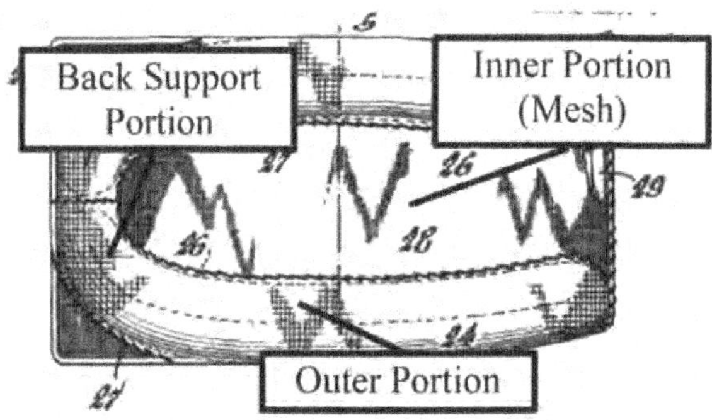 The '042 patent discloses a panel with an inner portion, an outer portion, and a back support portion.

	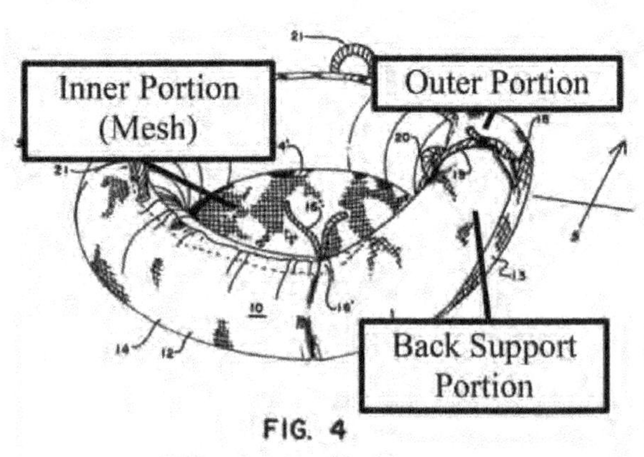 FIG. 4 The Intex King Kool Lounge discloses a panel with an inner portion, an outer portion, and a back support portion. 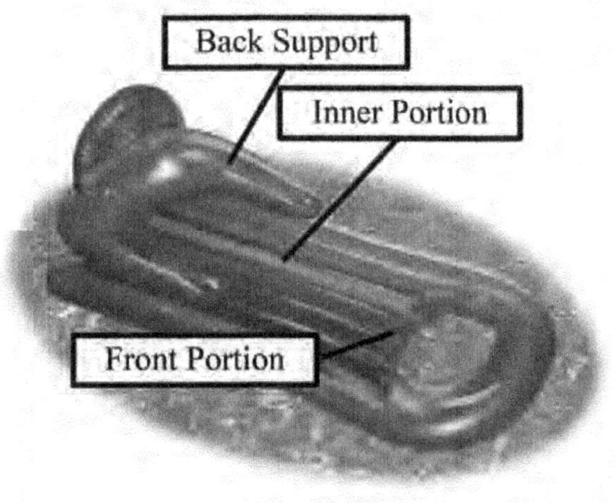
the inner portion of the panel including a mesh material,	The '404 patent discloses that its inner portion includes mesh material. The '344 patent discloses that its inner portion includes mesh material. The '474 patent discloses that its inner portion includes mesh material.

	The '042 patent discloses that its inner portion includes mesh material.
the panel defining an opening,	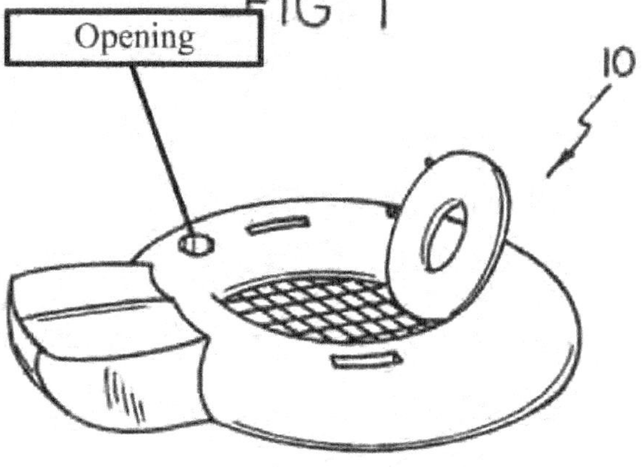 The '404 patent discloses a panel with an opening The '344 patent discloses a panel with an opening.

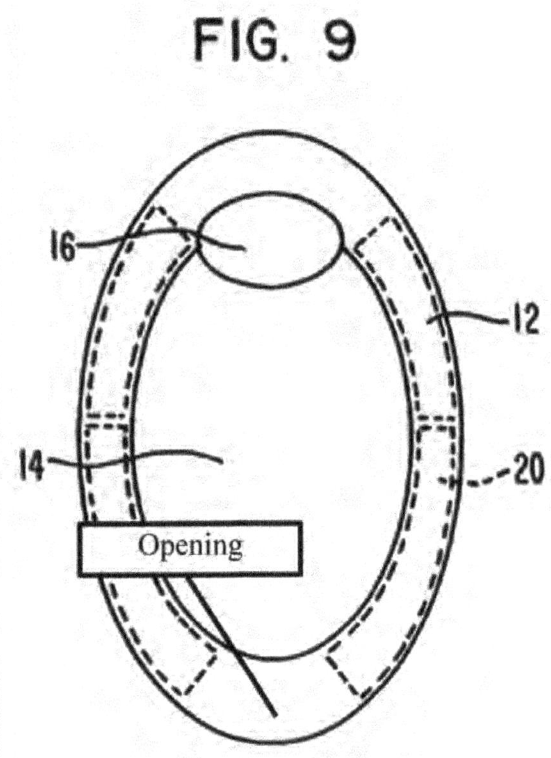

The '474 patent discloses a panel with an opening.

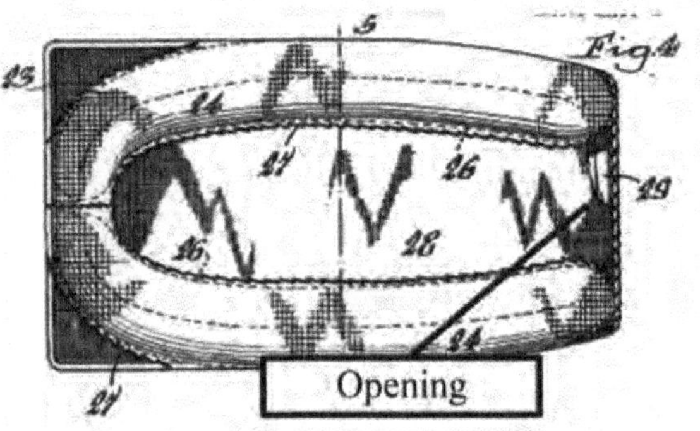

The Intex King Kool Lounge discloses a panel with an opening.

	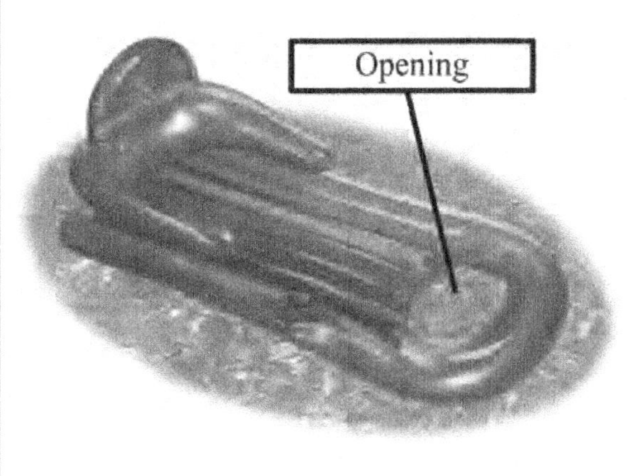
the back support portion being inflatable, the mesh material being disposed at least between the back support portion and a support portion defined by the panel;	The '404 patent discloses that its back support portion is inflatable, that the mesh material is disposed between the back support portion and a support portion of the panel. 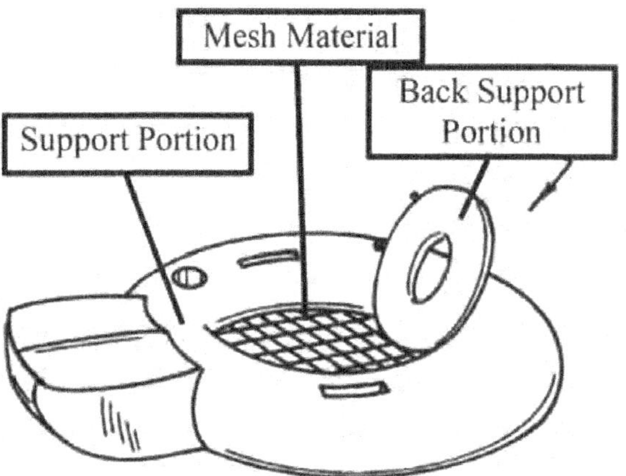 The '344 patent discloses that its back support portion is inflatable, that the mesh material is disposed between the back support portion and a support portion of the panel.

	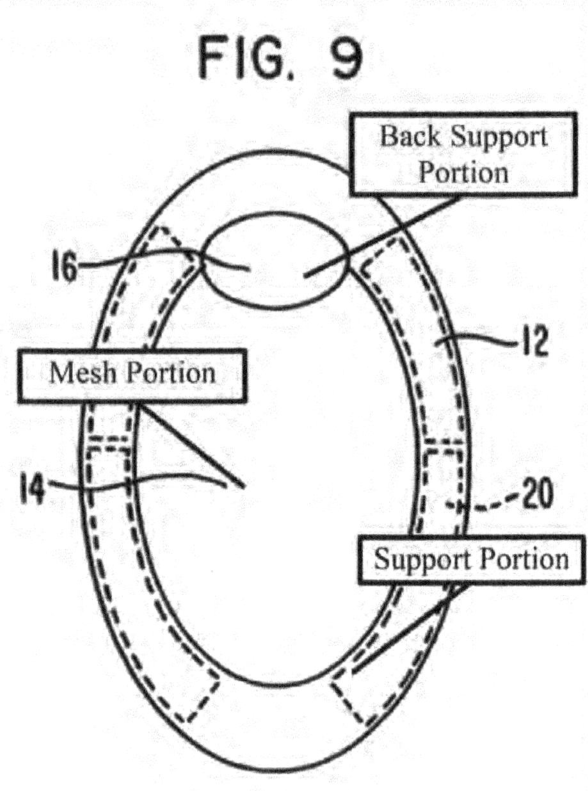 The '474 patent discloses that its back support portion is inflatable, that the mesh material is disposed between the back support portion and a support portion of the panel. 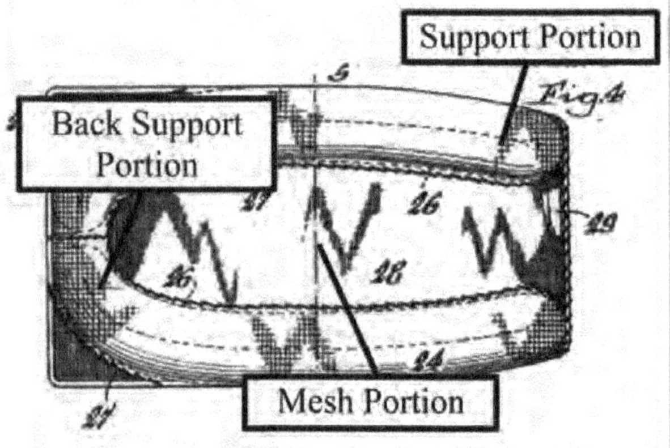 The '042 patent discloses that its back support portion is inflatable, that the mesh material is

	disposed between the back support portion and a support portion of the panel. 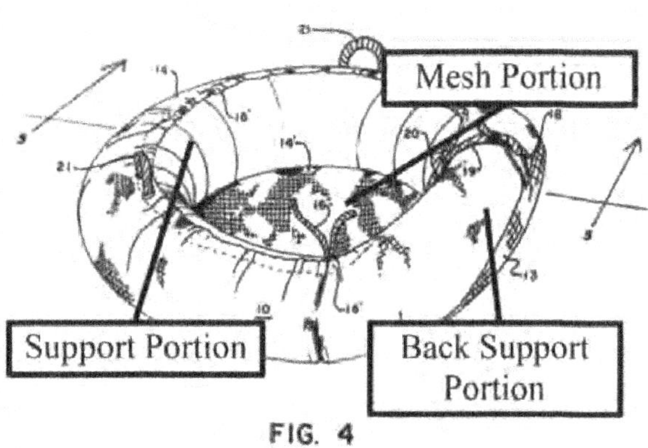 FIG. 4
a buoyant member disposed about at least a portion of the outer portion of the panel, the combination of the buoyant member, the panel and the back support portion being collectively configured to support a user in a seated position; and	The '404 patent discloses a buoyant member around the outer portion, its combination with the panel and back support supports a user in a seated position. 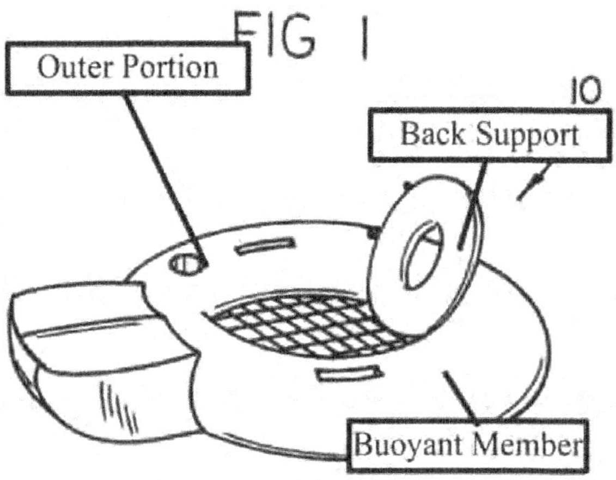 The '344 patent discloses a buoyant member around the outer portion, its combination with the panel and back support supports a user in a seated position.

	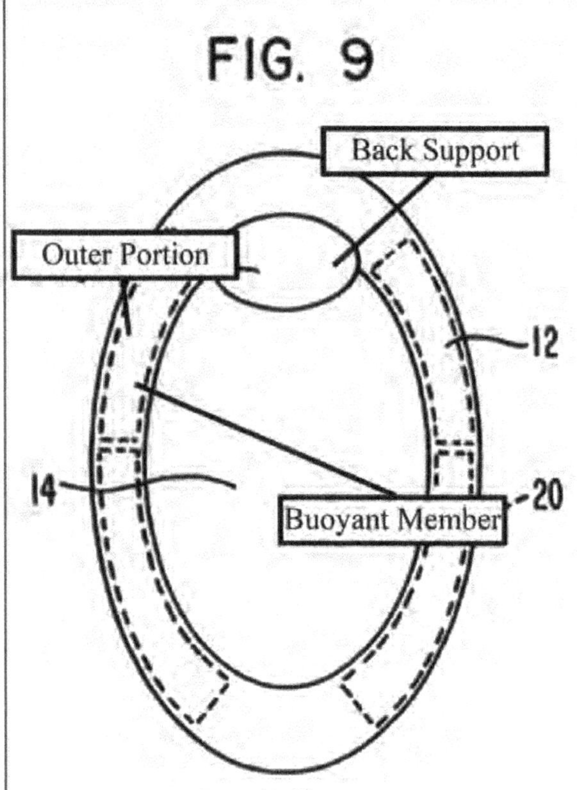 The '474 patent discloses a buoyant member around the outer portion, its combination with the panel and back support supports a user in a seated position. 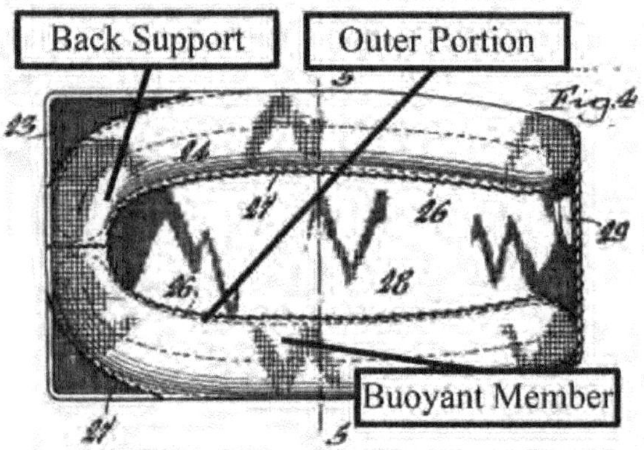 The '042 patent discloses a buoyant member around the outer portion, its combination with

	the panel and back support supports a user in a seated position. 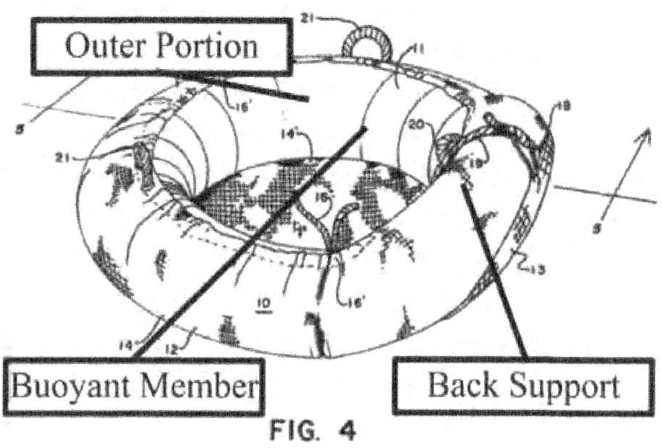 FIG. 4 The Intex King Kool Lounge discloses a buoyant member around the outer portion, its combination with the panel and back support supports a user in a seated position. 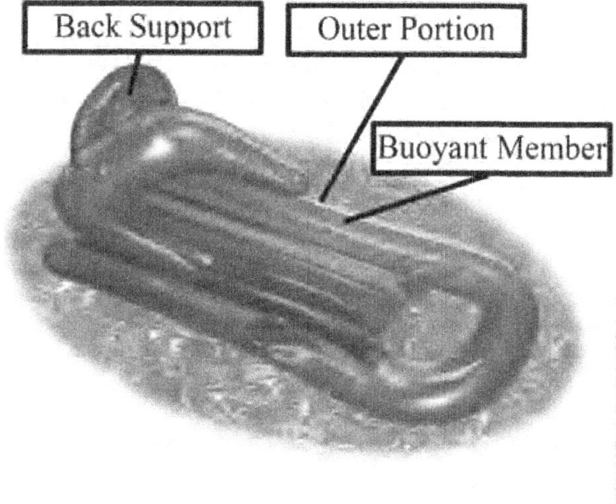
a foot support disposed at an end portion of the panel, the opening disposed between the foot support and the support portion, the foot	The '404 patent discloses a foot support at an end portion of the panel and that the opening is between the foot support and the support

support configured to buoyantly support a weight of the user's feet.	portion and that the foot support buoyantly supports a weight of a user's feet. 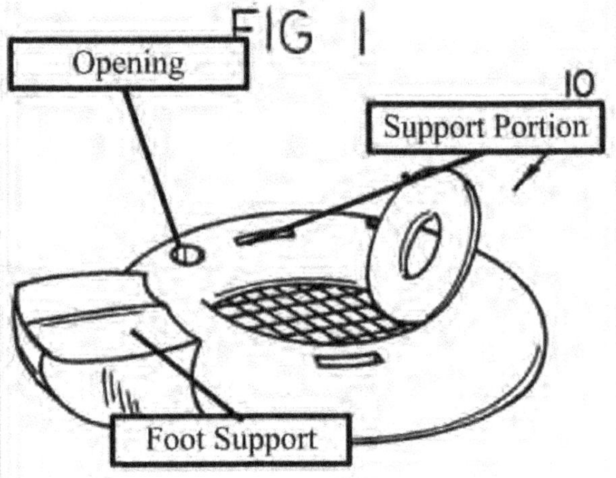 The '344 patent discloses a foot support at an end portion of the panel and that the opening is between the foot support and the support portion and that the foot support buoyantly supports a weight of a user's feet.

	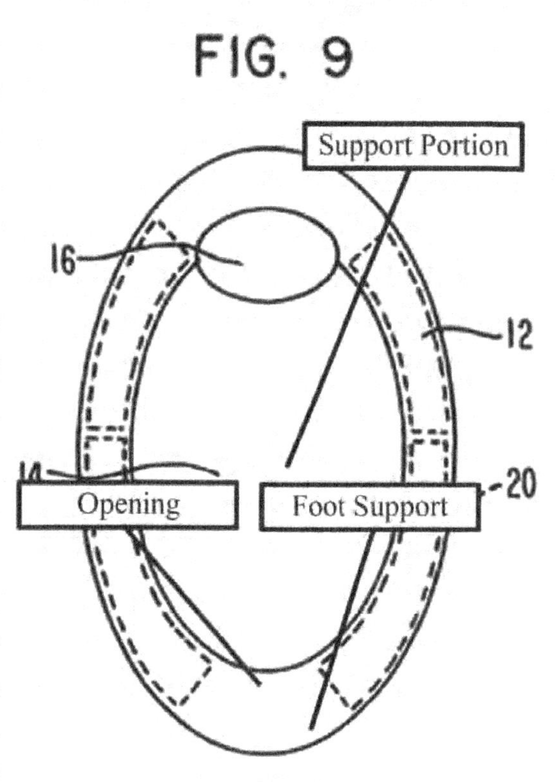 The '474 patent discloses a foot support at an end portion of the panel and that the opening is between the foot support and the support portion and that the foot support buoyantly supports a weight of a user's feet. 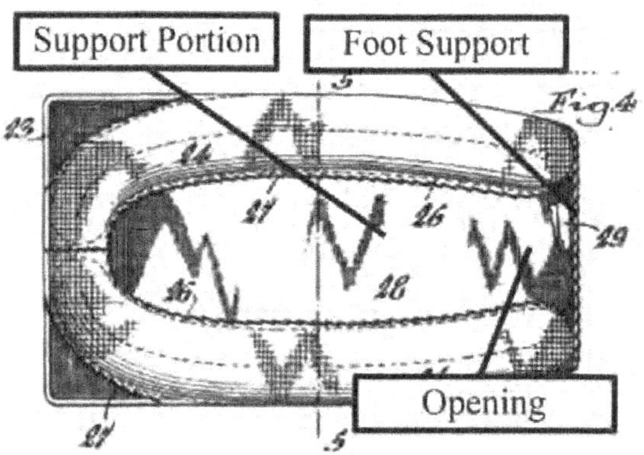 The Intex King Kool Lounge discloses a foot support at an end portion of the panel and that

	the opening is between the foot support and the support portion and that the foot support buoyantly supports a weight of a user's feet. 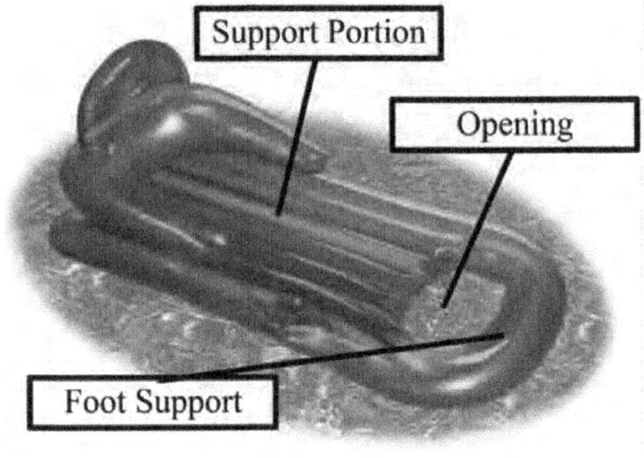

Exhibit C

Prior Art

Intex King Kool Lounge Product

U.S. Patent 1,960,474

U.S. Patent 3,602,930

U.S. Patent 3,871,042

U.S. Patent 5,476,404

U.S. Patent 6,485,344

U.S. Patent D293,012

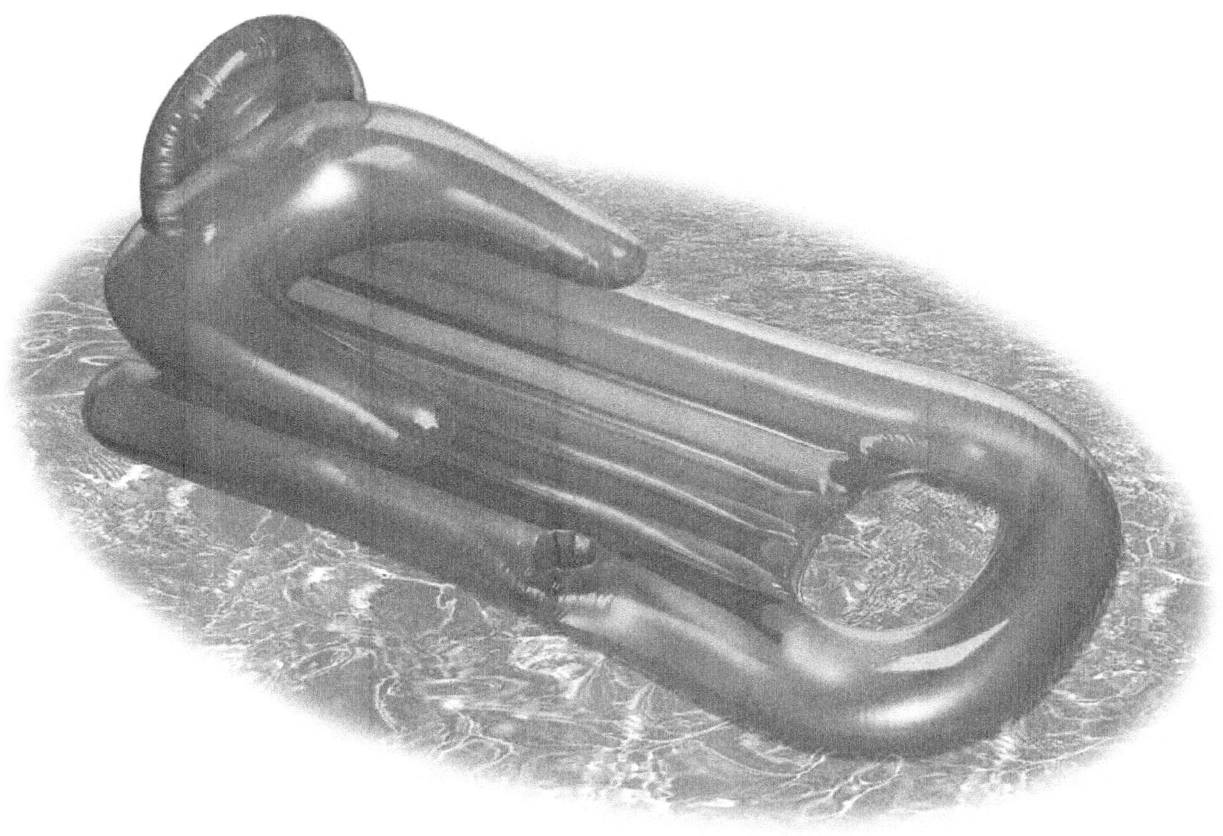

Intrex King Kool Lounge Product

[*Note*: To view this image in color, please refer to the CD-ROM accompanying this book.]

May 29, 1934. M. P. BROWNE 1,960,474

BUOYANT BATHING DEVICE

Filed Dec. 8, 1931 4 Sheets-Sheet 1

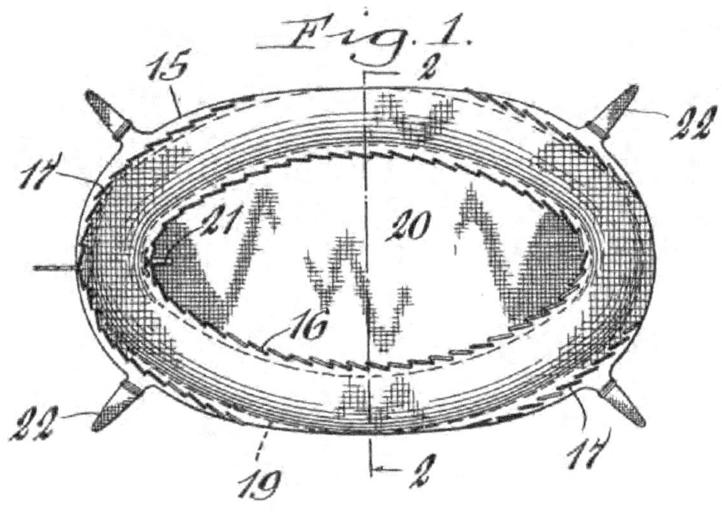

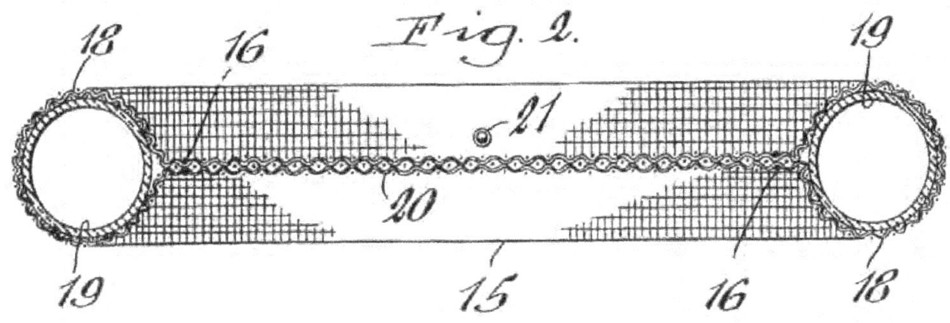

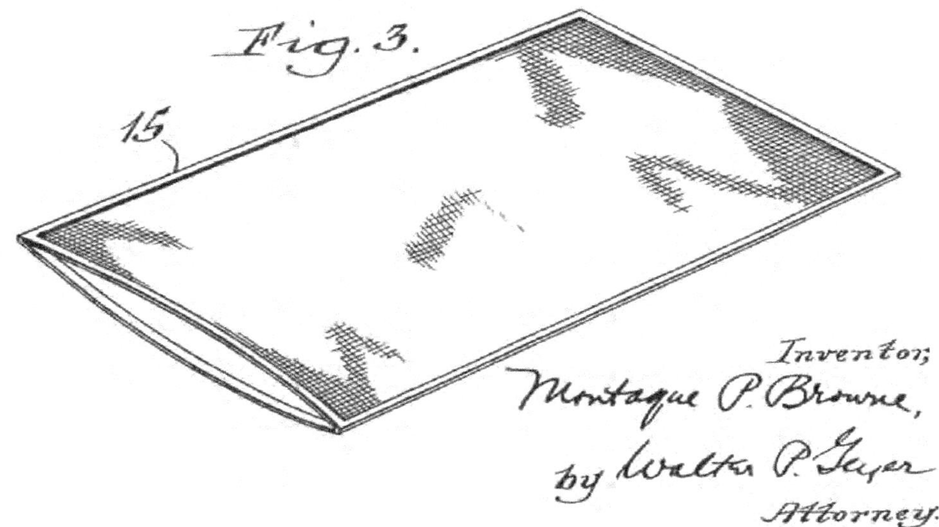

Inventor;
Montague P. Browne,
by Walter P. Geyer
Attorney.

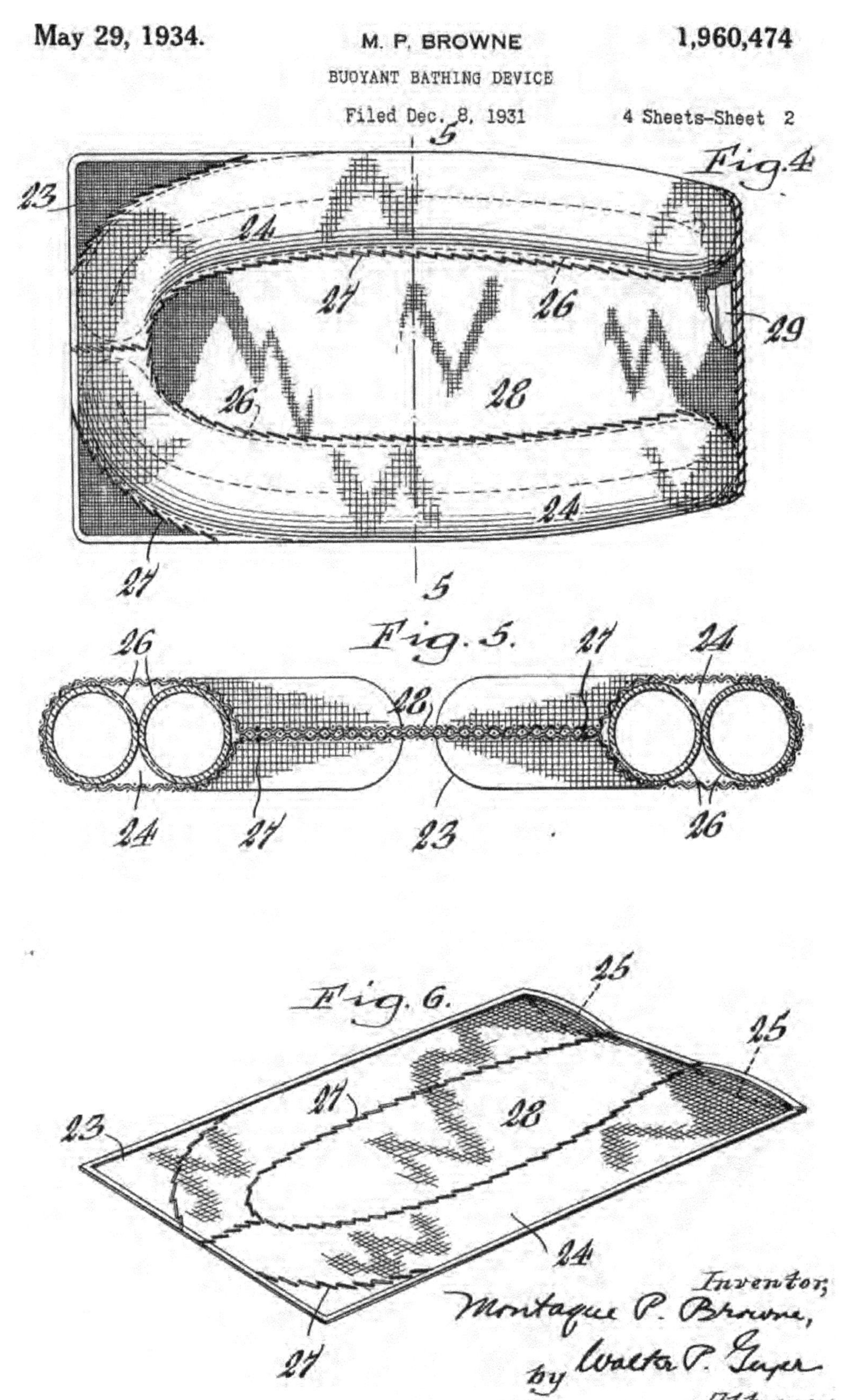
May 29, 1934.
M. P. BROWNE
1,960,474
BUOYANT BATHING DEVICE
Filed Dec. 8, 1931
4 Sheets-Sheet 2
Fig. 4
Fig. 5.
Fig. 6.
Inventor;
Montague P. Browne,
by Walter P. Geyer
Attorney.

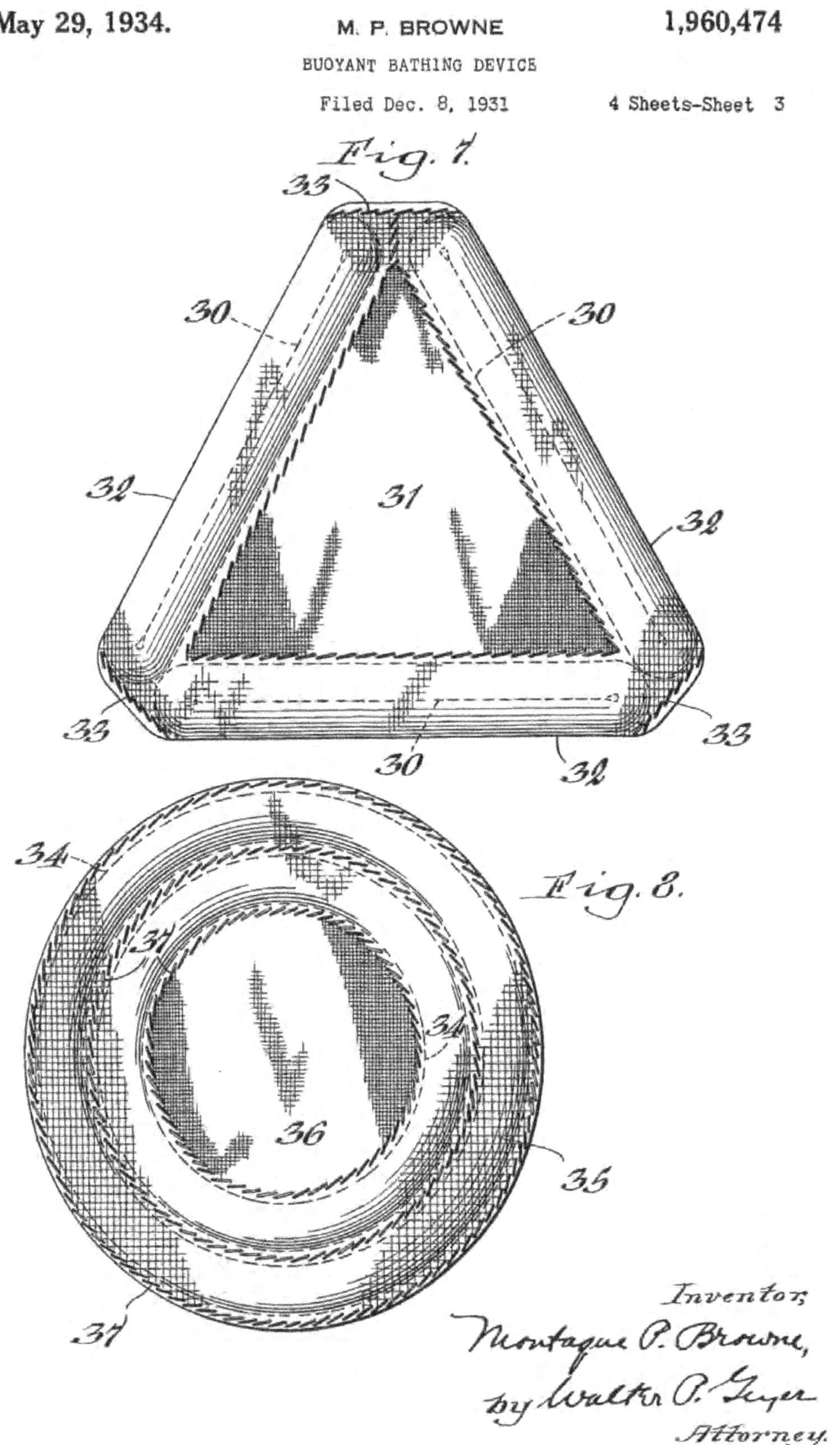
May 29, 1934.
M. P. BROWNE
1,960,474
BUOYANT BATHING DEVICE
Filed Dec. 8, 1931
4 Sheets-Sheet 3
Fig. 7.
33
30
30
32
31
32
33
33
30
32
34
Fig. 8.
34
34
36
35
37
Inventor;
Montague P. Browne,
by Walter P. Geyer
Attorney.

May 29, 1934. M. P. BROWNE 1,960,474

BUOYANT BATHING DEVICE

Filed Dec. 8, 1931 4 Sheets-Sheet 4

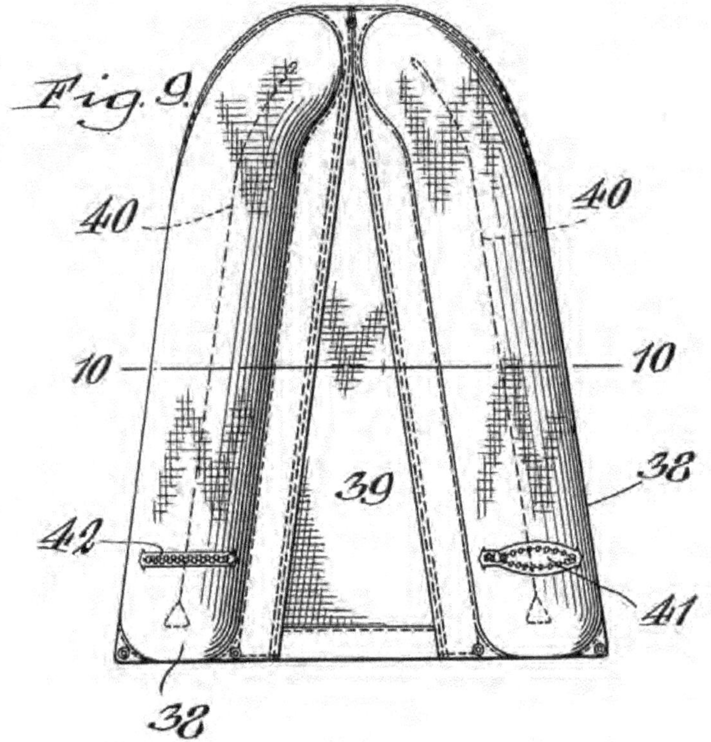

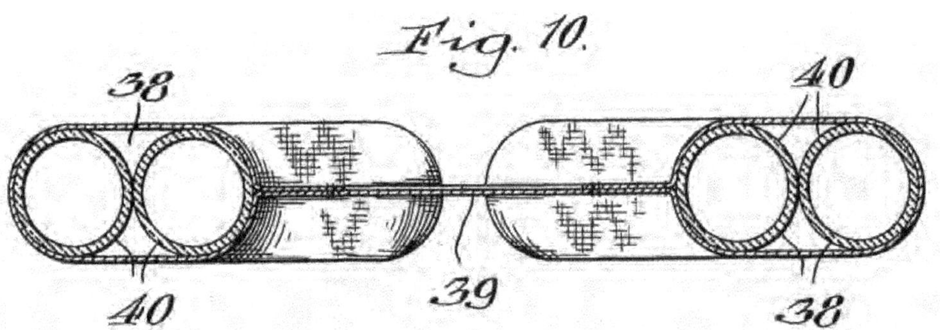

Inventor;
Montague P. Browne,
by Walter P. Geyer
Attorney.

Patented May 29, 1934 **1,960,474**

UNITED STATES PATENT OFFICE

1,960,474

BUOYANT BATHING DEVICE

Montague P. Browne, Buffalo, N. Y.

Application December 8, 1931, Serial No. 579,718

5 Claims. (Cl. 9—17)

This invention relates generally to improvements in water sport devices or appliances and particularly to a device designed for the amusement of bathers.

One of its objects is the provision of a buoyant water appliance of this character which is so designed as to not only protect its buoyant elements from over expansion, but also to afford absolute safety to the bathers by the elimination of parts with which the bather is liable to becomes entangled or accidentally caught.

Another object of the invention is the provision of a water sport device which is designed particularly for use with the inner tubes of automobile tires, whereby such tubes may be readily inserted and removed to and from the device.

A still further object is the provision of a water appliance of this character which is simple, compact and inexpensive in construction, and which when not in use may be compactly folded.

In the accompanying drawings:—

Figure 1 is a top plan view of a water sport device embodying my invention. Figure 2 is an enlarged transverse section thereof, taken on line 2—2, Figure 1. Figure 3 is a perspective view of the fabric bag or body from which the device is made. Figure 4 is a top plan view of a modified form of the invention. Figure 5 is an enlarged transverse section thereof, taken on line 5—5, Figure 4. Figure 6 is a perspective view of the body of the device shown in Figure 4 with the inflated tubes removed. Figures 7 and 8 are top plan views of other modifications of the invention. Figure 9 is a top plan view of a further modification of my invention. Figure 10 is an enlarged cross section taken on line 10—10, Figure 9.

Similar characters of reference indicate corresponding parts throughout the several views.

In its general organization, my improved water sport device or appliance is in the form of a buoyant body designed for use with the inner tubes of automobile tires, although not limited to such use, and consists of a flexible body of woven fabric or webbing material formed to provide one or more pockets, protective or envelope-like sections for receiving the inflatable tubes or like buoyant elements and completely encasing them and limiting their expansion so as to prevent breakage of the tubes, and a substantially flat platform-like section disposed between the pockets and constituting a support for the bather.

Referring now to Figures 1, 2 and 3, showing one form of my invention, 15 indicates a woven fabric bag of netting, canvas or like material which is provided adjacent its outer or marginal edges with concentric inner and outer rows of stitching or lacing 16 and 17 to provide a substantially circular pocket or envelope 18 for the reception of a buoyant element such as an inflatable tube 19. Contained within the area defined by the tube-pocket 18 is a substantially flat or platform-like section 20, the inflatable tube maintaining the same taut and distended to form a convenient platform for the user. In assembling the tube, the same is inserted in a deflated condition into the bag 15, after which the stitching or lacings 16 and 17 are made to form the pocket 18. As seen in Figure 1, the tube-valve 21 projects inwardly over one side of the platform 20 where it is exposed for conveniently inflating or deflating the tube when desired.

At its opposite ends, the device may be provided with suitable hand-holds or grips 22, which may be formed by drawing in the resulting corners of the bag produced when forming the tube-pocket 18, as seen in Figure 1.

In the modification of the invention shown in Figures 4, 5 and 6, the same is designed to receive two buoyant elements or inflatable tubes, and to this end the fabric body 23 is provided along its opposite sides and adjoining rear ends with separate pockets or envelopes 24 which are open at their front ends, as indicated at 25 in Figure 6, to permit of the insertion and removal of the tubes 26. As shown in Figure 4, the tubes are first folded upon themselves and then inserted with the two halves of the tube disposed in overlying relation. The pockets 24 may be formed by stitching or lacing 27 and the open ends 25 of the pockets may be detachably closed in any suitable manner, as by lacing or otherwise. Disposed between the tube-pockets is a platform-section 28, and contraction of the front end of the device may be prevented by inserting a stay or like element 29 between the open ends of the pockets 24, as shown in Figure 4.

In the modified form of the invention shown in Figure 7, the same is designed to receive three inflatable tubes 30 and is of triangular shape in plan, consisting of an intermediate or platform section 31 and surrounding pocket-sections 32, which pocket-sections may be integrally formed with the intermediate section 31, or if desired, these pocket-sections may be separate and suitably attached to such intermediate section by stitching, lacings or otherwise. Each pocket is open at one end to permit of the insertion and removal of the tubes 30 which are folded upon themselves in the same manner as set forth in the previously described construction, and the open ends of the pockets may be closed by stitching or lacing 33 or any other appropriate means.

In the modification of the invention shown in Figure 8, the device is circular in shape and utilizes two tubes 34 disposed in concentric relation to provide an outer buoyant section 35 and a central or intermediate platform-section 36. In this case the device may be made from two pieces of fabric or like material disposed in overlying relation with the tubes 34 disposed between them, the tubes being confined in circular pockets formed by annular rows of stitching or lacing 37.

The modified form of the invention shown in Figures 9 and 10 is similar to that shown in Figure 4, and consists of two forwardly-converging pockets or envelopes 38 joined at their inner edges to a platform section 39, the whole being made from a single blank of fabric material. Removably arranged in these pockets are inflatable tubes 40 which may be folded upon themselves in the manner previously described. In one side thereof, each pocket is provided with an opening 41 through which its tube may be inserted and removed and such opening may be closed by any appropriate fastening means 42.

I claim as my invention:—

1. A water sport device, comprising a body of web-like material having a platform-like section and an envelope section bordering thereon and adapted to receive, in a folded, deflated condition an inflatable ring-like buoyant element, said envelope section having an opening therein for the insertion and removal of said buoyant element when folded upon itself in a deflated condition.

2. A water sport device, comprising a body of webbing material having longitudinal pockets along its opposite sides open at one end and an intermediate platform-like section between said pockets, individual buoyant elements arranged in said pockets and each consisting of an inflatable tube folded upon itself to provide overlying longitudinal portions, said tubes being insertable and removable through the open ends of said pockets, and means for closing the pockets at their open ends.

3. A water sport device, comprising a body of fabric material having longitudinal pockets along its opposite sides converging toward one end for receiving individual and incommunicable buoyant elements, and an intermediate section disposed crosswise between said pockets, and a stay disposed between the opposite ends of said pockets.

4. A device of the character described, comprising a plurality of comparatively long and narrow envelope-like sections made of flexible material and disposed in adjoining relation to provide a support for the user, and buoyant elements arranged in said sections and protected thereby against expansion beyond a safe limit, each of said elements consisting of an inflatable tube folded upon itself to provide overlying portions arranged lengthwise of its envelope-like section.

5. A buoyant bathing device, comprising a body including a comparatively long pocket-shaped member of flexible material having an opening at one end, and an inflatable tube arranged in said pocket and insertable therein through said opening, said tube being circular and folded upon itself to provide overlying portions arranged lengthwise in the pocket.

MONTAGUE P. BROWNE.

United States Patent

[11] **3,602,930**

[72] Inventor **Robert M. Channon**
524 Leeridge Terrace, Glendale, Calif. 91206

[21] Appl. No. **851,175**
[22] Filed **Aug. 19, 1969**
[45] Patented **Sept. 7, 1971**

[54] **FLOATING SAUCER CHAIR**
4 Claims, 4 Drawing Figs.

[52] **U.S. Cl.** 9/347
[51] **Int. Cl.** **B63c 9/30**
[50] **Field of Search** 9/347, 311, 348, 400

[56] **References Cited**

UNITED STATES PATENTS

856,279	6/1907	Moore	9/347
2,207,025	7/1940	Rison	9/347
2,803,839	8/1957	Mosely	9/347
3,117,327	1/1964	Mathews	9/347
3,161,897	12/1964	Hill	9/347

Primary Examiner—Milton Buchler
Assistant Examiner—Paul E. Sauberer
Attorneys—Clarence A. O'Brien and Harvey B. Jacobson

ABSTRACT: A relaxing, sunbathing and floating chair idealy suitable for use in a pool, lake or the like and characterized by a ringlike ethafoam float encompassing and supporting a polypropylene mesh basket constituting a seat. This seat permits the occupant to nestle therein and sit or lie back. It is form fitting and balanced with requisite nicety. A cushioned headrest is adjustably mounted by paired upstanding polyethylene tubes on a suitably selected segmental portion of the float.

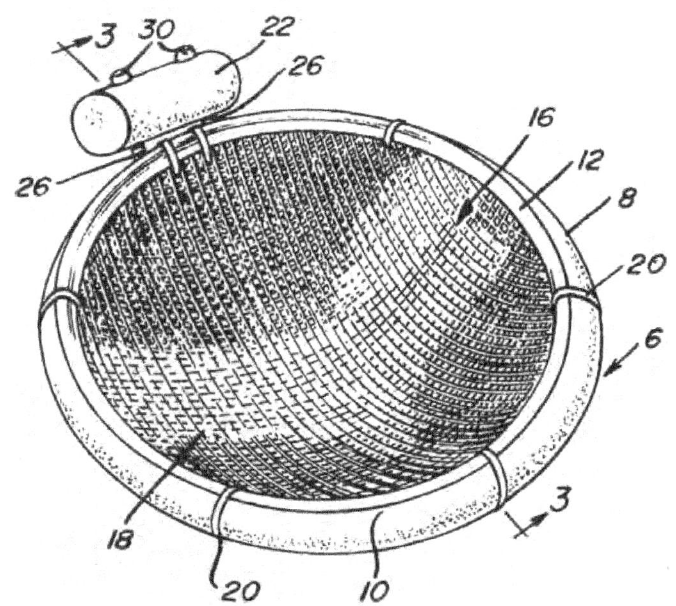

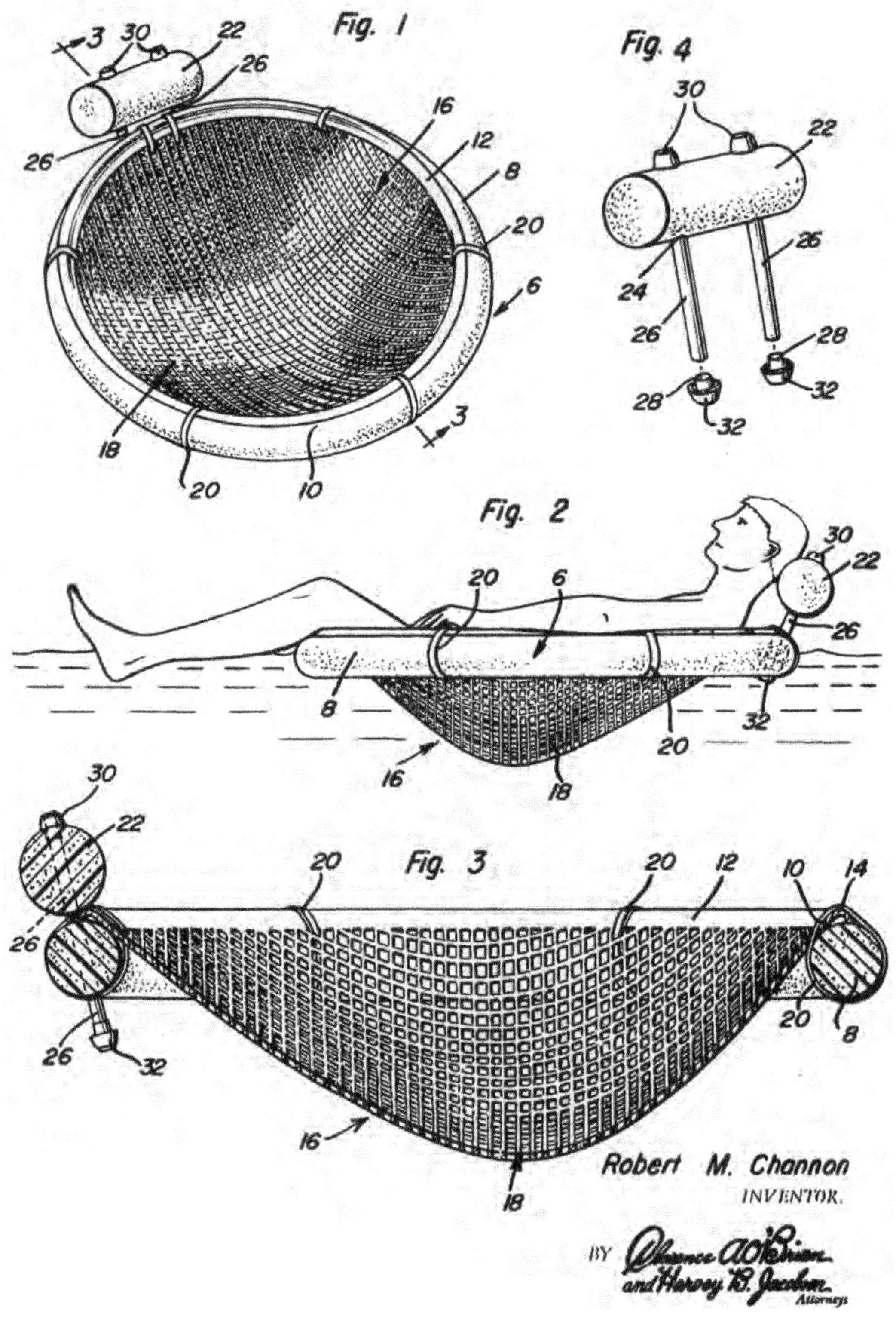
PATENTED SEP 7 1971
3,602,930
Fig. 1
Fig. 4
Fig. 2
Fig. 3
Robert M. Channon
INVENTOR.
BY
Attorneys

3,602,930

1

FLOATING SAUCER CHAIR

This invention relates to a floating saucerlike chair which lends itself to safe and acceptably reliable use in a swimming pool, lake, river or the like and which, broadly construed, comprises a formfitting well balanced openwork mesh seat in which the occupant can nestle and cradle, can sit, lie back in comfort and prop the head and neck on an adaptable headrest.

More specifically, the invention comprises a buoyant endless ring which serves as a float and which encompasses a dished or basket-type seat, said seat being made of molded polypropylene of webbed or openwork form, said seat being strapped by loops or the like to the float and being provided with a suitably attached and elevated headrest.

As will be hereinafter more fully appreciated, the chair herein comprehended weighs only 3 or 4 pounds and is uniquely safe in that it has no sharp corners or metal components that could be injurious to the occupant. It is such in construction that it can be conveniently transported to and from the beach or pool and because of the concavo-convex shape of the seat any number of correspondingly constructed chairs can be nested and stacked one atop the other for storage, shipping or handling. Then, too, the openwork webbing or mesh permits the water to circulate through the available openings and serves to keep the occupant cool. Repeated experience has shown that this innovation can be used by lying on it face down but is commonly and best used by sitting in it or cradling one's self and lying back with ease and comfort. The attached headrest props the head and neck and is adjustable for all users. In addition, the chair can be used for engaging in a floating basket ball game or as a floating planter. As a matter of fact, the circular basket can be hung on a wall when not in use to serve as an ornament or decoration. The contour enables the user to get in and out of the seat. Finally, the seat with its component parts is readily maneuverable in the water.

Briefly, the herein disclosed prefabricated adaptation provides a relaxing and floating chair for use in any suitable body of water. By preference it embodies a stout buoyant ring which constitutes an occupant encircling float. The concave upwardly opening suitably contoured seat has a substantially rigid marginal flange which constitutes a rim. The rim-equipped seat is fitted within the encompassing confines of the ring or float. In fact the rim is supportively seated atop the floating ring and is securely cooperatively strapped thereto by looping straps. The seat is made of self-shape-sustaining openwork material. It is contoured, form fitting and saucerlike in general appearance and is of predetermined depth in plan dimension to conformingly and comfortably balance the seated occupant and permits the occupant to sit and nestle therein while being cradled about, while lying back or otherwise supported for safe relaxation.

In carrying out a preferred embodiment of the invention the headrest means preferably takes the form of a compressibly resilient plastic pillowlike bolster. This component is of requisite length and cross section and is provided with a pair of spaced parallel supporting plastic tubes. Appropriate knobs on the upper and lower ends of the tubes serve to connect the tubes to apertured portions of a predetermined segmental part of the aforementioned ringlike float.

These together with other objects and advantages which will become subsequently apparent reside in the details of construction and operation as more fully hereinafter described and claimed, reference being had to the accompanying drawings forming a part hereof, wherein like numerals refer to like parts throughout, and in which:

FIG. 1 is a view in perspective of a floating saucer chair showing the principal component parts and how they are constructed and united for advantageous swimming pool or equivalent sunbathing use.

FIG. 2 is a view in side elevation of the saucer chair shown in FIG. 1 and illustrating the same in use in a body of water

2

and showing the occupant in one cradled position with the head propped on the compressibly resilient headrest.

FIG. 3 is an enlarged detail sectional view taken approximately on the plane of the section line 3—3 of FIG. 1 looking in the direction of the arrows.

And FIG. 4 is a view in perspective showing the headrest means.

The endless generally circular buoyant ring is denoted by the numeral **6**. It comprises a stout ring and is of appropriate diameter to provide the cradling support suggested in FIG. 1. More explicitly this ring is usually about 3 inches in diameter and is accordingly stout and of appropriate cross section and, more specifically, is a closed cell flexible foam ring, more explicitly, a ring made of ethafoam material. This floatable ring or float is circular in cross section as at **8**. The upper convex surface portion **10** (FIG. 3) serves to accommodatingly receive and support a substantially rigid annular flange **12** of channel-shaped cross section as designated at **14** in FIG. 3. This flange provides the integral outer marginal edge portion of the aforementioned dished or concavo-convex occupant seat. The seat is denoted, generally stated, by the numeral **16** and is of the depth suggested at **18** in FIG. 3. This seat constitutes a significant part of the overall chair and is preferably made of moldable polypropylene and is in some instances designated as a mesh basket. It can and usually is circular in plan and may be some 29 inches more or less in diameter with a depth of 10 inches at the seat portion **18**. Nylon or equivalent looplike straps **20** are circumferentially spaced and are laced through the openings in the marginal or rim portion of the seat and are snugly fitted around the float to thus join the seat and float in desired unified relationship.

The headrest means comprises a compressibly resilient cylindrical pillow or bolster **22** having openings **24** therethrough for the upper end portions of a pair of spaced parallel plastic tubes **26** which serve as struts and which are connected to the floatable ring. The knoblike caps are provided with attaching plugs as at **28**. These caps or knobs are identified as upper knobs **30** (FIG. 4) which are connected to the upper protruding ends of the struts or tubes, and lower caplike knobs **32** which are plugged into the lower ends of the tubes or struts. By utilizing a cushion **22** of requisite cross section it is possible to slide and adjust the same up and down on the tubular support members to attain the desired elevation. In practice it is possible and sometimes desirable to use two headrests, the second headrest being like the headrest **22** but not herein disclosed.

Experience has shown that the polypropylene basket is sturdy, comfortable and light in weight and is long lasting. The ethafoam ring or float is virtually indestructible. There are no metals parts and no component parts to chip. The construction of the chair is such that it weighs only 3 or 4 pounds and is easy to store. Anyone who desires can use it with reliability and can sit or lie back. The contour of the float and chair ensures form fitting balance. It follows that a chair embodying the component parts herein shown, described and assembled well serves the purposes for which it is intended. Accordingly, a more extended description is believed to be unnecessary.

The foregoing is considered as illustrative only of the principles of the invention. Further, since numerous modifications and changes will readily occur to those skilled in the art, it is not desired to limit the invention to the exact construction and operation shown and described, and accordingly all suitable modifications and equivalents may be resorted to, falling within the scope of the invention.

What is claimed as new is as follows:

1. For floating and sunbathing in a swimming pool, lake, or similar body of water, a prefabricated relaxing and floating chair comprising a dished upwardly opening seat having a marginal edge provided with an attached encompassing float, said seat being made of self-shape-sustaining openwork material which is adapted to promote free circulation of water about that part of the occupants body which is nested and seated in the receptacle portion of said seat, said material

comprising injection molded polypropylene mesh, said float comprising a closed cell compressibly resilient ethafoam relatively stout ring, said marginal edge having a rigid annular rim which is channel shaped in cross section and is superimposed on a top surface portion of said ring and is fastened thereon by plastic straps which are snugly and firmly looped around the rim and ring, respectively.

2. The chair defined in and according to claim 1 and wherein said seat is contoured, form fitting and saucerlike in overall shape and appearance and is of a prescribed depth to comfortably balance the occupant when sitting, lying back or when otherwise supported for floating.

3. The chair defined in and according to claim 1, and, in combination, a compressibly resilient pad constituting a headrest, and means operatively and adjustably mounting said headrest on a predetermined coacting portion of said float ring.

4. A prefabricated relaxing and floating chair for use in a swimming pool, a lake or similar body of water comprising, a stout buoyant ring constituting an occupant encircling float, a

concave upwardly opening seat having a substantially rigid marginal flange defining a rim, said seat being fitted within the encompassing confines of said ring, said rim resting upon and being supportively seated atop said ring and securely cooperatively strapped to said ring, said seat being made of self-shape-sustaining openwork material, said seat being contoured, form fitting and saucerlike in general appearance and being of a predetermined depth and plan dimension to conformingly and comfortably balance the occupant when sitting and nestled therein, while seated and lying back, or otherwise supported for floating, said material comprising injection molded plastic mesh, said float comprising a closed cell compressibly resilient relatively stout ring, and, in combination, a compressibly resilient pillowlike bolster constituting a headrest, and a pair of spaced parallel like bolster assembling tubes disposed at right angles to said bolster and buoyant ring, respectively, and operatively and adjustably mounting said bolster on a predetermined coacting portion of said ring.

United States Patent [19]

Farmer

[11] **3,871,042**

[45] **Mar. 18, 1975**

[54] **INFLATABLE VEHICLE CONSTRUCTION**

[76] Inventor: **Gary W. Farmer,** 310 W. Ash, Caldwell, Idaho 83605

[22] Filed: **Jan. 20, 1974**

[21] Appl. No.: **437,279**

Related U.S. Application Data

[63] Continuation-in-part of Ser. No. 310,741, Nov. 30, 1972, abandoned.

[52] **U.S. Cl.** .... **9/1 A,** 9/11 A, 280/12 B

[51] **Int. Cl.** **B63c 9/04**

[58] **Field of Search** .... 9/1 A, 11 R, 11 A, 310 F, 9/310 G, 311, 347; 280/12 B; 272/1 B

[56] **References Cited**

UNITED STATES PATENTS

2,223,625	12/1940	Krupp	9/11 A
2,246,108	6/1941	Sermon	9/347
2,876,467	3/1959	Lund	9/11 A
3,432,182	3/1969	Solipasso	9/11 A
3,435,471	4/1969	Drennen, Jr.	9/310 F
3,628,206	12/1971	Mecham	9/1 A

Primary Examiner—Trygve M. Blix
Assistant Examiner—Jesus D. Sotelo
Attorney, Agent, or Firm—John W. Kraft; Charles L. Kraft

[57] **ABSTRACT**

The inflatable vehicle construction for inflatable rings and the like comprises a cuff made of fabric portions operable to conform to the outer walls of the ring, a vehicle bottom fastened to the cuff about the lower portion of the cuff, and a drawcord at the upper terminal edge of the cuff.

5 Claims, 5 Drawing Figures

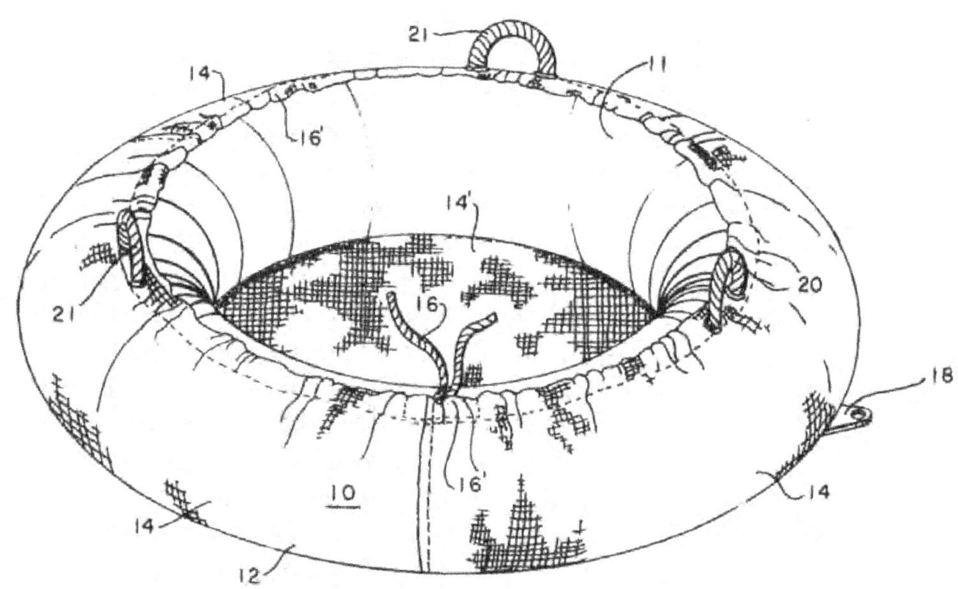

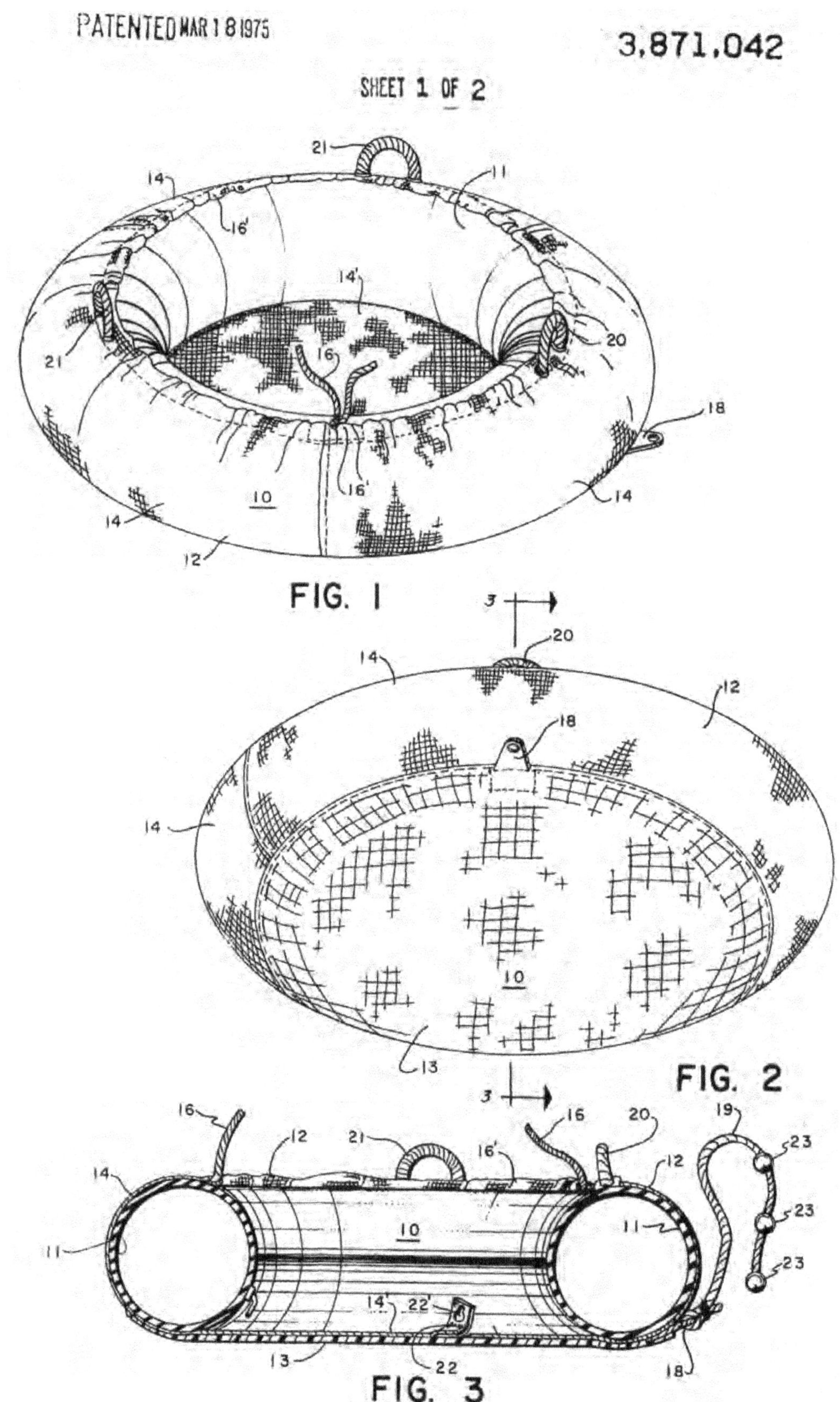
PATENTED MAR 18 1975
3,871,042
SHEET 1 OF 2
FIG. 1
FIG. 2
FIG. 3

PATENTED MAR 18 1975

3,871,042

SHEET 2 OF 2

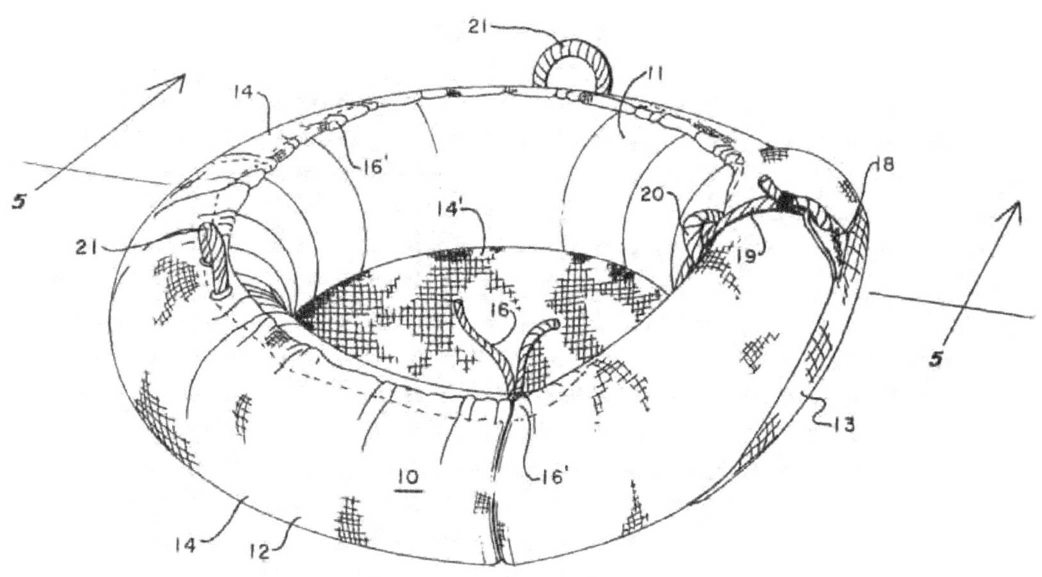

FIG. 4

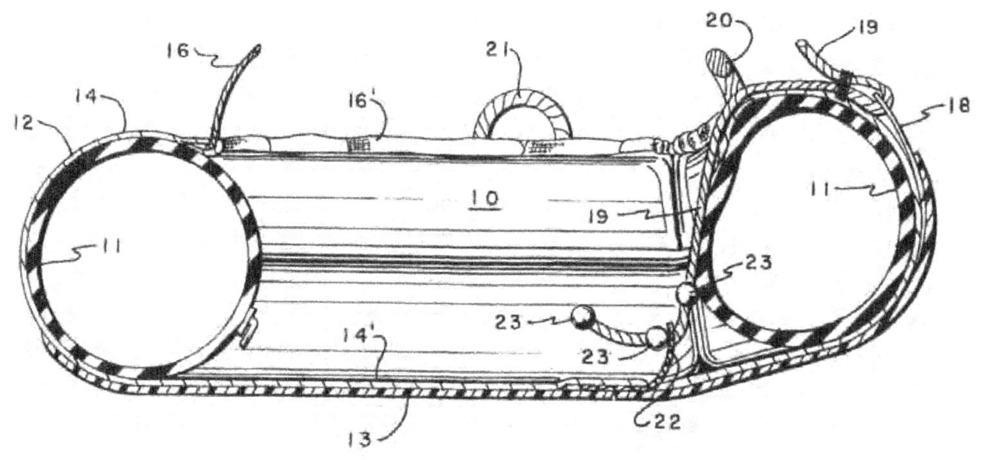

FIG. 5

3,871,042

1

INFLATABLE VEHICLE CONSTRUCTION

REFERENCE TO OTHER APPLICATIONS

This is a continuation-in-part of my application serial 310,741, filed November 30, 1972 now abandoned.

FIELD OF INVENTION

The present invention relates to inflatable vehicles and more particularly to inflatable vehicle constructions which may be applied to inflatable rings and the like.

DESCRIPTION OF THE PRIOR ART

Inflatable vehicles, such as inflatable rafts, are typically fabricated as a single construction. Inherent in this unitary construction is a complicated means of constructing inflatable vehicles and a complicated and laborious method of maintaining and repairing inflatable vehicles. Typically, this means that an imperfection or a tear in one of the air-retaining cells results in extensive patching or in complete loss of the vehicle. Further, it has been found that inflatable vehicles, which find great favor in certain aquatic recreation, are difficult to store, are not fully suited to recreational uses, and may be expensive owing to the typical unitary fabricating means. A primary characteristic of inflatable vehicles has been the lack of means for fluid planing, particularly when the vehicle is used in tow or as a river float vehicle. This characteristic is evident in one-man and two-man vehicles.

Accordingly, it is a primary object of the present invention to provide an inflatable vehicle having means for planing for tow, river floats, surfing, and the like.

It is an object of the present invention to provide an inflatable vehicle construction which may employ an inflatable ring, such as an inner tube and the like.

It is a further object of this invention to provide an inflatable vehicle construction which may be removed from the inflatable ring.

It is an object of this invention to provide an inflatable vehicle construction which may be provided with a mesh bottom to facilitate passage of water.

It is another of this invention to provide an inflatable vehicle construction which may be provided with suitably fastened tow rings and handles.

These and other objects shall become apparent from the description following, it being understood that modifications may be made without affecting the teachings of the invention here set out.

SUMMARY OF THE INVENTION

The inflatable vehicle construction for inflatable rings and the like comprises a cuff made of fabric portions operable to conform to the outer walls of the rings, a vehicle bottom fastened to the cuff about the lower portion of the cuff, and a drawcord at the upper terminal edge of the cuff. The inflatable vehicle construction may include a tow ring fastened within the inner face of the cuff and the vehicle bottom, and handles suitably fastened at intervals about the cuff.

A more thorough and comprehensive understanding may be had from the detailed description of the preferred embodiment when read in connection with the drawings forming a part of this specification.

2

BRIEF DESCRIPTION OF THE DRAWINGS

FIG. 1 is a top perspective view of the inflatable vehicle construction of this invention.

FIG. 2 is a bottom perspective view of the apparatus of the FIG. 1.

FIG. 3 is a cross-sectional view taken along the lines 3—3 of the FIG. 2 showing the interior configuration thereof.

FIG. 4 is a perspective view of the construction shown in its operating position.

FIG. 5 is a cross-sectional view taken along lines 5—5 of the FIG. 4 of the construction in its operating position.

DETAILED DESCRIPTION OF THE PREFERRED EMBODIMENT:

Referring now to the drawings and more particularly to the FIGS. 1 and 2, the inflatable vehicle construction of this invention is shown to advantage and generally identified by the numeral **10**. The vehicle construction **10** is intended to be mounted over an inflatable ring, such as a commonly known inner tube **11**. The vehicle construction **10** comprises a ring cuff **12** and a vehicle bottom **13**.

The vehicle cuff **12** may be fabricated of any of a variety of suitably bound fabric side portions **14** and a bottom portion **14'**. It is to be understood that the vehicle cuff **12** may also be fabricated from a single piece of bound fabric, if found convenient in production. The side portions **14** are bound so that the portions **14** cover a curved portion about the outer periphery of the tube **11** distally interior of the uppermost and lowermost apexes or invert portions of the tube **11**. The lower portion **14'** is circumferentially, tangentially disposed to the lowermost apex, and may be suitably fastened at the bottom of the vehicle construction **10** distally upwardly of the cuff **12**. Portions **14** and **14'** are intended to tightly conform to this curved configuration when the vehicle construction **10** is drawn over the tube **11**, before and after inflation as herein later described. The cuff **12** may be fabricated of any of a variety of suitable materials, such as canvas, polyvinyl-covered cloth and flexible polymer sheet. The uppermost terminal side of the vehicle bottom **13** is adjacently disposed, in face to face relationship to the lowermost terminal side of the bottom portion **14'** of the cuff **12**, and is suitably fastened at the bottom of the vehicle construction **10** distally upwardly from the cuff **12** as shown in the FIG. 3. The vehicle bottom **13** may be fabricated from any of a variety of suitable materials, such as polymer sheeting laminated to canvas or flexible polymer sheeting laminated to canvas. It is to be understood that when the vehicle bottom wall **13** is laminated to canvas and suitably fastened to portions **14**, the bottom portion **14'** of the cuff **12** would become integral with the portions **14**. The vehicle bottom **13** may also be fabricated of a flexible mesh fabric suitable for some recreational uses. The vehicle construction **10** is secured on the tube **11** by means of a drawcord **16** which is slidably carried within a cord-carrying means, such as a hem **16'**, about the upper terminal edge of the cuff **12**. A variety of other binding reams retaining the cord **16** may be used, such as rings, grommets and the like. A tow ring **18** may be securely fastened at the joint between the inner face of the cuff **12** and the vehicle bottom **13**. The tow ring **18** may be used in securing the

3,871,042

3

vehicle construction **10** and the inner tube **11** in transport, or may be employed with a towrope **19**, shown in the FIGS. **3, 4,** and **5** hereinafter described. A handle **20** is fastened distally from the upper terminal edge of the cuff **12,** distally above the tow ring **18.** A plurality of handles **21** may be provided at preselected intervals about the circumference of the cuff **12.**

As seen in the FIGS. **3, 4** and **5,** a tie means **22** is mounted centrally in the vehicle bottom **13,** and is operable to receive a shackle means disposed distally on the tow rope **19** opposite the tow ring **18.** The shackle means may be a plurality of balls **23** engageable with a concentrical hole **22'** disposed centrally in the tie ring **22.** It may be seen that a variety of other shackles may be employed to similar effect. The material forming the tie ring **22** may be secured to and disposed between the layers of the bottom **13** and the bottom portion **14'** of the cuff **12** and bound by suitable stitching. The tie rings **22** may also be suitably secured with rivets, grommets and the like.

The vehicle construction **10** may be secured on a deflated inner tube **11** by pulling the cuff **12** over the outermost walls of the tube **11,** drawing the draw cord **16** until the cuff **12** is taut about and conforms with the tube **11,** and tieing the cord **16.** A bow-like configuration is achieved by pulling the two rope **19** over the exterior of the covered innertube **11,** thus deforming the innertube **11.** The ball-like shackle **23** is engaged with the hole **22'** in the tie ring **22** to secure the innertube in the configuration. The rider may then employ the handles **20** and **21** to guide the construction **10** in the desired direction of travel. It has been found to advantage to dispose the handles **20** and **21** at approximately 90° with the tow ring **18** disposed between handles **20** and **21.**

One use of the vehicle **10** is as a hydroplane. In this way, a rider may pull the handle **20** upwardly and toward the side opposite the vehicle in a planing-like or ski-like configuration, This presents a smooth planing portion to overcome resistance on snow or water. The handle **20** may be used to distort the planing portion of the vehicle with respect to the line of attack of the

4

water or snow to provide steering. The amount by which the handle **20** is raised may be used to influence speed. This use is operable in river and snow floats, surfing, or by tows including the tow ring **18.**

Having thus described in detail a preferred apparatus which embodies the concepts and principles of the invention and which accomplishes the various objects, purposes and aims thereof, it is to be appreciated and will be apparent to those skilled in the art that many physical changes could be made in the apparatus without altering the inventive concepts and principles embodied therein. Hence, it is intended that the scope of the invention be limited only to the extent indicated in the appended claims.

I claim:

1. In combination with inflatable annular ring, an inflatable vehicle construction comprising a cuff fabricated to conform about the circumference of said ring over a portion of the outside periphery of said ring distally interior of the upper and lower apexes of said ring, a drawcord slidably carried in a suitable cord-carrying means disposed about the upper terminal edge of said cuff, a flexible bottom fastened about the lower terminal edge on the ring-contacting side of said cuff, a tow ring disposed distally from the lower edge of said cuff, and a tie ring secured centrally in the upper side of said bottom engageable with the two rope section which provides means for deforming said ring covered by said vehicle construction into a bow-like configuration and for securing said construction into said configuration.

2. The article of claim **1** including a plurality of handles fastened at approximately 90° to each other in the upper portion of said cuff with said two ring disposed centrally between said handles.

3. The article of claim **1** including a plurality of handles fastened at intervals distally from the upper terminal edge of said cuff.

4. The article of claim **1** wherein said bottom is fabricated of sheeting of suitable material.

5. The article of claim **1** wherein said bottom is fabricated of a flexible mesh fabric.

* * * * *

US005476404A

United States Patent [19]

Price

[11] **Patent Number: 5,476,404**

[45] **Date of Patent: Dec. 19, 1995**

[54] **INFLATABLE RECREATIONAL INNER TUBE TOY**

[76] Inventor: **John B. Price**, 16040 150th, Bonner Springs, Kans. 66012

[21] Appl. No.: **324,795**

[22] Filed: **Oct. 18, 1994**

[51] **Int. Cl.**[6] **A63H 3/06**; A63H 23/00; B63B 1/00; B63C 9/30

[52] **U.S. Cl.** **446/221**; 446/153; 441/67; 441/126; 441/131; 472/129; 472/134

[58] **Field of Search** 446/29, 71, 72, 446/73, 153, 220, 221, 222, 223, 225, 226; 441/66, 67, 126, 129, 130, 131, 132; 472/128, 129, 134; 5/644

[56] **References Cited**

U.S. PATENT DOCUMENTS

3,860,976	1/1975	Suyama	446/67 X
4,302,003	11/1981	Hughes	472/129
4,687,452	8/1987	Hull	441/131
5,004,296	4/1991	Ziegenfuss, Jr.	441/132 X
5,090,930	2/1992	Walden	441/131
5,122,086	6/1992	Remy	441/129 X
5,186,667	2/1993	Wang	441/130 X

Primary Examiner—Robert A. Hafer
Assistant Examiner—D. Neal Muir

[57] **ABSTRACT**

An inflatable recreational inner tube toy comprising a seat further including a toroid-shaped inflatable primary tube having a bottom surface, a top surface, an inner periphery defining a hollow interior, an outer periphery, a plurality of straps extended across the interior and coupled to the inner periphery, a generally-inflatable leg rest integrally coupled to and extended outwards from the outer periphery of the primary tube, and a valve for allowing the seat to be inflated and deflated; and a back rest formed of a toroid-shaped inflatable secondary tube sized smaller than the primary tube with the back rest coupled to the inner periphery of the primary tube and extended upwards therefrom and with the back rest further including a valve coupled thereto for allowing it to be inflated and deflated.

1 Claim, 3 Drawing Sheets

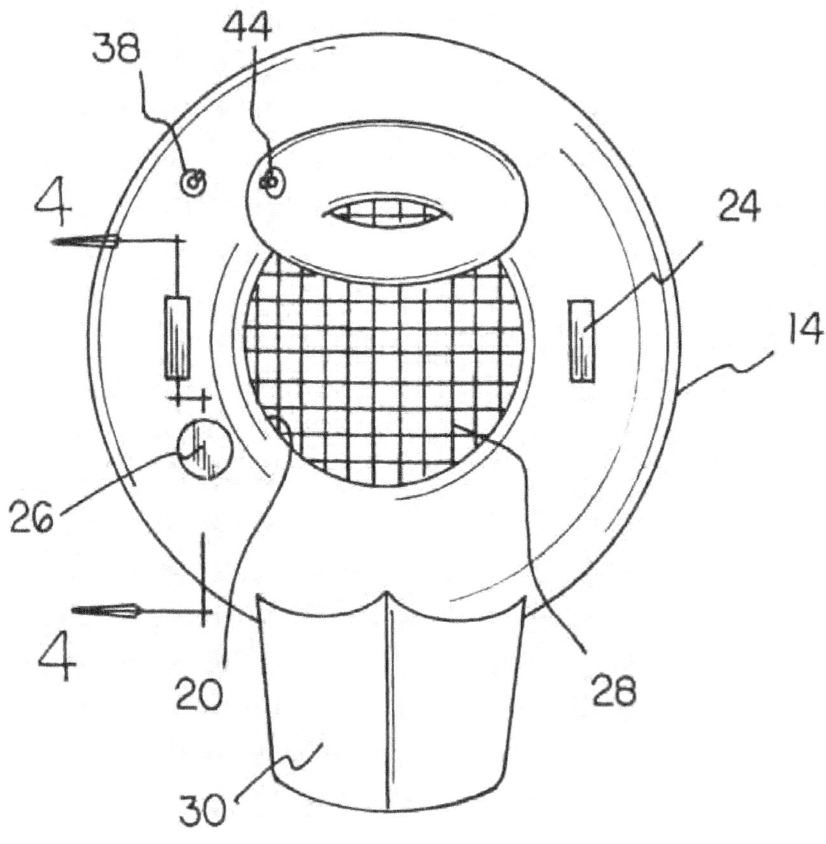

U.S. Patent Dec. 19, 1995 Sheet 1 of 3 **5,476,404**

FIG 1

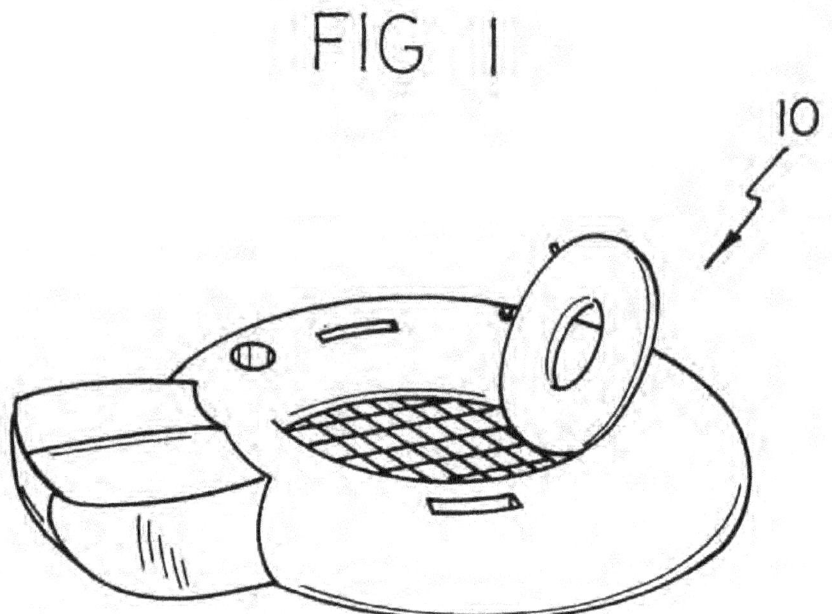

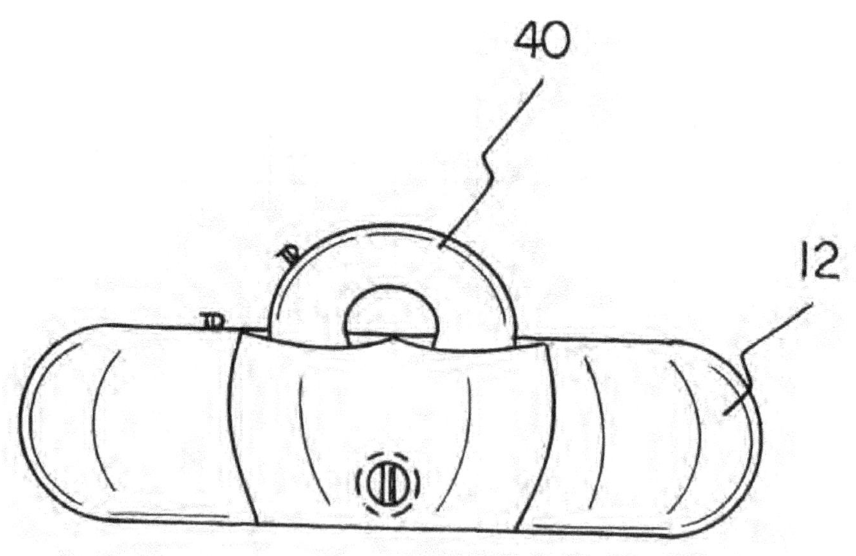

FIG 2

U.S. Patent **Dec. 19, 1995** **Sheet 2 of 3** **5,476,404**

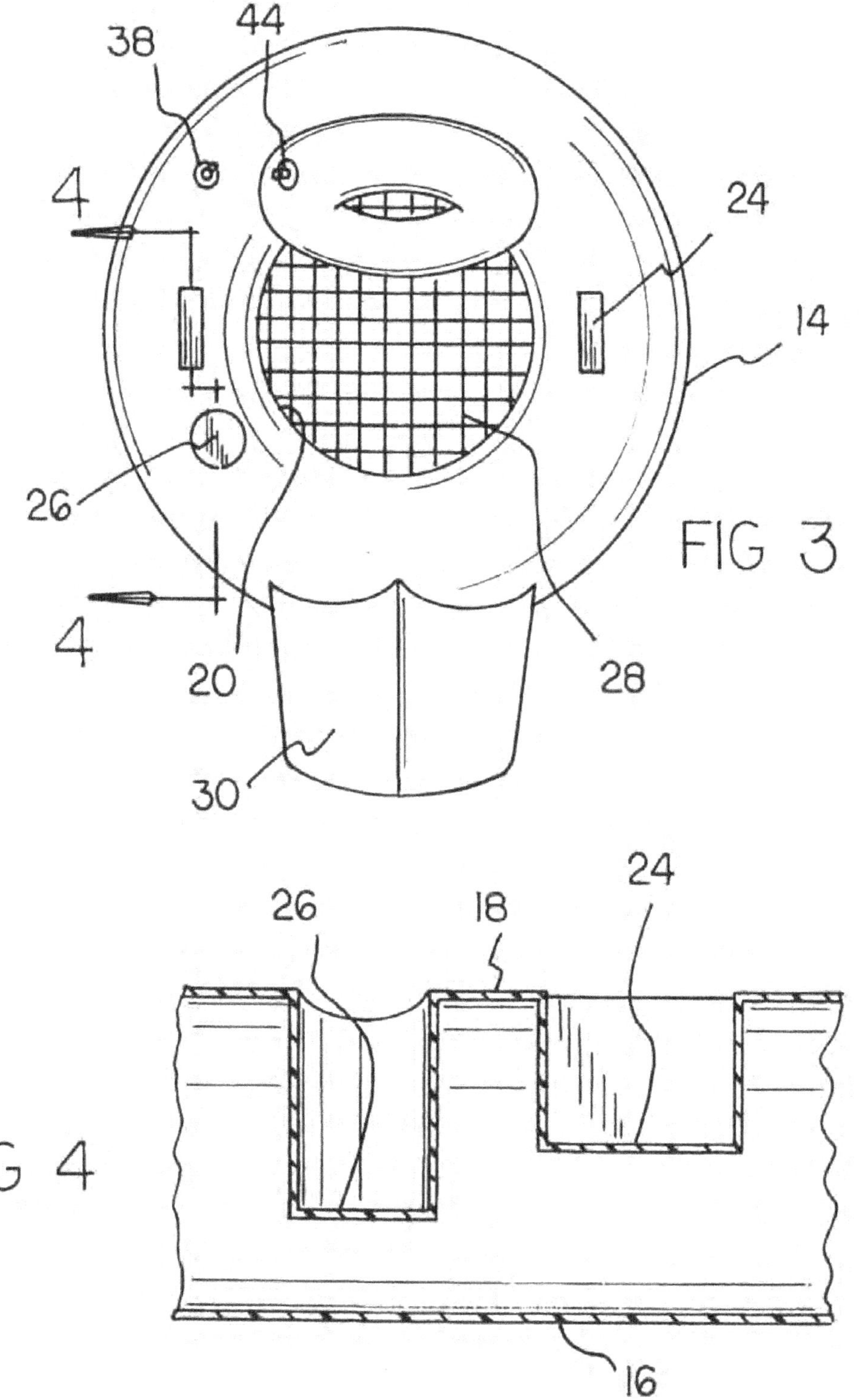

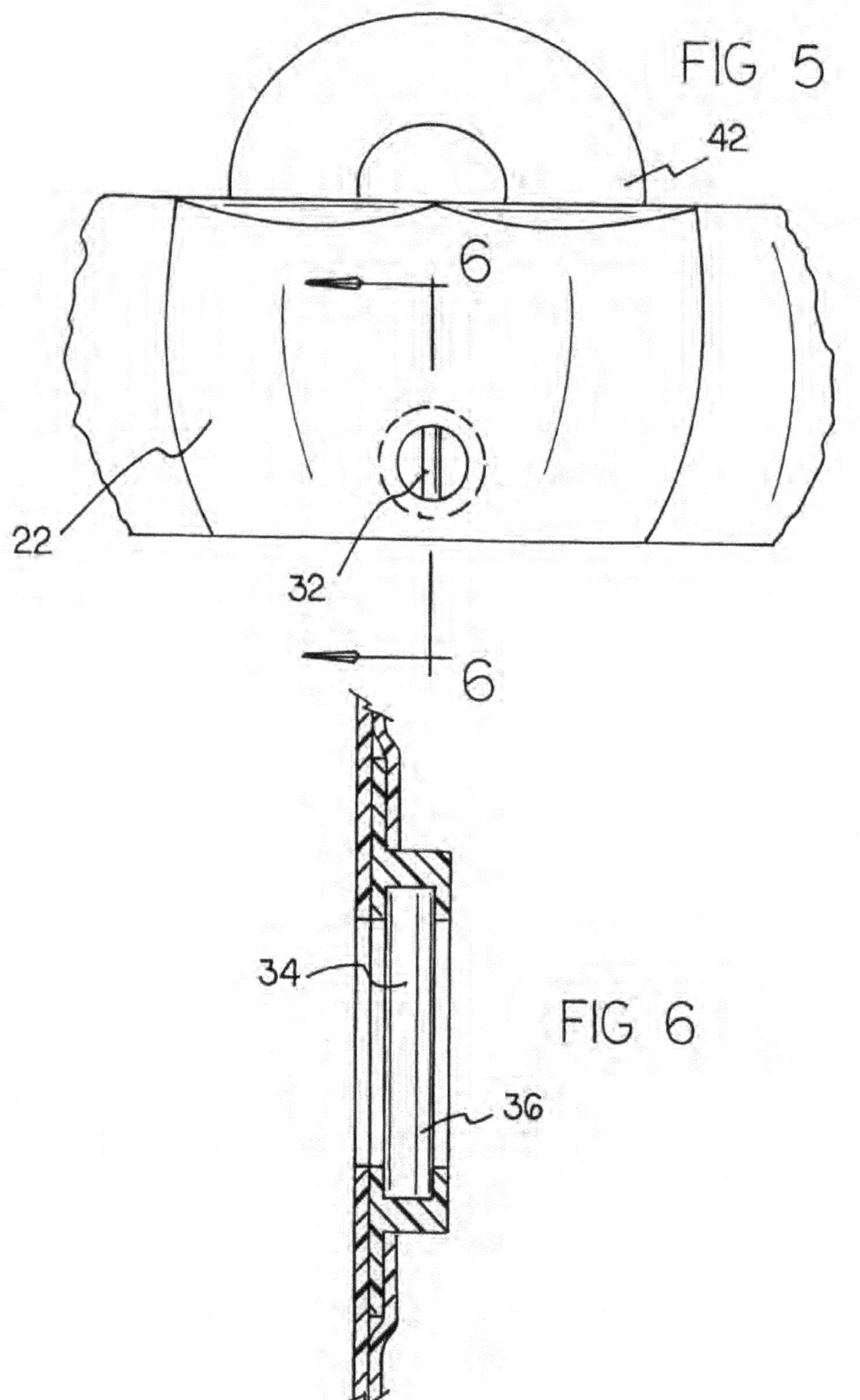
U.S. Patent
Dec. 19, 1995
Sheet 3 of 3
5,476,404
FIG 5
42
6
22
32
6
34
FIG 6
36

5,476,404

1

INFLATABLE RECREATIONAL INNER TUBE TOY

BACKGROUND OF THE INVENTION

1. Field of the Invention

The present invention relates to an inflatable recreational inner tube toy and more particularly pertains to use in recreational activities with an inflatable recreational inner tube toy.

2. Description of the Prior Art

The use of inner tube apparatuses is known in the prior art. More specifically, inner tube apparatuses heretofore devised and utilized for the purpose of use in recreational activities are known to consist basically of familiar, expected and obvious structural configurations, notwithstanding the myriad of designs encompassed by the crowded prior art which have been developed for the fulfillment of countless objectives and requirements.

By way of example, U. S. Pat. No. 3,928,879 to Britschinn discloses inflatable tube bodies. U. S. Pat. No. 4,367,689 to Lukehart et al. discloses a water recreational vehicle. U. S. Pat. No. 4,795,387 to Morgan discloses a collapsible inner tube seat insert. U. S. Pat. No. 5,046,978 to Howerton discloses a float tube with adjustable sling seat. U. S. Pat. No. 5,122,086 to Remy discloses a towable riding apparatus. U. S. Pat. No. 5,224,891 to Stephens discloses a recreational insert for an inner tube.

While these devices fulfill their respective, particular objective and requirements, the aforementioned patents do not describe an inflatable recreational inner tube toy that can be used in a variety of recreational activities such as sleding or skiing.

In this respect, the inflatable recreational inner tube toy according to the present invention substantially departs from the conventional concepts and designs of the prior art, and in doing so provides an apparatus primarily developed for the purpose of use in recreational activities.

Therefore, it can be appreciated that there exists a continuing need for new and improved inflatable recreational inner tube toy which can be used for use in recreational activities. In this regard, the present invention substantially fulfills this need.

SUMMARY OF THE INVENTION

In the view of the foregoing disadvantages inherent in the known types of inner tube apparatuses now present in the prior art, the present invention provides an improved inflatable recreational inner tube toy. As such, the general purpose of the present invention, which will be described subsequently in greater detail, is to provide a new and improved inflatable recreational inner tube toy and method which has all the advantages of the prior art and none of the disadvantages.

To attain this, the present invention essentially comprises, in combination a seat. The seat includes a toroid-shaped inflatable rubber primary tube having a bottom surface, a top surface, an inner periphery defining a hollow interior, an outer periphery, a pair of diametrically opposed sunken handles integrally coupled to the top surface, a cup holder formed as a recess integrally coupled to the top surface, a plurality of nylon straps extended across the interior and coupled to the inner periphery at a location near the bottom surface, a generally duckbill-shaped inflatable rubber leg rest integrally coupled to and extended outwards from the

2

outer periphery of the primary tube with the leg rest including an eye hook formed thereon for allowing attachment of an external pull rope, and a valve coupled to the primary tube for allowing the seat to be inflated and deflated. A back rest is also included and formed of a toroid-shaped inflatable rubber secondary tube sized smaller than the primary tube. The back rest is coupled to the inner periphery of the primary tube and extended angularly upwards therefrom. The back rest also has a valve coupled thereto for allowing it to be inflated and deflated.

There has thus been outlined, rather broadly, the more important features of the invention in order that the detailed description thereof that follows may be better understood, and in order that the present contribution to the art may be better appreciated. There are, of course, additional features of the invention that will be described hereinafter and which will form the subject matter of the claims appended hereto.

In this respect, before explaining at least one embodiment of the invention in detail, iris to be understood that the invention is not limited in its application to the details of construction and to the arrangements of the components set forth in the following description or illustrated in the drawings. The invention is capable of other embodiments and of being practiced and carried out in various ways. Also, it is to be understood that the phraseology and terminology employed herein are for the purpose of description and should not be regarded as limiting.

As such, those skilled in the art will appreciate that the conception, upon which this disclosure is based, may readily be utilized as a basis for the designing of other structures, methods and systems for carrying out the several purposes of the present invention. It is important, therefore, that the claims be regarded as including such equivalent constructions insofar as they do not depart from the spirit and scope of the present invention.

Further, the purpose of the foregoing abstract is to enable the U.S. Patent and Trademark Office and the public generally, and especially the scientists, engineers and practitioners in the art who are not familiar with patent or legal terms or phraseology, to determine quickly from a cursory inspection the nature and essence of the technical disclosure of the application. The abstract is neither intended to define the invention of the application, which is measured by the claims, nor is it intended to be limiting as to the scope of the invention in any way.

It is therefore an object of the present invention to provide a new and improved inflatable recreational inner tube toy which has all the advantages of the prior art inner tube apparatuses and none of the disadvantages.

It is another object of the present invention to provide a new and improved inflatable recreational inner tube toy which may be easily and efficiently manufactured and marketed.

It is a further object of the present invention to provide a new and improved inflatable recreational inner tube toy which is of durable and reliable construction.

An even further object of the present invention is to provide a new and improved inflatable recreational inner tube toy which is susceptible of a low cost of manufacture with regard to both materials and labor, and which accordingly is then susceptible of low prices of sale to the consuming public, thereby making such an inflatable recreational inner tube toy economically available to the buying public.

Still yet another object of the present invention is to provide a new and improved inflatable recreational inner tube toy which provides in the apparatuses and methods of the prior art some of the advantages thereof, while simultaneously overcoming some of the disadvantages normally associated therewith.

Even still another object of the present invention is to provide a new and improved inflatable recreational inner tube toy for use in recreational activities.

Lastly, it is an object of the present invention to provide a new and improved inflatable recreational inner tube toy comprising a seat further comprising a toroid-shaped inflatable primary tube having a bottom surface, a top surface, an inner periphery defining a hollow interior, an outer periphery, a plurality of straps extended across the interior and coupled to the inner periphery, a generally inflatable leg rest integrally coupled to and extended outwards from the outer periphery of the primary tube, and a valve for allowing the seat to be inflated and deflated; and a back rest formed of a toroid-shaped inflatable secondary tube sized smaller than the primary tube with the back rest coupled to the inner periphery of the primary tube and extended upwards therefrom, the back rest further including a valve coupled thereto for allowing it to be inflated and deflated.

These together with other objects of the invention, along with the various features of novelty which characterize the invention, are pointed out with particularity in the claims annexed to and forming a part of this disclosure. For a better understanding of the invention, its operating advantages and the specific objects attained by its uses, reference should be had to the accompanying drawings and descriptive matter in which there is illustrated preferred embodiments of the invention.

BRIEF DESCRIPTION OF THE DRAWINGS

The invention will be better understood and objects other than those set forth above will become apparent when consideration is given to the following detailed description thereof. Such description makes reference to the annexed drawings wherein:

FIG. 1 is a perspective view of the preferred embodiment of the inflatable recreational inner tube toy constructed in accordance with the principles of the present invention.

FIG. 2 is a side-elevational view of the present invention as viewed with respect to its leg rest.

FIG. 3 is a plan view of the preferred embodiment of the present invention.

FIG. 4 is a cross-sectional view of the seat of the present invention taken along the line **4—4** of **FIG. 3**.

FIG. 5 is an enlarged side-elevational view of the leg rest of the present invention.

FIG. 6 is a cross-sectional view of the eye hook of the leg rest taken along the line **6—6** of **FIG. 5**.

The same reference numerals refer to the same parts through the various Figures.

DESCRIPTION OF THE PREFERRED EMBODIMENT

With reference now to the drawings, and in particular, to **FIG. 1** thereof, the preferred embodiment of the new and improved inflatable recreational inner tube toy embodying the principles and concepts of the present invention and generally designated by the reference number **10** will be described.

Specifically, the present invention essentially includes two major components. The major components are the seat and back rest. These components are interrelated to provide the intended function.

More specifically, it will be noted in the various Figures that the first major component is the seat **12**. The seat is formed of a toroid-shaped inflatable primary tube **14**. The primary tube is formed of a flexible elastomeric material such as rubber. The primary tube has a bottom surface **16**, a top surface **18**, an inner periphery **20** defining and enclosing a hollow interior, and an outer periphery **221**. The primary tube also has a pair of diametrically opposed sunken handles **24** integrally coupled to the top surface and positioned about the interior. The primary tube also includes a cup holder **26**. The cup holder is formed as a generally cylindrical recess integrally coupled to the top surface near one, of the handles. The seat also includes a plurality of straps **28** extended across the interior in a matrix-type configuration. The straps are formed of nylon or other similar strong flexible material. The straps are coupled to the inner periphery at a location near the bottom surface. The straps in combination with the primary tube create a generally cup-shaped recess for holding a user. The seat also includes a generally duckbill-shaped inflatable leg rest. The leg rest is formed of a flexible elastomeric material such as rubber. The leg rest is integrally coupled to and extended outwards from the outer periphery of the primary tube. The leg rest includes an eye hook **32** formed thereon. The eye hook is formed of a rod **34** positioned within a generally circular recess **36**. The eye hook allows attachment of an external pull rope for pulling the present invention with a boat, snowmobile, or the like. Lastly, a valve **38** is coupled to the primary tube. The valve allows the seat to be inflated and deflated.

The second major component is the back rest **40**. The back rest is formed of a toroid-shaped inflatable secondary tube **42**. The secondary tube is formed of a flexible elastomeric material such as rubber. The secondary tube has an outer diameter smaller than that of the primary tube. The back rest is coupled to the inner periphery of the primary tube within the recess and extended angularly upwards therefrom. The back rest is generally aligned with the leg rest such that the recess is positioned therebetween. The back rest further includes a valve **44** coupled thereto. The valve allows the back rest to be inflated and deflated.

The present invention can be used for sled riding in snow or can be pulled by a vehicle such as a snow mobile, a four-wheeler, or a ski boat. The present invention can also be used for floating down a river or for general play in a body of water. The present invention is made of rubber except the nylon straps used in forming the seat. The outer diameter of the primary tube of the present invention is about 4 feet in length. The outer diameter of the back rest is about 18 inches in length. Thus, the ratio of the outer diameter of the back rest to the outer diameter of the seat is about 3:8. The bottom surface of the primary tube is formed of reinforced rubber with a thickness of about ¾ inch. The eye hook is formed of a polyester cord reinforced lug or rod. The eye hook is reinforced to insure that it does not rip under high-loading conditions. The eye hook is located on the outboard end of the leg rest is such that the present invention will ride in a level orientation when pulled by a vehicle.

As to the manner of usage and operation of the present invention, the same should be apparent from the above description. Accordingly, no further discussion relating to the manner of usage and operation will be provided.

With respect to the above description then, it is to be

5,476,404

5

realized that the optimum dimensional relationships for the parts of the invention, to include variations in size, materials, shape, form, function and the manner of operation, assembly and use, are deemed readily apparent and obvious to one skilled in the art, and all equivalent relationships to those illustrated in the drawings and described in the specification are intended to be encompassed by the present invention.

Therefore, the foregoing is considered as illustrative only of the principles of the invention. Further, since numerous modification and changes will readily occur to those skilled in the art, it is not desired to limit the invention to the exact construction and operation shown and described, and accordingly, all suitable modification and equivalents may be resorted to, falling within the scope of the invention.

What is claimed as being new and desired to be protected by LETTERS PATENT of the United States is as follows:

1. An inflatable recreational inner tube toy for use in recreational activities comprising, in combination:

a seat further comprising a toroid-shaped inflatable rubber primary tube having an outer diameter, a bottom surface, a top surface, an inner periphery defining a hollow interior, an outer periphery, a pair of diametrically opposed sunken handles integrally coupled to the top surface, a cup holder formed as a recess integrally

6

coupled to the top surface, a plurality of nylon straps extended across the interior in a matrix-type configuration and coupled to the inner periphery at a location near the bottom surface to create a generally cup-shaped recess for holding a user, a generally duckbill-shaped inflatable rubber leg rest integrally coupled to and extended outwards from the outer periphery of the primary tube with the leg rest including an eye hook disposed thereon for allowing attachment of an external pull rope and with the eye hook formed of a rod positioned across a generally circular recess, and a valve coupled to the primary tube for allowing the seat to be inflated and deflated; and

a back rest formed of a toroid-shaped inflatable rubber secondary tube having an outer diameter and with the ratio of the outer diameter of the back rest to the outer diameter of the seat being about 3:8 and with the back rest coupled to the inner periphery of the primary tube and extended angularly upwards therefrom, the back rest further having a valve coupled thereto for allowing it to be inflated and deflated.

* * * * *

(12) **United States Patent**
Arias

(10) **Patent No.: US 6,485,344 B2**
(45) **Date of Patent: Nov. 26, 2002**

(54) **COLLAPSIBLE FLOTATION DEVICE**

(75) Inventor: **David A. Arias**, Virginia Beach, VA (US)

(73) Assignee: **Gray Matter Holdings, LLC**, Baltimore, MD (US)

(*) Notice: Subject to any disclaimer, the term of this patent is extended or adjusted under 35 U.S.C. 154(b) by 0 days.

(21) Appl. No.: **09/772,739**

(22) Filed: **Jan. 30, 2001**

(65) **Prior Publication Data**

US 2002/0102889 A1 Aug. 1, 2002

Related U.S. Application Data

(60) Provisional application No. 60/238,988, filed on Oct. 10, 2000.

(51) **Int. Cl.**[7] **B63C 9/08**
(52) **U.S. Cl.** **441/131**
(58) **Field of Search** 5/417, 419, 420; 114/345; 441/40, 43, 80, 81, 125, 129, 130, 131, 136

(56) **References Cited**

U.S. PATENT DOCUMENTS

722,801 A	3/1903	Bourne, Jr.	
1,190,743 A *	7/1916	Fageol	441/131
1,479,903 A	1/1924	Erland	
1,960,474 A *	5/1934	Browne	441/129
2,119,023 A	5/1938	Pickard	
2,173,963 A *	9/1939	Eubank	441/131
2,190,566 A	2/1940	Julian	
2,344,010 A	3/1944	Walsh	
2,357,789 A	9/1944	Levy	
2,420,344 A	5/1947	Alexander	
2,442,105 A	5/1948	Vacheron	
2,637,861 A	5/1953	Kethledge	
2,731,997 A	1/1956	Muth et al.	
2,803,291 A	8/1957	Meyer	
2,870,464 A	1/1959	Lalick	
3,052,895 A	9/1962	Lo Vico	
3,336,610 A	8/1967	Geddings	
3,602,930 A *	9/1971	Channon	441/65
3,775,782 A *	12/1973	Rice et al.	5/82
3,862,876 A	1/1975	Graves	
3,960,161 A	6/1976	Norman	
3,990,463 A	11/1976	Norman	
4,097,944 A	7/1978	Yulish	
4,200,942 A	5/1980	Case	
4,231,125 A	11/1980	Tittl	
D261,464 S	10/1981	Smith	
4,296,788 A	10/1981	Slater	
4,478,587 A *	10/1984	Mackal	441/41

(List continued on next page.)

FOREIGN PATENT DOCUMENTS

EP 0 974 293 A2 1/2000

Primary Examiner—S. Joseph Morano
Assistant Examiner—Andrew Wright
(74) *Attorney, Agent, or Firm*—Cooley Godward LLP

(57) **ABSTRACT**

A collapsible flotation device has an uncollapsed configuration and a collapsed configuration. The device includes a spring which is forced to coil in upon itself by folding to achieve the collapsed configuration of the device and which is biased towards the uncoiled configuration. The spring is located along the perimeter of the device in a pocket formed along the perimeter of a panel of flexible material or on the external perimeter of the device. Also located within the pocket are one or more inflation chambers which are inflated to provide buoyancy. Additional or alternate pockets which include inflatable chambers may be located in the central portion of the flexible panel.

25 Claims, 5 Drawing Sheets

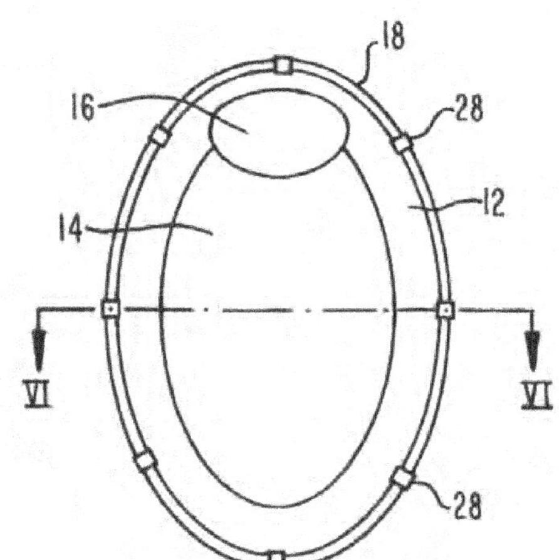

US 6,485,344 B2

Page 2

U.S. PATENT DOCUMENTS

Patent	Kind		Date	Name	Class
4,512,049	A		4/1985	Henry	
4,561,480	A		12/1985	Underwood et al.	
4,576,375	A	*	3/1986	Roberts	472/129
4,709,430	A		12/1987	Nicoll	
4,766,918	A	*	8/1988	Oderkirk	135/96
4,815,784	A		3/1989	Zheng	
4,825,892	A		5/1989	Norman	
4,858,634	A		8/1989	McLeese	
4,942,838	A	*	7/1990	Boyer et al.	114/345
4,946,067	A	*	8/1990	Kelsall	222/5
4,951,333	A		8/1990	Kaiser et al.	
4,976,642	A	*	12/1990	Wilkie	441/131
5,024,262	A		6/1991	Huang	
5,038,812	A		8/1991	Norman	
5,056,172	A		10/1991	Kaiser et al.	
5,059,463	A		10/1991	Peters	
5,070,807	A	*	12/1991	Lewis	114/361
D325,489	S		4/1992	Pratt	
5,116,273	A		5/1992	Chan	
5,163,192	A		11/1992	Watson	
5,163,461	A		11/1992	Ivanovich et al.	
5,206,964	A		5/1993	Wilson, Sr.	
5,213,147	A		5/1993	Zheng	
5,261,131	A		11/1993	Kilby	
5,299,331	A		4/1994	Badillo	
D349,593	S		8/1994	Hensley	
5,334,067	A	*	8/1994	Henry et al.	441/131
5,345,627	A		9/1994	Cammarata	
5,385,518	A	*	1/1995	Turner	482/23
5,396,917	A		3/1995	Hazinski et al.	
5,430,980	A		7/1995	Ferrier	
5,433,433	A		7/1995	Armell	
5,435,025	A		7/1995	Gerard et al.	
5,454,643	A		10/1995	Sullivan	
5,467,794	A		11/1995	Zheng	
D366,177	S		1/1996	Dean	
5,520,561	A	*	5/1996	Langenohl	441/129
5,533,653	A		7/1996	Kaufman	
5,560,385	A		10/1996	Zheng	
5,571,036	A	*	11/1996	Hannigan	441/129
5,579,799	A		12/1996	Zheng	
5,592,961	A		1/1997	Chin	
5,618,110	A		4/1997	Sullivan	
5,618,246	A		4/1997	Zheng	
RE35,571	E		7/1997	McLeese	
5,644,807	A		7/1997	Battistella	
5,688,052	A		11/1997	Compton	
5,693,398	A		12/1997	Granger	
D389,362	S		1/1998	Boulatian	
5,718,612	A	*	2/1998	Elsholz	441/38
5,729,846	A		3/1998	Sullivan	
5,730,529	A		3/1998	Fritz et al.	
5,810,695	A	*	9/1998	Sass	441/37
D400,749	S		11/1998	Bechtold, Jr.	
5,885,123	A	*	3/1999	Clifford	441/129
5,976,023	A		11/1999	Cho	
6,030,300	A		2/2000	Zheng	
D425,357	S		5/2000	Waring	
D426,415	S		6/2000	Le Gette et al.	
6,073,283	A		6/2000	Zheng	
6,170,100	B1		1/2001	Le Gette et al.	
6,192,635	B1		2/2001	Zheng	
6,223,673	B1	*	5/2001	Mears et al.	114/364
6,276,979	B1	*	8/2001	Saltel et al.	441/132
D447,661	S		9/2001	Le Gette et al.	
D449,193	S		10/2001	Le Gette et al.	

* cited by examiner

U.S. Patent Nov. 26, 2002 Sheet 1 of 5 US 6,485,344 B2

FIG. 1

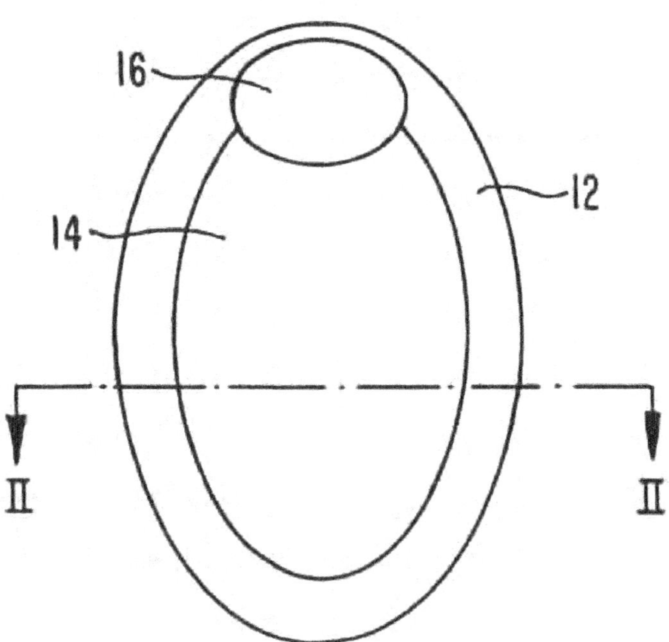

FIG. 2

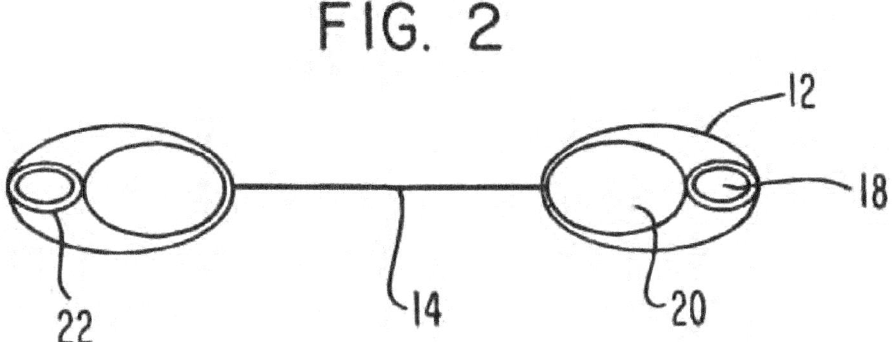

U.S. Patent Nov. 26, 2002 Sheet 2 of 5 US 6,485,344 B2

FIG. 3

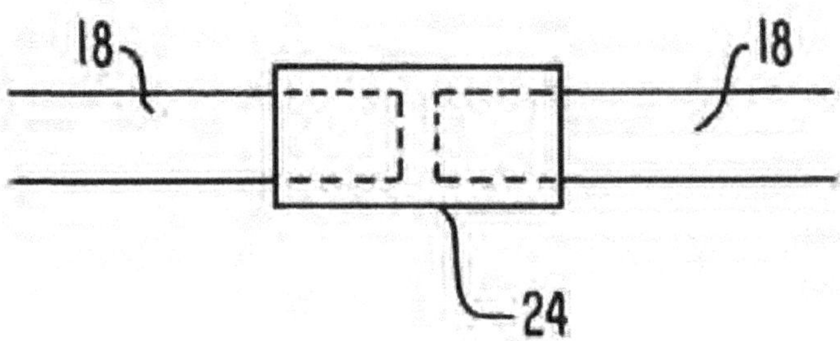

FIG. 4

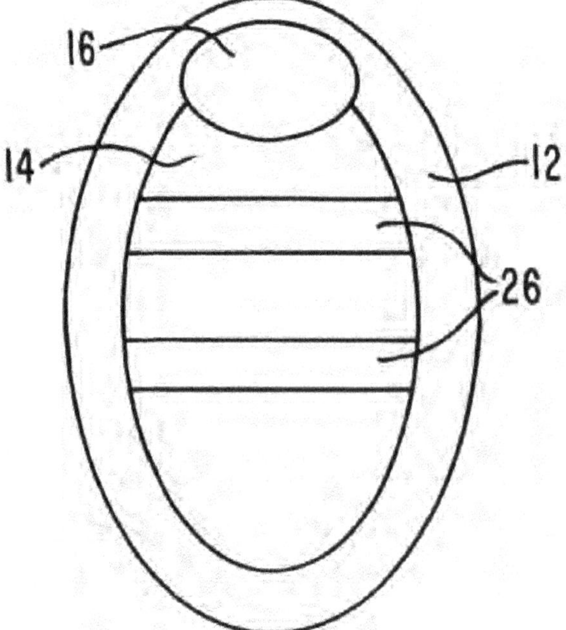

U.S. Patent Nov. 26, 2002 Sheet 3 of 5 US 6,485,344 B2

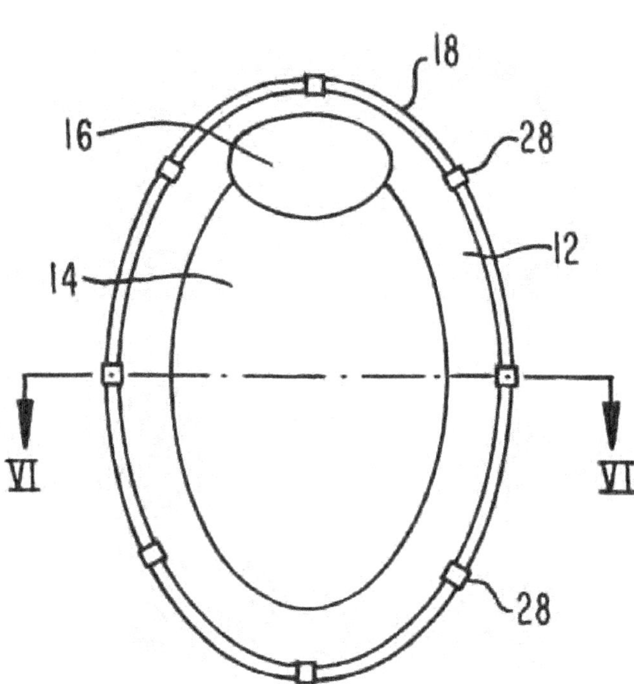

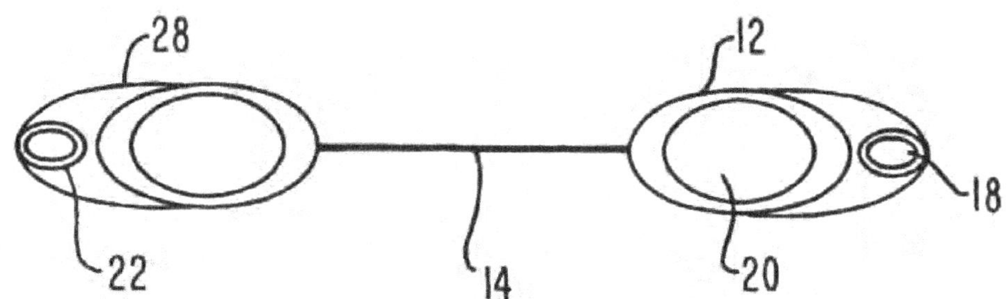

U.S. Patent Nov. 26, 2002 Sheet 4 of 5 US 6,485,344 B2

FIG. 7

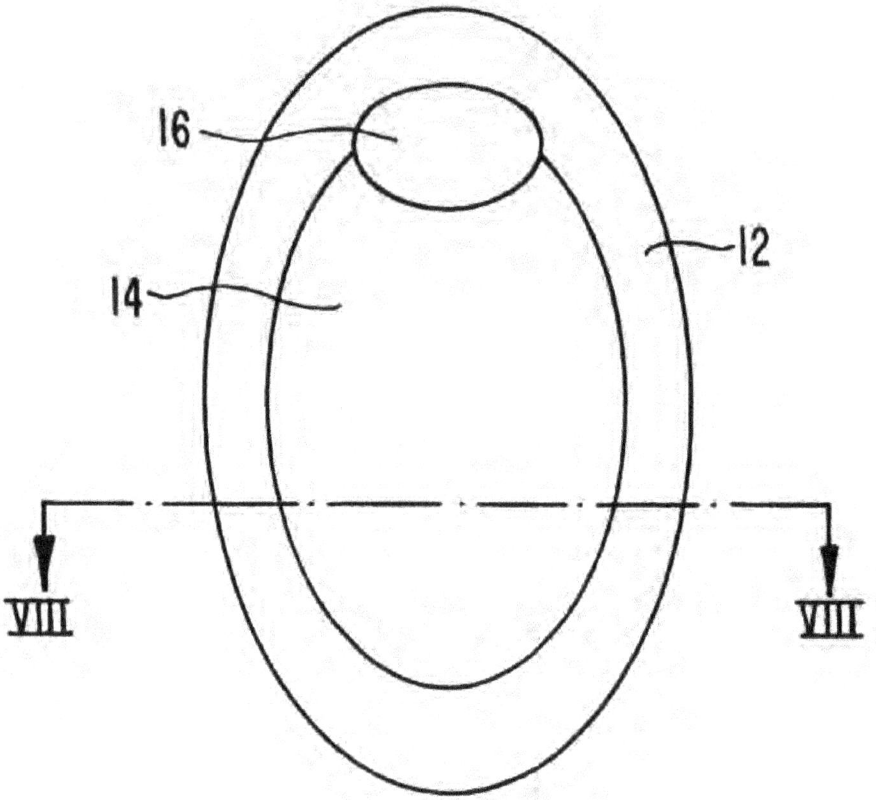

16
12
14
VIII
VIII

FIG. 8

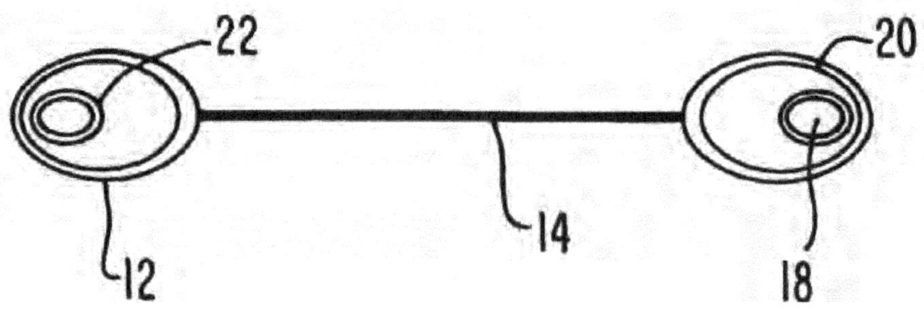

FIG. 9

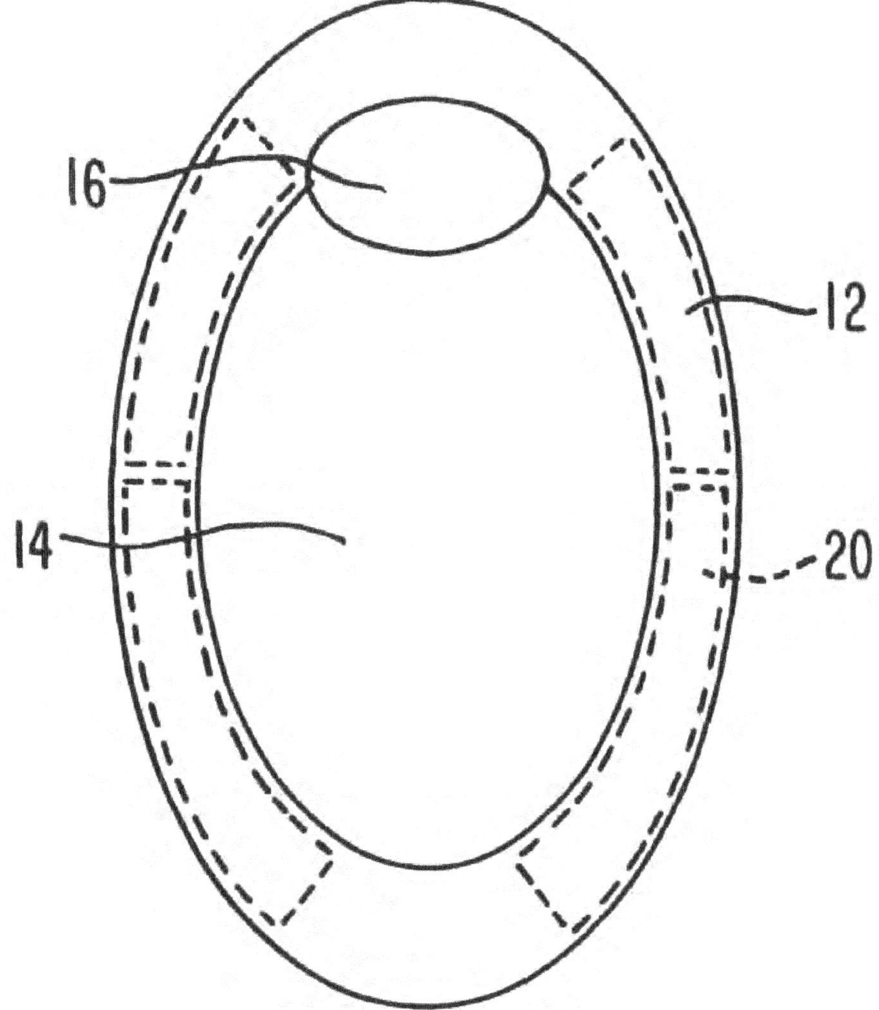

US 6,485,344 B2

1

COLLAPSIBLE FLOTATION DEVICE

CROSS REFERENCE TO RELATED APPLICATION

The present application claims priority from U.S. Provisional Application Ser. No. 60/238,988, filed Oct. 10, 2000.

BACKGROUND OF THE INVENTION

1. Field of the Invention

The present invention relates to inflatable flotation devices. In particular, the present invention relates to inflatable flotation devices which are collapsible through use of a spring mechanism.

2. Description of the Related Art

Inflatable flotation devices are well known in the form of floats, rafts, lifeboats, life preservers and other like devices. Previously known devices generally maintain their shape through air pressure alone and generally collapse when deflated.

In one of many examples, U.S. Pat. No. 3,775,782 issued to Rice et al. describes an inflatable rescue raft. When deflated, the raft can be rolled into a compact size.

Also well known in the art are collapsible items which are collapsible through the use of a collapsible metal or plastic spring. U.S. Pat. No. 4,815,784 shows an automobile sun shade which uses these collapsible springs. The springs are also used in children's play structures (U.S. Pat. Nos. 5,618,246 and 5,560,385) and tent-like shade structures (U.S. Pat. Nos. 5,579,799 and 5,467,794).

The collapsible springs are typically retained or held within fabric sleeves provided along the edges of a piece of fabric or other panel. The collapsible springs may be provided as one continuous loop, or may be a strip or strips of material connected at the ends to form a continuous loop. These collapsible springs are usually formed of flexible coilable steel, although other materials such as plastics are also used. The collapsible springs are usually made of a material which is relatively strong and yet is flexible to a sufficient degree to allow it to be coiled. Thus, each collapsible spring is capable of assuming two configurations, a normal uncoiled or expanded configuration, and a coiled or collapsed configuration in which the spring is collapsed into a size which is much smaller than its open configuration. The springs may be retained within the respective fabric sleeves without being connected thereto. Alternatively, the sleeves may be mechanically fastened, stitched, fused, or glued to the springs to retain them in position.

SUMMARY OF THE DISCLOSURE

A collapsible flotation device is described which includes a coilable spring and a flexible panel. Along the outer edge of the flexible panel is a perimeter pocket into which the coilable spring and at least one inflatable chamber are placed. The coilable spring can be made from steel which has been treated such that it is resistant to water damage or the coilable spring can be made from a waterproof material. The flexible panel can be made from any material which is appropriate for use in the water such as nylon. Alternatively, the flexible panel can be constructed from multiple materials. For example, the perimeter pocket can be made from nylon while the central portion can be made from mesh material. The inflatable chambers are made from any appropriate material but are preferably puncture resistant and each chamber includes a means for inflating and deflating the chamber such as a valve. The flotation device can also

2

include a pillow section to provide buoyant support for a user's head. This pillow section would also include an inflatable chamber to form the pillow. In addition to or instead of the perimeter pockets, the central portion of the flexible panel may include pockets into which inflatable chambers may be placed. Although the spring is normally placed within the perimeter pocket of the flexible panel, it would be possible to mechanically attach the coilable spring to the outer edge of the flexible panel.

It is therefore an object of the present invention to provide a collapsible flotation device.

It is another object of the present invention to provide a collapsible flotation device which is easily collapsed and extended to full size through a mechanical means.

It is yet another object of the present invention to provide a collapsible flotation device which is easily collapsed and extended to full size through the use of a spring.

It is yet a further object of the present invention to provide a collapsible flotation device which requires minimal force to twist and fold into the collapsed configuration.

Finally, it is an object of the present invention to accomplish the foregoing objectives in a simple and cost effective manner.

DESCRIPTION OF THE DRAWINGS

FIG. **1** is a top view of the preferred embodiment of the present invention;

FIG. **2** is a cross sectional view of the preferred embodiment of the present invention taken along line II—II of FIG. **1**;

FIG. **3** is a view of a joining method as used in one embodiment of the present invention;

FIG. **4** is a top view of an alternate embodiment of the present invention;

FIG. **5** is a top view of another alternate embodiment of the present invention; and

FIG. **6** is a cross section view of the alternate embodiment of the present invention across line VI—VI of FIG. **5**.

FIG. **7** is a top view of an alternative embodiment of the present invention;

FIG. **8** is a cross sectional view of the embodiment of the present invention, taken along line VIII—VIII of FIG. **7**;

FIG. **9** is a plan view of another embodiment of the present invention.

DETAILED DESCRIPTION OF THE PREFERRED EMBODIMENTS

The following detailed description is of the best presently contemplated modes of carrying out the invention. This description is not to be taken in a limiting sense, but is made merely for the purpose of illustrating general principles of embodiments of the invention.

The present invention provides a collapsible flotation device. The device includes a coilable metal or plastic spring. The coilable spring can be made from other materials, however, it is important that the coilable spring be made from a material that is strong and flexible. The spring must be coilable such that it folds on top of itself to become more compact. In its uncoiled state, the coilable spring can be round or oval or any shape satisfactory for use as a flotation device. Because it is to be used in water, the coilable spring is preferably either manufactured from a waterproof material or coated to protect any material which is not waterproof. The coilable spring can be a single

US 6,485,344 B2

3

continuous element or can include a joining means, such as a sleeve, for joining the ends of one or more spring elements together. The coilable spring can be of any appropriate shape and dimension. The coilable spring also has memory such that is biased to return to its uncoiled configuration when not held in the coiled configuration.

Stretched across the coilable spring is a flexible panel of material. The flexible panel can be one continuous piece or can be made up of several different types of material. In a preferred embodiment, the center portion of the flexible panel is mesh to allow water to flow through while the perimeter edges are nylon or polyester. At the edges of the flotation device, the material is a double thickness, forming a pocket around the perimeter of the flotation device. In this pocket are one or more inflatable chambers. One inflatable chamber may surround the entire perimeter of the flotation device or it may be divided into two or more inflatable chambers with each inflatable chamber having a means for inflating and deflating the inflatable chamber. In a preferred embodiment, one inflatable chamber is specifically designed to accommodate the user's head. In this embodiment, the pocket formed by the material is wider along a small portion of the perimeter of the flotation device to allow for a wider inflatable chamber. This will prevent the user's head from sinking below the rest of the user's body. The size of the inflatable chamber can vary significantly and need only be as wide as necessary to support the user's body weight. A preferred embodiment includes an inflatable chamber which is 3 inches in diameter when inflated. The inflatable chamber can be made from any appropriate float material but is preferably resistant to punctures. The coilable spring may also be located within the perimeter pocket. If one inflatable chamber is selected, the coilable spring can be placed inside or outside the inflatable chamber. If multiple inflatable chambers are used, the coilable spring will be outside the inflatable chambers. Alternatively, the coilable spring may be located outside the perimeter pocket along the outer edge of the flotation device. The coilable spring may be attached to the flexible panel through mechanical means such as fastening, stitching, fusing, or gluing.

A preferred embodiment of the flotation device is shown in FIGS. 1 and 2 in its expanded configuration. The perimeter pocket **12** portion of the flexible panel is nylon while the central portion **14** of the flexible panel is made from a mesh material. The pillow **16** is part of the perimeter pocket **12** as it includes a double layer of fabric to accept an inflatable chamber **20** between the layers of fabric. In this particular embodiment, there are two inflatable chambers **20** in the perimeter pocket of the flotation device and one in the pillow **16**, each of which includes a means for inflating the inflatable chamber **20**. The inflation means is a valve on the underside of the flotation device. The inflatable chambers **20** in the perimeter pocket of the flotation device expand to approximately a 3-inch diameter when inflated. The coilable spring **18** is made from flexible, collapsible steel and is coated with a layer of PVC **22** to protect the coilable spring **18** from corroding and rusting due to contact with water during normal use of the flotation device. The coilable spring **18** also has memory such that will open to its uncoiled configuration when not held in the coiled configuration. The coilable spring **18** can be a single unitary element or can include sleeves **24** for joining the ends of one or more strips as shown in FIG. **3** in which the ends of the coilable spring **18** within the sleeve **24** are shown in dashed lines for clarification.

Alternatively or in addition to the perimeter inflatable chambers, the device can include inflatable chambers **26** which cross the panel as shown in FIG. **4**. FIGS. **5** and **6** show a further alternate embodiment of the present invention in which the coilable spring **18** is attached to the external perimeter of the pocket portion **12** of the flexible panel through the use of a mechanical means. In this particular embodiment, several loops **28** are used to attach the coilable spring **18** to the pocket portion **12** of the flexible panel.

4

While the description above refers to particular embodiments of the present invention, it will be understood that many modifications may be made without departing from the spirit thereof The accompanying claims are intended to cover such modifications as would fall within the true scope and spirit of the present invention.

What is claimed is:

1. A collapsible device, comprising:

a panel having a central portion and a perimeter sleeve, said panel being permeable to a liquid;

a spring coupled substantially around the perimeter of the panel and moveable between a coiled and an uncoiled configuration, said spring being coiled while in a collapsed configuration and being uncoiled while in an expanded configuration; and

an inflatable bladder disposed circumferentially about, and being encapsulated within, at least a portion of said perimeter sleeve, said inflatable bladder configured to support a body weight of a user disposed on the panel.

2. A collapsible floatation device, comprising:

a panel having a central portion and a perimeter portion;

a coilable spring coupled substantially around the perimeter of the panel, said spring being coiled while in a collapsed configuration and being uncoiled while in an expanded configuration; and

an inflatable bladder disposed circumferentially about, and being coupled to, the panel and configured to support a body weight of a user disposed on the panel.

3. The collapsible floatation device of claim **2**, wherein said inflatable bladder is encapsulated within a perimeter sleeve defined by said perimeter portion.

4. The collapsible floatation device of claim **3**, wherein said coilable spring is disposed within at least a portion of said perimeter sleeve.

5. The collapsible floatation device of claim **3**, wherein said coilable spring is disposed within at least a portion of said inflatable bladder.

6. The collapsible floatation device of claim **2**, wherein said coilable spring is coupled to said perimeter portion.

7. The collapsible floatation device of claim **2**, further comprising:

a sleeve extending through said central portion; and

a second inflatable bladder disposed within at least a portion of said sleeve extending through said central portion.

8. The collapsible floatation device of claim **2**, said inflatable bladder being a first inflatable bladder, further comprising:

a pillow section configured to encapsulate a second inflatable bladder.

9. A collapsible device, comprising:

a panel having a central portion and a perimeter sleeve;

a coilable spring coupled substantially around the perimeter of the panel, said spring being coiled while in a collapsed configuration and being uncoiled while in an expanded configuration; and

an inflatable bladder disposed circumferentially about, and being encapsulated within, at least a portion of said perimeter sleeve.

US 6,485,344 B2

5

10. The collapsible device of claim 9, wherein said spring is moveable between a coiled configuration and an uncoiled configuration.

11. The collapsible device of claim 9, wherein said inflatable bladder is configured to support the body weight of a user.

12. The collapsible device of claim 9, wherein said coilable spring is disposed within at least a portion of said perimeter sleeve.

13. The collapsible device of claim 9, wherein said coilable spring is disposed within at least a portion of said inflatable bladder.

14. The collapsible device of claim 9, wherein said coilable spring is coupled outside of said perimeter sleeve and outside of a perimeter of the panel.

15. The collapsible device of claim 9, further comprising:

a pillow section configured to encapsulate at least a portion of said inflatable bladder.

16. The collapsible device of claim 9, said inflatable bladder being a first inflatable bladder, further comprising:

a pillow section configured to encapsulate a second inflatable bladder.

17. The collapsible device of claim 9, wherein said panel is configured to allow water to flow through said central portion.

18. A collapsible device, comprising:

a panel having a central portion and a perimeter sleeve;

a coilable spring coupled substantially around the perimeter of said panel, said spring being coiled while in a collapsed configuration and being uncoiled while in an expanded configuration; and

a plurality of inflatable bladders disposed circumferentially about, and being encapsulated within, at least a portion of said perimeter sleeve, the plurality of inflatable bladders include a first inflatable bladder and a second inflatable bladder being disposed on opposite sides of the panel.

6

19. The collapsible device of claim 18, wherein said coilable spring is disposed within at least a portion of said perimeter sleeve.

20. The collapsible device of claim 18, wherein said coilable spring is coupled outside of said perimeter sleeve and outside of a perimeter of said panel.

21. The collapsible device of claim 18, further comprising:

a pillow section configured to encapsulate one of said plurality of inflatable bladders.

22. A device, comprising:

a panel having a central portion and a perimeter sleeve;

a spring moveable between a coiled configuration and an uncoiled configuration, said spring disposed within at least a portion of said perimeter sleeve and coupled substantially around the perimeter of said panel such that said panel is collapsed when said spring is in the coiled configuration and said panel is expanded when said spring is in the uncoiled configuration; and

an inflatable bladder disposed circumferentially about, and extending substantially throughout, said perimeter sleeve.

23. A device, comprising:

a spring configured to form a closed loop, the spring being moveable between a coiled configuration when the spring is collapsed and an uncoiled configuration when the spring is expanded, the spring defining an interior area within at least a portion of the closed loop when the spring is in the uncoiled configuration; and

an inflatable bladder coupled to said spring and being disposed circumferentially within said interior area.

24. The device of claim 23, said inflatable bladder defining a second interior area, further comprising:

a panel coupled within said second interior area.

25. The device of claim 24, wherein said panel is permeable to a liquid.

* * * * *

United States Patent [19]

Storey et al.

[11] **Patent Number: Des. 293,012**

[45] **Date of Patent: ** Dec. 1, 1987**

[54] **POOL LOUNGER**

[75] Inventors: **William R. Storey**, Sunnyvale; **Leon H. Tager**, San Carlos, both of Calif.

[73] Assignee: **Poolmaster, Inc.**, Menlo Park, Calif.

[**] Term: **14 Years**

[21] Appl. No.: **785,971**

[22] Filed: **Oct. 10, 1985**

[52] U.S. Cl. **D21/237**

[58] **Field of Search** D12/316; D21/237; 441/129-132, 88, 40, 41

[56] **References Cited**

U.S. PATENT DOCUMENTS

D. 187,313	2/1960	Denyer	441/132
2,623,574	12/1952	Damsch	441/129
3,740,095	6/1973	Nail	441/130

FOREIGN PATENT DOCUMENTS

1432404	2/1966	France	441/131
2462332	3/1981	France	441/130

OTHER PUBLICATIONS

FAO Schwarz, Sprg./Summer, 1974, Cat. p. A, D See-through Aqua Lounge.

FAO Schwarz, Sprg./Summer, 1974, Cat. p. 1, D Sun-Lounge with Pillow.

FAO Schwarz, Sprg./Summer, 1974, Cat. p. 1, E See-thru Aqua Float.

Primary Examiner—James M. Gandy

Assistant Examiner—Kay H. Chin

Attorney, Agent, or Firm—Flehr, Hohbach, Test, Albritton & Herbert

[57] **CLAIM**

The ornamental design for a pool lounger, as shown.

DESCRIPTION

FIG. 1 is a perspective view of a pool lounger showing our new design;

FIG. 2 is a top plan view thereof;

FIG. 3 is a side elevational view thereof;

FIG. 4 is a bottom plan view thereof;

FIG. 5 is a front elevational view thereof.

FIG. 6 is a rear elevational view thereof.

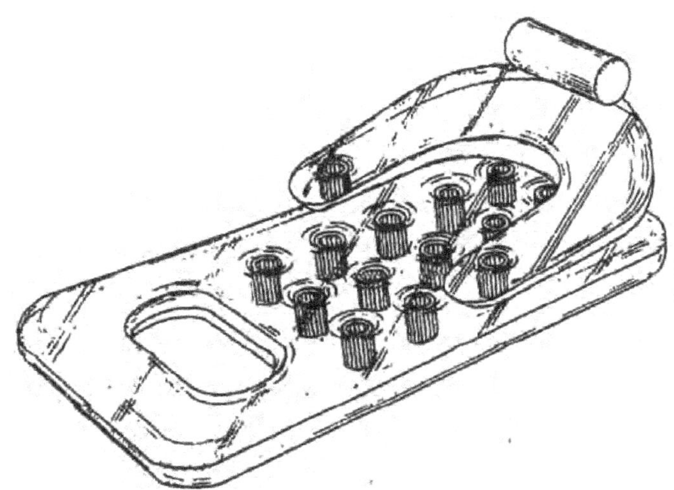

U.S. Patent Dec. 1, 1987 Sheet 1 of 2 **D293,012**

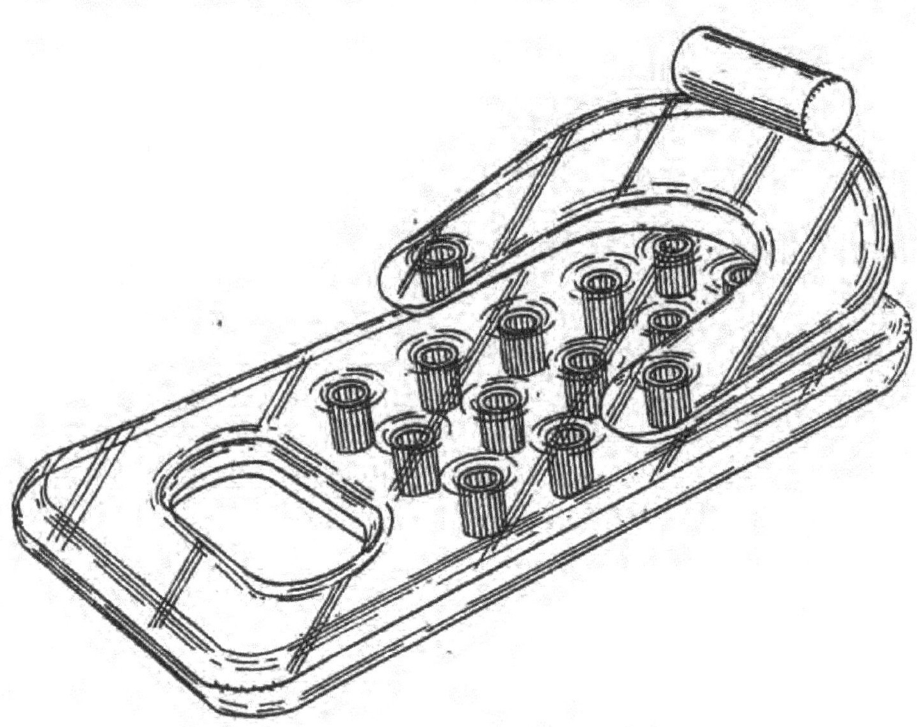

FIG.—1

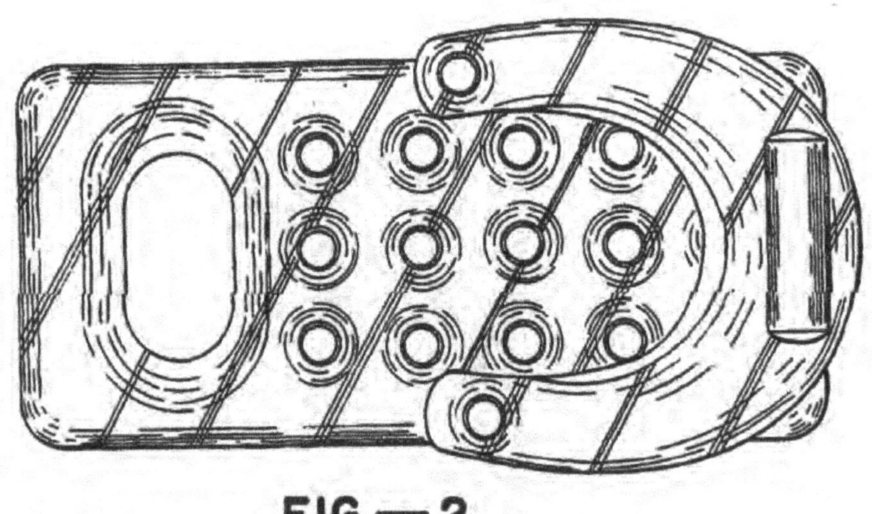

FIG.—2

U.S. Patent Dec. 1, 1987 Sheet 2 of 2 **D293,012**

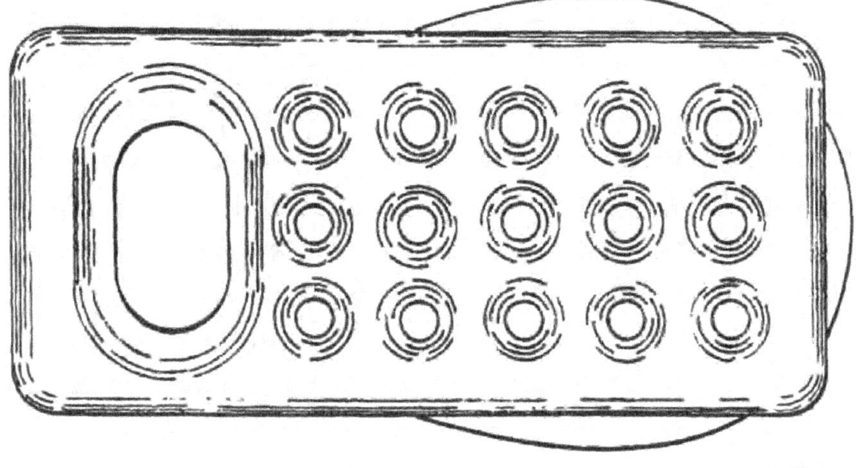

FIG.—4

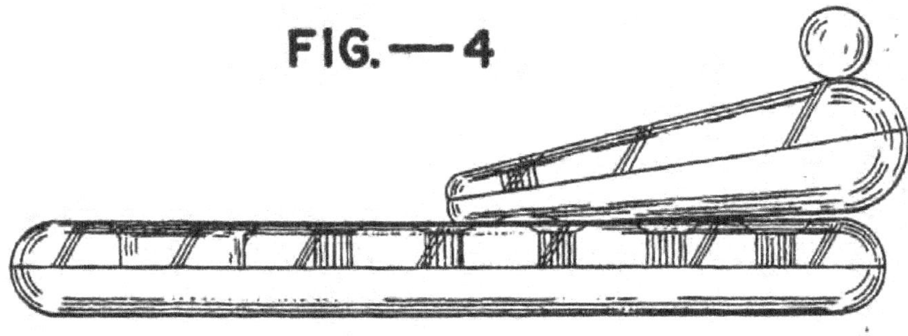

FIG.—3

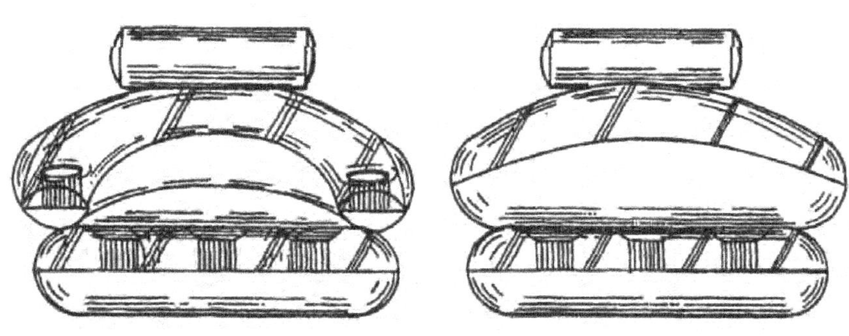

FIG.—5 FIG.—6

UNITED STATES DISTRICT COURT
FOR THE DISTRICT OF NITA

Nita City Division

SWIMTIME CORPORATION, Plaintiff, v. WATER-FUN, INC., Defendant.	)))))))	Civil Action No. 1:Y00-cv-00100

DEFENDANT'S RESPONSIVE EXPERT REPORT ON NON-INFRINGEMENT

I. INTRODUCTION

My name is Drew Clark. I have been retained by counsel for Water-Fun to review materials relating to the above-referenced patent infringement matter and to provide my opinion on whether any claim of U.S. Patent Number 8,197,517 ("the '517 patent") is infringed by the Water-Fun (Holey) Recliner or the Water-Fun (Mesh) Recliner, as these Water-Fun product have been called by SwimTime Corporation's ("SwimTime") expert, Pat Thurman.

I am being compensated at the rate of $600 per hour for my efforts in this matter.

This report is submitted by the undersigned pursuant to Rule 26(a)(2)(B) of the Federal Rules of Civil Procedure.

Photographs of the accused products are provided below.

Water-Fun (Holey) Recliner: Water-Fun (Mesh) Recliner:

[*Note*: To view these images in color, please refer to the CD-ROM accompanying this book.]

II. SUMMARY OF MY OPINIONS

None of claims 1, 2, or 3 of the '517 patent are infringed by the Water-Fun (Holey) Recliner or the Water-Fun (Mesh) Recliner.

III. APPLICABLE LAW

Only a valid patent claim can be infringed and, as I explained in my opening report, each claim of the '517 patent is invalid as anticipated, obvious, or as lacking proper support in the specification of the patent. However, even if any of these claims were not invalid, which is not the case, to be infringed the accused devices would have to incorporate each and every limitation or element of the respective claim, either literally or under the doctrine of equivalents. SwimTime has not alleged infringement under the doctrine of equivalents for any claim element and, thus, here we are only presented with allegations of direct, literal infringement.

A party is liable for direct infringement if he, she, or it, without the authority of the patent holder, makes, uses, offers to sell, or sells the patented invention within the United States; or imports a patented invention into the United States. To prevail with a patent infringement claim, a patent owner must prove that each patent claim element is present or practiced by a preponderance of the evidence by the accused device or method.

In determining whether a claim element is present in an accused device, the claims must be properly construed. Here, the Court has construed the claims of the '517 patent to resolve any disputes over claim meaning or scope. I have applied the Court's construction, where appropriate, and elsewhere read the claims from the perspective of one of ordinary skill in the art as of the invention date. The Court's claim construction was as follows:

> *The Court defines the term "panel" as "a layer of material that is mostly flat, but does not necessarily contain a spring."*
>
> *The Court defines the term "substantially planar" as "mostly flat."*
>
> *The Court determines that no construction of the term "different" is necessary and that this term shall have its plain and ordinary meaning. The plain and ordinary meaning of the term does not require the limitation that different members be dissimilar in character or quality.*
>
> *The Court defines the term "disposed about" to mean "around but not necessarily on all sides."*
>
> *The Court defines the term "seated position" to mean "includes an upright-seated position and reclined seated position, but not a prone position."*
>
> *The Court defines the term "foot support" to mean "a member that supports a user's feet, but not necessarily different or separate from the buoyant member."*

IV. NON-INFRINGEMENT ANALYSIS

A. Claim 1 is not infringed by the Water-Fun (Holey) Recliner or the Water-Fun (Mesh) Recliner.

Claim 1 of the '517 patent states as follows:

> *1. An apparatus, comprising:*
>
> *a panel including an inner portion, an outer portion and a back support portion,*

> *the inner portion of the panel having a first edge and a second edge on an opposite side of the inner portion of the panel from the first edge, a distance between the first edge of the inner portion of the panel and the second edge of the inner portion of the panel defining a width of the inner portion of the panel,*
>
> *the inner portion of the panel being substantially planar across the width of the inner portion of the panel,*
>
> *the back support portion being inflatable; and*
>
> *a buoyant member disposed about at least the inner portion of the panel, at least a portion of the buoyant member being disposed within at least a portion of the outer portion of the panel,*
>
> *the buoyant member having a first portion and a second portion different from the first portion, the first portion of the buoyant member and the second portion of the buoyant member being disposed at opposite locations of the inner portion of the panel and separated by the width of the inner portion of the panel,*
>
> *the inner portion of the panel extending continuously between the first portion of the buoyant member and the second portion of the buoyant member without an intervening buoyant member;*
>
> *at least one of the outer portion of the panel within which the first portion of the buoyant member is at least partially disposed or the first portion of the buoyant member being in contact with the first edge of the inner portion of the panel,*
>
> *at least one of the outer portion of the panel within which the second portion of the buoyant member is at least partially disposed or the second portion of the buoyant member being in contact with the second edge of the inner portion of the panel,*
>
> *the buoyant member having an outermost width that substantially defines an outermost width of the apparatus, the apparatus being configured to support a user in a seated position.*

First, the Court construed "panel" as "a layer of material that is mostly flat, but does not necessarily contain a spring." As is apparent from the photos of the two Water-Fun products, neither is mostly flat. Thus, this limitation is not met.

Second, as is apparent from the photographs of the two Water-Fun products, neither has an edge on it. They are each substantially rounded and generally tubular. Thus, the limitation of "a first edge" and "a second edge" are not met. No limitation requiring an "edge" of any kind is met.

Third, in the Water-Fun products, the floatation device is an internal tube that surrounds the seat portion (there is also a second internal tube that surrounds the foot portion and a third bladder in the seat back), but this internal tube has but one portion. Thus, the limitation "the buoyant member having a first portion and a second portion different from the first portion" is not met.

For at least these reasons, claim 1 is not infringed.

B. Claim 2 is not infringed by the Water-Fun (Holey) Recliner or the Water-Fun (Mesh) Recliner.

Claim 2 of the '517 patent states as follows:

2. An apparatus, comprising:

a panel including an inner portion, an outer portion and a back support portion, the inner portion of the panel including a mesh material,

the panel defining an opening configured to collectively receive a user's legs there-through, the opening being outside the inner portion of the panel,

the back support portion being inflatable; and

a buoyant member disposed about at least a portion of the outer portion of the panel, the buoyant member having a front portion, the front portion of the buoyant member and the back support member being disposed at opposite locations of the inner portion of the panel and separated by a length of the inner portion of the panel,

the front portion of the buoyant member being disposed between the inner portion of the panel and the opening,

the combination of the buoyant member, the panel and the back support portion being collectively configured to support the user in a seated position.

The Court construed "panel" as "a layer of material that is mostly flat, but does not necessarily contain a spring." As is apparent from the photos of the two Water-Fun products, neither is mostly flat. Thus, this limitation is not met.

Also, in the accused products, the front-most part of the buoyant member (there is a single inflatable tube) is not between the opening and the inner portion. Thus, the limitation, "the front portion of the buoyant member being disposed between the inner portion of the panel and the opening," is not satisfied.

For at least these reasons, the Water-Fun products do not infringe claim 2.

C. Claim 3 is not infringed by the Water-Fun (Holey) Recliner or the Water-Fun (Mesh) Recliner.

Claim 3 of the '517 patent states as follows:

3. An apparatus, comprising:

a panel including an inner portion, an outer portion and a back support portion,

the inner portion of the panel including a mesh material,

the panel defining an opening,

the back support portion being inflatable, the mesh material being disposed at least between the back support portion and a support portion defined by the panel;

a buoyant member disposed about at least a portion of the outer portion of the panel, the combination of the buoyant member, the panel and the back support portion being collectively configured to support a user in a seated position; and a foot support disposed at an end portion of the panel, the opening disposed between the foot support and the support portion, the foot support configured to buoyantly support a weight of the user's feet.

The Court construed "panel" as "a layer of material that is mostly flat, but does not necessarily contain a spring." As is apparent from the photos of the two Water-Fun products, neither is mostly flat. Thus, this limitation is not met.

For at least this reason, the Water-Fun products do not infringe claim 3.

V. CONCLUSION

For at least the reasons set forth above, it is my opinion that the claims of the '517 patent are not infringed by the Water-Fun products. I reserve the right to supplement or update my opinions based on subsequent discovery in this case.

Respectfully submitted,

Drew Clark

UNITED STATES DISTRICT COURT
FOR THE DISTRICT OF NITA

Nita City Division

SWIMTIME CORPORATION, Plaintiff,	))	Civil Action No. 1:Y00-cv-00100
	)	
v.	))	
WATER-FUN, INC., Defendant.	))	

PLAINTIFF'S RESPONSIVE EXPERT REPORT ON VALIDITY

I. INTRODUCTION

I, Pat Thurman, am a United States citizen residing in Deaconville, Nita. I have been retained by the Plaintiffs in this case as a technical expert in this action for patent infringement filed against Water-Fun, Inc. ("Water-Fun"). As part of that litigation, Plaintiffs have accused Water-Fun of infringing United States Patent Number 8,197,517 ("the '517 patent"). I have previously provided an expert report ("Infringement Report") that presented in detail my opinions concerning Water-Fun's infringement of the '517 patent.

Water-Fun has submitted an expert report ("Clark Report" or "Clark") in support of its contention that the '517 patent is invalid. This rebuttal report is in response to the Clark Report and is submitted pursuant to Rule 26(a)(2)(B) of the Federal Rules of Civil Procedure. I specifically reserve the right to formulate and offer additional opinions to those given in this report and in my previous Infringement Report based on any additional information or discovery that may be provided or derived; and I likewise reserve the right to supplement my opinions based on future Court rulings, agreements between the parties, and additional evidence submitted by either party either prior to or at trial.

II. BACKGROUND AND QUALIFICATIONS

My background and qualifications as presented in my earlier Infringement Report remain the same as stated therein. The terms of my compensation also remain the same.

III. SUMMARY OF OPINIONS

If asked to testify at trial regarding this matter, I am prepared to explain in detail, with appropriate visual aids, the opinions expressed in this report.

As explained in more detail in the following sections, it is my opinion that, contrary to Clark's conclusions, 1) the prior art relied on by Clark does not disclose each and every limitation of any of the asserted claims of the '517 patent; 2) the prior art relied on by Clark would not have rendered the inventions of any of the asserted claims obvious to a person of ordinary skill in the art at the time the invention was made; and 3) the original written description in the application that issued as the '517 patent would have conveyed to a person having ordinary skill in the art that, at the time of the filing of the patent application, the inventor of the '517 patent had possession of the claimed subject matter as of the filing date. I have analyzed validity using the claim constructions adopted by the Court in its *Markman* Order.

IV. LEGAL FRAMEWORK FOR ANALYSIS

In developing my opinions on the alleged invalidity of the '517 patent set forth herein, I have relied upon the following legal framework.

One of Ordinary Skill in the Art

I understand that claims are interpreted from the perspective of one of ordinary skill in the art at the time of the invention and not from the perspective of the judge, a layperson, those skilled in remote arts, or geniuses in the art at hand.

I further understand that the characteristics of this hypothetical person having ordinary skill in the art should be defined before engaging in any infringement or invalidity analysis. Factors that can be considered in determining the level of ordinary skill in the art include 1) the educational level of the inventor; 2) the type of problems encountered in the art; 3) the prior art solutions to those problems; 4) the rapidity with which innovations are made; 5) the sophistication of the technology; and 6) the educational level of active workers in the field.

For purposes of this analysis, I have considered the characteristics of a person having ordinary skill in the art with respect to the inventions claimed in the '517 Patent, and have concluded that, at a minimum, such a person would have 1) at least two years' experience in designing inflatable products, or 2) a bachelor's degree in industrial design or mechanical engineering.

I am a person having at least this level of skill in the art, and in fact, I possess skill significantly beyond this level as a result of my education and experience, but I understand what such person would know and understand. For example, I have worked with designers and technicians who have little or no formal engineering training, but who have worked with such systems in a design and manufacturing capacity.

Clark identified what he considers to be the skill level of one having ordinary skill in the art as "someone with a competency and skill level comparable to a college degree and at least three to five years' experience in the recreational flotation device industry." If this level of ordinary skill in the art were found to be applicable, my opinion that the asserted claims are not invalid remains unchanged.

Claim Construction

The property right protected by a patent is defined by the claims of the patent, which appear as numbered paragraphs at the end of the text. Each claim stands on its own when determining infringement or validity. These are the "metes and bounds" that define the scope of the property right. Thus, the first step in analyzing either the infringement or validity of a patent claim begins with an analysis of the claim itself, also referred to as "claim construction."

The first step in construing a claim is an analysis of how the claim language would be understood by a person having ordinary skill in the art. To understand the perspective of a person of ordinary skill in the art, one must determine the field of art to which the patent pertains, and then the background of one of ordinary skill in that art. Dictionaries, encyclopedias, and treatises may be used to demonstrate how one skilled in the art would understand a specific term or phrase recited in a claim. Such terms or phrases are also referred to as "claim limitations," because, as discussed below, they limit what is covered by a claim.

After reviewing the precise language used in the claim, the patent specification and prosecution history are reviewed to ensure that they do not alter the way one skilled in the art would understand a claim limitation. At times, the specification might provide further clarification as to the meaning of a claim limitation.

Statements and amendments made by a patent applicant during prosecution of the patent application might provide further clarification as to the meaning of a claim limitation. For example, the applicant may argue that certain prior art raised by the examiner is outside the scope of a claim because it fails to disclose a certain claim limitation. The claims cannot be construed to cover that which was surrendered during prosecution. In addition to the claim language, patent specification, and prosecution history, which are the preferred sources for claim construction, outside sources may be referenced to construe a claim limitation.

Patent Validity—Presumption of Validity

An issued patent is presumed to be valid. A party challenging the validity of a patent can do so only by establishing invalidity on the basis of clear and convincing evidence. Validity, like infringement, is determined on a claim-by-claim basis. Thus, even if certain claims are shown to be invalid, the remaining claims are presumed to be valid until shown otherwise by clear and convincing evidence.

Patent Validity—Prior Art

"Prior art" refers, in some cases, to matters that were known before the filing of the patent application and that therefore can establish that the claimed inventions are not new or were obvious. The patent laws provide that the claims are not new if the invention claimed is disclosed in certain prior art references. This encompasses any printed publication in this or a foreign country as well as any public use or sale in the U.S. of the claimed subject matter.

Patent Validity—Anticipation

A patent claim is invalid as anticipated (i.e., the claimed invention is not new or novel) under section 102 of the Patent Act when a single prior art reference (e.g., a patent or publication) discloses within the four corners of the document every limitation recited in the claimed, arranged or combined in the same way as recited in the claim.

This analysis is very similar to an infringement analysis. In an infringement analysis, the claims are first construed, and then the properly construed claims are compared to the product that is being accused of infringement. If the accused product includes all limitations of the claim combined or arranged as recited in the claim, it infringes that claim. Anticipation analysis is much the same, except that the properly construed claims are compared to a prior art reference, not to the accused product. If that prior art reference teaches all the limitations combined or arranged as recited in the claim in a manner that would enable one skilled in the art to practice the claimed invention, that claim is not new, but is "anticipated" by the prior art reference.

For example, if a claim simply specifies the limitations of A, B, and C, and the accused products contains at least those three elements arranged as required by the claim, then the accused product infringes. Likewise, if a prior art reference teaches at least elements A, B, and C arranged as required by the claim, the claim is anticipated.

For a prior art reference to "teach" the limitations of a claim, a person of ordinary skill in the art must recognize the limitations as disclosed, expressly or inherently, in that single reference and, to the extent the claim specifies a relationship between the limitations, the disclosed limitations must be in the same relationship as recited in the claim. Additionally, a disclosure can "teach" a limitation only if the disclosure of the reference is enabling. This means that a person of ordinary skill in the art, having become familiar with the prior art, must be enabled thereby to practice the invention without undue experimentation.

A prior art reference may anticipate a claimed invention when the claim limitations not expressly found in that reference are nonetheless "inherent" in it. However, a single prior art reference may only anticipate a claimed invention by inherent disclosure when the prior art reference must necessarily include the accused limitation. To establish inherency, the extrinsic evidence (evidence outside the document) must make clear that the missing descriptive matter is necessarily present in the thing described in the reference, and that it would be so recognized by persons of ordinary skill.

Patent Validity—Obviousness

Where a single prior art reference does not disclose all limitations of a claim, that claim may nonetheless be proven invalid as obvious under section 103 of the Patent Act. For a claim to be obvious, all limitations of the claimed invention must be present in one or more prior art references, or in prior art references combined with the knowledge generally possessed by one of ordinary skill in the art. Thus, if a claim specifies the limitations A, B, and C, and one reference shows only A and B, C must be disclosed in a separate and combinable reference or, alternatively, must be part of the knowledge of one of ordinary skill in the art.

An obviousness finding cannot be made solely on the basis that all of the claim limitations are found in the prior art; most inventions are new combinations of known components. Instead, there must be some reason or motive to combine the limitations in the fashion claimed by the invention at issue.

A patent claim is invalid as obvious if the differences between the claimed subject matter and the prior art are such that the subject matter as a whole at the time of the invention would have been obvious to a person having ordinary skill in the art of the subject matter to which the patent claim pertains. It is improper, however, to use hindsight in assessing obviousness.

Finally, even if an invention is found prima facie obvious, this finding can be rebutted upon a finding of sufficient secondary indicia of non-obviousness, sometimes called "secondary considerations," that may have existed at the time of the invention and afterwards, such as:

a. whether the invention was commercially successful as a result of the merits of the claimed invention (rather than the result of design needs or market-pressure advertising or similar activities);

b. whether the invention satisfied a long-felt need;

c. whether others had tried and failed to make the invention;

d. whether others invented the invention at roughly the same time;

e. whether others copied the invention;

f. whether there were changes or related technologies or market needs contemporaneous with the invention;

g. whether the invention achieved unexpected results;

h. whether others in the field praised the invention;

i. whether persons having ordinary skill in the art of the invention expressed surprise or disbelief regarding the invention;

j. whether others sought or obtained rights to the patent from the patent holder;

k. whether the inventor proceeded contrary to accepted wisdom in the field; and

l. whether products embodying the invention have achieved commercial success.

Patent Validity—Written Description

I understand that, to comply with the "written description" requirement of section 112 of the Patent Act, a patent must convey with reasonable clarity to those skilled in the art that, as of the filing date, the inventor was in possession of the full scope of each and every limitation of the claimed invention. I understand that the level of skill required to satisfy the written description requirement varies depending on the nature and scope of the claims and on the complexity and predictability of the relevant technology.

V. BACKGROUND ON THE '517 PATENT AND THE ASSERTED CLAIMS

Summary of the '517 Patent

The '517 patent discloses a collapsible flotation device. Figure 1 of the patent provides a perspective view of a collapsible flotation device 100 according to one embodiment of the invention. The flotation device 100 includes a panel 102 that has an outer portion 101 and an inner portion. The outer portion includes a back support member 110 and a foot support member 112. An inner portion 103 provides a seating area. The inner portion 103 of the panel 102 can be a membrane made from a mesh, or similar material, while the material of the outer portion 101 of the panel 102 can be a nylon, or other suitable material. When the flotation device 100 has a user seated thereon, the inner portion 103 of the panel 102 is partially submerged in water. By using a mesh, or other similar material for the inner portion 103, water can freely pass, thereby partially submerging a user seated in the inner portion 103 of the panel 102. The flotation device 100 can also include a coilable spring 104 to provide rigidity to the flotation device 100 while the flotation device 100 is in an expanded configuration. The flotation device 100 can include a hole or opening 114 through which water may pass or through which a user may place his legs.

Asserted Claims of the '517 Patent

It is my understanding that Plaintiff is currently asserting infringement of claims 1, 2, and 3.

The Court's Claim Construction of Disputed Terms

I have performed my validity analysis using the claim constructions adopted by the Court. Those constructions are summarized below:

> *The Court defines the term "panel" as "a layer of material that is mostly flat, but does not necessarily contain a spring."*
>
> *The Court defines the term "substantially planar" as "mostly flat."*

The Court determines that no construction of the term "different" is necessary and that this term shall have its plain and ordinary meaning. The plain and ordinary meaning of the term does not require the limitation that different members be dissimilar in character or quality.

The Court defines the term "disposed about" to mean "around but not necessarily on all sides."

The Court defines the term "seated position" to mean "includes an upright-seated position and reclined seated position, but not a prone position."

The Court defines the term "foot support" to mean "a member that supports a user's feet, but not necessarily different or separate from the buoyant member."

VI. VALIDITY ANALYSIS

A. Claims 1 through 3 of the '517 Patent are not anticipated or rendered obvious by U.S. Patent No. 3,871,042.

I disagree with Clark's conclusion that U.S. Patent No. 3,871,042 ("the '042 patent") discloses each and every limitation of claims 1 through 3.

The '042 patent discloses a "vehicle" 10 configured to be mounted over an inflatable ring, such as a commonly known inner tube 11. The vehicle construction comprises a ring cuff 12 and a vehicle bottom 13. The vehicle bottom 13 may be fabricated from a suitable mesh fabric. The '042 patent discloses that an object of the invention is to provide an inflatable vehicle having means for planing on water during tow, river floats, surfing, and the like.

The '042 patent at least does not disclose an inflatable "back support portion" or the apparatus "being configured to support a user in a seated position" as recited by claims 1 through 3.

Moreover, in my opinion, it would not have been obvious to a person of ordinary skill in the art to modify the '042 patent to include these limitations. The focus of the '042 patent is on the use of two separate entities: the cuff and common inner tube. The addition of an inflatable back support portion and/or configuring the apparatus to support a user in a seated position would have required the use of a specialized inner tube or an additional back support segment on the cuff.

B. Claims 1 through 3 of the '517 Patent are not anticipated or rendered obvious by U.S. Patent No. 1,960,474.

I disagree with Clark's conclusion that U.S. Patent No. 1,960,474 ("the '474 patent") discloses each and every limitation of claims 1 through 3. The '474 patent discloses an extremely basic "buoyant bathing device" comprising a woven fabric bag that houses a buoyant element such as an inflatable tube.

The '474 patent discloses that one object of the invention is the provision of a water sport device that is designed particularly for use with the inner tubes of automobile tires, whereby such tubes may be readily inserted and removed to and from the device. The '474 patent discloses that another object of the invention is the provision of a water appliance that is simple, compact, and inexpensive in construction, and which when not in use may be completely folded.

The '474 patent at least does not disclose an inflatable "back support portion" or the apparatus "being configured to support a user in a seated position" as recited by claims 1 through 3.

Moreover, in my opinion, it would not have been obvious to a person of ordinary skill in the art to modify the '474 patent to include these limitations. As noted above, one object of the invention is to provide a simple and inexpensive device that can be used with inner tubes of (historic) automobile tires (modern automobile tires do not use inner tubes). The addition of an inflatable back support portion and/or configuring the apparatus to support a user in a seated position would have required a significantly more complex and expensive design and/or the use of specialized inner tubes.

C. Claims 1 through 3 of the '517 Patent are not anticipated or rendered obvious by U.S. Patent No. 6,485,344.

I disagree with Clark's conclusion that U.S. Patent No. 6,485,344 ("the '344 patent") discloses each and every limitation of claims 1 through 3.

The '344 patent discloses a collapsible flotation device that includes a coilable spring and a flexible panel. The coilable spring is disposed within a perimeter pocket along with one or more inflatable chambers. The central portion of the panel can be made from a mesh material. The flotation device can also include a pillow section to provide buoyant support to a user's head.

The '344 patent at least does not disclose an inflatable "back support portion" or the apparatus "being configured to support a user in a seated position" as recited by claims 1 through 3.

Moreover, in my opinion, it would not have been obvious to a person of ordinary skill in the art to modify the '344 patent to include these limitations as they would have greatly changed the character and use of the '344 patent's design, in addition to requiring substantial changes to the design including the provision of additional structural support. Clark does not explain how a person of ordinary skill in the art would have made the required changes or why they would have allegedly been motivated to do so.

D. Claims 1 through 3 of the '517 Patent are not anticipated or rendered obvious by U.S. Patent No. 5,476,404.

I disagree with Clark's conclusion that U.S. Patent No. 5,476,404 ("the '404 patent") discloses each and every limitation of claims 1 through 3.

The '404 patent discloses an inflatable recreational inner tube toy having a seat formed of a toroid-shaped inflatable primary tube 14 formed of a flexible elastomeric material such as rubber. The primary tube has a bottom surface 16, a top surface 18, an inner periphery 20 defining and enclosing a hollow interior, and an outer periphery 221. The seat also includes a plurality of straps 28 extended across the interior in a matrix-type configuration. The seat also includes a generally duckbill-shaped inflatable leg rest. The leg rest is formed of a flexible elastomeric material such as rubber. The leg rest is integrally coupled to and extended outwards from the outer periphery of the primary tube.

The '404 patent at least does not disclose a "panel" and "buoyant member" with the claimed relationship as recited in claims 1 through 3, e.g., the "buoyant member disposed about at least the inner portion of the panel, at least a portion of the buoyant member being disposed within at least a portion of the outer portion of the panel." If, e.g., one attempted to take the primary tube as the "buoyant member," there is no "panel" within which at least a portion of the primary tube is disposed. I also note that the '404 patent was explicitly considered by the examiner during prosecution, who determined that the issued claims were patentable over this reference.

E. Claims 2 and 3 are not obvious over the '042 Patent or the '474 Patent in view of the prior art products with openings.

I disagree with Clark's conclusion that claims 2 and 3 would have been obvious to a person of ordinary skill in the art over the '042 patent or the '474 patent in view of any of the "prior art products with openings."

The '042 patent and the '474, described above, at least do not disclose an inflatable "back support portion" or the apparatus "being configured to support a user in a seated position" as recited by Claims 2 and 3, an "opening" with the characteristics recited in Claims 2 and 3, or a "foot support" with the characteristics recited in Claim 3. Clark cites the "Prior Art Products with Openings," listed in the chart attached to the Clark Report, as allegedly disclosing the "opening" and "foot support" limitations. However, Clark's report fails to describe how these limitation are allegedly met or how the '042 patent or the '474 patent would have been modified in light of the prior art to arrive at the claimed invention.

Furthermore, as described above, the focus of the '042 patent is on the use of two separate entities: the cuff and common inner tube. Modifying the '042 patent's design to include the "opening" and "foot support" limitations would have required the use of a specialized inner tube or additional structure on the cuff. Similarly, the required modifications to the '474 patent's design would have been extensive and would have negated several objects of that invention, e.g., the provision of a device that is simple, inexpensive, and can be used with conventional inner tubes. In my opinion, the proposed combination makes use of impermissible hindsight bias and improperly assumes that a person of ordinary skill in the art would have known the end result to be achieved.

F. Claims 2 and 3 are not obvious over the '042 Patent in view of the Intex King Kool Lounge.

I disagree with Clark's conclusion that claims 1 through 3 would have been obvious to a person of ordinary skill in the art over the '042 patent in view of the Intex King Kool Lounge.

Clark incorporates his prior arguments, and I incorporate my response to those arguments set forth in the previous section. Clark also refers to his claim chart, but fails to provide any further explanation regarding the bases for his opinion. The chart that Clark refers to is only a partial chart. For numerous limitations, the claim chart of his report does not include a corresponding entry for the King Kool Lounge.

In my opinion, the Intex King Kool Lounge at least does not disclose a "panel" and "buoyant member" with the claimed relationship as recited in claim 1, e.g., the "buoyant member disposed about at least the inner portion of the panel, at least a portion of the buoyant member being disposed within at least a portion of the outer portion of the panel"; as recited in claim 2, e.g., "a buoyant member disposed about at least a portion of the outer portion of the panel"; or as recited in claim 3, e.g., "a buoyant member disposed about at least a portion of the outer portion of the panel." The entirety of the King Kool Lounge appears to consist of an inflatable raft, no portion of which is disposed within a separate "panel." Furthermore, the Intex King Kool Lounge does not disclose an inner portion of a panel having a mesh material as required by claims 2 and 3.

G. Claims 1 through 3 are not anticipated by, nor obvious over, the Intex King Kool Lounge.

Clark states his opinion that "in the event that any of the accused products are determined to contain all of the elements of claims 1 through 3 of the '517 Patent, the Intex King Kool Lounge similarly contains all of the elements of those claims." Clark fails to provide any support for this conclusion.

Furthermore, for at least the reasons set forth in the previous section, I do not agree that the Intex King Kool Lounge teaches all of the limitations of any of the asserted claims. Nor do I agree that the Intex King Kool Lounge would have rendered obvious any of the asserted claims.

H. Claims 2 and 3 are not obvious over the '344 patent in view of the prior art products with openings.

I disagree with Clark's conclusion that Claims 2 and 3 would have been obvious to a person of ordinary skill in the art over the '344 patent in view of any of the "prior art products with openings."

The '344, as described above, at least does not disclose an inflatable "back support portion" or the apparatus "being configured to support a user in a seated position" as recited by claims 2 and 3, an "opening" with the characteristics recited in claims 2 and 3, or a "foot support" with the characteristics recited in claim 3.

Clark points to his claim chart as allegedly disclosing the "opening" and "foot support" limitations. However, neither Clark's report nor his claim chart describe how these limitations are allegedly met or how the '344 patent would have been modified in light of the prior art to arrive at the claimed invention. Furthermore, modifying the '344 patent to arrive at the claimed invention would have required extensive modifications to the design, including the provision of additional structure, and would have greatly changed the device's character and use.

In my opinion, the proposed combination makes use of impermissible hindsight bias and improperly assumes that a person of ordinary skill in the art would have known the end result to be achieved.

I. Claims 2 and 3 are not obvious over the '404 patent in view of the prior art products with openings.

I disagree with Clark's conclusion that claims 1 through 3 would have been obvious to a person of ordinary skill in the art over the '404 patent in view of the "prior art products with openings."

The '344, described above, at least does not disclose a "panel" and "buoyant member" with the claimed relationship as recited in Claim 2, e.g., "a buoyant member disposed about at least a portion of the outer portion of the panel"; or as recited in Claim 3, e.g., "a buoyant member disposed about at least a portion of the outer portion of the panel." Nor does the '404 patent disclose an "opening" with the characteristics recited in Claims 2 and 3, or a "foot support" with the characteristics recited in Claim 3.

Clark cites the "Prior Art Products with Openings," listed in the chart attached to his report, as allegedly disclosing the "opening" and "foot support" limitations. However, Clark's report fails to describe how these limitations are allegedly met or how the '404 patent would have been modified in light of the prior art to arrive at the claimed invention.

Furthermore, the toy disclosed in the '404 patent is designed to be towable by a boat, snowmobile, or the like. It would not have been desirable to modify the design to include the claimed opening as this may have made the toy unsuitable for its intended purpose. In my opinion, the proposed combination makes use of impermissible hindsight bias and improperly assumes that a person of ordinary skill in the art would have known the end result to be achieved.

J. Secondary considerations of non-obviousness.

It is my opinion that, even if the subject matter of the claims is found to have been obvious over any of the above-identified combinations of prior art references, it is nonetheless not obvious because of the strong evidence of secondary indicia of non-obviousness, as follows.

The invention of the '517 patent, which is embodied in the SwimTime Spring Float product, was and continues to be very commercially successful as a result of the merits of the claimed invention. The overall configuration of components and features of claims 1, 2, and 3 have made this product a true standout in the industry, which has resulted in millions of dollars of sales and its position as the number-one luxury pool float on the market.

It is quite apparent that Water-Fun specifically copied the invention of the '517 patent and the SwimTime Spring Float. Upon seeing the Spring Float on sale, Water-Fun made the affirmative decision to copy it and sell a competing product, which has itself been quite popular in the marketplace.

The Spring Float has received praise from others in the industry. Retailers, such as Walmart, Kmart, Amazon, Frontgate, Herrington, and others have expressed their appreciation for the Spring Float and noted its good sales in their outlets.

For at least these reasons, the claims of the '517 patent are not invalid.

K. The '517 Patent's claims comply with the written description requirement.

I disagree with Clark's conclusion that the original description in the application that issued as the '517 patent would not have conveyed to a person of ordinary skill in the art that the inventor had invented a device that did not contain a spring for collapsing the device.

As alleged support for his opinion, Clark cites a single excerpt from the specification that describes "[t]he various collapsible flotation devices of the invention" and refers to a spring. In my opinion, Berenson is improperly attempting to limit the claims to a preferred embodiment and disregarding the Court's *Markman* Order, which explicitly held that the "panel" of the claimed invention "does not necessarily contain a spring."

The fact that the preferred embodiments are disclosed as including the feature of a spring would not have suggested to a person of ordinary skill in the art that the inventors were not in possession of an invention that did not include this feature. Nothing in the specification suggests that the inclusion of a spring is essential to the function of the disclosed inflation devices, or that it would not have been possible to construct a flotation device that did not include a spring. To the contrary, in my opinion, a person of ordinary skill in the art would have recognized that the use of a spring was not required to construct a flotation device meeting the limitations of the asserted claims.

In further support of my opinion, I note that the '517 patent's "Field of the Invention" section does not reference a spring, but instead describes the invention as "directed to a collapsible flotation device having a support member that allows a user to float thereon in a seated position." Col 1, ll. 20-25.

I also note that the use of a coilable spring is specifically identified as being exemplary. See, e.g., col. 4, ll. 51-53 ("A rigid support member, or shape-retaining member, 104 (e.g., a coilable spring) is disposed about the outer portion 101 of the panel 102.").

The '517 patent repeatedly describes the invention in broad terms and as encompassing numerous alternative designs. See, e.g., col. 4, ll. 7-9 ("The collapsible flotation device of the invention may also make use of a variety of configurations to provide maximum utility to a user."); col. 4, ll. 24-25 ("The flotation device of the invention can be constructed from a variety of different materials."); col. 10, ll. 44-48 ("Furthermore, it will be appreciated that the choice of materials and size and shape of the various elements of the invention could be varied according to particular design specifications or constrains requiring a flotation device according to the invention.").

Finally, I note that the '517 patent expressly states that the disclosed embodiments are "considered in all respects to be illustrative and not restrictive" and that "[t]he scope of the invention is indicated by the appended claims, rather than the foregoing description...." Col. 14, ll. 49-53.

VII. CONCLUSION

For the reasons discussed and illustrated above, it is my opinion 1) the prior art relied on by Berenson does not disclose each and every limitation of any of the asserted claims of the '517 patent; 2) the prior art relied on by Berenson would not have rendered the inventions of any of the asserted claims obvious to a person of ordinary skill in the art at the time the invention was made; and 3) the original written description in the application that issued as the '517 patent would have conveyed to a person having ordinary skill in the art that, at the time of the filing of the patent application, the inventor of the '517 patent had possession of the claimed subject matter as of the filing date.

Respectfully Submitted,

Pat Thurman

UNITED STATES DISTRICT COURT
FOR THE DISTRICT OF NITA

Nita City Division

SWIMTIME CORPORATION, Plaintiff,	))	Civil Action No. 1:Y00-cv-00100
	)	
v.	)	
	)	
WATER-FUN, INC., Defendant.	))	

PLAINTIFF SUMMARY JUDGMENT MOTION: ISSUES RAISED

Pursuant to Federal Rule of Civil Procedure 56, Plaintiff SwimTime Corporation (SwimTime), by counsel, respectively moves this Court for an order granting summary judgment in favor of Plaintiff on the grounds that:

Issue 1: Defendant Water-Fun, Inc. (Water-Fun) has infringed claims 1, 2, and 3 of U.S. Patent No. 8,197,517 ("the '517 patent");

Issue 2: Claims 1, 2, and 3 of the '517 patent are valid as a matter of law.

UNITED STATES DISTRICT COURT
FOR THE DISTRICT OF NITA

Nita City Division

SWIMTIME CORPORATION, Plaintiff, v. WATER-FUN, INC., Defendant.	)))))))	Civil Action No. 1:Y00-cv-00100

DEFENDANT'S SUMMARY JUDGMENT MOTION: ISSUES RAISED

The defendant, Water-Fun, Inc. ("Water-Fun"), hereby moves for an order granting Water-Fun summary judgment with respect to all remaining claims of the complaint. Water-Fun is entitled to summary judgment as to the single count of the complaint because:

1. Claims 1 through 3 of the '517 Patent are invalid because the invention described in those claims is not disclosed in the patent's written description;
2. Water-Fun's accused products do not infringe claim 1 of the '517 Patent because the accused devices' buoyant member does not have a second portion different from the first portion; and
3. Water-Fun's accused "Mesh" recliner products do not infringe claims 2 and 3 of the '517 Patent because those products do not contain an opening.

(*Note:* If the class chooses to brief and argue summary judgment motions, refrain from reading on until the mock oral argument has taken place. The Court's order on cross-summary judgment motions follows.)

UNITED STATES DISTRICT COURT
FOR THE DISTRICT OF NITA

Nita City Division

SWIMTIME CORPORATION, Plaintiff,	)	Civil Action No. 1:Y00-cv-00100
	)	
v.	)	
	)	
WATER-FUN, INC., Defendant.	)	

COURT'S ORDER ON CROSS-MOTIONS FOR SUMMARY JUDGMENT

This matter comes before the Court on the parties' cross-motions for summary judgment and motions to exclude expert testimony.

For the reasons stated from the bench, the Court orders the following:

1. The Court DENIES the cross-motions for summary judgment.
2. The Court DENIES the motions to exclude expert testimony. Both experts will be permitted to testify, but the Court will not permit either expert to testify to legal conclusions.

It is so ORDERED.

Let the Clerk send a copy of this Order to all counsel of record.

FEDERAL AND NITA STATUTES

The case will follow the Federal Rules of Civil Procedure and Federal Rules of Evidence, as well as the local rules of the E.D. Nita. U.S. patent law will apply.

FEDERAL PATENT ACT (RELEVANT PORTIONS: 35 U.S.C. §§ 101, 102, 103, 271)

35 U.S.C. § 101

Whoever invents or discovers any new and useful process, machine, manufacture, or composition of matter, or any new and useful improvement thereof, may obtain a patent therefor, subject to the conditions and requirements of this title.

35 U.S.C. § 102[1]

(a) Novelty; Prior Art.—A person shall be entitled to a patent unless—

1. Note, pre-AIA (America Invents Act) § 102 may be applied to patents filed prior to March 16, 2013, and reads as follows:

A person shall be entitled to a patent unless—

(a) the invention was known or used by others in this country, or patented or described in a printed publication in this or a foreign country, before the invention thereof by the applicant for patent, or

(b) the invention was patented or described in a printed publication in this or a foreign country or in public use or on sale in this country, more than one year prior to the date of the application for patent in the United States, or

(c) he has abandoned the invention, or

(d) the invention was first patented or caused to be patented, or was the subject of an inventor's certificate, by the applicant or his legal representatives or assigns in a foreign country prior to the date of the application for patent in this country on an application for patent or inventor's certificate filed more than twelve months before the filing of the application in the United States, or

(e) the invention was described in—(1) an application for patent, published under section 122(b), by another filed in the United States before the invention by the applicant for patent or (2) a patent granted on an application for patent by another filed in the United States before the invention by the applicant for patent, except that an international application filed under the treaty defined in section 351(a) shall have the effects for the purposes of this subsection of an application filed in the United States only if the international application designated the United States and was published under Article 21(2) of such treaty in the English language; or

(f) he did not himself invent the subject matter sought to be patented, or

(g)

(1) during the course of an interference conducted under section 135 or section 291, another inventor involved therein establishes, to the extent permitted in section 104, that before such person's invention thereof the invention was made by such other inventor and not abandoned, suppressed, or concealed, or

(2) before such person's invention thereof, the invention was made in this country by another inventor who had not abandoned, suppressed, or concealed it. In determining priority of invention under this subsection, there shall be considered not only the respective dates of conception and reduction to practice of the invention, but also the reasonable diligence of one who was first to conceive and last to reduce to practice, from a time prior to conception by the other.

This Pre-AIA version of § 102 shall be used in case file exercises until the year 2023 (the patent-in-suit has a priority date of February 21, YR-10, thus until February 21, 2023, this priority date will be before the effective date of the AIA).

(1) the claimed invention was patented, described in a printed publication, or in public use, on sale, or otherwise available to the public before the effective filing date of the claimed invention; or

(2) the claimed invention was described in a patent issued under section 151, or in an application for patent published or deemed published under section 122(b), in which the patent or application, as the case may be, names another inventor and was effectively filed before the effective filing date of the claimed invention.

(b) Exceptions.—

(1) Disclosures made 1 year or less before the effective filing date of the claimed invention.—A disclosure made 1 year or less before the effective filing date of a claimed invention shall not be prior art to the claimed invention under subsection (a)(1) if—

(A) the disclosure was made by the inventor or joint inventor or by another who obtained the subject matter disclosed directly or indirectly from the inventor or a joint inventor; or

(B) the subject matter disclosed had, before such disclosure, been publicly disclosed by the inventor or a joint inventor or another who obtained the subject matter disclosed directly or indirectly from the inventor or a joint inventor.

(2) Disclosures appearing in applications and patents.—A disclosure shall not be prior art to a claimed invention under subsection (a)(2) if—

(A) the subject matter disclosed was obtained directly or indirectly from the inventor or a joint inventor;

(B) the subject matter disclosed had, before such subject matter was effectively filed under subsection (a)(2), been publicly disclosed by the inventor or a joint inventor or another who obtained the subject matter disclosed directly or indirectly from the inventor or a joint inventor; or

(C) the subject matter disclosed and the claimed invention, not later than the effective filing date of the claimed invention, were owned by the same person or subject to an obligation of assignment to the same person.

(c) Common Ownership Under Joint Research Agreements.—Subject matter disclosed and a claimed invention shall be deemed to have been owned by the same person or subject to an obligation of assignment to the same person in applying the provisions of subsection (b)(2)(C) if—

(1) the subject matter disclosed was developed and the claimed invention was made by, or on behalf of, 1 or more parties to a joint research agreement that was in effect on or before the effective filing date of the claimed invention;

(2) the claimed invention was made as a result of activities undertaken within the scope of the joint research agreement; and

(3) the application for patent for the claimed invention discloses or is amended to disclose the names of the parties to the joint research agreement.

(d) Patents and Published Applications Effective as Prior Art.—For purposes of determining whether a patent or application for patent is prior art to a claimed invention under subsection (a)(2), such patent or application shall be considered to have been effectively filed, with respect to any subject matter described in the patent or application—

(1) if paragraph (2) does not apply, as of the actual filing date of the patent or the application for patent; or

(2) if the patent or application for patent is entitled to claim a right of priority under section 119, 365(a), or 365(b), or to claim the benefit of an earlier filing date under section 120, 121, or 365(c), based upon 1 or more prior filed applications for patent, as of the filing date of the earliest such application that describes the subject matter.

35 U.S.C. § 103[2]

A patent for a claimed invention may not be obtained, notwithstanding that the claimed invention is not identically disclosed as set forth in section 102, if the differences between the claimed invention and

2. Note, pre-AIA (America Invents Act) § 103 may be applied to patents filed prior to March 16, 2013, and reads as follows:

(a) A patent may not be obtained though the invention is not identically disclosed or described as set forth in section 102, if the differences between the subject matter sought to be patented and the prior art are such that the subject matter as a whole would have been obvious at the time the invention was made to a person having ordinary skill in the art to which said subject matter pertains. Patentability shall not be negatived by the manner in which the invention was made.

(b)

(1) Notwithstanding subsection (a), and upon timely election by the applicant for patent to proceed under this subsection, a biotechnological process using or resulting in a composition of matter that is novel under section 102 and nonobvious under subsection (a) of this section shall be considered nonobvious if—

(A) claims to the process and the composition of matter are contained in either the same application for patent or in separate applications having the same effective filing date; and

(B) the composition of matter, and the process at the time it was invented, were owned by the same person or subject to an obligation of assignment to the same person.

(2) A patent issued on a process under paragraph (1)—

(A) shall also contain the claims to the composition of matter used in or made by that process, or

(B) shall, if such composition of matter is claimed in another patent, be set to expire on the same date as such other patent, notwithstanding section 154.

(3) For purposes of paragraph (1), the term "biotechnological process" means—

(A) a process of genetically altering or otherwise inducing a single- or multi-celled organism to—

(i) express an exogenous nucleotide sequence,

(ii) inhibit, eliminate, augment, or alter expression of an endogenous nucleotide sequence, or

(iii) express a specific physiological characteristic not naturally associated with said organism;

the prior art are such that the claimed invention as a whole would have been obvious before the effective filing date of the claimed invention to a person having ordinary skill in the art to which the claimed invention pertains. Patentability shall not be negated by the manner in which the invention was made.

35 U.S.C. § 112[3]

(a) IN GENERAL.—The specification shall contain a written description of the invention, and of the manner and process of making and using it, in such full, clear, concise, and exact terms as to enable any person skilled in the art to which it pertains, or with which it is most nearly connected, to make and

---

(B) cell fusion procedures yielding a cell line that expresses a specific protein, such as a monoclonal antibody; and

(C) a method of using a product produced by a process defined by subparagraph (A) or (B), or a combination of subparagraphs (A) and (B).

(c)

(1) Subject matter developed by another person, which qualifies as prior art only under one or more of subsections (e), (f), and (g) of section 102, shall not preclude patentability under this section where the subject matter and the claimed invention were, at the time the claimed invention was made, owned by the same person or subject to an obligation of assignment to the same person.

(2) For purposes of this subsection, subject matter developed by another person and a claimed invention shall be deemed to have been owned by the same person or subject to an obligation of assignment to the same person if—

(A) the claimed invention was made by or on behalf of parties to a joint research agreement that was in effect on or before the date the claimed invention was made;

(B) the claimed invention was made as a result of activities undertaken within the scope of the joint research agreement; and

(C) the application for patent for the claimed invention discloses or is amended to disclose the names of the parties to the joint research agreement.

(3) For purposes of paragraph (2), the term "joint research agreement" means a written contract, grant, or cooperative agreement entered into by two or more persons or entities for the performance of experimental, developmental, or research work in the field of the claimed invention.

This pre-AIA version of § 103 shall be used in case file exercises until the year 2023 (the patent-in-suit has a priority date of February 21, YR-10, thus until February 21, 2023, this priority date will be before the effective date of the AIA).

3. Note, pre-AIA (America Invents Act) § 112 may be applied to patents filed prior to March 16, 2013, and reads as follows:

The specification shall contain a written description of the invention, and of the manner and process of making and using it, in such full, clear, concise, and exact terms as to enable any person skilled in the art to which it pertains, or with which it is most nearly connected, to make and use the same, and shall set forth the best mode contemplated by the inventor of carrying out his invention.

The specification shall conclude with one or more claims particularly pointing out and distinctly claiming the subject matter which the applicant regards as his invention.

A claim may be written in independent or, if the nature of the case admits, in dependent or multiple dependent form.

Subject to the following paragraph, a claim in dependent form shall contain a reference to a claim previously set forth and then specify a further limitation of the subject matter claimed. A claim in dependent form shall be construed to incorporate by reference all the limitations of the claim to which it refers.

A claim in multiple dependent form shall contain a reference, in the alternative only, to more than one claim previously set forth and then specify a further limitation of the subject matter claimed. A multiple dependent claim shall not serve as a basis for any other multiple dependent claim. A multiple dependent claim shall be construed to incorporate by reference all the limitations of the particular claim in relation to which it is being considered.

use the same, and shall set forth the best mode contemplated by the inventor or joint inventor of carrying out the invention.

(b) CONCLUSION.—The specification shall conclude with one or more claims particularly pointing out and distinctly claiming the subject matter which the inventor or a joint inventor regards as the invention.

(c) FORM.—A claim may be written in independent or, if the nature of the case admits, in dependent or multiple dependent form.

(d) REFERENCE IN DEPENDENT FORMS.—Subject to subsection (e), a claim in dependent form shall contain a reference to a claim previously set forth and then specify a further limitation of the subject matter claimed. A claim in dependent form shall be construed to incorporate by reference all the limitations of the claim to which it refers.

(e) REFERENCE IN MULTIPLE DEPENDENT FORM.—A claim in multiple dependent form shall contain a reference, in the alternative only, to more than one claim previously set forth and then specify a further limitation of the subject matter claimed. A multiple dependent claim shall not serve as a basis for any other multiple dependent claim. A multiple dependent claim shall be construed to incorporate by reference all the limitations of the particular claim in relation to which it is being considered.

(f) ELEMENT IN CLAIM FOR A COMBINATION.—An element in a claim for a combination may be expressed as a means or step for performing a specified function without the recital of structure, material, or acts in support thereof, and such claim shall be construed to cover the corresponding structure, material, or acts described in the specification and equivalents thereof.

35 U.S.C. § 271

(a) Except as otherwise provided in this title, whoever without authority makes, uses, offers to sell, or sells any patented invention, within the United States, or imports into the United States any patented invention during the term of the patent therefor, infringes the patent.

(b) Whoever actively induces infringement of a patent shall be liable as an infringer.

(c) Whoever offers to sell or sells within the United States or imports into the United States a component of a patented machine, manufacture, combination, or composition, or a material or apparatus for use in practicing a patented process, constituting a material part of the invention, knowing the same to be especially made or especially adapted for use in an infringement of such patent, and not a staple article or commodity of commerce suitable for substantial noninfringing use, shall be liable as a contributory infringer.

An element in a claim for a combination may be expressed as a means or step for performing a specified function without the recital of structure, material, or acts in support thereof, and such claim shall be construed to cover the corresponding structure, material, or acts described in the specification and equivalents thereof.

This pre-AIA version of § 112 shall be used in case file exercises until the year 2023 (the patent-in-suit has a priority date of February 21, YR-10, thus until February 21, 2023, this priority date will be before the effective date of the AIA).

(d) No patent owner otherwise entitled to relief for infringement or contributory infringement of a patent shall be denied relief or deemed guilty of misuse or illegal extension of the patent right by reason of his having done one or more of the following: (1) derived revenue from acts which if performed by another without his consent would constitute contributory infringement of the patent; (2) licensed or authorized another to perform acts which if performed without his consent would constitute contributory infringement of the patent; (3) sought to enforce his patent rights against infringement or contributory infringement; (4) refused to license or use any rights to the patent; or (5) conditioned the license of any rights to the patent or the sale of the patented product on the acquisition of a license to rights in another patent or purchase of a separate product, unless, in view of the circumstances, the patent owner has market power in the relevant market for the patent or patented product on which the license or sale is conditioned.

(e)

(1) It shall not be an act of infringement to make, use, offer to sell, or sell within the United States or import into the United States a patented invention (other than a new animal drug or veterinary biological product (as those terms are used in the Federal Food, Drug, and Cosmetic Act and the Act of March 4, 1913) which is primarily manufactured using recombinant DNA, recombinant RNA, hybridoma technology, or other processes involving site specific genetic manipulation techniques) solely for uses reasonably related to the development and submission of information under a Federal law which regulates the manufacture, use, or sale of drugs or veterinary biological products.

(2) It shall be an act of infringement to submit —

(A) an application under section 505(j) of the Federal Food, Drug, and Cosmetic Act or described in section 505(b)(2) of such Act for a drug claimed in a patent or the use of which is claimed in a patent,

(B) an application under section 512 of such Act or under the Act of March 4, 1913 (21 U.S.C. 151-158) for a drug or veterinary biological product which is not primarily manufactured using recombinant DNA, recombinant RNA, hybridoma technology, or other processes involving site specific genetic manipulation techniques and which is claimed in a patent or the use of which is claimed in a patent, or

(C)

(i) with respect to a patent that is identified in the list of patents described in section 351(l)(3) of the Public Health Service Act (including as provided under section 351(l)(7) of such Act), an application seeking approval of a biological product, or

(ii) if the applicant for the application fails to provide the application and information required under section 351(l)(2)(A) of such Act, an application seeking approval of a biological product for a patent that could be identified pursuant to section 351(l)(3)(A)(i) of such Act, if the purpose of such submission is to obtain approval under such Act to engage in the commercial manufacture, use, or sale of a drug, veterinary biological product, or biological product claimed in a patent or the use of which is claimed in a patent before the expiration of such patent.

(3) In any action for patent infringement brought under this section, no injunctive or other relief may be granted which would prohibit the making, using, offering to sell, or selling within the United States or importing into the United States of a patented invention under paragraph (1).

(4) For an act of infringement described in paragraph (2)—

(A) the court shall order the effective date of any approval of the drug or veterinary biological product involved in the infringement to be a date which is not earlier than the date of the expiration of the patent which has been infringed,

(B) injunctive relief may be granted against an infringer to prevent the commercial manufacture, use, offer to sell, or sale within the United States or importation into the United States of an approved drug, veterinary biological product, or biological product,

(C) damages or other monetary relief may be awarded against an infringer only if there has been commercial manufacture, use, offer to sell, or sale within the United States or importation into the United States of an approved drug, veterinary biological product, or biological product, and

(D) the court shall order a permanent injunction prohibiting any infringement of the patent by the biological product involved in the infringement until a date which is not earlier than the date of the expiration of the patent that has been infringed under paragraph (2)(C), provided the patent is the subject of a final court decision, as defined in section 351(k)(6) of the Public Health Service Act, in an action for infringement of the patent under section 351(l)(6) of such Act, and the biological product has not yet been approved because of section 351(k)(7) of such Act.

The remedies prescribed by subparagraphs (A), (B), (C), and (D) are the only remedies which may be granted by a court for an act of infringement described in paragraph (2), except that a court may award attorney fees under section 285.

(5) Where a person has filed an application described in paragraph (2) that includes a certification under subsection (b)(2)(A)(iv) or (j) (2)(A)(vii)(IV) of section 505 of the Federal Food, Drug, and Cosmetic Act (21 U.S.C. 355), and neither the owner of the patent that is the subject of the certification nor the holder of the approved application under subsection (b) of such section for the drug that is claimed by the patent or a use of which is claimed by the patent brought an action for infringement of such patent before the expiration of 45 days after the date on which the notice given under subsection (b)(3) or (j)(2)(B) of such section was received, the courts of the United States shall, to the extent consistent with the Constitution, have subject matter jurisdiction in any action brought by such person under section 2201 of title 28 for a declaratory judgment that such patent is invalid or not infringed.

(6)

(A) Subparagraph (B) applies, in lieu of paragraph (4), in the case of a patent—

(i) that is identified, as applicable, in the list of patents described in section 351(l)(4) of the Public Health Service Act or the lists of patents described in section 351(l)(5)(B) of such Act with respect to a biological product; and

(ii) for which an action for infringement of the patent with respect to the biological product—

(I) was brought after the expiration of the 30-day period described in subparagraph (A) or (B), as applicable, of section 351(l)(6) of such Act; or

(II) was brought before the expiration of the 30-day period described in subclause (I), but which was dismissed without prejudice or was not prosecuted to judgment in good faith.

(B) In an action for infringement of a patent described in subparagraph (A), the sole and exclusive remedy that may be granted by a court, upon a finding that the making, using, offering to sell, selling, or importation into the United States of the biological product that is the subject of the action infringed the patent, shall be a reasonable royalty.

(C) The owner of a patent that should have been included in the list described in section 351(l)(3)(A) of the Public Health Service Act, including as provided under section 351(l)(7) of such Act for a biological product, but was not timely included in such list, may not bring an action under this section for infringement of the patent with respect to the biological product.

(f)

(1) Whoever without authority supplies or causes to be supplied in or from the United States all or a substantial portion of the components of a patented invention, where such components are uncombined in whole or in part, in such manner as to actively induce the combination of such components outside of the United States in a manner that would infringe the patent if such combination occurred within the United States, shall be liable as an infringer.

(2) Whoever without authority supplies or causes to be supplied in or from the United States any component of a patented invention that is especially made or especially adapted for use in the invention and not a staple article or commodity of commerce suitable for substantial non-infringing use, where such component is uncombined in whole or in part, knowing that such component is so made or adapted and intending that such component will be combined outside of the United States in a manner that would infringe the patent if such combination occurred within the United States, shall be liable as an infringer.

(g) Whoever without authority imports into the United States or offers to sell, sells, or uses within the United States a product which is made by a process patented in the United States shall be liable as an infringer, if the importation, offer to sell, sale, or use of the product occurs during the term of such process patent. In an action for infringement of a process patent, no remedy may be granted for infringement on account of the noncommercial use or retail sale of a product unless there is no adequate remedy under this title for infringement on account of the importation or other use, offer to sell, or sale of that product. A product which is made by a patented process will, for purposes of this title, not be considered to be so made after—

(1) it is materially changed by subsequent processes; or

(2) it becomes a trivial and nonessential component of another product.

(h) As used in this section, the term "whoever" includes any State, any instrumentality of a State, any officer or employee of a State or instrumentality of a State acting in his official capacity. Any State, and any such instrumentality, officer, or employee, shall be subject to the provisions of this title in the same manner and to the same extent as any nongovernmental entity.

(i) As used in this section, an "offer for sale" or an "offer to sell" by a person other than the patentee or any assignee of the patentee, is that in which the sale will occur before the expiration of the term of the patent.

E.D. NITA LOCAL PATENT RULES

P.R. 1—Infringement Contentions.

A party claiming patent infringement must serve on all parties a "Disclosure of Asserted Claims and Infringement Contentions." Separately for each opposing party, the "Disclosure of Asserted Claims and Infringement Contentions" shall contain the following information:

(a) Each claim of each patent in suit that is allegedly infringed by each opposing party;

(b) Separately for each asserted claim, each accused apparatus, product, device, process, method, act, or other instrumentality ("Accused Instrumentality") of each opposing party of which the party is aware. This identification shall be as specific as possible. Each product, device, and apparatus must be identified by name or model number, if known. Each method or process must be identified by name, if known, or by any product, device, or apparatus which, when used, allegedly results in the practice of the claimed method or process;

(c) A chart identifying specifically where each element of each asserted claim is found within each Accused Instrumentality, including for each element that such party contends is governed by 35 U.S.C. § 112(6), the identity of the structure(s), act(s), or material(s) in the Accused Instrumentality that performs the claimed function;

(d) Whether each element of each asserted claim is claimed to be literally present or present under the doctrine of equivalents in the Accused Instrumentality;

(e) For any patent that claims priority to an earlier application, the priority date to which each asserted claim allegedly is entitled; and

(f) If a party claiming patent infringement wishes to preserve the right to rely, for any purpose, on the assertion that its own apparatus, product, device, process, method, act, or other instrumentality practices the claimed invention, the party must identify, separately for each asserted claim, each such apparatus, product, device, process, method, act, or other instrumentality that incorporates or reflects that particular claim.

P.R. 2—Invalidity Contentions.

Not later than forty-five days after service upon it of the "Disclosure of Asserted Claims and Infringement Contentions," each party opposing a claim of patent infringement, shall serve on all parties its "Invalidity Contentions," which must contain the following information:

(a) The identity of each item of prior art that allegedly anticipates each asserted claim or renders it obvious. Each prior art patent shall be identified by its number, country of origin, and date of issue. Each prior art publication must be identified by its title, date of publication, and where feasible, author and publisher. Prior art under 35 U.S.C. § 102 shall be identified by specifying the item offered for sale or publicly used or known, the date the offer or use took place or the information became known, and the identity of the person or entity which made the use or which made and received the offer, or the person or entity which made the information known or to whom it was made known; providing the name of the person(s) from whom and the circumstances under which the invention or any part of it was derived; providing the identities of the person(s) or entities involved in and the circumstances surrounding the making of the invention before the patent applicant(s);

(b) Whether each item of prior art anticipates each asserted claim or renders it obvious. If a combination of items of prior art makes a claim obvious, each such combination, and the motivation to combine such items, must be identified;

(c) A chart identifying where specifically in each alleged item of prior art each element of each asserted claim is found, including for each element that such party contends is governed by 35 U.S.C. § 112(6), the identity of the structure(s), act(s), or material(s) in each item of prior art that performs the claimed function; and

(d) Any grounds of invalidity based on indefiniteness under 35 U.S.C. § 112(2) or enablement or written description under 35 U.S.C. § 112(1) of any of the asserted claims.

UNITED STATES DISTRICT COURT
FOR THE DISTRICT OF NITA

Nita City Division

SWIMTIME CORPORATION, Plaintiff,	))	Civil Action No. 1:Y00-cv-00100
	)	
v.	)	
	)	
WATER-FUN, INC., Defendant.	))	

INSTRUCTIONS TO BE GIVEN PRIOR TO OPENING STATEMENTS

PROPOSED JURY INSTRUCTIONS

WHAT A PATENT IS AND HOW ONE IS OBTAINED

This case involves a dispute relating to a United States patent. Before summarizing the positions of the parties and the issues involved in the dispute, let me take a moment to explain what a patent is and how one is obtained.

Patents are granted by the United States Patent and Trademark Office (sometimes called "the PTO"). A valid United States patent gives the patent holder the right for up to twenty years from the date the patent application was filed to prevent others from making, using, offering to sell, or selling the patented invention within the United States, or from importing it into the United States, without the patent holder's permission. A violation of the patent holder's rights is called infringement. The patent holder may try to enforce a patent against persons believed to be infringers by a lawsuit filed in federal court.

The process of obtaining a patent is called patent prosecution. To obtain a patent, one must first file an application with the PTO. The PTO is an agency of the federal government and employs trained examiners who review applications for patents. The application includes what is called a "specification," which contains a written description of the claimed invention telling what the invention is, how it works, how to make it, and how to use it. The specification concludes with one or more numbered sentences. These are the patent "claims." When the patent is eventually granted by the PTO, the claims define the boundaries of its protection and give notice to the public of those boundaries.

After the applicant files the application, an examiner reviews the application to determine whether the claims are patentable (appropriate for patent protection) and whether the specification adequately describes the invention claimed. In examining a patent application, the examiner reviews certain information about the state of the technology at the time the application was filed. The PTO searches for and reviews information that is publicly available or that is submitted by the applicant. This information is called "prior art." The examiner reviews this prior art to determine whether the invention is truly an advance over the state of the art at the time. Prior art is defined by law, and I will give you, at a later time during these instructions, specific instructions as to what constitutes prior art. However, in general, prior art includes information that demonstrates the state of technology that existed before the claimed invention was made or before the application was filed. A patent lists the prior art that the examiner considered; this list is called the "cited references."

After the prior art search and examination of the application, the examiner informs the applicant in writing of what the examiner has found and whether the examiner considers any claim to be patentable and, thus, would be "allowed." This writing from the examiner is called an "Office Action." If the examiner rejects the claims, the applicant has an opportunity to respond to the examiner to try to persuade the examiner to allow the claims, and to change the claims or to submit new claims. This process may go back and forth for some time until the examiner is satisfied that the application meets the requirements for a patent and the application issues as a patent, or that the application should be rejected and no patent should issue. Sometimes, patents are issued after appeals within the PTO or to a court. The papers generated during these communications between the examiner and the applicant are called the "prosecution history."

The fact that the PTO grants a patent does not necessarily mean that any invention claimed in the patent, in fact, deserves the protection of a patent. For example, the PTO may not have had available to it all other prior art that will be presented to you. A person accused of infringement has the right to argue here in federal court that a claimed invention in the patent is invalid because it does not meet the requirements for a patent. It is your job to consider the evidence presented by the parties and determine independently whether Water-Fun has proven that the patent is invalid.

Summary of Contentions

To help you follow the evidence, I will now give you a summary of the positions of the parties.

The parties in this case are SwimTime Corporation and Water-Fun, Inc. The case involves United States Patent No. 8,197,517, which has been called the '517 patent during this trial, obtained by Eric(a) Flax, Richard Pruitt, August LaCata, Reba Sparks, Leon Holbrook, and Susan Kolb, and transferred by these inventors to SwimTime.

SwimTime filed suit in this court seeking money damages from Water-Fun for allegedly infringing the '517 patent by making, selling, and offering for sale in the United States products that SwimTime argues are covered by claims 1, 2, and 3 of the '517 patent.

The products that are alleged to infringe are the Water-Fun Recliner Fabric Comfort Lounge, called the "Water-Fun Recliner" (in "Holey" and "Mesh" versions) during this trial. Water-Fun denies that it has infringed claims 1 through 3 of the '517 patent. Water-Fun also argues that claims 1 through 3 are invalid. I will instruct you later as to the ways in which a patent may be invalid. In general, however, a patent is invalid if it is not new or is obvious in view of the state of the art at the relevant time, or if the description in the patent does not meet certain requirements.

Your job will be to decide whether or not claims 1, 2, and/or 3 of the '517 patent have been infringed and whether those claims are invalid. If you decide that any claim of the '517 patent has been infringed and is not invalid, you do not need to decide any money damages to be awarded to compensate it for the infringement, as such matters have been stipulated to in advance of trial.

Patent at Issue

I have already determined the meaning of the claims of the '517 patent. You have been given a document reflecting those meanings. For a claim term for which I have not provided you with a definition, you should apply the ordinary meaning. You are to apply my definitions of these terms throughout this case. However, my interpretation of the language of the claims should not be taken as an indication that I have a view regarding issues such as infringement and invalidity. Those issues are yours to decide. I will provide you with more detailed instructions on the meaning of the claims before you retire to deliberate your verdict.

Overview of Applicable Law

In deciding the issues I just discussed, you will be asked to consider specific legal standards. I will give you an overview of those standards now and will review them in more detail before the case is submitted to you for your verdict.

The first issue you will be asked to decide is whether Water-Fun has infringed the claims of the '517 patent. Infringement is assessed on a claim-by-claim basis. Therefore, there may be infringement as to one claim, but not infringement as to another. In general, Water-Fun may infringe the '517 patent by making, using, selling, or offering for sale in the United States, or by importing into the United States, a product or by using a method meeting all the requirements of a claim of the '517 patent.

Another issue you will be asked to decide is whether the '517 patent is invalid. A patent may be invalid for a number of reasons, including because it claims subject matter that is not new or is obvious. For a claim to be invalid because it is not new, Water-Fun must show, by clear and convincing evidence, that all of the elements of a claim are present in a single previous device or method, or sufficiently described in a single previous printed publication or patent. We call these "prior art." If a claim is not new, it is said to be anticipated.

Another way that a claim may be invalid is that it may have been obvious. Even though every element of a claim is not shown or sufficiently described in a single piece of "prior art," the claim may still be invalid if it would have been obvious to a person of ordinary skill in the field of technology of the patent at the relevant time. You will need to consider a number of questions in deciding whether the invention(s) claimed in the '517 patent are obvious.

A patent may also be invalid if its description in the specification does not meet certain requirements. To be valid, a patent must meet the "written description" requirement. In order to meet this written description requirement, the description of the invention in the specification portion of the patent must be detailed enough to demonstrate that the applicant actually possessed the invention as broadly as claimed in the claims of the issued patent. The disclosure of a patent must also meet the "enablement" requirement. To meet this requirement, the description in the patent has to be sufficiently full and clear to have allowed persons of ordinary skill in the field of technology of the patent to make and use the invention without undue experimentation, at the time the patent application was originally filed.

Outline of Trial

The trial will now begin. First, each side may make an opening statement. An opening statement is not evidence. It is simply an opportunity for the lawyers to explain what they expect the evidence will show.

There are two standards of proof that you will apply to the evidence, depending on the issue you are deciding. On some issues, you must decide whether certain facts have been proven by a preponderance of the evidence. A preponderance of the evidence means that the fact that is to be proven is more likely true than not, i.e., that the evidence in favor of that fact being true is sufficient to tip the scale, even if slightly, in its favor. On other issues that I will identify for you, you must use a higher standard and decide whether the fact has been proven by clear and convincing evidence, i.e., that you have been left with a clear conviction that the fact has been proven.

These standards are different from what you may have heard about in criminal proceedings where a fact must be proven beyond a reasonable doubt. On a scale of these various standards of proof, as you move from preponderance of the evidence, where the proof need only be sufficient to tip the scale in favor of the party proving the fact, to beyond a reasonable doubt, where the fact must be proven to a very high degree of certainty, you may think of clear and convincing evidence as being between the two standards.

After the opening statements, SwimTime will present its evidence in support of its contention that the claims of the '517 patent have been and continue to be infringed by Water-Fun. To prove infringement of any claim, SwimTime must persuade you that it is more likely than not that Water-Fun has infringed that claim. This is the preponderance of the evidence standard of proof, which applies to proof of patent infringement.

Water-Fun will then present its evidence that the claims of the '517 patent are invalid. To prove invalidity of any claim, Water-Fun must persuade you by clear and convincing evidence that the claim is invalid.

SwimTime may then put on additional evidence responding to Water-Fun's evidence that the claims of the '517 patent are invalid, and to offer any additional evidence of infringement. This is referred to as "rebuttal" evidence. SwimTime's "rebuttal" evidence may respond to any evidence offered by Water-Fun.

Finally, Water-Fun may have the option to put on its own "rebuttal" evidence to support its contentions as to the invalidity of the claims of the '517 patent by responding to any evidence offered by SwimTime on that issue.

After the evidence has been presented, the attorneys will make closing arguments and I will give you final instructions on the law that applies to the case. These closing arguments by the attorneys are not evidence. After the closing arguments and instructions, you will then decide the case.

Instructions to be Given at the Close of Evidence

Summary of Contentions

As I did at the start of the case, I will first give you a summary of each side's contentions in this case. I will then provide you with detailed instructions on what each side must prove to win on each of its contentions.

As I previously told you, SwimTime seeks money damages from Water-Fun for allegedly infringing the '517 patent by making, using, selling, and offering for sale products that SwimTime argues are covered by claims 1, 2, and 3 of the '517 patent. These are the asserted claims of the '517 patent. The products that are alleged to infringe are those sold as the Water-Fun Recliner Fabric Comfort Lounge, called the "Water-Fun Recliner" (in both a "Holey" and a "Mesh" version) during this trial.

Water-Fun denies that it has infringed the asserted claims of the '517 patent and argues that, in addition, claims 1 through 3 are invalid.

Your job is to decide whether Water-Fun has infringed the asserted claims of the '517 patent and whether any of the asserted claims of the '517 patent are invalid.

Level of Ordinary Skill

In deciding what the level of ordinary skill in the field of [invention] is, you should consider all the evidence introduced at trial, including but not limited to 1) the levels of education and experience of the inventor and other persons actively working in the field; 2) the types of problems encountered in the field; 3) prior art solutions to those problems; 4) rapidity with which innovations are made; and 5) the sophistication of the technology.

The level of ordinary skill in the art will play an important role in several determinations with regard to the '517 patent's infringement and validity, as I will explain in a moment.

Claim Construction—
The Role of the Claims of a Patent

Before you can decide many of the issues in this case, you will need to understand the role of patent "claims." The patent claims are the numbered sentences at the end of each patent. The claims are important because it is the words of the claims that define what a patent covers. The figures and text in the rest of the patent provide a description and/or examples of the invention and provide a context for the claims, but it is the claims that define the breadth of the patent's coverage. Each claim is effectively treated as if it were a separate patent, and each claim may cover more or less than another claim. Therefore, what a patent covers depends, in turn, on what each of its claims covers.

You will first need to understand what each claim covers in order to decide whether there is infringement of the claim and to decide whether the claim is invalid. The law says that it is my role to define the terms of the claims and it is your role to apply my definitions to the issues that you are asked to decide in this case. Therefore, as I explained to you at the start of the case, I have determined the meaning of the claims and I will provide to you my definitions of certain claim terms. You must accept my definitions of these words in the claims as being correct. It is your job to take these definitions and apply them to the issues that you are deciding, including the issues of infringement and validity.

How a Claim Defines what it Covers

I will now explain how a claim defines what it covers.

A claim sets forth, in words, a set of requirements. Each claim sets forth its requirements in a single sentence. If a device or a method satisfies each of these requirements, then it is covered by the claim.

There can be several claims in a patent. Each claim may be narrower or broader than another claim by setting forth more or fewer requirements. The coverage of a patent is assessed claim by claim. In patent law, the requirements of a claim are often referred to as "claim elements" or "claim limitations." When a thing (such as a product or a process) meets all of the requirements of a claim, the claim is said to "cover" that thing, and that thing is said to "fall" within the scope of that claim. In other words, a claim covers a product or process where each of the claim elements or limitations is present in that product or process.

Sometimes the words in a patent claim are difficult to understand, and therefore it is difficult to understand what requirements these words impose. It is my job to explain to you the meaning of the words in the claims and the requirements these words impose.

As I just instructed you, there are certain specific terms that I have defined and you are to apply the definitions that I provide to you. By understanding the meaning of the words in a claim and by understanding that the words in a claim set forth the requirements that a product or process must meet in order to be covered by that claim, you will be able to understand the scope of coverage for each claim. Once you understand what each claim covers, then you are prepared to decide the issues that you will be asked to decide, such as infringement and invalidity.

Claim Interpretation

I will now explain to you the meaning of some of the words of the claims in this case. In doing so, I will explain some of the requirements of the claims. As I have previously instructed you, you must accept my definition of these words in the claims as correct. For any words in the claim for which I have not provided you with a definition, you should apply their common meaning. You should not take my definition of the language of the claims as an indication that I have a view regarding how you should decide the issues that you are being asked to decide, such as infringement and invalidity. These issues are yours to decide.

[The court gives its claim interpretation. This instruction may be divided up into claim-by-claim sub-instructions if the court believes it would be helpful.]

Infringement Generally

I will now instruct you how to decide whether Water-Fun has infringed the '517 patent. Infringement is assessed on a claim-by-claim basis. Therefore, there may be infringement as to one claim but no infringement as to another.

In order to prove infringement, SwimTime must prove that the requirements are met by a preponderance of the evidence, i.e., that it is more likely than not that all of the requirements of infringement have been proved.

Direct Infringement by "Literal Infringement"

There are two types of "direct infringement": 1) "literal infringement" and 2) "infringement under the doctrine of equivalents." In order to prove direct infringement by literal infringement, SwimTime must prove by a preponderance of the evidence—i.e., that it is more likely than not—that Water-Fun made, used, sold, offered for sale within, or imported into the United States a product that meets all of the requirements of a claim and did so without the permission of SwimTime during the time the '517 patent was in force. You must compare the product with each and every one of the requirements of a claim to determine whether all of the requirements of that claim are met.

You must determine, separately for each asserted claim, whether there is infringement. Regular literal infringement means that each required limitation of any given claim is actually (i.e., literally) found in the accused product. If any one or more limitations of a claim are not literally found in the accused product, the accused product may still be found to infringe if those missing limitations are nonetheless found to be present as equivalent features. A feature is equivalent to a claimed limitation if, in the view of the person of ordinary skill in the art at the time of invention, it differs in mere insubstantial ways from the claimed feature, that is, it performs the substantially the same function, in substantially the same way, to achieve substantially the same results.

The prior art may preclude a finding of infringement under the doctrine of equivalents. I will explain what "prior art" is, but, generally speaking, "prior art" is things that were already known or done before the invention. In reaching your decisions in this case, you must use the definition of "prior art" that I provide to you. The doctrine of equivalents cannot allow a claim limitation to stretch so far as to include those things that would have been in or obvious in view of the prior art. If in considering a "hypothetical claims" using equivalents that would cover the accused product literally you find that such a claim would have been anticipated or obvious over the prior art, the doctrine of equivalents will not apply in finding infringement.

Actions taken and arguments made by the patent holder or patent applicant during the prosecution of the patent before the USPTO can also preclude an application of the doctrine of equivalents. Specifically, in order to find equivalents, you must first also find one or more of the following: 1) the amendment that is asserted by Water-Fun to limit the scope of equivalents substituted a broader requirement for a narrower requirement or replaced a requirement of equal scope; 2) the reason for making this amendment was not related to patentability; 3) a person having ordinary skill in the field of technology of the patent at the time of the amendment would not have foreseen the potential substitution of the allegedly "equivalent" alternative for the unmet claim requirement; 4) the reason for the amendment is tangential or relates to some issue other than the assertion of equivalence at issue; or 5) some other reason, such as the shortcomings of language, prevented the applicant from using claim language that included the allegedly "equivalent" alternative. You may not find that the alternative feature of the Water-Fun recliner is an equivalent to an unmet requirement of a claim if that requirement was added to the claim (or to any claim of the '517 patent) by amendment during the prosecution of the applications that led to issuance of the '517 patent, unless you also find that at least one of these factors that I have identified to you.

Invalidity—Burden of Proof

I will now instruct you on the rules you must follow in deciding whether Water-Fun has proven that claims 1, 2, and/or 3 of the '517 patent are invalid. To prove that any claim of a patent is invalid,

Water-Fun must persuade you by clear and convincing evidence, i.e., you must be left with a clear conviction that the claim is invalid.

Prior Art

Prior art may include items that were publicly known or that have been used or offered for sale, publications, or patents that disclose the claimed invention or elements of the claimed invention. To be prior art, the item or reference must have been made, known, used, published, or patented either before the invention was made or February 21, YR-10, or more than one year before the filing date of the patent application. However, prior art does not include a publication that describes the inventor's own work and was published less than one year before the date of invention.

For anticipation:

For the claim to be invalid because it is not new, Water-Fun must show that all of the requirements of that claim were present in a single previous device or method that was known of, used, or described in a single previous printed publication or patent. We call these things "anticipating prior art." To anticipate the invention, the prior art does not have to use the same words as the claim, but all of the requirements of the claim must have been disclosed, either stated expressly or implied to a person having ordinary skill in the art in the technology of the invention, so that looking at that one reference, that person could make and use the claimed invention.

For obviousness:

Even though an invention may not have been identically disclosed or described before it was made by an inventor, in order to be patentable, the invention must also not have been obvious to a person of ordinary skill in the field of technology of the patent at the time the invention was made.

Water-Fun may establish that a patent claim is invalid by showing, by clear and convincing evidence, that the claimed invention would have been obvious to persons having ordinary skill in the art at the time the invention was made in the field of pool accessories.

In determining whether a claimed invention is obvious, you must consider the level of ordinary skill in the field of the invention that someone would have had at the time the claimed invention was made, the scope and content of the prior art, and any differences between the prior art and the claimed invention.

Keep in mind that the existence of each and every element of the claimed invention in the prior art does not necessarily prove obviousness. Most, if not all, inventions rely on building blocks of prior art. In considering whether a claimed invention is obvious, you may but are not required to find obviousness if you find that at the time of the claimed invention there was a reason that would have prompted a person having ordinary skill in the field of the invention to combine the known elements in a way the claimed invention does, taking into account such factors as 1) whether the claimed invention was merely the predictable result of using prior art elements according to their known function(s); 2) whether the claimed invention provides an obvious solution to a known problem in the relevant field; 3) whether the prior art teaches or suggests the desirability of combining elements claimed in the invention; 4) whether the prior art teaches away from combining elements in the claimed invention; 5) whether it would have been obvious to try the combinations of elements, such as when there is a design need or market pressure to solve a problem and there are a finite number of identified, predictable solutions; and 6) whether the change resulted more from design incentives or other market forces. To find it rendered the invention obvious, you must find that the prior art provided a reasonable expectation of success. Obvious to try is not sufficient in unpredictable technologies.

In determining whether the claimed invention was obvious, consider each claim separately. Do not use hindsight, i.e., consider only what was known at the time of the invention. In making these assessments, you should take into account any objective evidence (sometimes called "secondary considerations") that may have existed at the time of the invention and afterwards that may shed light on the obviousness or not of the claimed invention, such as:

a. whether the invention was commercially successful as a result of the merits of the claimed invention (rather than the result of design needs or market-pressure advertising or similar activities);

b. whether the invention satisfied a long-felt need;

c. whether others had tried and failed to make the invention;

d. whether others invented the invention at roughly the same time;

e. whether others copied the invention;

f. whether there were changes or related technologies or market needs contemporaneous with the invention;

g. whether the invention achieved unexpected results;

h. whether others in the field praised the invention;

i. whether persons having ordinary skill in the art of the invention expressed surprise or disbelief regarding the invention;

j. whether others sought or obtained rights to the patent from the patent holder;

k. whether the inventor proceeded contrary to accepted wisdom in the field; and

l. whether the invention has achieved commercial success.

<u>Scope and Content of the Prior Art</u>

In considering whether the claimed invention was obvious at the time it was made, you should consider the scope and content of the following prior art: Intex King Kool Lounge Product; U.S. Patent 6,485,344; U.S. Patent 5,476,404; U.S. Patent 3,871,042; U.S. Patent 1,960,474; U.S. Patent D293,012; U.S. Patent 3,602,930.

In considering whether the claimed invention was obvious, you must first determine the scope and content of the prior art. The scope and content of prior art for deciding whether the invention was obvious includes prior art in the same field as the claimed invention, regardless of the problem addressed by the item or reference, and prior art from different fields that a person of ordinary skill in the art using common sense might combine if familiar so as to solve the problem, like fitting together the pieces of a puzzle. When a party attacking the validity of a patent relies on prior art that was specifically considered by the examiner during the prosecution of the application leading to the issuance of the patent, that party bears the burden of overcoming the deference due a qualified government agency official presumed to have performed his or her job.

Written Description Requirement

The patent law contains certain requirements for the part of the patent called the specification. Water-Fun contends that claims 1 through 3 of SwimTime's '517 patent are invalid because the specification of the '517 patent does not contain an adequate written description of the invention. To succeed, Water-Fun must show by clear and convincing evidence that the specification fails to meet the law's requirements for written description of the invention. In the patent application process, the applicant may keep the originally filed claims, or change the claims between the time the patent application is first filed and the time a patent is issued. An applicant may amend the claims or add new claims. These changes may narrow or broaden the scope of the claims. The written description requirement ensures that the issued claims correspond to the scope of the written description that was provided in the original application.

In deciding whether the patent satisfies this written description requirement, you must consider the description from the viewpoint of a person having ordinary skill in the field of technology of the patent when the application was filed. The written description requirement is satisfied if a person having ordinary skill reading the original patent application would have recognized that it describes the full scope of the claimed invention as it is finally claimed in the issued patent and that the inventor actually possessed that full scope by the filing date of the original application.

The written description requirement may be satisfied by any combination of the words, structures, figures, diagrams, formulas, etc., contained in the patent application. The full scope of a claim or any particular requirement in a claim need not be expressly disclosed in the original patent application if a person having ordinary skill in the field of technology of the patent at the time of filing would have understood that the full scope or missing requirement is in the written description in the patent application.

Enablement

The patent law contains certain requirements for the part of the patent called the specification. Water-Fun contends that claims 1 through 3 of SwimTime's '517 patent are invalid because the specification does not contain a sufficiently full and clear description of how to make and use the full scope of the claimed invention. To succeed, Water-Fun must show by clear and convincing evidence that the '517 patent does not contain a sufficiently full and clear description of the claimed invention. To be sufficiently full and clear, the description must contain enough information to have allowed a person having ordinary skill in the field of technology of the patent to make and use the full scope of the claimed invention at the time the original patent application was filed. This is known as the "enablement" requirement. If a patent claim is not enabled, it is invalid.

In order to be enabling, the patent must permit persons having ordinary skill in the field of technology of the patent to make and use the full scope of the claimed invention at the time of original filing without having to conduct undue experimentation. However, some amount of experimentation to make and use the invention is allowable. In deciding whether a person having ordinary skill would have to experiment unduly in order to make and use the invention, you may consider several factors:

1. the time and cost of any necessary experimentation;
2. how routine any necessary experimentation is in the field of pool accessories;
3. whether the patent discloses specific working examples of the claimed invention;

4. the amount of guidance presented in the patent;
5. the nature and predictability of the field of pool accessories;
6. the level of ordinary skill in the field of pool accessories; and
7. the scope of the claimed invention.

No one or more of these factors is alone dispositive. Rather, you must make your decision whether the degree of experimentation required is undue based upon all of the evidence presented to you. You should weigh these factors and determine whether, in the context of this invention and the state of the art at the time of the original application, a person having ordinary skill would need to experiment unduly to make and use the full scope of the claimed invention.

Glossary

Some of the terms in this glossary will be defined in more detail in the legal instructions you are given. The definitions in the instructions must be followed and must control your deliberations. [*The jury may be given a copy of this glossary.*]

Abstract: A brief summary of the technical disclosure in a patent to enable the U.S. Patent and Trademark Office and the public to determine quickly the nature and gist of the technical disclosure in the patent.

Amendment: A patent applicant's change to one or more claims or to the specification either in response to an office action taken by an examiner or independently by the patent applicant during the patent application examination process.

Anticipation: A situation in which a claimed invention describes an earlier invention and, therefore, is not considered new and is not entitled to be patented.

Assignment: A transfer of patent rights to another called an "assignee" who, upon transfer, becomes the owner of the rights assigned.

Best Mode: The best way the inventor actually knew to make or use the invention at the time of the patent application. If the applicant had a best mode as of the time the application was first filed, it must be set forth in the patent specification.

Claim: Each claim of a patent is a concise, formal definition of an invention and appears at the end of the specification in a separately numbered paragraph. In concept, a patent claim marks the boundaries of the patent in the same way that a legal description in a deed specifies the boundaries of land, i.e., similar to a landowner who can prevent others from trespassing on the bounded property, the inventor can prevent others from using what is claimed. Claims may be independent or dependent. An independent claim stands alone. A dependent claim does not stand alone and refers to one or more other claims. A dependent claim incorporates whatever the other referenced claim or claims say.

Conception: The complete mental part of the inventive act which must be capable of proof, as by drawings, disclosure to another, etc.

Drawings: The drawings are visual representations of the claimed invention contained in a patent application and issued patent, and usually include several figures illustrating various aspects of the claimed invention.

Elements: The required parts of a device or the required steps of a method. A device or method infringes a patent if it contains each and every requirement of a patent claim.

Embodiment: A product or method that contains the claimed invention.

Enablement: A description of the invention that is sufficient to enable persons skilled in the field of the invention to make and use the invention. The specification of the patent must contain such an enabling description.

Examination: Procedure before the U.S. Patent and Trademark Office whereby an examiner reviews the filed patent application to determine if the claimed invention is patentable.

Filing Date: Date a patent application, with all the required sections, has been submitted to the U.S. Patent and Trademark Office.

Infringement: Violation of a patent occurring when someone makes, uses, or sells a patented invention, without permission of the patent holder, within the United States during the term of the patent. Infringement may be direct, by inducement, or contributory. Direct infringement is making, using, or selling the patented invention without permission.

Limitation: A required part of an invention set forth in a patent claim. A limitation is a requirement of the invention. The word "limitation" is often used interchangeably with the word "requirement."

Nonobviousness: One of the requirements for securing a patent. To be valid, the subject matter of the invention must not have been obvious to a person of ordinary skill in the field at the time of the earlier of the filing date of the patent application or the date of invention.

Office Action: A written communication from the examiner to the patent applicant in the course of the application examination process.

Patent: A patent is an exclusive right granted by the U.S. Patent and Trademark Office to an inventor to prevent others from making, using, or selling an invention for a term of twenty years from the date the patent application was filed. When the patent expires, the right to make, use, or sell the invention is dedicated to the public. The patent has three parts, which are a specification, drawings and claims. The patent is granted after examination by the U.S. Patent and Trademark Office of a patent application filed by the inventor which has these parts, and this examination is called the prosecution history.

Patent and Trademark Office (PTO or USPTO): An administrative branch of the U.S. Department of Commerce that is charged with overseeing and implementing the federal laws of patents and trademarks. It is responsible for examining all patent applications and issuing all patents in the United States.

Prior Art: Previously known subject matter in the field of a claimed invention for which a patent is being sought. It includes issued patents, publications, and knowledge deemed to be publicly available, such as trade skills, trade practices, and the like.

Prosecution History: The prosecution history is the complete written record of the proceedings in the PTO from the initial application to the issued patent. The prosecution history includes the office actions taken by the PTO and the amendments to the patent application filed by the applicant during the examination process.

Reads On: A patent claim "reads on" a device or method when each required part (requirement) of the claim is found in the device or method.

Reduction to Practice: The invention is "reduced to practice" when it is sufficiently developed to show that it would work for its intended purpose.

Requirement: A required part or step of an invention set forth in a patent claim. The word "requirement" is often used interchangeably with the word "limitation."

Royalty: A royalty is a payment made to the owner of a patent by a nonowner in exchange for rights to make, use, or sell the claimed invention.

Specification: The specification is a required part of a patent application and an issued patent. It is a written description of the invention and of the manner and process of making and using the claimed invention.

UNITED STATES DISTRICT COURT
FOR THE DISTRICT OF NITA

Nita City Division

SWIMTIME CORPORATION, Plaintiff,	))	Civil Action No. 1:Y00-cv-00100
	)	
v.	))	
WATER-FUN, INC., Defendant.	))	

JURY VERDICT FORM

When answering the following questions and filling out this Verdict Form, please follow the directions provided throughout the form. Your answer to each question must be unanimous. Some of the questions contain legal terms that are defined and explained in detail in the Jury Instructions. Please refer to the Jury Instructions if you are unsure about the meaning or usage of any legal term that appears in the questions below.

We, the jury, unanimously agree to the answers to the following questions and return them under the instructions of this court as our verdict in this case.

Findings on Infringement Claims

(The questions regarding infringement should be answered regardless of your findings with respect to the validity or invalidity of the patent.)

A. Direct Infringement

1. Has SwimTime proven that it is more likely than not that every requirement of any claim of its '517 patent is included in the Water-Fun Recliner product?

Yes _____ No _____

If your answer to question 1 is "yes," list the infringed claims: ____________________.

(If you have not included any one of the asserted claims in this list, go to question 2. If all claims are included, go to question 3.)

B. Infringement under the Doctrine of Equivalents

2. For any claim not found to be literally infringed, has SwimTime proven that it is more likely than not that the accused product includes parts that are identical or equivalent to every requirement of any claim of the '517 patent? In other words, for any requirement that is not literally found in the Water-Fun Recliner product, does the accused product have an equivalent part to that requirement?

Yes _____ No _____

If your answer to question 2 is "yes," list the respective infringed claims: _________________.

Findings on Invalidity Defenses

(The questions regarding invalidity should be answered regardless of your findings with respect to infringement.)

A. Written Description Requirement

3. Has Water-Fun proven that it is highly probable that the specification of the '517 patent does not contain an adequate written description of the claimed invention of any one or more of the asserted claims?

Yes _____ No _____

If your answer to question 3 is "yes," list the invalid claims: _____________________.

B. Enablement

4. Has Water-Fun proven that it is highly probable that the specification of the '517 patent does not contain a description of the claimed invention of any one of the asserted claims that is sufficiently full and clear to enable persons of ordinary skill in the field to make and use the invention?

Yes _____ No _____

If your answer to question 4 is "yes," list the invalid claims: _____________________.

C. Anticipation

5. Has Water-Fun proven that it is highly probable that any claim of the '517 patent was "anticipated," or, in other words, not new?

Yes _____ No _____

If your answer to question 5 is "yes," list the invalid claims: _____________________.

D. Obviousness

6. The ultimate conclusion that must be reached on the obviousness question is whether Water-Fun has proven that it is highly probable that the claimed invention would have been obvious to a person of ordinary skill in the field at the time the patent application was filed.

Do you find that the Water-Fun has proven that it is highly probable that any claim of the '517 patent would have been obvious to a person of ordinary skill in the field at the time the respective patent application was filed?

Yes _____ No _____

If your answer to question 6 is "yes," list the invalid claims: _____________________.

* * *

You have now reached the end of the verdict form and should review it to ensure it accurately reflects your unanimous determinations. The foreperson should then sign and date the verdict form in the spaces below and notify the security guard that you have reached a verdict. The foreperson should retain possession of the verdict form and bring it when the jury is brought back into the courtroom.

Dated: ________________, YR-___

By: ___________________________

Foreperson

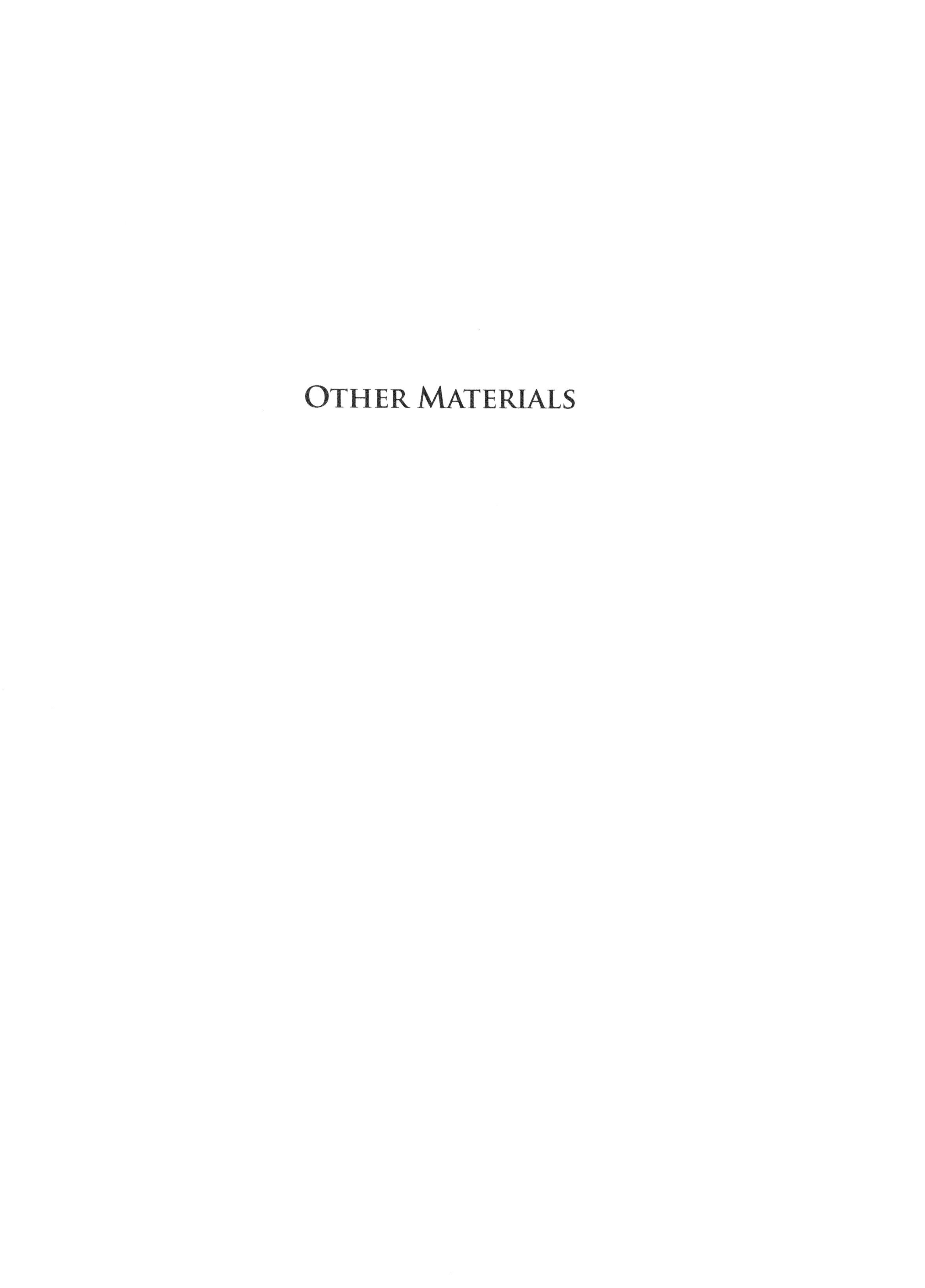

Other Materials

From: Berenson, Glenn (CEO)   Sent: Mon 12/20/YR-4 11:01 AM
To: Kim, Barry (Head R&D)
Cc:
Subject: New Product Design

Message | Photos Spring Float (3MB)

Barry,

Take a look at the attached photos of SwimTime's new product. They call it the "spring float". I just saw it on the shelves at Walmart. Did some checking - this product is everywhere and it's selling like hot cakes. I love the design and apparently so do our customers. Please get cracking on a competitive product. We can't afford to lose any more market share to these guys.

Glenn Berenson
Chief Executive Officer
Water-Fun, Inc

UNITED STATES PATENT AND TRADEMARK OFFICE

UNITED STATES DEPARTMENT OF COMMERCE
United States Patent and Trademark Office
Address: COMMISSIONER FOR PATENTS
P.O. Box 1450
Alexandria, Virginia 22313-1450
www.uspto.gov

APPLICATION NUMBER	FILING or 371(c) DATE	GRP ART UNIT	FIL FEE REC'D	ATTY.DOCKET.NO	TOT CLAIMS	IND CLAIMS
12/123,456	Oct. 15, YR-8	3617	1006	SWIM-016/03US 301393-2256	3	3

CONFIRMATION NO. 6713

58249
Clark Nikole LLP
Attn: Patent Group
Ste. 1000
777 6th Street
Nita City, NT (US)

FILING RECEIPT

Date Mailed: 10/19/YR-8

Receipt is acknowledged of this non-provisional patent application. The application will be taken up for examination in due course. Applicant will be notified as to the results of the examination. Any correspondence concerning the application must include the following identification information: the U.S. APPLICATION NUMBER, FILING DATE, NAME OF APPLICANT, and TITLE OF INVENTION. Fees transmitted by check or draft are subject to collection. Please verify the accuracy of the data presented on this receipt. **If an error is noted on this Filing Receipt, please submit a written request for a Filing Receipt Correction. Please provide a copy of this Filing Receipt with the changes noted thereon. If you received a "Notice to File Missing Parts" for this application, please submit any corrections to this Filing Receipt with your reply to the Notice. When the USPTO processes the reply to the Notice, the USPTO will generate another Filing Receipt incorporating the requested corrections**

Applicant(s)
Eric Flax, Nita City, NT (US);
Richard Pruitt, Nita City, NT (US);
August LaCata, Nita City, NT (US);
Reba Sparks, Nita City, NT (US);
Leon Holbrook, Nita City, NT (US);
Susan Kolb, Nita City, NT (US)

Power of Attorney: None

Domestic Priority data as claimed by applicant
This application is a CON of 11/234,567 **05/31**YR-9 **PAT** 4,249,454
which is a CON of 10/345,678 **02/21**YR-10**PAT** 3,401,020

Foreign Applications

If Required, Foreign Filing License Granted: Oct. 15, YR-8

The country code and number of your priority application, to be used for filing abroad under the Paris Convention, is **US** 12/123,456

Projected Publication Date: Sep. 16, YR-7

Non-Publication Request: No

Early Publication Request: No
**** SMALL ENTITY ****

page 1 of 3

UNITED STATES PATENT AND TRADEMARK OFFICE

UNITED STATES DEPARTMENT OF COMMERCE
United States Patent and Trademark Office
Address: COMMISSIONER FOR PATENTS
P.O. Box 1450
Alexandria, Virginia 22313-1450
www.uspto.gov

APPLICATION NO.	FILING DATE	FIRST NAMED INVENTOR	ATTORNEY DOCKET NO.	CONFIRMATION NO.
12/123,456	Oct. 15, YR-8	Eric Flax	SWIM-016/03US 301393-2256	6713

58249 7590
Clark Nikole LLP
Attn: Patent Group
Ste. 1000
777 6th Street
Nita City, NT (US)

EXAMINER	
VENNE, DANIEL V	

ART UNIT	PAPER NUMBER
3617	

MAIL DATE	DELIVERY MODE
12/19/YR-8	PAPER

Please find below and/or attached an Office communication concerning this application or proceeding.

The time period for reply, if any, is set in the attached communication.

PTOL-90A (Rev. 04/07)

Office Action Summary	Application No.	Applicant(s)	
	12/123,456	Flax et al.	
	Examiner	Art Unit	
	DANIEL V. VENNE	3617	

-- The MAILING DATE of this communication appears on the cover sheet with the correspondence address --

Period for Reply

A SHORTENED STATUTORY PERIOD FOR REPLY IS SET TO EXPIRE 3 MONTH(S) OR THIRTY (30) DAYS, WHICHEVER IS LONGER, FROM THE MAILING DATE OF THIS COMMUNICATION.

- Extensions of time may be available under the provisions of 37 CFR 1.136(a). In no event, however, may a reply be timely filed after SIX (6) MONTHS from the mailing date of this communication.
- If NO period for reply is specified above, the maximum statutory period will apply and will expire SIX (6) MONTHS from the mailing date of this communication.
- Failure to reply within the set or extended period for reply will, by statute, cause the application to become ABANDONED (35 U.S.C. § 133). Any reply received by the Office later than three months after the mailing date of this communication, even if timely filed, may reduce any earned patent term adjustment. See 37 CFR 1.704(b).

Status

1)☒ Responsive to communication(s) filed on Oct. 15, YR-8

2a)☐ This action is **FINAL**. 2b)☒ This action is non-final.

3)☐ Since this application is in condition for allowance except for formal matters, prosecution as to the merits is closed in accordance with the practice under *Ex parte Quayle*, 1935 C.D. 11, 453 O.G. 213.

Disposition of Claims

4)☒ Claim(s) 1-3 is/are pending in the application.

4a) Of the above claim(s) _____ is/are withdrawn from consideration.

5)☐ Claim(s) _____ is/are allowed.

6)☒ Claim(s) 1-3 is/are rejected.

7)☐ Claim(s) _____ is/are objected to.

8)☐ Claim(s) _____ are subject to restriction and/or election requirement.

Application Papers

9)☐ The specification is objected to by the Examiner.

10)☒ The drawing(s) filed on Oct. 15, YR-8 is/are: a)☒ accepted or b)☐ objected to by the Examiner.

Applicant may not request that any objection to the drawing(s) be held in abeyance. See 37 CFR 1.85(a).

Replacement drawing sheet(s) including the correction is required if the drawing(s) is objected to. See 37 CFR 1.121(d).

11)☐ The oath or declaration is objected to by the Examiner. Note the attached Office Action or form PTO-152.

Priority under 35 U.S.C. § 119

12)☐ Acknowledgment is made of a claim for foreign priority under 35 U.S.C. § 119(a)-(d) or (f).

a)☐ All b)☐ Some * c)☐ None of:

1.☐ Certified copies of the priority documents have been received.

2.☐ Certified copies of the priority documents have been received in Application No. _____.

3.☐ Copies of the certified copies of the priority documents have been received in this National Stage application from the International Bureau (PCT Rule 17.2(a)).

* See the attached detailed Office action for a list of the certified copies not received.

Attachment(s)

1)☒ Notice of References Cited (PTO-892)

2)☐ Notice of Draftsperson's Patent Drawing Review (PTO-948)

3)☒ Information Disclosure Statement(s) (PTO/SB/08)
Paper No(s)/Mail Date Oct. 15, YR-8

4)☐ Interview Summary (PTO-413)
Paper No(s)/Mail Date _____

5)☐ Notice of Informal Patent Application

6)☐ Other _____

U.S. Patent and Trademark Office
PTOL-326 (Rev. 08-06) **Office Action Summary** Part of Paper No./Mail Date 1219YR-8

Application/Control Number: 12/123,456 Page 2
Art Unit: 3617

DETAILED ACTION

1. This application is a continuation of application 11/234,567 which is now U.S. Patent 4,249,454 .

2. Claims 1-23 are pending in the application.

Double Patenting

3. The nonstatutory double patenting rejection is based on a judicially created doctrine grounded in public policy (a policy reflected in the statute) so as to prevent the unjustified or improper timewise extension of the "right to exclude" granted by a patent and to prevent possible harassment by multiple assignees. A nonstatutory obviousness-type double patenting rejection is appropriate where the conflicting claims are not identical, but at least one examined application claim is not patentably distinct from the reference claim(s) because the examined application claim is either anticipated by, or would have been obvious over, the reference claim(s). See, e.g., *In re Berg*, 140 F.3d 1428, 46 USPQ2d 1226 (Fed. Cir. 1998); *In re Goodman*, 11 F.3d 1046, 29 USPQ2d 2010 (Fed. Cir. 1993); *In re Longi*, 759 F.2d 887, 225 USPQ 645 (Fed. Cir. 1985); *In re Van Ornum*, 686 F.2d 937, 214 USPQ 761 (CCPA 1982); *In re Vogel*, 422 F.2d 438, 164 USPQ 619 (CCPA 1970); and *In re Thorington*, 418 F.2d 528, 163 USPQ 644 (CCPA 1969).

A timely filed terminal disclaimer in compliance with 37 CFR 1.321(c) or 1.321(d) may be used to overcome an actual or provisional rejection based on a nonstatutory double patenting ground provided the conflicting application or patent either is shown to

Application/Control Number: 12/123,456 Page 3
Art Unit: 3617

be commonly owned with this application, or claims an invention made as a result of activities undertaken within the scope of a joint research agreement.

Effective January 1, 1994, a registered attorney or agent of record may sign a terminal disclaimer. A terminal disclaimer signed by the assignee must fully comply with 37 CFR 3.73(b).

4. Claims 1-3 of the present application are rejected on the ground of nonstatutory obviousness-type double patenting as being unpatentable over claims 1-36 of U.S. Patent No. 4,249,454 . Although the conflicting claims are not identical, they are not patentably distinct from each other because claims 1-3 of the present application are generic to all that is recited in claims 1-36 of US 4,249,454 . Thus, claims 1-36 of US 4,249,454 fully encompass the subject matter of claims 1-23 of the present application. Since claims 1-23 are fully encompassed and/or anticipated by claims 1-36 of US 4,249,454 , claims 1-23 of the present application are not patentably distinct from claims 1-36 of US 4,249,454 , regardless of any additional subject matter presented in claims 1-36 of US 4,249,454 .

Obviousness

The following is a quotation of 35 U.S.C. 103 which forms the basis for all obviousness rejections set forth in this Office action:

> A patent for a claimed invention may not be obtained, notwithstanding that the claimed invention is not identically disclosed as set forth in section 102 of this title, if the differences between the claimed invention and the prior art are such that the claimed invention as a whole would have been obvious before the effective filing date of the claimed invention to a person having ordinary skill in the art to which the claimed invention pertains. Patentability shall not be negated by the manner in which the invention was made.

5. Claims 1-3 of the present application are rejected as being drawn to obvious subject matter in view of U.S. Patent 5,476,404 to Price. Price, at figure 3 discloses the recited panel (14) with inner and outer portions, the inner portion having a first and second edge that define a width. The Price device is inflatable and is intended to support a person in

Application/Control Number: 12/123,456 **Page 4**
Art Unit: 3617

water in a seated position. A buoyant member is disposed within the panel and has a first portion (44 or 14) and a second portion (14 or 30) (alternatively, the first and second portions of the Price apparatus could be the left and right sides thereof). A panel extends between these portions without an intervening buoyant member (28).

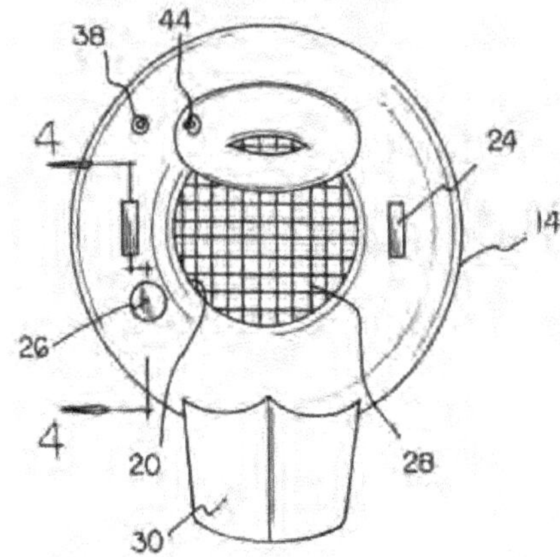

6. The Price apparatus is also disclosed to have the buoyant member in contact with a first edge and second edge of the inner panel as shown in figure 3. Price also discloses a foot support (30) and mesh material as the panel seat (28).
7. The price apparatus also discloses a hole (26) as recited by claim 3.
8. It would have been obvious to combine Price with the abundance of prior art, e.g., U.S. Patent D293,012 to add a foot rest hole, as recited by claim 2. There would have been motivation to do so based on knowledge of those of skill in the art.
9. Price, alone or in combination, renders the claims obvious. Claims 1-3 are unpatentable as obvious under 35 U.S.C. § 103(a) over Price.

Conclusion

10. **The prior art cited and not relied upon is considered pertinent to applicant's disclosure. Ziegenfuss, Jr. (US 5004296) discloses a panel (lounge chair) with buoyant member, back support and foot support.**

Application/Control Number: 12/123,456 Page 5
Art Unit: 3617

Any inquiry concerning this communication or earlier communications from the examiner should be directed to Daniel V. Venne whose telephone number is (571) 272-7947. The examiner can normally be reached between 7:30AM - 4:00PM. If attempts to reach the examiner by telephone are unsuccessful, the examiner's supervisor, Samuel J. Morano can be reached on (571) 272-6684. The fax phone number for the organization where this application or proceeding is assigned is 571-273-8300. Information regarding the status of an application may be obtained from the Patent Application Information Retrieval (PAIR) system. Status information for published applications may be obtained from either Private PAIR or Public PAIR. Status information for unpublished applications is available through Private PAIR only. For more information about the PAIR system, see http://pair-direct.uspto.gov. Should you have questions on access to the Private PAIR system, contact the Electronic Business Center (EBC) at 866-217-9197 (toll-free). If you would like assistance from a USPTO Customer Service Representative or access to the automated information system, call 800-786-9199 (IN USA OR CANADA) or 571-272-1000.

If you would like assistance from a USPTO Customer Service Representative or access to the automated information system, call 800-786-9199 (IN USA OR CANADA) or 571-272-1000.

/Daniel V Venne/ 12/19/YR-8

Primary Examiner, Art Unit 3617

Attorney Docket No. SWIM-016/03US 301393-2256 **PATENT**

IN THE UNITED STATES PATENT AND TRADEMARK OFFICE

In Re Application of:	Eric Flax et al.	Confirmation No.:	6713
Serial No.:	12/123,456	Group Art Unit:	3617
Filed:	Oct. 15, YR-8	Examiner:	Daniel V. Venne

For: **COLLAPSIBLE FLOTATION DEVICE**

Via EFS
U.S. Patent and Trademark Office
Randolph Building
401 Dulany Street
Alexandria, VA 22314

REPLY UNDER 37 C.F.R. 1.111

In response to the Office Action dated December 19, YR-8 the period for responding to which extends to March 19, YR-7 the Applicants submit the following remarks.

The Applicants do not believe that extensions of time or fees for net addition of claims are required beyond those that are submitted with the electronic filing of this response. However, if additional extensions of time are necessary to prevent abandonment of this application, then such extensions of time are hereby petitioned under 37 C.F.R. § 1.136(a), and any fees required therefore (including fees for net addition of claims) are hereby authorized to be charged to our Deposit Account No. 50-1283.

Amendments to the Specification are on page 2 of this paper.

Remarks begin on page 3 of this paper.

Attorney Docket No.: SWIM-016/03US 301393-2256
Serial No. 12/123,456
Page 2

In the Specification:

Please amend paragraph [0001] of the specification as follows. Additions are shown underlined and deletions are show in strikethrough text. No new matter is added.

[0001] This application is a continuation of U.S. Application Serial No. 11/234,567 filed May 31, YR-9 now U.S. Patent No. 4,249,454 which is a continuation of U.S. Application Serial No. 10/345,678 filed February 21, YR-10now U.S. Patent No. 3,401,020 each of the disclosures of which is incorporated herein by reference in its entirety.

Attorney Docket No.: SWIM-016/03US 301393-2256
Serial No. 12/123,456
Page 3

Remarks

Reconsideration of this Application is respectfully requested. Upon entry of this response, claims 1-3 are pending, with each one of claims 1, 2 and 3 **being the independent claims. The Applicants respectfully request that the Examiner reconsider and withdraw all outstanding rejections. No new matter is added.**

Double Patenting Rejection

Claims 1-3 **were rejected on the ground of nonstatutory obviousness-type double patenting as being unpatentable over claims 1-36 of U.S. Patent No.**4,249,454. **The Applicants have submitted herewith a Terminal Disclaimer to address this rejection. In addition, the Examiner indicated in the Office Action that claims** 1-3 **are pending; however, the Applicants note that claims** 1-3 **were originally-filed with the application and are currently pending. Accordingly, the Applicants have referenced claim** 3 **in this response and in the Terminal Disclaimer submitted herewith. Accordingly, the Applicants respectfully submit that claims 1-** 3 **are in condition for allowance.**

Claims 1-3 were rejected under 35 U.S.C. § 103(a) as directed to obvious subject matter over U.S. Patent 5,476,404 to Price ("Price"). Applicants respectfully traverse this rejection.

Price fails to disclose or render obvious the recited "panel" and "buoyant member" of claims 1-3, notably in the claimed relationship there between.

Independent claims 1-3 each recite that the apparatus includes "a buoyant member disposed about at least the inner portion of the panel, at least a portion of the buoyant member being disposed within at least a portion of the outer portion of the panel." Price discloses only a primary tube, which cannot be both the recited buoyant member and the panel.

Because Price fails to at least disclose these recited features of independent claims 1-3, Applicants respectfully request that the rejection of these claims over Price be withdrawn and the claims be passed on to allowance.

Conclusion

All of the stated grounds of rejection in the Office Action have been properly traversed or rendered moot. Applicants therefore respectfully request that the Examiner reconsider and withdraw all outstanding rejections. Applicants believe that a full and complete response has been made to the outstanding Office Action and, as such, the present application is in condition for allowance. If the Examiner believes that personal communication will expedite prosecution of this application, the Examiner is invited to telephone the undersigned at the number provided.

Prompt and favorable consideration of this Amendment is respectfully requested.

Dated: March 19, YR-7

Respectfully submitted,

By: Bill Bixby
Reg. No. 51,515

Clark Nikole LLP
Attn: Patent Group
Ste. 1000
777 6th Street
Nita City, NT (US)

464115 v1/RE

United States Patent and Trademark Office

UNITED STATES DEPARTMENT OF COMMERCE
United States Patent and Trademark Office
Address: COMMISSIONER FOR PATENTS
P.O. Box 1450
Alexandria, Virginia 22313-1450
www.uspto.gov

NOTICE OF ALLOWANCE AND FEE(S) DUE

Clark Nikole LLP
Attn: Patent Group
Ste. 1000
777 6th Street
Nita City, NT (US)

EXAMINER	
VENNE, DANIEL V	
ART UNIT	PAPER NUMBER
3617	

DATE MAILED: July 4, YR-6

APPLICATION NO.	FILING DATE	FIRST NAMED INVENTOR	ATTORNEY DOCKET NO.	CONFIRMATION NO.
12/123,456	Oct. 15, YR-8	Eric Flax	SWIM-016/03US 301393-2256	6713

TITLE OF INVENTION: COLLAPSIBLE FLOTATION DEVICE

APPLN. TYPE	SMALL ENTITY	ISSUE FEE DUE	PUBLICATION FEE DUE	PREV. PAID ISSUE FEE	TOTAL FEE(S) DUE	DATE DUE
nonprovisional	YES	$755	$300	$0	$1055	10/4/YR-6

THE APPLICATION IDENTIFIED ABOVE HAS BEEN EXAMINED AND IS ALLOWED FOR ISSUANCE AS A PATENT. PROSECUTION ON THE MERITS IS CLOSED. THIS NOTICE OF ALLOWANCE IS NOT A GRANT OF PATENT RIGHTS. THIS APPLICATION IS SUBJECT TO WITHDRAWAL FROM ISSUE AT THE INITIATIVE OF THE OFFICE OR UPON PETITION BY THE APPLICANT. SEE 37 CFR 1.313 AND MPEP 1308.

THE ISSUE FEE AND PUBLICATION FEE (IF REQUIRED) MUST BE PAID WITHIN THREE MONTHS FROM THE MAILING DATE OF THIS NOTICE OR THIS APPLICATION SHALL BE REGARDED AS ABANDONED. THIS STATUTORY PERIOD CANNOT BE EXTENDED. SEE 35 U.S.C. 151. THE ISSUE FEE DUE INDICATED ABOVE DOES NOT REFLECT A CREDIT FOR ANY PREVIOUSLY PAID ISSUE FEE IN THIS APPLICATION. IF AN ISSUE FEE HAS PREVIOUSLY BEEN PAID IN THIS APPLICATION (AS SHOWN ABOVE), THE RETURN OF PART B OF THIS FORM WILL BE CONSIDERED A REQUEST TO REAPPLY THE PREVIOUSLY PAID ISSUE FEE TOWARD THE ISSUE FEE NOW DUE.

HOW TO REPLY TO THIS NOTICE:

I. Review the SMALL ENTITY status shown above.

If the SMALL ENTITY is shown as YES, verify your current SMALL ENTITY status:

A. If the status is the same, pay the TOTAL FEE(S) DUE shown above.

B. If the status above is to be removed, check box 5b on Part B - Fee(s) Transmittal and pay the PUBLICATION FEE (if required) and twice the amount of the ISSUE FEE shown above, or

If the SMALL ENTITY is shown as NO:

A. Pay TOTAL FEE(S) DUE shown above, or

B. If applicant claimed SMALL ENTITY status before, or is now claiming SMALL ENTITY status, check box 5a on Part B - Fee(s) Transmittal and pay the PUBLICATION FEE (if required) and 1/2 the ISSUE FEE shown above.

II. PART B - FEE(S) TRANSMITTAL, or its equivalent, must be completed and returned to the United States Patent and Trademark Office (USPTO) with your ISSUE FEE and PUBLICATION FEE (if required). If you are charging the fee(s) to your deposit account, section "4b" of Part B - Fee(s) Transmittal should be completed and an extra copy of the form should be submitted. If an equivalent of Part B is filed, a request to reapply a previously paid issue fee must be clearly made, and delays in processing may occur due to the difficulty in recognizing the paper as an equivalent of Part B.

III. All communications regarding this application must give the application number. Please direct all communications prior to issuance to Mail Stop ISSUE FEE unless advised to the contrary.

IMPORTANT REMINDER: Utility patents issuing on applications filed on or after Dec. 12, 1980 may require payment of maintenance fees. It is patentee's responsibility to ensure timely payment of maintenance fees when due.

Page 1 of 3

PTOL-85 (Rev. 02/11)

United States Patent and Trademark Office

UNITED STATES DEPARTMENT OF COMMERCE
United States Patent and Trademark Office
Address: COMMISSIONER FOR PATENTS
P.O. Box 1450
Alexandria, Virginia 22313-1450
www.uspto.gov

APPLICATION NO.	ISSUE DATE	PATENT NO.	ATTORNEY DOCKET NO.	CONFIRMATION NO.
12/123,456	Oct. 26, YR-6	US 8,197,517 B2	SWIM-016/03US 301393-2256	6713

58249 7590

Clark Nikole LLP
Attn: Patent Group
Ste. 1000
777 6th Street
Nita City, NT (US)

ISSUE NOTIFICATION

The projected patent number and issue date are specified above.

Determination of Patent Term Adjustment under 35 U.S.C. 154 (b)
(application filed on or after May 29, 2000)

The Patent Term Adjustment is 0 day(s). Any patent to issue from the above-identified application will include an indication of the adjustment on the front page.

If a Continued Prosecution Application (CPA) was filed in the above-identified application, the filing date that determines Patent Term Adjustment is the filing date of the most recent CPA.

Applicant will be able to obtain more detailed information by accessing the Patent Application Information Retrieval (PAIR) WEB site (http://pair.uspto.gov).

Any questions regarding the Patent Term Extension or Adjustment determination should be directed to the Office of Patent Legal Administration at (571)-272-7702. Questions relating to issue and publication fee payments should be directed to the Application Assistance Unit (AAU) of the Office of Data Management (ODM) at (571)-272-4200.

APPLICANT(s) (Please see PAIR WEB site http://pair.uspto.gov for additional applicants):

Eric Flax, Nita City, NT (US);
Richard Pruitt, Nita City, NT (US);
August LaCata, Nita City, NT (US);
Reba Sparks, Nita City, NT (US);
Leon Holbrook, Nita City, NT (US);
Susan Kolb, Nita City, NT (US)

IR103 (Rev. 10/09)

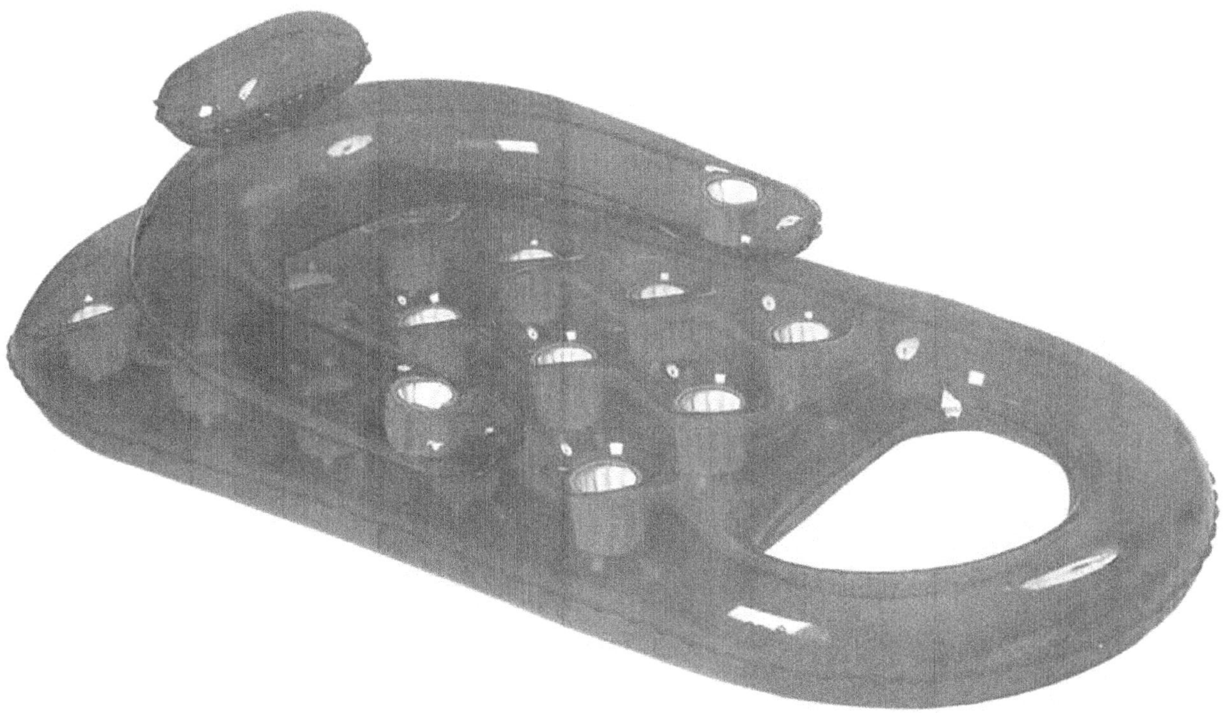

[*Note*: To view this image in color, please refer to the CD-ROM accompanying this book.]

From: Flax, Eric (Head R&D)
To: Miller, Morgan (CEO)
Cc:
Subject: The Spring Float

Sent Mon 3/13/YR-10 9:00 AM

Message

Mr. Morgan,

We've just finished the prototype of the new Spring Float product. Our design is based on the historically most successful pool float designs, but as you've requested, we've up'ed the lux factor by 10. The new products will incorporate an inflatable bladder designed around a spring-based opening system for instant opening and convenient closing by our customers. A simple twist and squeeze will fold the lounges in half for storage in an attractive stow bag and when wanted for use, simply remove from the bag and let it drop - the spring opens the lounge. We've got patent applications directed to the new design, too.

Eric Flax
Head of R&D
SwimTime Corporation

SwimTime

Infringement Demonstratives

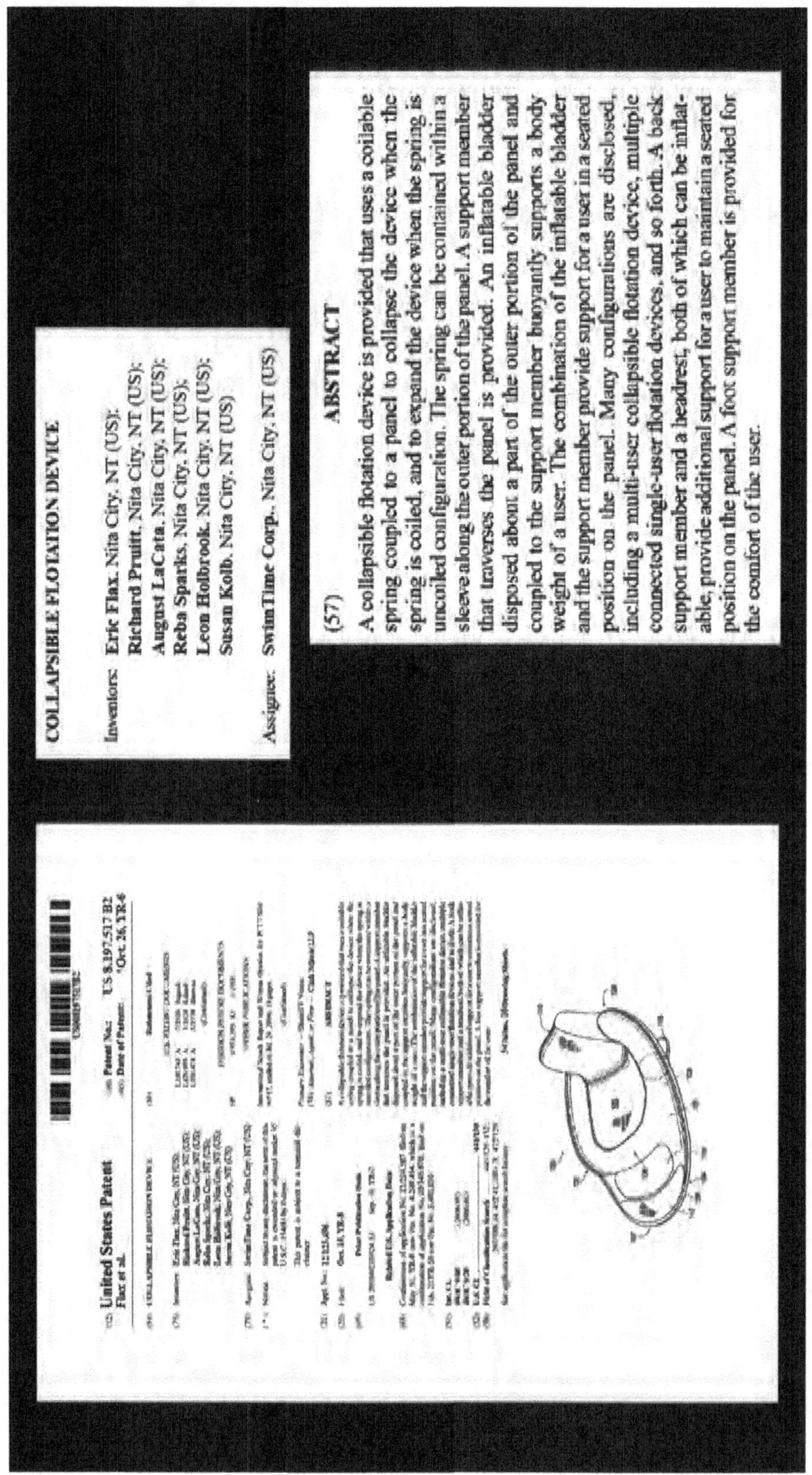

[*Note*: To view the following images in this demonstratives slideshow in color, please refer to the CD-ROM accompanying this book.]

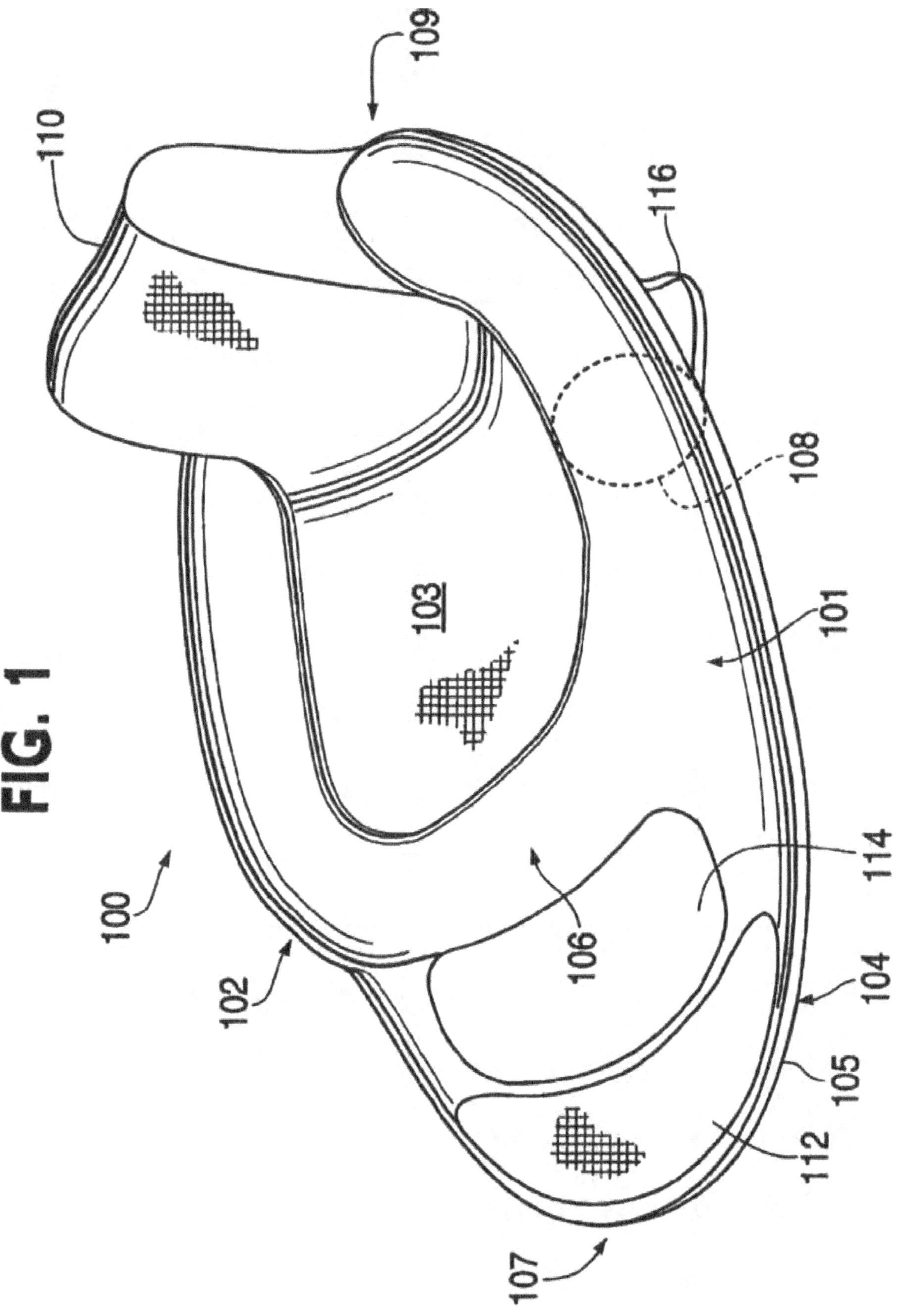
FIG. 1
100
101
102
103
104
105
106
107
108
109
110
112
114
116

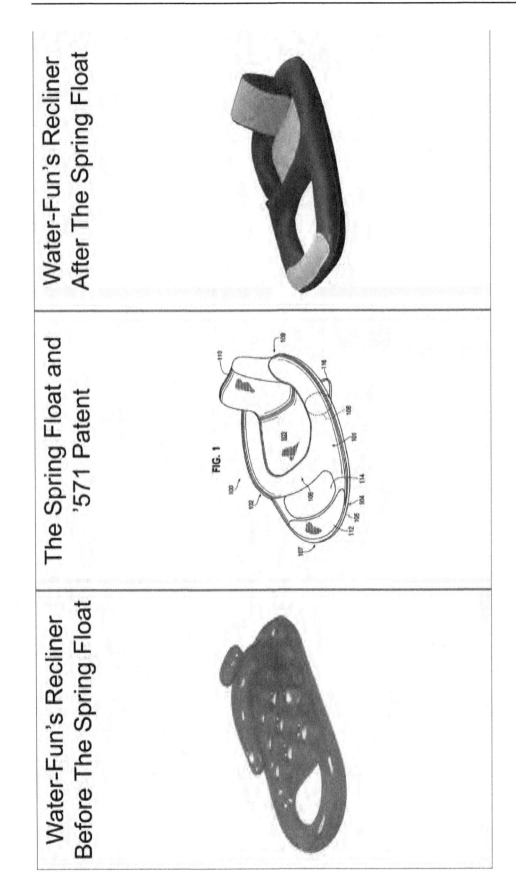

Water-Fun's Recliner Before The Spring Float	The Spring Float and '571 Patent	Water-Fun's Recliner After The Spring Float
	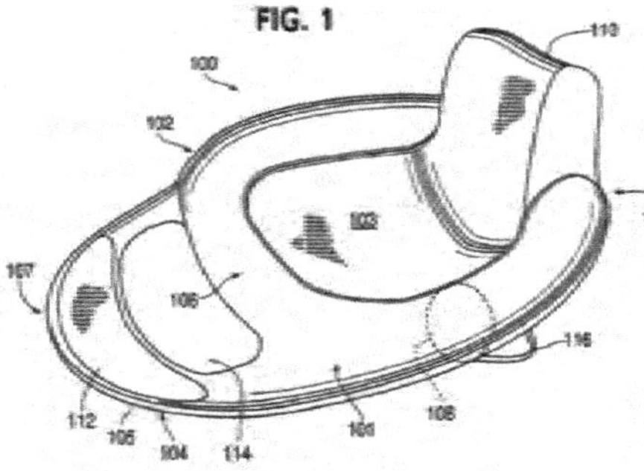 FIG. 1	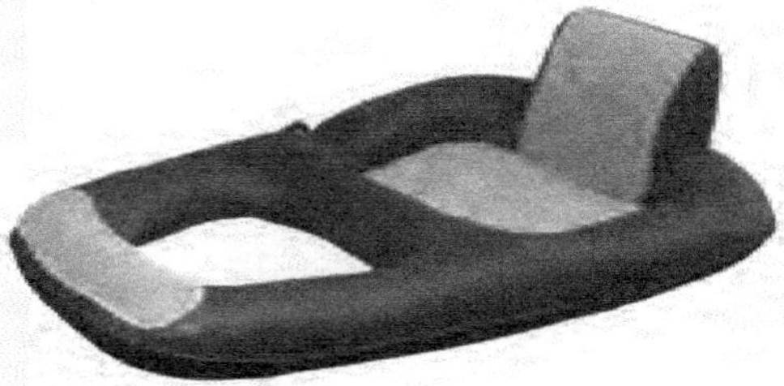

Court's Claim Construction

panel - "a layer of material that is mostly flat, but does not necessarily contain a spring"

substantially planar - "mostly flat"

disposed about - "around but not necessarily on all sides"

seated position - "includes an upright-seated position and reclined seated position, but not a prone position"

foot support - "a member that supports a user's feet, but not necessarily different or separate from the buoyant member"

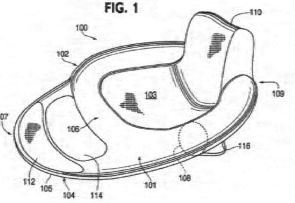

FIG. 1

1. An apparatus, comprising:

a panel including an inner portion, an outer portion and a back support portion, the inner portion of the panel having a first edge and a second edge on an opposite side of the inner portion of the panel from the first edge, a distance between the first edge of the inner portion of the panel and the second edge of the inner portion of the panel defining a width of the inner portion of the panel, the inner portion of the panel being substantially planar across the width of the inner portion of the panel, the back support portion being inflatable; and

a buoyant member disposed about at least the inner portion of the panel, at least a portion of the buoyant member being disposed within at least a portion of the outer portion of the panel, the buoyant member having a first portion and a second portion different from the first portion, the first portion of the buoyant member and the second portion of the buoyant member being disposed at opposite locations of the inner portion of the panel and separated by the width of the inner portion of the panel, the inner portion of the panel extending continuously between the first portion of the buoyant member and the second portion of the buoyant member without an intervening buoyant member,

at least one of the outer portion of the panel within which the first portion of the buoyant member is at least partially disposed or the first portion of the buoyant member being in contact with the first edge of the inner portion of the panel,

at least one of the outer portion of the panel within which the second portion of the buoyant member is at least partially disposed or the second portion of the buoyant member being in contact with the second edge of the inner portion of the panel,

the buoyant member having an outermost width that substantially defines an outermost width of the apparatus, the apparatus being configured to support a user in a seated position.

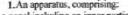

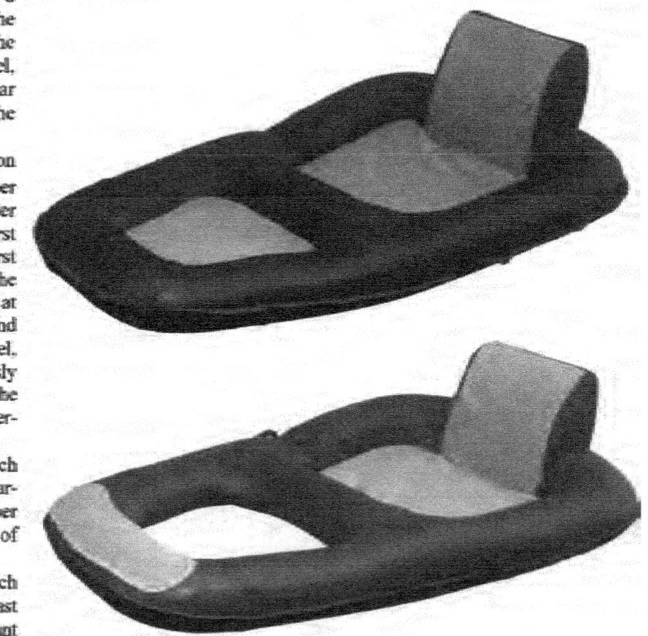

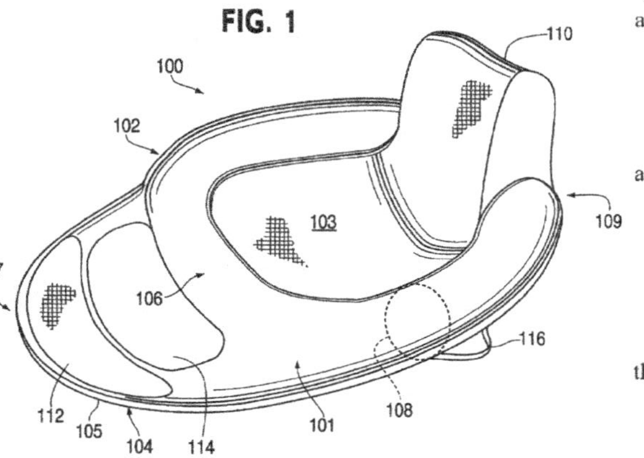

2. An apparatus, comprising:

a panel including an inner portion, an outer portion and a back support portion, the inner portion of the panel including a mesh material, the panel defining an opening configured to collectively receive a user's legs there-through, the opening being outside the inner portion of the panel, the back support portion being inflatable; and

a buoyant member disposed about at least a portion of the outer portion of the panel, the buoyant member having a front portion, the front portion of the buoyant member and the back support member being disposed at opposite locations of the inner portion of the panel and separated by a length of the inner portion of the panel, the front portion of the buoyant member being disposed between the inner portion of the panel and the opening,

the combination of the buoyant member, the panel and the back support portion being collectively configured to support the user in a seated position.

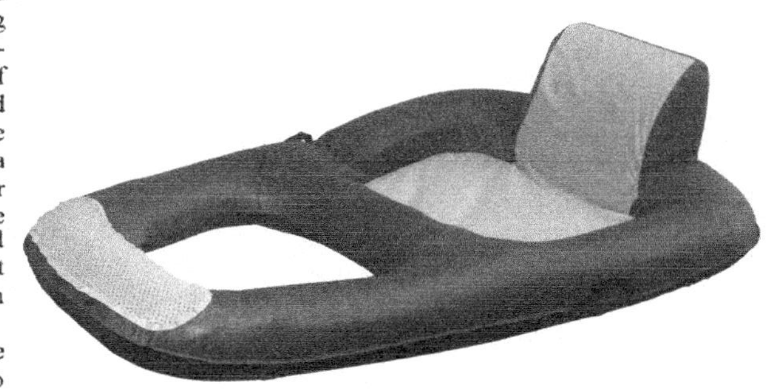

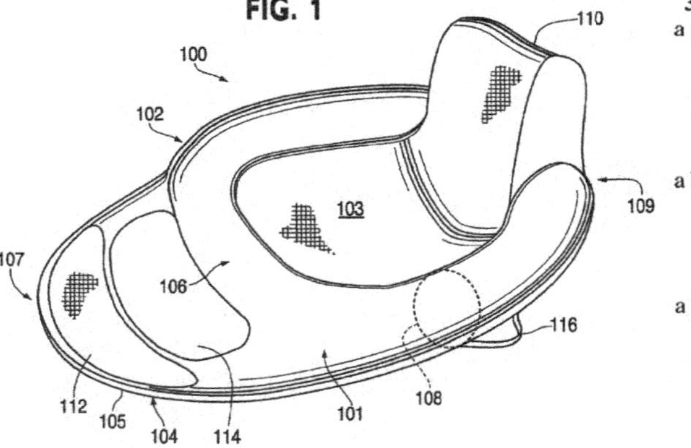

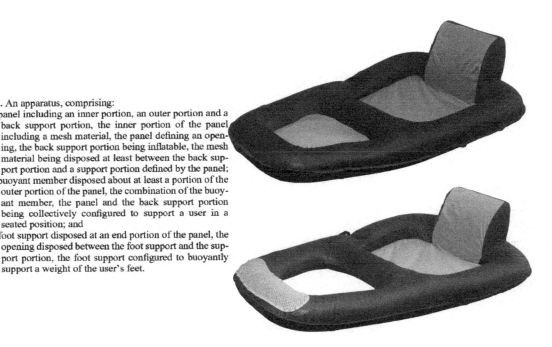

3. An apparatus, comprising:

a panel including an inner portion, an outer portion and a back support portion, the inner portion of the panel including a mesh material, the panel defining an opening, the back support portion being inflatable, the mesh material being disposed at least between the back support portion and a support portion defined by the panel;

a buoyant member disposed about at least a portion of the outer portion of the panel, the combination of the buoyant member, the panel and the back support portion being collectively configured to support a user in a seated position; and

a foot support disposed at an end portion of the panel, the opening disposed between the foot support and the support portion, the foot support configured to buoyantly support a weight of the user's feet.

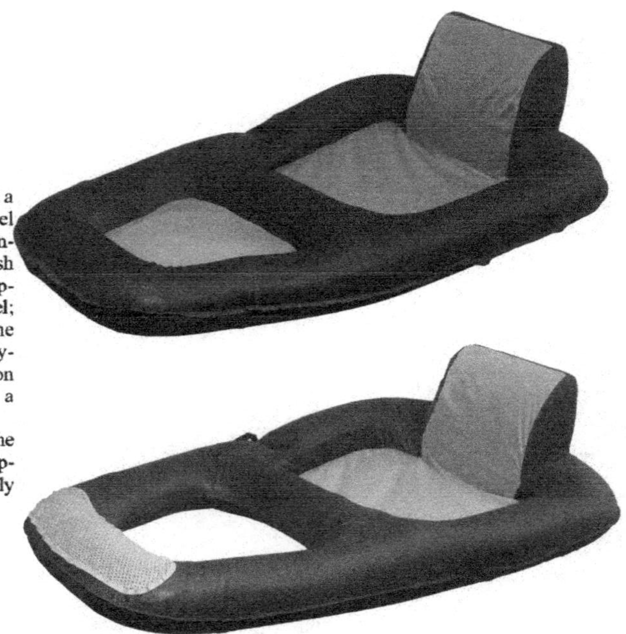

Claim Limitation	Water-Fun (Holey) Recliner	Water-Fun (Mesh) Recliner
1. An apparatus, comprising:		
a panel including an inner portion, an outer portion and a back support portion,		
the inner portion of the panel having a first edge and a second edge on an opposite side of the inner portion of the panel from the first edge, a distance between the first edge of the inner portion of the panel and the second edge of the inner portion of the panel defining a width of the inner portion of the panel,		
the inner portion of the panel being substantially planar across the width of the inner portion of the panel,		
the back support portion being inflatable; and		
a buoyant member disposed about at least the inner portion of the panel, at least a portion of the buoyant member being disposed within at least a portion of the outer portion of the panel,		
the buoyant member having a first portion and a second portion different from the first portion, the first portion of the buoyant member and the second portion of the buoyant member being disposed at opposite locations of the inner portion of the panel and separated by the width of the inner portion of the panel,		
the inner portion of the panel extending continuously between the first portion of the buoyant member and the second portion of the buoyant member without an intervening buoyant member,		
at least one of the outer portion of the panel within which the first portion of the buoyant member is at least partially disposed or the first portion of the buoyant member being in contact with the first edge of the inner portion of the panel,		
at least one of the outer portion of the panel within which the second portion of the buoyant member is at least partially disposed or the second portion of the buoyant member being in contact with the second edge of the inner portion of the panel,		
the buoyant member having an outermost width that substantially defines an outermost width of the apparatus, the apparatus being configured to support a user in a seated position.		

Claim Limitation	Water-Fun (Holey) Recliner
2. An apparatus, comprising:	
a panel including an inner portion, an outer portion and a back support portion, the inner portion of the panel including a mesh material,	
the panel defining an opening configured to collectively receive a user's legs therethrough, the opening being outside the inner portion of the panel,	
the back support portion being inflatable; and	
a buoyant member disposed about at least a portion of the outer portion of the panel, the buoyant member having a front portion, the front portion of the buoyant member and the back support member being disposed at opposite locations of the inner portion of the panel and separated by a length of the inner portion of the panel,	
the front portion of the buoyant member being disposed between the inner portion of the panel and the opening,	
the combination of the buoyant member, the panel and the back support portion being collectively configured to support the user in a seated position.	

Claim Limitation	Water-Fun (Holey) Recliner	Water-Fun (Mesh) Recliner
3. An apparatus, comprising:		
a panel including an inner portion, an outer portion and a back support portion,		
the inner portion of the panel including a mesh material,		
the panel defining an opening,		
the back support portion being inflatable, the mesh material being disposed at least between the back support portion and a support portion defined by the panel;		
a buoyant member disposed about at least a portion of the outer portion of the panel, the combination of the buoyant member, the panel and the back support portion being collectively configured to support a user in a seated position; and		
a foot support disposed at an end portion of the panel, the opening disposed between the foot support and the support portion, the foot support configured to buoyantly support a weight of the user's feet.		

Water-Fun

Invalidity Demonstratives

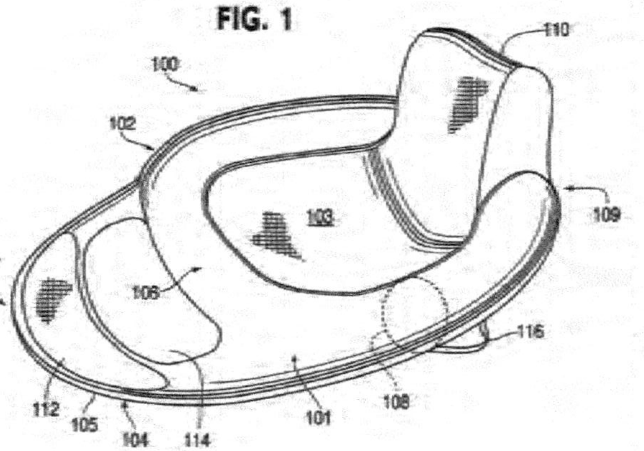

1. An apparatus, comprising:

a panel including an inner portion, an outer portion and a back support portion, the inner portion of the panel having a first edge and a second edge on an opposite side of the inner portion of the panel from the first edge, a distance between the first edge of the inner portion of the panel and the second edge of the inner portion of the panel defining a width of the inner portion of the panel, the inner portion of the panel being substantially planar across the width of the inner portion of the panel, the back support portion being inflatable; and

a buoyant member disposed about at least the inner portion of the panel, at least a portion of the buoyant member being disposed within at least a portion of the outer portion of the panel, the buoyant member having a first portion and a second portion different from the first portion, the first portion of the buoyant member and the second portion of the buoyant member being disposed at opposite locations of the inner portion of the panel and separated by the width of the inner portion of the panel, the inner portion of the panel extending continuously between the first portion of the buoyant member and the second portion of the buoyant member without an intervening buoyant member,

at least one of the outer portion of the panel within which the first portion of the buoyant member is at least partially disposed or the first portion of the buoyant member being in contact with the first edge of the inner portion of the panel,

at least one of the outer portion of the panel within which the second portion of the buoyant member is at least partially disposed or the second portion of the buoyant member being in contact with the second edge of the inner portion of the panel,

the buoyant member having an outermost width that substantially defines an outermost width of the apparatus, the apparatus being configured to support a user in a seated position.

U.S. Patent 5,476,404

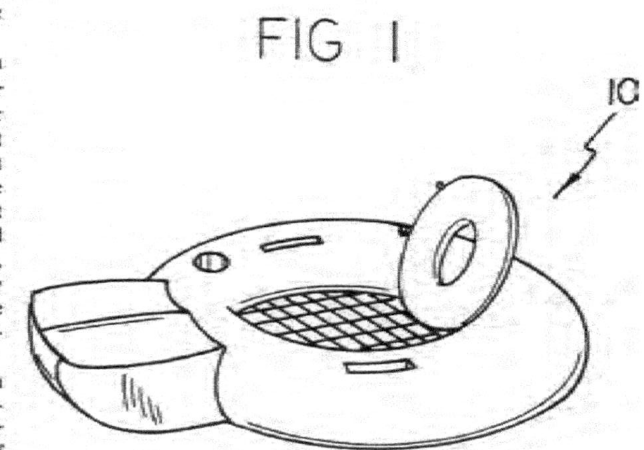

FIG I

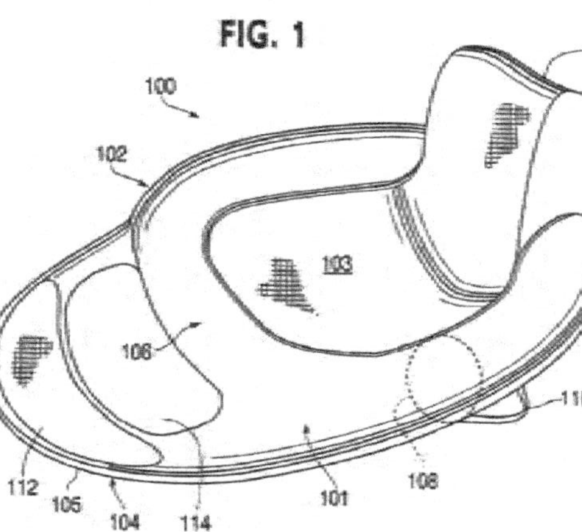

1. An apparatus, comprising:

a panel including an inner portion, an outer portion and a back support portion, the inner portion of the panel having a first edge and a second edge on an opposite side of the inner portion of the panel from the first edge, a distance between the first edge of the inner portion of the panel and the second edge of the inner portion of the panel defining a width of the inner portion of the panel, the inner portion of the panel being substantially planar across the width of the inner portion of the panel, the back support portion being inflatable; and

a buoyant member disposed about at least the inner portion of the panel, at least a portion of the buoyant member being disposed within at least a portion of the outer portion of the panel, the buoyant member having a first portion and a second portion different from the first portion, the first portion of the buoyant member and the second portion of the buoyant member being disposed at opposite locations of the inner portion of the panel and separated by the width of the inner portion of the panel, the inner portion of the panel extending continuously between the first portion of the buoyant member and the second portion of the buoyant member without an intervening buoyant member.

at least one of the outer portion of the panel within which the first portion of the buoyant member is at least partially disposed or the first portion of the buoyant member being in contact with the first edge of the inner portion of the panel,

at least one of the outer portion of the panel within which the second portion of the buoyant member is at least partially disposed or the second portion of the buoyant member being in contact with the second edge of the inner portion of the panel,

the buoyant member having an outermost width that substantially defines an outermost width of the apparatus, the apparatus being configured to support a user in a seated position.

U.S. Patent 6,485,344

FIG. 9

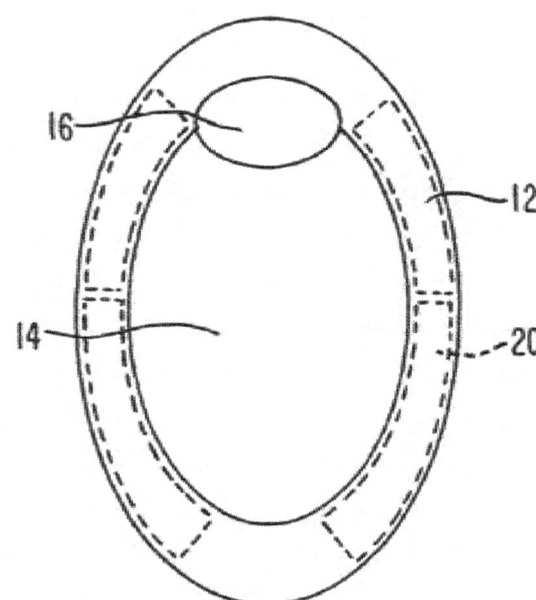

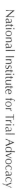

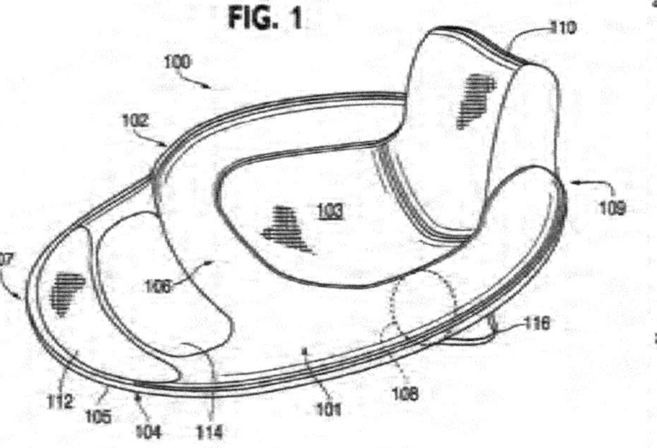

1. An apparatus, comprising:

a panel including an inner portion, an outer portion and a back support portion, the inner portion of the panel having a first edge and a second edge on an opposite side of the inner portion of the panel from the first edge, a distance between the first edge of the inner portion of the panel and the second edge of the inner portion of the panel defining a width of the inner portion of the panel, the inner portion of the panel being substantially planar across the width of the inner portion of the panel, the back support portion being inflatable; and

a buoyant member disposed about at least the inner portion of the panel, at least a portion of the buoyant member being disposed within at least a portion of the outer portion of the panel, the buoyant member having a first portion and a second portion different from the first portion, the first portion of the buoyant member and the second portion of the buoyant member being disposed at opposite locations of the inner portion of the panel and separated by the width of the inner portion of the panel, the inner portion of the panel extending continuously between the first portion of the buoyant member and the second portion of the buoyant member without an intervening buoyant member,

at least one of the outer portion of the panel within which the first portion of the buoyant member is at least partially disposed or the first portion of the buoyant member being in contact with the first edge of the inner portion of the panel,

at least one of the outer portion of the panel within which the second portion of the buoyant member is at least partially disposed or the second portion of the buoyant member being in contact with the second edge of the inner portion of the panel,

the buoyant member having an outermost width that substantially defines an outermost width of the apparatus, the apparatus being configured to support a user in a seated position.

U.S. Patent 1,960,474

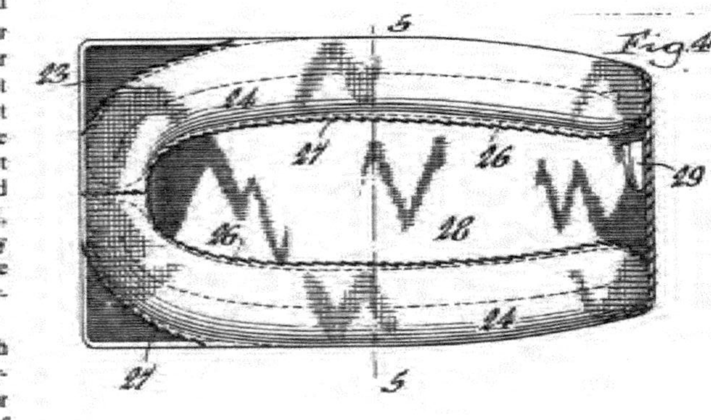

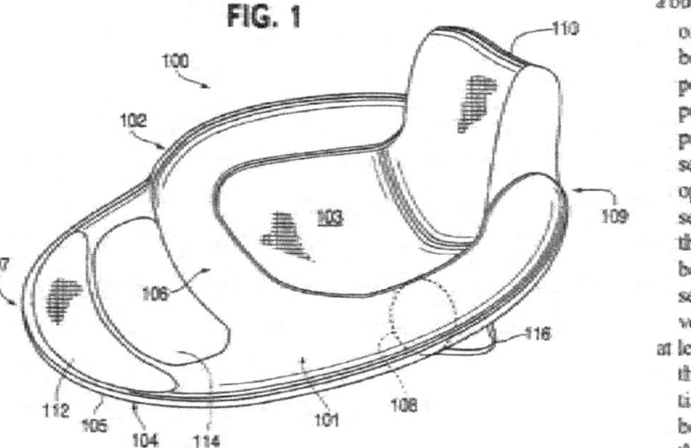

FIG. 1

1. An apparatus, comprising:

a panel including an inner portion, an outer portion and a back support portion, the inner portion of the panel having a first edge and a second edge on an opposite side of the inner portion of the panel from the first edge, a distance between the first edge of the inner portion of the panel and the second edge of the inner portion of the panel defining a width of the inner portion of the panel, the inner portion of the panel being substantially planar across the width of the inner portion of the panel, the back support portion being inflatable; and

a buoyant member disposed about at least the inner portion of the panel, at least a portion of the buoyant member being disposed within at least a portion of the outer portion of the panel, the buoyant member having a first portion and a second portion different from the first portion, the first portion of the buoyant member and the second portion of the buoyant member being disposed at opposite locations of the inner portion of the panel and separated by the width of the inner portion of the panel, the inner portion of the panel extending continuously between the first portion of the buoyant member and the second portion of the buoyant member without an intervening buoyant member,

at least one of the outer portion of the panel within which the first portion of the buoyant member is at least partially disposed or the first portion of the buoyant member being in contact with the first edge of the inner portion of the panel,

at least one of the outer portion of the panel within which the second portion of the buoyant member is at least partially disposed or the second portion of the buoyant member being in contact with the second edge of the inner portion of the panel,

the buoyant member having an outermost width that substantially defines an outermost width of the apparatus, the apparatus being configured to support a user in a seated position.

U.S. Patent 3,871,042

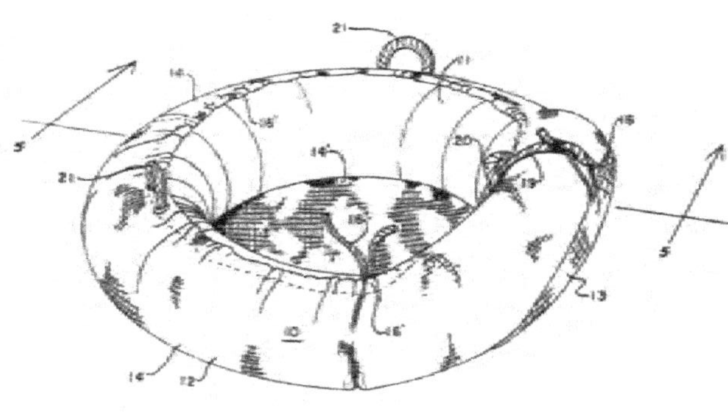

FIG. 4

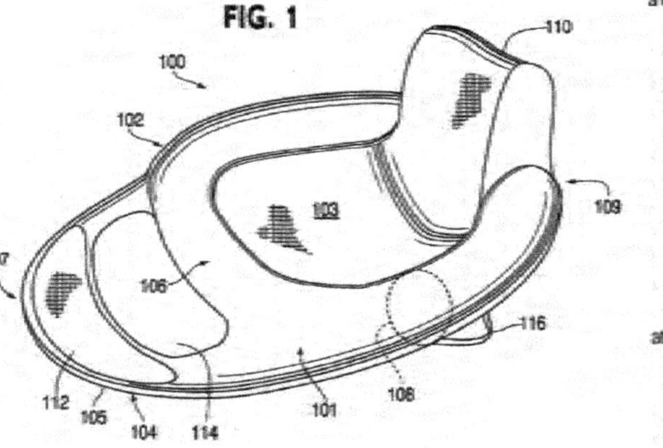

1. An apparatus, comprising:

a panel including an inner portion, an outer portion and a back support portion, the inner portion of the panel having a first edge and a second edge on an opposite side of the inner portion of the panel from the first edge, a distance between the first edge of the inner portion of the panel and the second edge of the inner portion of the panel defining a width of the inner portion of the panel, the inner portion of the panel being substantially planar across the width of the inner portion of the panel, the back support portion being inflatable; and

a buoyant member disposed about at least the inner portion of the panel, at least a portion of the buoyant member being disposed within at least a portion of the outer portion of the panel, the buoyant member having a first portion and a second portion different from the first portion, the first portion of the buoyant member and the second portion of the buoyant member being disposed at opposite locations of the inner portion of the panel and separated by the width of the inner portion of the panel, the inner portion of the panel extending continuously between the first portion of the buoyant member and the second portion of the buoyant member without an intervening buoyant member,

at least one of the outer portion of the panel within which the first portion of the buoyant member is at least partially disposed or the first portion of the buoyant member being in contact with the first edge of the inner portion of the panel,

at least one of the outer portion of the panel within which the second portion of the buoyant member is at least partially disposed or the second portion of the buoyant member being in contact with the second edge of the inner portion of the panel,

the buoyant member having an outermost width that substantially defines an outermost width of the apparatus, the apparatus being configured to support a user in a seated position.

Intex King Cool Loung

U.S. Patent 5,476,404

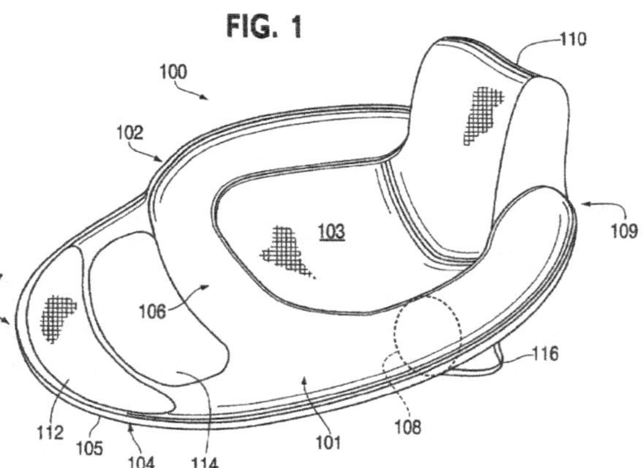

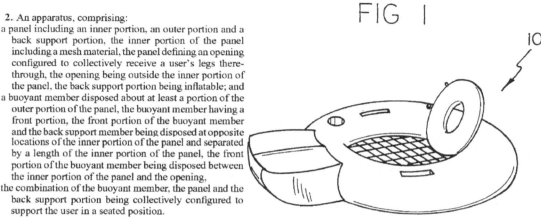

2. An apparatus, comprising:

a panel including an inner portion, an outer portion and a back support portion, the inner portion of the panel including a mesh material, the panel defining an opening configured to collectively receive a user's legs therethrough, the opening being outside the inner portion of the panel, the back support portion being inflatable; and

a buoyant member disposed about at least a portion of the outer portion of the panel, the buoyant member having a front portion, the front portion of the buoyant member and the back support member being disposed at opposite locations of the inner portion of the panel and separated by a length of the inner portion of the panel, the front portion of the buoyant member being disposed between the inner portion of the panel and the opening,

the combination of the buoyant member, the panel and the back support portion being collectively configured to support the user in a seated position.

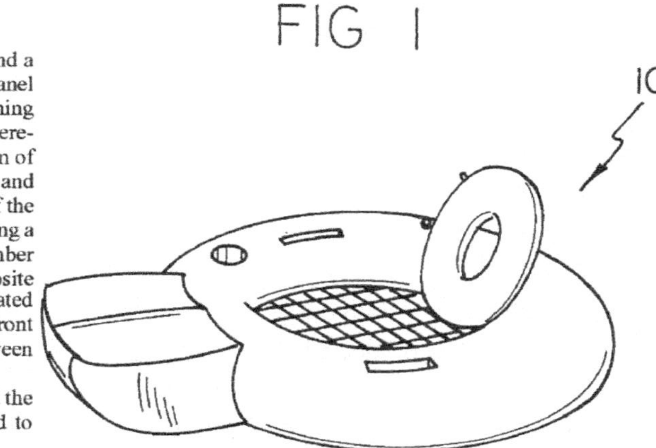

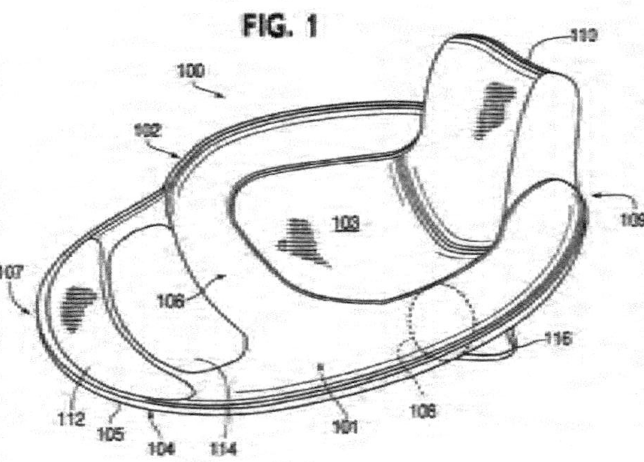

2. An apparatus, comprising:

a panel including an inner portion, an outer portion and a back support portion, the inner portion of the panel including a mesh material, the panel defining an opening configured to collectively receive a user's legs therethrough, the opening being outside the inner portion of the panel, the back support portion being inflatable; and

a buoyant member disposed about at least a portion of the outer portion of the panel, the buoyant member having a front portion, the front portion of the buoyant member and the back support member being disposed at opposite locations of the inner portion of the panel and separated by a length of the inner portion of the panel, the front portion of the buoyant member being disposed between the inner portion of the panel and the opening,

the combination of the buoyant member, the panel and the back support portion being collectively configured to support the user in a seated position.

U.S. Patent 6,485,344

FIG. 9

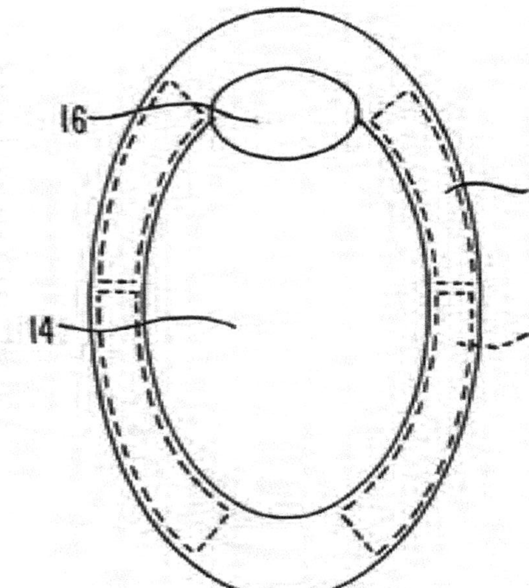

U.S. Patent 1,960,474

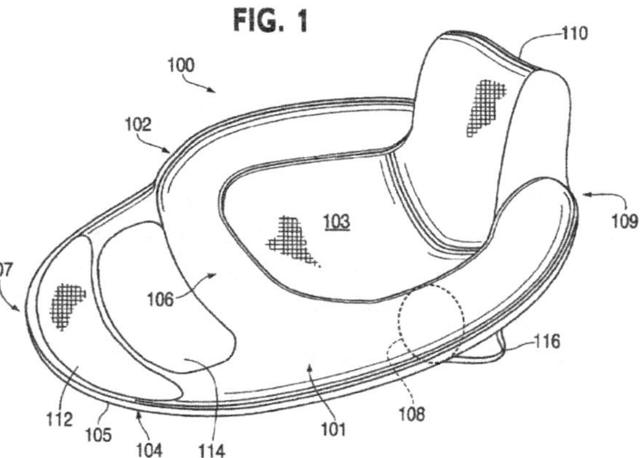

FIG. 1

2. An apparatus, comprising:
a panel including an inner portion, an outer portion and a back support portion, the inner portion of the panel including a mesh material, the panel defining an opening configured to collectively receive a user's legs therethrough, the opening being outside the inner portion of the panel, the back support portion being inflatable; and
a buoyant member disposed about at least a portion of the outer portion of the panel, the buoyant member having a front portion, the front portion of the buoyant member and the back support member being disposed at opposite locations of the inner portion of the panel and separated by a length of the inner portion of the panel, the front portion of the buoyant member being disposed between the inner portion of the panel and the opening,
the combination of the buoyant member, the panel and the back support portion being collectively configured to support the user in a seated position.

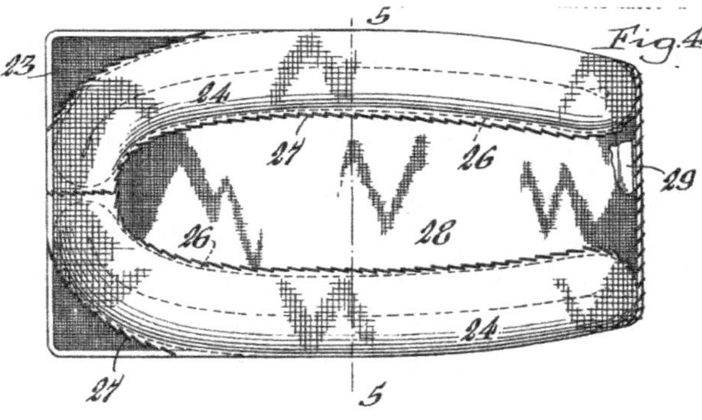

Fig. 4

U.S. Patent 3,871,042

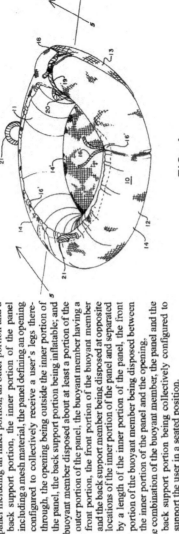

FIG. 1

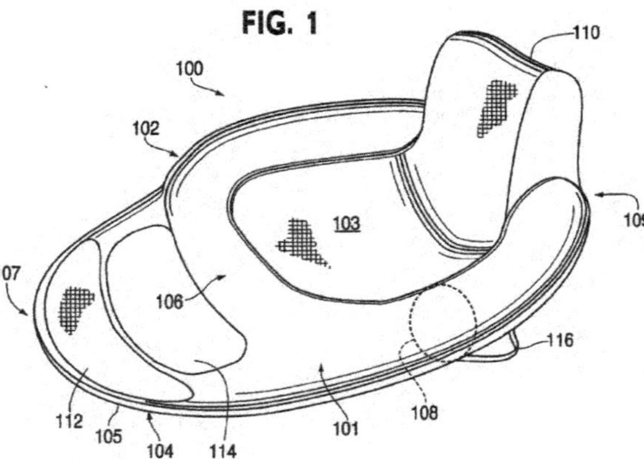

2. An apparatus, comprising:

a panel including an inner portion, an outer portion and a back support portion, the inner portion of the panel including a mesh material, the panel defining an opening configured to collectively receive a user's legs therethrough, the opening being outside the inner portion of the panel, the back support portion being inflatable; and

a buoyant member disposed about at least a portion of the outer portion of the panel, the buoyant member having a front portion, the front portion of the buoyant member and the back support member being disposed at opposite locations of the inner portion of the panel and separated by a length of the inner portion of the panel, the front portion of the buoyant member being disposed between the inner portion of the panel and the opening,

the combination of the buoyant member, the panel and the back support portion being collectively configured to support the user in a seated position.

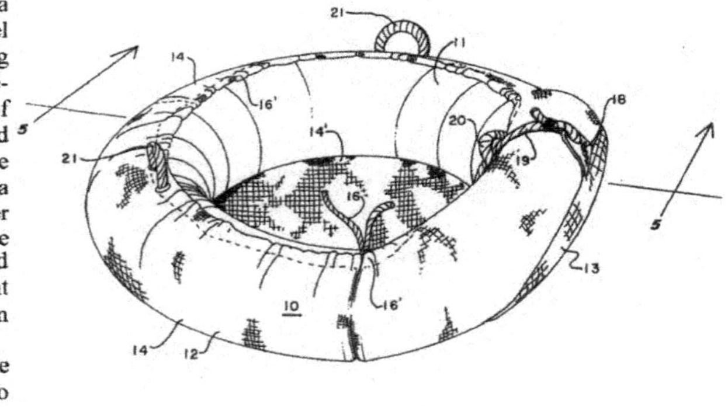
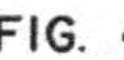

FIG. 4

Intex King Cool Loung

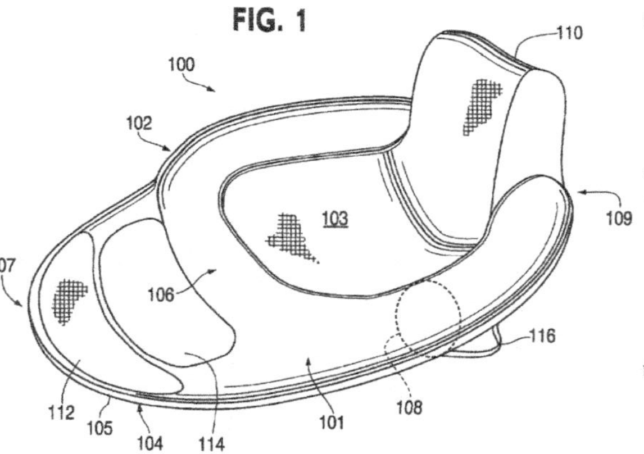

2. An apparatus, comprising:

a panel including an inner portion, an outer portion and a back support portion, the inner portion of the panel including a mesh material, the panel defining an opening configured to collectively receive a user's legs therethrough, the opening being outside the inner portion of the panel, the back support portion being inflatable; and

a buoyant member disposed about at least a portion of the outer portion of the panel, the buoyant member having a front portion, the front portion of the buoyant member and the back support member being disposed at opposite locations of the inner portion of the panel and separated by a length of the inner portion of the panel, the front portion of the buoyant member being disposed between the inner portion of the panel and the opening,

the combination of the buoyant member, the panel and the back support portion being collectively configured to support the user in a seated position.

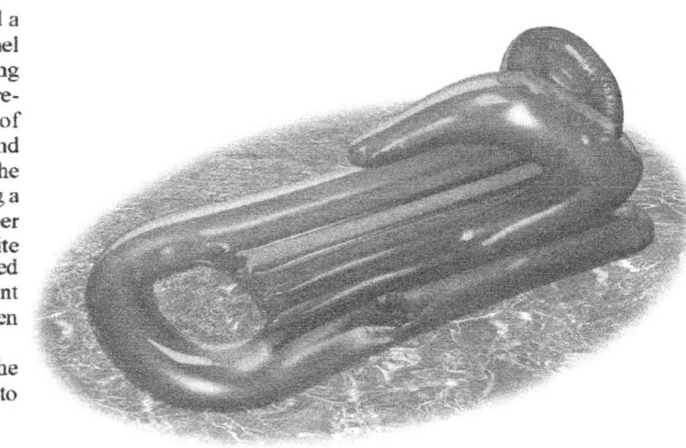

U.S. Patent 5,476,404

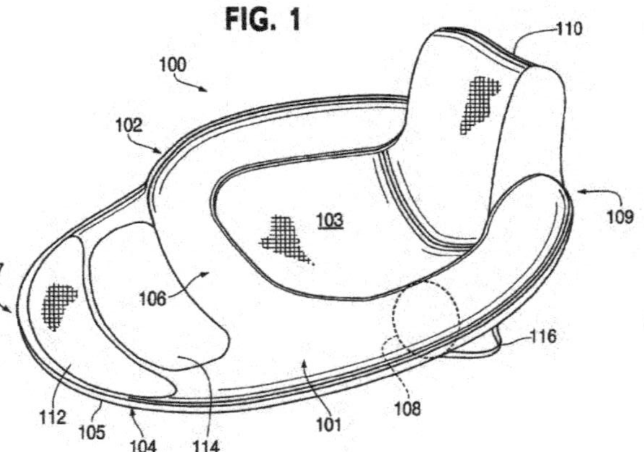

3. An apparatus, comprising:

a panel including an inner portion, an outer portion and a back support portion, the inner portion of the panel including a mesh material, the panel defining an opening, the back support portion being inflatable, the mesh material being disposed at least between the back support portion and a support portion defined by the panel;

a buoyant member disposed about at least a portion of the outer portion of the panel, the combination of the buoyant member, the panel and the back support portion being collectively configured to support a user in a seated position; and

a foot support disposed at an end portion of the panel, the opening disposed between the foot support and the support portion, the foot support configured to buoyantly support a weight of the user's feet.

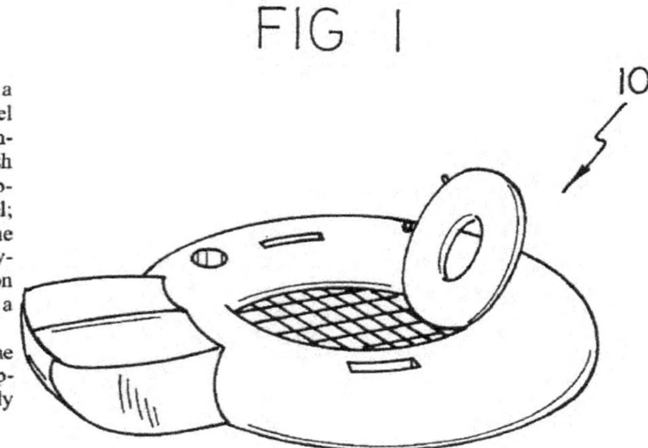

U.S. Patent 6,485,344

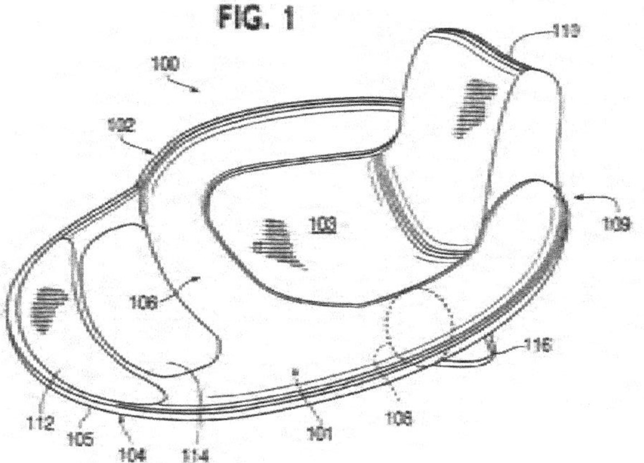

3. An apparatus, comprising:

a panel including an inner portion, an outer portion and a back support portion, the inner portion of the panel including a mesh material, the panel defining an opening, the back support portion being inflatable, the mesh material being disposed at least between the back support portion and a support portion defined by the panel;

a buoyant member disposed about at least a portion of the outer portion of the panel, the combination of the buoyant member, the panel and the back support portion being collectively configured to support a user in a seated position; and

a foot support disposed at an end portion of the panel, the opening disposed between the foot support and the support portion, the foot support configured to buoyantly support a weight of the user's feet.

FIG. 9

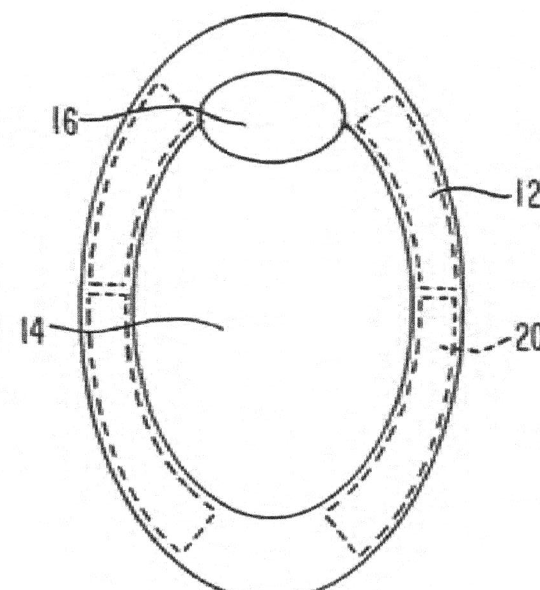

U.S. Patent 1,960,474

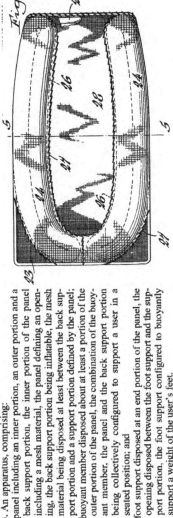

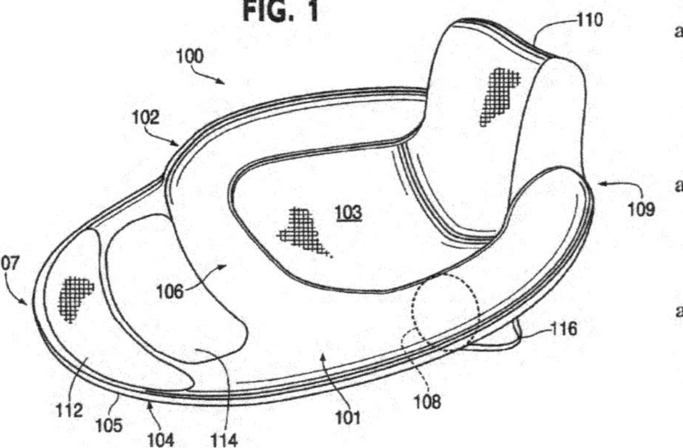

3. An apparatus, comprising:

a panel including an inner portion, an outer portion and a back support portion, the inner portion of the panel including a mesh material, the panel defining an opening, the back support portion being inflatable, the mesh material being disposed at least between the back support portion and a support portion defined by the panel;

a buoyant member disposed about at least a portion of the outer portion of the panel, the combination of the buoyant member, the panel and the back support portion being collectively configured to support a user in a seated position; and

a foot support disposed at an end portion of the panel, the opening disposed between the foot support and the support portion, the foot support configured to buoyantly support a weight of the user's feet.

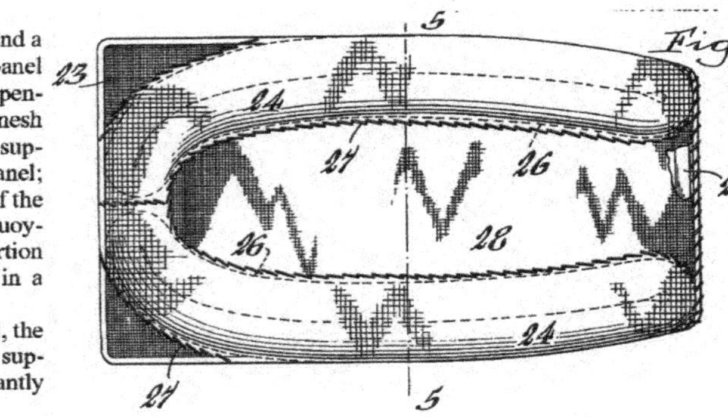

U.S. Patent 3,871,042

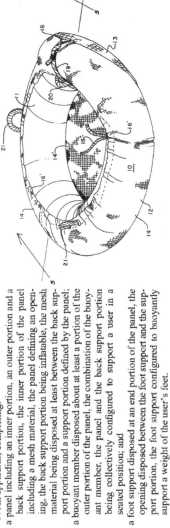

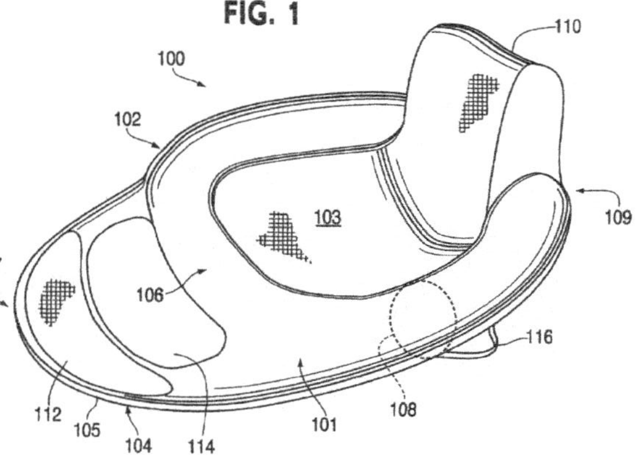

FIG. 1

3. An apparatus, comprising:

a panel including an inner portion, an outer portion and a back support portion, the inner portion of the panel including a mesh material, the panel defining an opening, the back support portion being inflatable, the mesh material being disposed at least between the back support portion and a support portion defined by the panel;

a buoyant member disposed about at least a portion of the outer portion of the panel, the combination of the buoyant member, the panel and the back support portion being collectively configured to support a user in a seated position; and

a foot support disposed at an end portion of the panel, the opening disposed between the foot support and the support portion, the foot support configured to buoyantly support a weight of the user's feet.

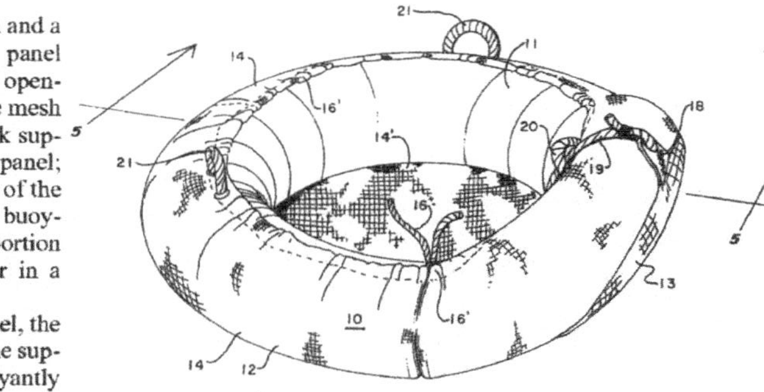
FIG. 4

Intex King Cool Loung

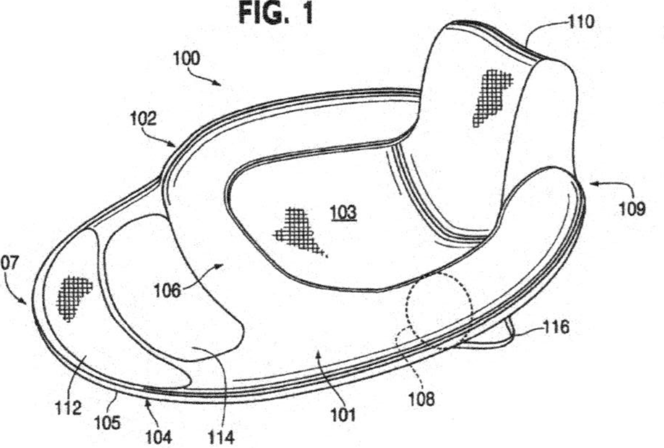

FIG. 1

3. An apparatus, comprising:

a panel including an inner portion, an outer portion and a back support portion, the inner portion of the panel including a mesh material, the panel defining an opening, the back support portion being inflatable, the mesh material being disposed at least between the back support portion and a support portion defined by the panel;

a buoyant member disposed about at least a portion of the outer portion of the panel, the combination of the buoyant member, the panel and the back support portion being collectively configured to support a user in a seated position; and

a foot support disposed at an end portion of the panel, the opening disposed between the foot support and the support portion, the foot support configured to buoyantly support a weight of the user's feet.

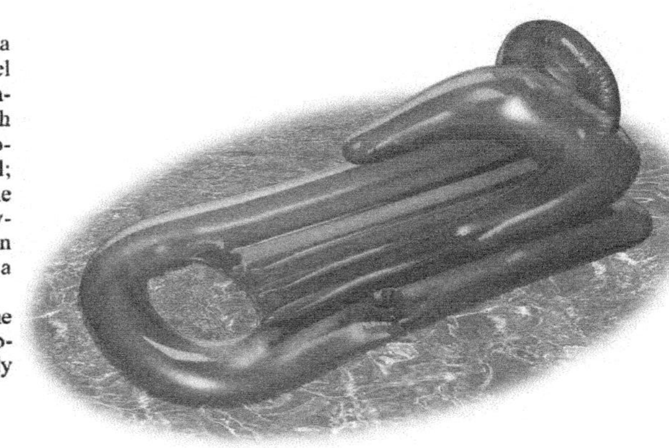

United States Patent
Flax et al.

Patent No.: US 8,197,517 B2
Date of Patent: *Oct. 26, YR-6

(57) **ABSTRACT**

A collapsible flotation device is provided that uses a coilable spring coupled to a panel to collapse the device when the spring is coiled, and to expand the device when the spring is uncoiled configuration. The spring can be contained within a sleeve along the outer portion of the panel. A support member that traverses the panel is provided. An inflatable bladder disposed about a part of the outer portion of the panel and coupled to the support member buoyantly supports a body weight of a user. The combination of the inflatable bladder and the support member provide support for a user in a seated position on the panel. Many configurations are disclosed, including a multi-user collapsible flotation device, multiple connected single-user flotation devices, and so forth. A back support member and a headrest, both of which can be inflatable, provide additional support for a user to maintain a seated position on the panel. A foot support member is provided for the comfort of the user.

SUMMARY

A collapsible device provides a panel with an inner portion and an outer portion. A spring is disposed about the outer portion of the panel and is movable between a coiled configuration and an uncoiled configuration. A support member that traverses the panel is also provided. An inflatable bladder is disposed about at least a part of an outer portion of the panel, and is disposed proximate to the support member. The inflatable bladder is configured to buoyantly support the body weight of a user disposed on the panel.

Further features of the invention, and the advantages offered thereby, are explained in greater detail hereinafter with references to specific embodiments illustrated in the accompanying drawings, wherein like elements are indicated by like reference designators.

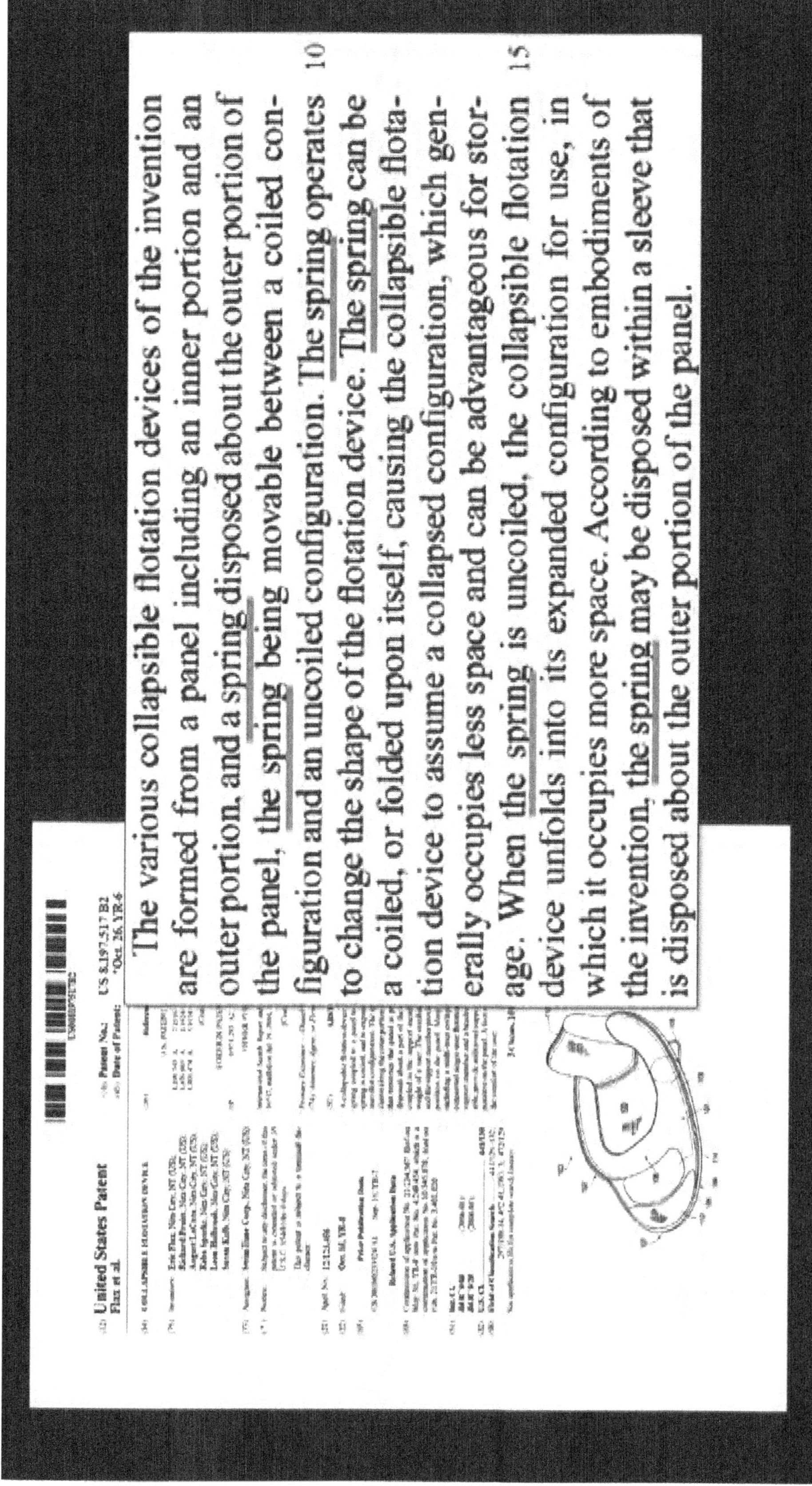

United States Patent
Flax et al.

Patent No.: US 8,197,517 B2
Date of Patent: *Oct. 26, YR-6

The various collapsible flotation devices of the invention are formed from a panel including an inner portion and an outer portion, and a spring disposed about the outer portion of the panel, the spring being movable between a coiled configuration and an uncoiled configuration. The spring operates to change the shape of the flotation device. The spring can be a coiled, or folded upon itself, causing the collapsible flotation device to assume a collapsed configuration, which generally occupies less space and can be advantageous for storage. When the spring is uncoiled, the collapsible flotation device unfolds into its expanded configuration for use, in which it occupies more space. According to embodiments of the invention, the spring may be disposed within a sleeve that is disposed about the outer portion of the panel.

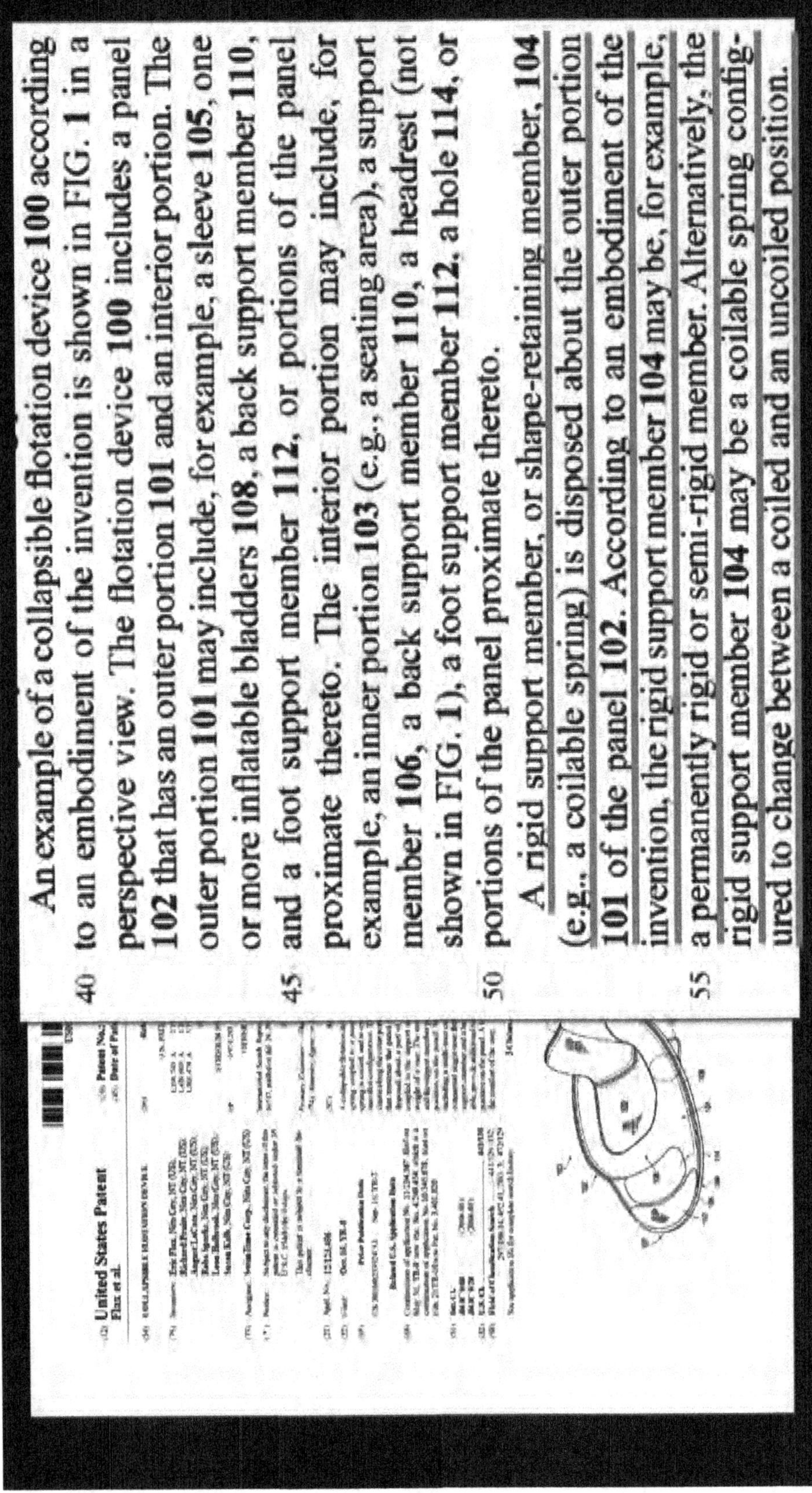

An example of a collapsible flotation device **100** according to an embodiment of the invention is shown in FIG. **1** in a perspective view. The flotation device **100** includes a panel **102** that has an outer portion **101** and an interior portion. The outer portion **101** may include, for example, a sleeve **105**, one or more inflatable bladders **108**, a back support member **110**, and a foot support member **112**, or portions of the panel proximate thereto. The interior portion may include, for example, an inner portion **103** (e.g., a seating area), a support member **106**, a back support member **110**, a headrest (not shown in FIG. 1), a foot support member **112**, a hole **114**, or portions of the panel proximate thereto.

A rigid support member, or shape-retaining member, **104** (e.g., a coilable spring) is disposed about the outer portion **101** of the panel **102**. According to an embodiment of the invention, the rigid support member **104** may be, for example, a permanently rigid or semi-rigid member. Alternatively, the rigid support member **104** may be a coilable spring configured to change between a coiled and an uncoiled position.

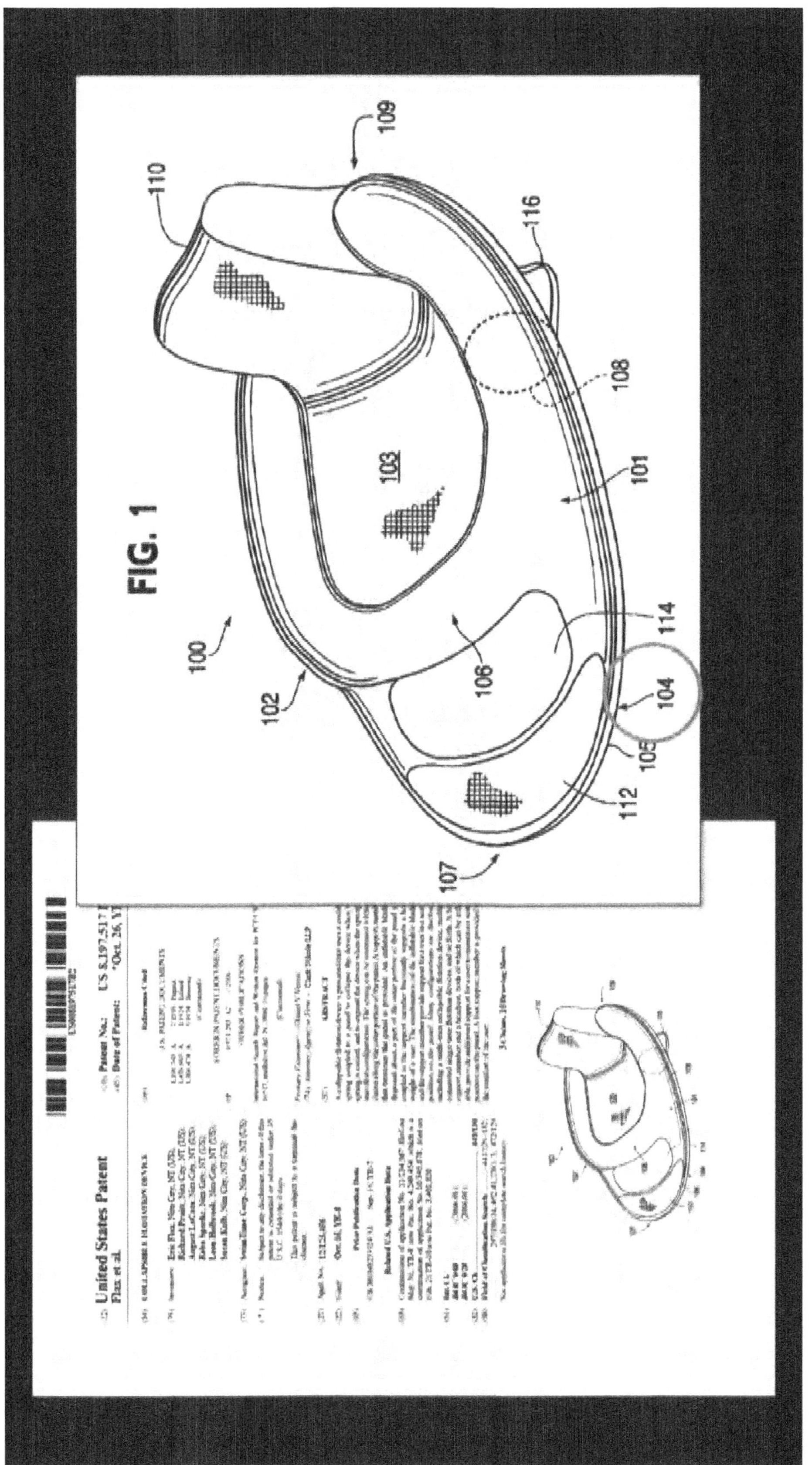
FIG. 1
100
101
102
103
104
105
106
107
108
109
110
112
114
116

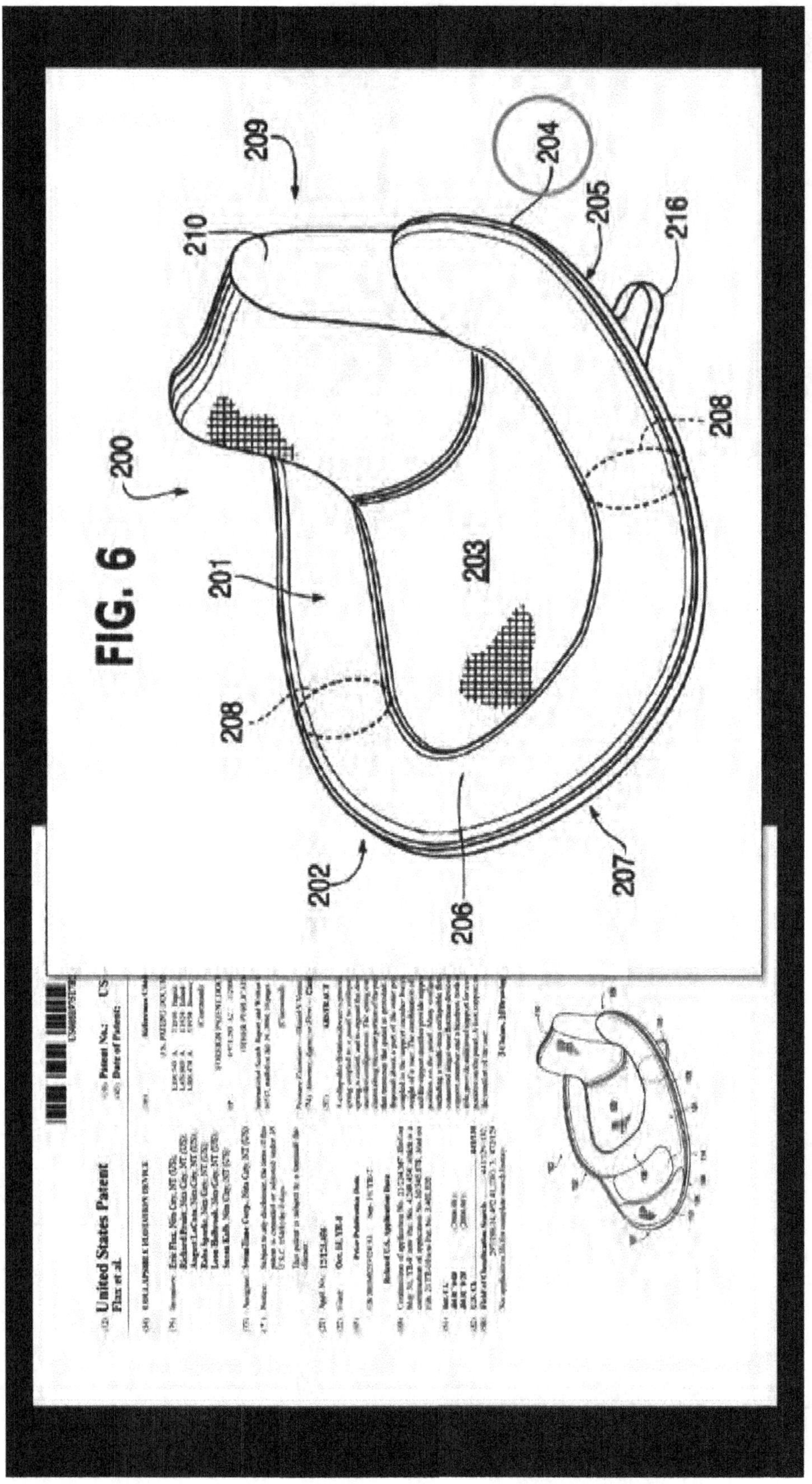
FIG. 6
200
201
202
203
204
205
206
207
208
208
209
210
216
United States Patent
Flax et al.

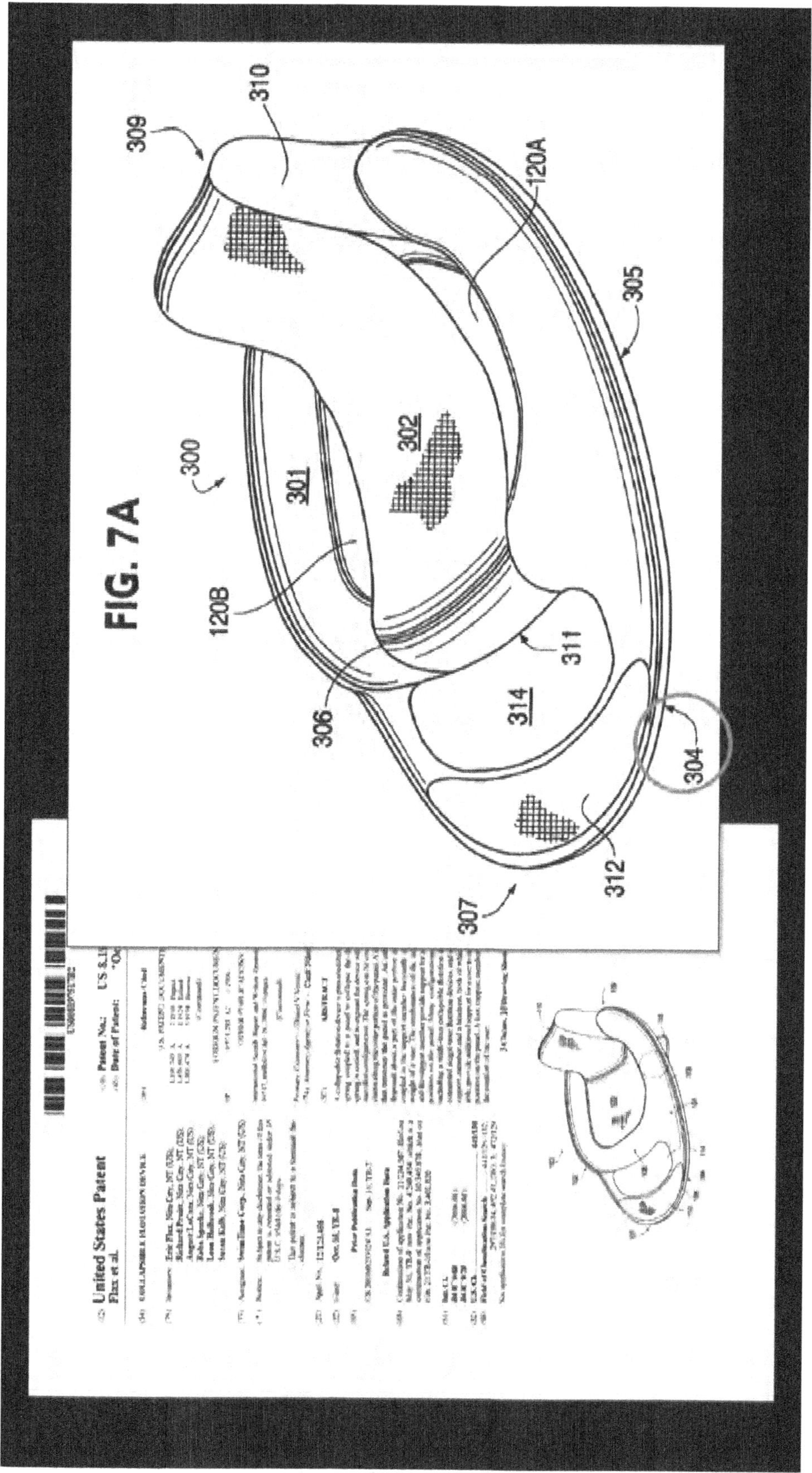
FIG. 7A
300
301
302
304
305
306
307
309
310
311
312
314
120A
120B
United States Patent
Flax et al.

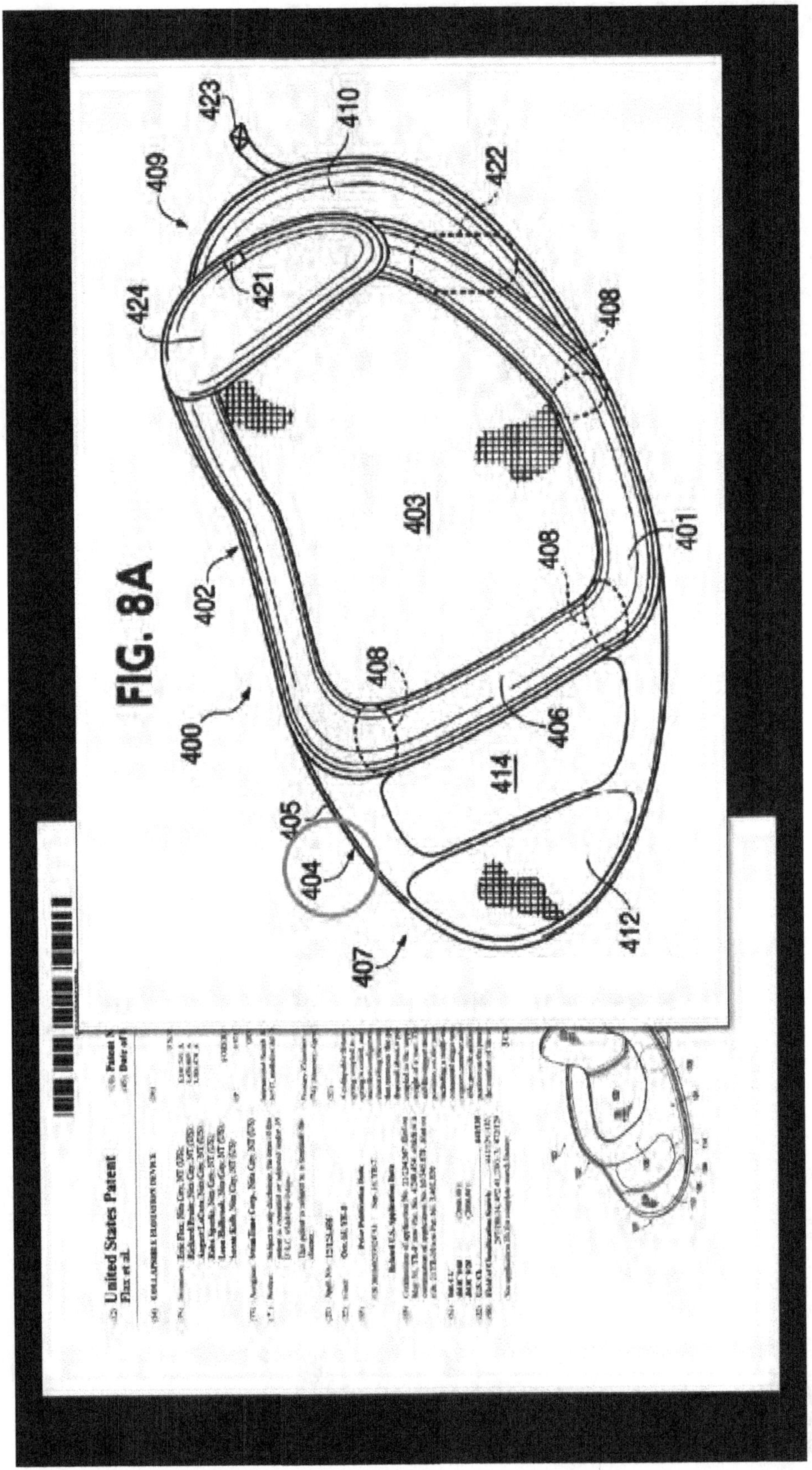
FIG. 8A
400
402
403
401
405
404
406
407
408
409
410
412
414
421
422
423
424